DATE DUE

PRINTED IN U. S. A.

D1572554

A RAIN OF DARTS

THE MEXICA AZTECS

The Texas Pan American Series

A Rain of Darts

THE MEXICA AZTECS

by Burr Cartwright Brundage

UNIVERSITY OF TEXAS PRESS, AUSTIN & LONDON

The Texas Pan American Series is published
with the assistance of a revolving publication
fund established by the Pan American Sulphur
Company and other friends of Latin America
in Texas.

Library of Congress Cataloging in Publication Data

Brundage, Burr Cartwright, 1912–
  A rain of darts.

  (Texas pan-American series)
  Bibliography: p.
  1. Aztecs—History. I. Title.
F1219.B89   970.3   72-680
ISBN 0-292-77002-2

Composition by G&S Typesetters, Austin
Printing by The University of Texas Printing Division, Austin
Binding by Universal Bookbindery, Inc., San Antonio

TO ARNOLD TOYNBEE

in friendship and gratitude

CONTENTS

MAPS

PREFACE

This book came about because, as a historian, I have long felt the lack of a dependable and informative history of one discrete Aztec state. Books written up to now on the Aztecs have mingled bits of several histories along with heavy doses of the culture of all the Aztec states together, as if the many Aztec states had had no separate existence of their own. I have chosen to concentrate on that one Aztec state with the most abundant records and with certainly the most renown, Mexico.

This is a political history; it depicts customs, cults, and myths only insofar as these are necessary to clarify the narrative. Those who wish to immerse themselves in the social, literary, technological and economic details of Aztec life—all of which is of the greatest interest—are advised to go to general surveys of the culture, of which there are many.

The story of how a certain people comported themselves in their years on earth is then the essential task here, and if the story falters or the narrative becomes muddy, I have failed. I should particularly like to draw attention to the fact that there is a theme to this history: the keen realization by the Mexica of the illegitimacy of their claim to the land and their expectation of the proprietorial return of the god. This theme appears throughout Mexican history—in the origination legends, in the final catastrophe that befell the state, and in all the fury and arrogance of the interim years.

To the uninitiated, Nahuatl names appear unpronounceable, and where there was any choice I have used their shorter forms or those least offensive to the untutored eye, such as Cuacuauhtzin for the more correct Cuacuauhpitzahuac. All Nahuatl words are accented on the penultimate syllable. The letter *x* is pronounced like *sh* in English.

The records relied on in writing this history have been the well-known primary and secondary sources, ranging from the *Anales de Tlatilulco* down through Veytia and Clavigero. Tertiary sources (from Orozco y Berra to Barlow, Krickeberg, Kirchhoff, Piña-Chan, Bernal, et al.) have been read and very occasionally cited. The *Handbook of Middle American Indians* has aided me in many matters of geography and culture. Volumes 10 and 11 of that series were issued when this work was in proofs. Consequently, none of the pertinent material there could be assimilated for this writing. This is regrettable, particularly in the case of articles such as that by Charles Gibson on the geographical extension of the Aztec empire. By and large, however, the work rests directly on the sixteenth-, seventeenth-, and eighteenth-century sources. The quantity of such sources, both published and in manuscript, is vast and I make no claim to have consulted more than the essential works.

Due to the sporadic and somewhat unusual circumstances of note-taking in preparation for this book, it has inadvertently happened that two or three primary sources used have been cited in the bibliography and notes in more than one translation or edition. This will appear awkward to the eye of the critic, but it in no wise lessens the work, for, in regard to each statement of fact, the citation will lead the interested party to the proper source.

A word on chronology. In this area I have been immeasurably helped by Dr. Howard F. Cline, late director of the Hispanic Foundation of the Library of Congress. He not only read this work in manuscript and offered valuable suggestions, but he allowed me access to an article of his on Christian-Aztec synchronology, which is to be published in the *Journal des Américainistes* in Paris. This article and his own personal advice convinced me that the traditional founding date for Tenochtitlan (1325) was in error and that Kirchhoff's date of 1369-1370 was correct. (See Paul Kirchhoff, "The Mexican Calendar and the Founding of Tenochtitlan-Tlatilulco," New York Academy of Science, *Transactions*, series 2, 12:126–132.) After making this fundamental correction, all surrounding dates could then be more accurately placed. Dr. Cline also brought to my attention the latest datings of Teotihuacan and Tula, which I have also incorporated in this work. Because Dr. Cline, at the time of his death, was preparing a book to be published by the University of Texas Press, which will discuss this antecedent material at length, I have only briefly touched on it here.

We differed on one important point. Dr. Cline (private communication) set 1380 as the true date for the founding of Tlatilulco, eleven years after the founding of Tenochtitlan. I cannot give a precise date to that founding, but I believe it to have been several years before 1369 and I have so depicted it in these pages.

I wish to express my gratitude for the help given me by Dr. Cline and for his interest in this book. His untimely death was a very great loss to the scholarly world.

The three maps in this volume have been painstakingly drawn by Mr. Geza Knipfer of The University of Texas at Austin; his skill is greatly appreciated.

My efforts to gain competence in the field of Aztec studies have been supported by a grant from the Board of Higher Education of the Presbyterian Church. Additionally my own institution, Eckerd College (formerly Florida Presbyterian College), has taken a real and continuing interest in both the inception and the realization of this study and with numerous grants of money has supported my library acquisitions and sent me to Mexico to carry on my research. I received gracious help in an important matter of translation from Dr. A. J. O. Anderson of San Diego State College and Dr. Charles Dibble of the University of Utah. It is a pleasure to acknowledge this aid and to express my gratitude.

INTRODUCTION

The story of the Aztecs, whatever else it may be, is a tale of midnight murders, intrigues, and wild revenges. Disguises and espionage were commonplace and came to their culmination in the most hair-raising escapades. The din of battle was relentless and unceasing. All this, added to the constantly shifting loyalties that marked the relationships among the various Aztec states during the short period of their floruit, sows confusion in the mind of the scholar, tempting him to believe that Aztec history is before all else passionate and episodic in character.

The Mexica, that branch of the Aztec people investigated in this book, seem to exemplify nicely this view of Aztec history. Indeed the Tlascalans described them as a "people who seem to have been born never to rest, never to leave anyone in peace,"[1] while the Otomí cried out to all who would hear: "The Mexican is an inhuman person. He is very wicked. . . . The Mexicans are supremely bad. There is none who can surpass the Mexican in evil." [2]

The history of the Mexica—microcosmic of the whole Aztec world—has a lurid quality not often met with in the chronicles of nations. The historian feels that he is looking back upon a people adrift in a great tempest of their own making.

Yet these same Mexica were in no sense a heaven-storming people; they were, on the contrary, most submissive and melancholy servants of their gods. The perturbations and egotisms in their political lives were merely enchantments thrown upon them. In fact they formed a steadfast and sacred society, disciplined by their belief in the sacrament of human sacrifice and forever humble under the bans and demands of gods and demons. The lordship of the heavens was the salient fact in all their calculations. Deep under the tumults of their daily lives, they were eminently quiet slaves.

The personage who stood in the very center of Aztec history was the *teuctli*. We will have much to say about him later, but a short introduction is necessary here. He was both the hero and the victim of his society. The word *teuctli* referred primarily to the successful warrior, but beyond that it carried implications of superior social status. Proper translations of the title should undoubtedly be taken from among that constellation of words so well known to us from the Middle Ages: "knight," "baron," and "lord." Certainly all of the connotations of those terms are present in the Nahuatl word, as well as others that are specific to the Aztec world.

It was this *teuctli* whose voracious hunger for battle, whose boastfulness, whose monstrous dignity and unending search for honors form the dynamic in Aztec history. The Aztec states were institutions shaped by his hand and geared to the fulfillment of his needs. These states were therefore platforms displaying him in all his armorial gaudiness to the world at large. Out of his knightly enterprise was to come the energy, the treachery, and the tumult of the times.

But this Aztec baron was in addition the high priest of his culture, scrupulously intent on advancing the millenial purposes of the gods. More was asked of the *teuctli* than of any man. The sacrifices he was called upon to make were very great indeed, and his death on the field of battle or on the sacrificial stone was in every sense redemptive for his people. Still he knew himself to be a defeated man whose end was certain, and in bitterness he could and did lament the enchantment in which he was locked:

> We came here only to sleep,
> Only to dream—
> It is not true that we came to live on the earth.[3]

The basic stuff of Aztec history is the appearance of this *teuctli*, his seizure of power (or rather his reformulation of it) upon the ruins of the Toltec empire, and his attempts to find a legitimacy for that power. Mexican history shares in this common Aztec history but is unique both in the high intensity of its political life and in its final solution to the problem of legitimacy.

The Mexica are probably as controversial to us today as they were to themselves in their own times. Their catastrophic end is better known to most than the events of the fall of Rome, but their beginnings and their corporate life as they lived it for a few fleeting decades are generally not known to the majority of serious readers. The whole tale is, as it were, a skeleton, its bones split and scattered about by the years. These we can inspect one by one and even curiously reassemble them. Within those bones lies, still fat, the historic marrow of an amazing people. Their tale should be known and is here offered.

A RAIN OF DARTS

THE MEXICA AZTECS

Tlacochquiaui tlalticpac
in nepapan xochitli on yohuala ica
ya tetecuica in ilhuicatl.

A rain of darts falls on the earth.
Flowers of many hues wilt under the dark cloud
And the heavens in anguish bellow.

From a poem attributed to Cacama

1. The Fall of Tula

The present borders of the Republic of Mexico do not adequately define the scene of the events we are about to describe. The name given by the Aztecs to the central portion of the Mesoamerican plateau that would become their world was Anahuac, meaning literally "in the vicinity of the waters" or "on the shore." Specifically, the word Anahuac referred to the lacustrine world within the present Basin of Mexico, but in a more extended sense it also was used to include the lands just over the mountains to the east, which lands were sometimes called Tlateputzco, "the land at the back." We shall treat this greater Anahuac not as a political but as a cultural province, keeping its geographic outlines purposefully vague.[1]

Long before the arrival of the Aztecs in the area, Anahuac was a much coveted and beautiful land, being then a part of the Toltec empire. Four gigantic mountains, among the most majestic in the world, dominate the landscape: the snow-capped pair, Popocatepetl and Iztaccihuatl define the eastern wall of the Basin, the other two, Malinche and the Nevado de Toluca, respectively, post the eastern and western boundaries of greater Anahuac. As long as the traveler could keep any one of these four peaks within sight, he was still in Anahuac or skirting its frontiers.

At the center of Anahuac was the great central Basin of Mexico, which was defined by circumambient mountains clothed with immense forests. Streams carried the melted snows into Lake Tezcoco, which, shallow and vast, glittered like a mirror. Its edges were crowded with beds of stiff reeds, the air over it was filled with squalling, wheeling flights of aquatic birds, while monstrous volcanic islands invaded the surface of the lake like great wedges that had been lazily shoved out into the waters and left there. Cities and cultivated fields ringed the lake, adding the touch of man to the vastness and solemnity of the scene.

The northern portion of the Basin differed from the other three sides in being unimpressive and far less verdant. Here the hills were low and widely spaced, and they gave easy access to the arid lands beyond where there grew thickets of cactus trees and mesquite and often little else. When one had gone north beyond the old city of Tula, the last outposts of Anahuac were left behind and one entered a territory roamed over by a near-naked and barbaric people called the Chichimecs. This steppe country, austere and endless, was to loom largely in the background of all the Aztec peoples; it was always mentioned with as much aversion as respect. It was called Teotlalli, "Godland."[2] "It is a place of misery, pain, suffering, fatigue, poverty, torment. It is a place of dry rocks, of failure; a place of lamentation; a place of death from thirst; a place of starvation. It is a place of much hunger, of much death. It is to the north."[3]

Teotihuacan and the Fall of Tula[4]

The geographic backgrounds of our history are these northern fringes of Anahuac. By A.D. 200 certain peoples had formed themselves in the northern part of the Basin into the first of the great cities of Mesoamerica, which we refer to by its later Aztec name, Teotihuacan.

The knowledge the Aztecs had of this vast urban site—totally ruined even in their day—was confused with that of another city, Tula, successor in time and in prestige to Teotihuacan. As an imperial center Teotihuacan was destroyed possibly about A.D. 650 and thereafter for a century sheltered only a weak and dwindling population. Tula, situated to the northwest, carried on the torch, itself to give way and founder on a date that has been traditionally accepted as sometime in the twelfth century. Both Teotihuacan and Tula had created empires and an indelible way of life, but details are vague and shifting, for the Aztecs afterwards telescoped these two cities and their histories together. Here in a brief sketch is what the Aztecs cared to remember of them.

The ancient splendors of Teotihuacan finally came to an end, its resounding fall marking in the mythology of later people the end of a cosmic aeon as well. In this cataclysm the sun and all the heavenly bodies flared out leaving the world in darkness. A new aeon had to be created, and this act was accordingly performed in the silent temple courtyards of Teotihuacan, a new sun and a new moon being called up out of the ashes of two gods who voluntarily immolated themselves to this end.

The first men of this latest aeon were the Toltecs, intruders from the upper Atoyac watershed near Cholula. They were wise beyond knowing, curers, magicians, builders, in all ways fantastically accomplished; their name in fact (Tolteca) would eventually come to mean "men wise in the arts."

In 770 the Toltecs elected their first prince and prepared the foundations of their capital city. Here in Tula they worshipped Quetzalcoatl, a god peculiarly their own, for he represented to them the highest reaches of sanctity and wisdom. In that pre-Aztec state the royal office seems to have been dual; the conduct of war was carried on by a functionary called the *huemac*, and the priestly charge was in the care of a personage called the *quetzalcoatl*.[5] The Toltecs spoke that most elegant of tongues, Nahuatl, while the peoples round about spoke, in addition, Otomí. Out from Tula a vigorous empire soon spread to engulf many peoples and to provide fiefs for the Toltec barons. The land of Anahuac was a part of this empire.

A legend was born out of this period that was later to become of paramount importance to the Aztecs. It goes as follows. A certain prince who bore the name Topiltzin became the *quetzalcoatl*, but he was a divisive figure in the state, for his strange ways of doing things included cult innovations featuring prohibitions on human sacrifice. Factions arose to oppose him. Even the gods, it was believed, became envious of him and his righteousness, and they instituted a successful cabal to tempt him from his self-imposed state of purity. His eventual fall from grace into sin brought about his expulsion from the city. The party that had shared in his career and accomplishments accompanied him on the legendary peregrinations that now followed. Finally, on the shores of the Mexican Gulf near Coatzacoalcos, he threw himself upon a pyre and perished in the flames. His heart rose upward as that rare scintilla of brightness, the morning star. Before his end he had prophesied that he would return on the anniversary of his birth date, Ce Acatl ("one-Reed"), and that he would then reclaim the empire of Tula as his, ruling as Quetzalcoatl's anointed one, his exile behind him and the legitimacy of his rule at last vindicated. All of this took place at a time close to the end of the Toltec empire.

So much for the legend. The facts appear to have been that the last *quetzalcoatl* of Tula was indeed a prince called Topiltzin, and that he greatly alarmed the traditional cultists of that city. His tenure of office was contemporary with a period of severe drought and consequent famine. The political structure of the empire underwent a rapid erosion in his time, and with this came the appearance of ghastly signs and wonders. Guilt became attached to him and he was forced out. He fled southward with a band of loyal followers and eventually came out on the Gulf coast. From here in a fleet of canoes he departed eastward to Yucatan, possibly to Chichén Itzá, a city which for many years previous to this had been subject to the Toltecs.

In 1168 Tula was burned and broken up in a great act of vengeance.[6] Its stately pillars were tumbled down and its treasures dispersed. The last *huemac* of Tula fled from the conflagration southward.[7] Folk memory pretended to know what happened to him. Leading his last veterans he moved down into the midst of the plundered Toltec cities around Lake Tezcoco and settled at the foot of the rock of Chapulte-

pec. This was a Toltec community that had been weakened in the wars and famine and consequently offered him little refuge. On the rock he met his end. Whether shot with arrows or dying by his own hand, he was still supposed to have cheated death by magically disappearing into a holy cave called Cincalco.[8] Here in the deep heart of the mountain he was revived to rule a land where all was beauty and freshness and where those fortunate enough to pass the scrutiny of his gimlet-eyed guardians lived forever.

In the distant future a Mexican king, Moteuczoma II, in fear of the ominous appearance of certain bearded men from the sea, would seek refuge in this paradise of Cincalco—but would find it closed to him.[9]

The People of Godland

Toltec rule had undoubtedly weakened from internal excesses as well as from the treasons of the great earls, but the storm that finally swept it away came from the north and west, from Teotlalli. It came not with the force of a single hurricane but in wild gusts and squalls with intervals of quiet. We refer to it *in toto* as the Chichimec invasion, but even that oversimplifies the matter.

In the succeeding centuries, most of the Aztec groups were to point in pride to their Chichimec descent. They believed that their Chichimec blood endowed them with toughness, independence, endurance, valor —all the virtues befitting a warlike people—and one may guess without fear of error that their ancestors did indeed evince these very characteristics. Certainly the perils of Teotlalli would not have produced a feeble people. In later times distinguished Aztec warriors took pride in the designation of themselves as Chichimecs.

Know that when our ancestors lived in the wilds, in the thorny deserts, they lived by the bow and arrow—if they were not assiduous they did not eat—and that was in the days of those godlike Chichimecs, our ancestors.[10]

What distinguished the Chichimecs was not their language, for in addition to Nahuatl they spoke other tongues, but rather the stringent way of life imposed upon them by the steppe. The Chichimecs comprised three major groups, which can be placed in a descending order of cultural sophistication: Otomí, Tamime, and Teochichimecs.[11] The

first group spoke their own language, which was quite distinct from
the Nahuatl tongue spoken by the Toltecs and the Aztecs. They differed
from the other two divisions of the Chichimecs by being part-time ag-
riculturalists while still remaining adept at hunting and collecting. As
warriors, there were none hardier. Though they had a priesthood and a
sense of confederacy, their preference was to live in small and disparate
communities on the mountain slopes and in rough piney country. They
were the southernmost of the Chichimecs and had inhabited western
and northern Anahuac and large areas of the Basin well before the fall
of Tula. Indeed they must have been one of the component peoples of
the Toltec empire. No doubt they had learned the arts of agriculture
from Tula.

Far north and west of the Otomí in Teotlalli were the Teochichimecs, sometimes referred to as "Chichimecs of the steppe" or as Zacateca, "people of the plains," which implied wild men.[12] Nomads, they
lived by the bow and arrow and digging stick. They went either naked
or draped in a few skins, moving about in small monogamous bands.
During the day the women foraged for roots and other vegetable
foods, leaving their papooses slung high up in the thin shade of the
mesquite tree. These groups recognized certain headmen who resided
for extended periods of time in caves or grass stalls marked by a white
pennon that was the symbol of their holiness or command. They were
generally hostile to the incursion of Toltec merchants into their territory. In herbal lore the Chichimec people were unsurpassed. There was
not a plant, lichen, or fruit to be found in the desert or clinging to the
sides of the ravines of which they did not have elaborate knowledge.
They had used the hallucinogenic mushoom and peyote since time
immemorial, and from the spiny *tzihuactli* they made an intoxicating
drink. In the desperation and near starvation of their daily lives, all
members of the band had to find food. The sick and aged were killed
when their usefulness was at an end. Every evening a smoke signal
went up and called in the hunting bands with their kill. The headman
received a portion of all game caught. Meat was eaten uncooked.

Though they made no idols of him, the presence of their god was
indicated by inserting an upright arrow in a matted mass of desert grass
or marking the spot with the white banner of divinity. He was the

numen in the flight of the arrow through their sky, thus perhaps the origin of his Nahuatl name Mixcoatl, "cloud serpent."[13] By him alone they were fed and lived. He was their luck in the chase and their fortune in life, whether good or bad.[14] Mixcoatl is said to have possessed a fetish of great power, which he carried about on his back in a sacred bundle. This was an obsidian knife blade and was the locus of a powerful female oracle, Itzpapalotl, "butterfly knife." We shall see it later in Mexican history as the blood-stained knife of sacrifice.

These Chichimecs constantly encroached on the two regions of Mesoamerica neighboring them that were civilized, coastal Huaxteca on the east and Anahuac to the south. It is for this reason that we find many of the Chichimecs speaking tongues other than their own, such as Huaxtec, Otomí, or Nahuatl.[15] Chichimec bands were wont to appear suddenly among the establishments of the Toltec empire, among the gardens and ditches of the tribute-paying peoples, or simply coursing about on the hills behind the cities; they traded a bit, spied out the land with practised eyes, raided where their small numbers permitted, served for periods as rough mercenaries, and even occasionaly learned to grow a bit of maize. These slightly more acculturated groups we call the Tamime.[16] Nevertheless, like their ruder brothers up in the heart of Teotlalli, they never entirely put aside their desert habits and every man slept always with his bow beside his head.

It is the Tamime who blazed the ways down from Teotlalli into Anahuac, feeding their blood into the land wherever opportunities for temporary settlement presented themselves or, inversely, as refugees and prodigals, moving back into the steppe to present themselves to their fellows there with some shreds of a new culture or with news of the land of cities and marvels to recount of the south. They were a fringe folk and perhaps ancestral to the Aztecs.

The Teochichimecs or "pure" Chichimecs in the far north were not essentially a warlike people, for war is a matter of policy and masses and they were always few and hungry in a nearly empty land. Nevertheless when, like the Tamime, they moved itinerantly among the warring Toltec cities, they had many opportunities to watch the evolutions and tactics of trained armies from their stations high up among the crags. Whenever in fact they themselves, in a loose tributary subjection to Toltec earls, sometimes fought in the same battles—then the hardness of their lives in nature was transformed overnight into a ferocious valor on the field of battle. Skill in ambush and tracking, incredible marksmanship with arrows and darts, ability to move about in the dust of the melee with the agility of the mountain lion and the deadliness of the rattlesnake—such qualities would have become for them easy passports into the warrior class.

But their skill in war provided them only with the cruder means, not with the incentives, of civilization. Our knowledge of the breakup of the Toltec empire is meager, but we are able to see great marcher lords forming up in the outer provinces and coming at Tula from many sides with armies. A protracted period of disarray in a state, along with endemic warfare, provides a perfect culture for a people such as the Chichimecs to assimilate. It is in fact probable that the Toltec armies, after decades of intestine warfare, had become heavily Chichimec in personnel. In turn the Tamime would have begun to alter their own institutions and beliefs, adopting with little difficulty the warrior cult and the warrior mentality of the highly organized Toltecs. We have no real evidence that this is what happened, but it is probable.

We are surely correct in believing that the Chichimecs far back in Teotlalli were affected by the rumors and rumblings south of them and that there began among them as a consequence a slow osmotic move in that direction, perhaps stimulated also by an increasing desiccation in the steppe.[17] One such movement of peoples—traditionally seven bands loosely united—listened to the urgings of their gods and took up the southward trek. These Chichimecs were to become the Aztecs of later history, mingling their blood with the refugee Toltecs who, following the sack of Tula, were moving south ahead of them.

Culhuacan and the Legitimacy

Rulers often seem to be preoccupied with the matter of discovering, establishing, and justifying the transfer of legitimacy. Legendary Troy was the home of great kings. After its sack there ensued a dispersal of its peoples led by daring and piratical princes, each carrying pieces of the legitimacy. Under Aeneas and in the persons of his descendants, this inchoate kingship was carried to Alba Longa in distant Italy. Here it was nurtured until that day when the descendants of Aeneas should reinstitute Trojan rule by founding a city out of which flowed a great empire. Rome was this new city, but essential to it was the antiquity of its claim to exercise legitimate power.

This makes a suitable scenario for our own tale. In the eyes of all the peoples of Mesoamerica, Tula was the very fountain of rule, and only a Toltec ruler, whether a *quetzalcoatl* or a *huemac*, could be considered a true suzerain. The authority wielded by Chichimec kinglets or chieftains had no such prestige. After the dispersion of the Toltec princes and magnates, one of them led a band of people who called themselves Culua down to the southern shore of Lake Tezcoco, where they settled.[18] Their community was named Culhuacan after them and was located under the sacred hill, Huixachtlan, today the Cerro de la Estrella. Here the legitimacy which the Culua claimed as carriers of the blood royal remained and grew strong until it was finally to be carried off to the city of Mexico, just as Trojan legitimacy in Alba Longa was carried off to Rome.

Since Culhuacan, therefore, is the neo-Toltec city from which the Mexica were later to derive their claim to rule Anahuac and the world, it is best to sketch here its early history. Whether the Culua were pure-blooded Toltecs with an immaculate tradition behind them is immaterial. The point is that they claimed such high prestige and made their claim stick. Culhuacan was accepted by the other new immigrant cities arising in Anahuac as something of a successor to Tula.[19] It seemed for a short while as if indeed out of the ashes of the Toltec empire would rise this phoenix of a new Tula, able again to exercise true political sovereignty. But this was not to occur. Though Culhuacan quickly became a center of revived Toltec skills and culture, it was never powerful enough to exercise more than a nominal suzerainty over the south shore of the lake.

The first ruler may have been of the former line of Toltec kings, or he may have simply strengthened ties to Tula by marrying his daughter to one of its last pauper princes. Whichever is the case, the line of kings he headed in Culhuacan felt itself descended in a direct line from the great Toltec emperors. Culhuacan was thus a rump Toltec state on its own promulgation and by the acquiescence of the other rulers of Anahuac. This right to rule had first been enunciated by Teotihuacan in the cloudy past; it had passed thence to Tula and was now in Culhuacan. On the erosion of the imperial pretensions of Culhuacan, legitimate Toltec rule would finally settle in Mexico, the fourth and last Mesoamerican capital in this tradition.

The date of the founding of Culhuacan is in dispute; 1179 has been suggested, and this is quite consistent with the chronology we have been following.[20] There had undoubtedly been an urban center on the spot before the entry of the Culua, so in effect what we are talking about is the refounding of a city.

The new state suffered from the pervasive restlessness of the times; internal dissensions periodically forced groups out to found daughter colonies or to merge into the growing populations of other cities. Culhuacan was never given time to mature and become great. The claims of its house to an antique imperial dignity brought forth in due time the inevitable challenge. A person named Xolotl, one of the great conquerors in Mesoamerican history, had just led a Chichimec horde into the northern part of the Basin. This incursion of peoples and its meaning for Aztec history will be discussed later; here it is sufficient to state that Xolotl and his son Nopaltzin resented the claim of Culhuacan to dominion everywhere in the Basin. Nopaltzin accordingly demanded that Culhuacan recognize his house as overlord. On receiving an insulting reply he threw his wild bowmen against the city and took it.[21] The Culua ruler was ousted, and the victorious Chichimecs set up in his place a related Toltec ruler who could equally claim the blood royal from Tula. While this defeat frustrated the advance of further Culua claims, it inhibited neither the growth nor the disputatiousness of the city.

All over Anahuac other cities were springing into renewed life as migrations and invasions poured down like spring freshets from the north, swelling the population and increasing conflict. Chichimec, Otomí, Toltec, or intermingled groups of all three were moving now in force into older urban foundations, either as petitioning settlers or as autocratic conquerors. New lines of petty kings sprang up overnight; some of them were fortunate and lasted out several generations, some were eclipsed almost at their first appearance, but all without exception ruled over rapidly growing populations. Contests between cities were to become perennial, and there seemed to be no respite from war. Culhuacan found itself engaged against a strong neighbor, Xochimilco, for supremacy in the southern part of the Basin. Culhuacan never let it be forgotten that she had been the first city in the Basin to anoint a king, to establish an aristocracy, and to care for the perpetuation of Toltec records and culture. While there was no denial of this—for her princesses were much in demand by aspiring kings of other cities eager to further their own legitimacy—her authority extended only to where her armies might travel without fear of ambush. Furthermore, her aristocracy soon became so inextricably mingled through marriage with new Chichimec houses that distinctions between Toltec and Chichimec prestige were difficult to make.

The Entry of Xolotl

The history of Anahuac can be rightly understood only as the confluence of two streams, Chichimec and Toltec, each bringing complementary skills and traditions to the making of the new Aztec city-states. Xolotl, the Chichimec leader previously mentioned, stands at the source of the first of those streams.[22] His name is Nahautl.[23] It was probably given to him by the late Toltecs and bears witness to the horror and fear he inspired in them. The word has several meanings, but that intended here is probably "monster" or "prodigy"; it describes a chimera or apparition in the world of men. The epitome of a great and fortunate steppe leader, he was by far the most outstanding ruler of his age.

Somewhere in Godland was a place called Oyome, no longer identifiable but probably a client kingdom out beyond Tula's northern frontier.[24] Here ruled a line of shadowy Chichimec chieftains during the penultimate days of the great Toltec capital. Their power rested on tribal custom, and wherever they sat in that wilderness, the symbolic white flag was placed near an overhang of rock or under a judging tree to designate the spot as their chancery. Whenever this court moved, the pennon streamed out in the van of the straggling lines of men, no doubt marking the royal presence in imitation of the more polished Toltec custom. This cactus kingdom, Oyome, could have contained at most only a few villages and certain ceremonial centers where periodically the tribes met. Otherwise it was a land of campsites scattered over the hundreds of thousands of square miles of broken country where its denizens ranged in their unending quest for food.

The long reverberations of Tula's death agonies were profoundly felt in Godland and necessitated finally a recasting of the crude policy of the barbarians. In the years contemporary with Toltec decline, clans and small pillaging groups had been constantly drifting south, violating the frontiers of civilization with impunity. Moving through the interstices of what was thus a crumbling society, these Chichimecs pressed closer and closer to the central Basin of Anahuac. Caught between their love of the wild and the lure of a higher civilization, their descents were random. The most significant of these Chichimec migrations was that under the leadership of Xolotl, younger brother of the ruler of Oyome. More aggressive—or more discontented—than others, he put himself at the head of a formidable group of followers and took the road southward. His dates are greatly in doubt, but it is probable that he began his career of conquest about the middle of the thirteenth century, some seventy-five years after the destruction of Tula.

But it was not just Oyome that was sending its blood south. As the times became more and more parlous and as a devastating drought was added to the tale of man-made disasters, the demise of Tula became a certainty. Chichimec groups outside Oyome, from widely separated areas in the north and west, joined the exodus until it seemed that a whole world was on the move, not only piecemeal bits of the broken Toltec state but also multitudes of border peoples as well.

The stars favored Xolotl, bringing additional vagrant and warrior bands to his banner. By the time he had passed through the debris and broken streets of Tula, he had become the charismatic leader of a great horde.[25] As this swarm of people became increasingly aware of its power, casting the terror of its name like a shadow on the road ahead,

its desires grew and its composition changed to accommodate them. Rapidly, though unconsciously, the horde was changing into a primitive state. It was beginning to be aware of the fact that it had definitively cast its lot in Anahuac, that loot was not now its only objective, and that its objectives included the winning of cities and even the establishment of baronial seats in those cities.

The Xolotl horde was indeed responding to civilization. Its loosely federative structure would in a short time give way to a kind of imperial feudalism knit around a man and not a geographical center. The cities in the Basin and its environs had been under an uninterrupted Toltec influence or had been refounded by refugee Toltec bands; these Xolotl scorned and desired at the same time. He was proposing that a new dispensation be given to this old world, based no longer on Tula's ancient legitimacy of rule but instead on the prescriptive right of effective leadership.

Whether or not Xolotl invented the title which was to express this new constellation of political power—*chichimeca teuctli*—is unknown. It is a Nahuatl term and is literally translated "lord of the Chichimecs." It suggests an office of archaic and untutored grandeur.[26]

The horde settled temporarily in a vast campsite just north of the ruins of Teotihuacan, outside the Basin proper. Appropriately, this stopping place was called Xoloc or "the Place of Xolotl," and it was from here that the first entry was planned. A story that was current among his descendants said that Xolotl climbed a high mountain on the north side of the Basin and cast his eyes down into the summering expanse below to behold blue water everywhere, craggy islands, and all around the edges of the lakes innumerable columns of smoke rising from cities and villages awakening into a new life. To Chichimec eyes, used to parched landscapes and stony fields of cactus, such gleaming habitations with their surrounding maize plots represented another world entirely. What could be thought of a people who insisted on wearing cotton garments instead of the durable pelts of deer and coyote! What of people who licked salt and spent their days laboring in fields! Of people who could not run with the wind or course over the mountain! But it was a beautiful land and it called to them. Xolotl returned to his temporary capital and set in motion the necessary reconnoitering, dispatching his son Nopaltzin into the Basin country at the head of a band of co-adventurers.

On the basis of the reports from this party, Xolotl finally broke up his camp and pushed southwest to the former Toltec city of Tenayuca and subdued it. From the peak of a nearby mountain he shot four arrows into space, one into each of the four sacred directions, as was the Chichimec custom on taking formal possession of a new land.[27] Henceforth, according to his promulgation, Anahuac was to be the hunting preserve of the Chichimecs. Xolotl established at Tenayuca the first capital of the *chichimeca teuctli* in Anahuac.

There were now two polar powers in the Basin, in the north the Chichimecs actively campaigning out from their center in Tenayuca, in the south the Culua capital of Culhuacan, less warlike but more prestigious. The population of the capital in the north was being constantly replenished by new Chichimec and related bands trekking in from the hinterland; the population of the southern center was sustained as well by the increase natural to an urbanized folk. Their respective polities also were different, yet the amalgamation of the two was producing the civilization we know as Aztec.

In his center in Tenayuca, Xolotl received chieftains crowding in with their warriors and women, enlisting them in his inchoate and ill-defined imperial state. He had paid off his own early followers by assigning them either to unoccupied areas reserved for the chase or to designated cities if they wished to adopt that style of life. In all cases they were required to create great hunting parks so they might more easily provide him with his customary tax on the game they took. Those more recently arrived who had also demonstrated their usefulness to him were granted parcels of land that they were expected to conquer and to bring under tribute by themselves. In certain cases the baronies granted to these later retainers were merely small enclaves inserted into states being consolidated under the rule of members of his original horde— this being designed to keep the latecomers under adequate surveillance. One notable and important exception to this caution was made in Xolotl's later years when three strong chieftains did homage to him and were consequently assigned to the strategic cities of Xaltocan, Coatli-

chan, and Azcapotzalco.[28] These three had come in at the head of Otomí or Otomí-related groups from the Toluca area west of the Basin,
and their history subsequently was to form one of the persistent themes
in Aztec life. In any case the holders of royal patents—whether the
original bands or latecomers such as these—were all obligated to appear in Tenayuca to perform homage to Xolotl. The annual gathering
here was one of the few institutions of the Chichimec state.

Far different was the state system practiced by Culhuacan. As important to her as her warriors were her nubile princesses. These young
women in whose veins ran the blood of Quetzalcoatl were more than
items of great worth and beauty—they were indispensable pawns in
the harsh and guileful game of alliance politics just beginning. Culhuacan was not an amorphous and seething body of barons as was, in
some respects, the state of Xolotl. It was a single city; it called on no
increment to its strength from adventurers and starvelings, for it presumed to be exclusive and thoroughly Toltec. Its claims were prodi-
gious but its actual means were limited, for hostile cities like Xochimilco neighbored it and allowed it little room for expansion. Craft and
legitimacy were its lance and buckler as it faced the aborning Aztec
world of which it was a part.

Tezcoco

The great Xolotl died at an advanced age and was
buried in a cave in the mountain behind Tenayuca. His able son and co-
adjutant Nopaltzin, after a long lifetime of wars and alarms, died and
was buried in the cave beside the bones of his father.[29] Between them,
they had carved out a permanent place for their crude empire in the
northern part of Anahuac.

But the tempo of events had significantly speeded up. What had
been a sprawling Chichimec world had emerged into a toughened but
trimmed-down empire on the east side of the Basin. This state was to
be known as Acolhuacan. Its capital city was to be Tezcoco, and its
first acknowledged ruler was a grandson of Xolotl named Tlotzin. It
is permissible to refer to Tlotzin now as an Aztec ruler.

The site of Tezcoco was one of rare beauty, and in later and more
prosperous years the city would come right down to the lake to which

it gave its name. Behind it was green country—corn country—rolling up to the slumberous bulk of Mount Tlaloc. It was in the foothills just behind Tezcoco where Xolotl had first settled upon a certain wild and yet intimate area as a deer run reserved for his hunting pleasure. Nopaltzin had tightened the imperial grip on the forests and ravines of the area by prohibitions against setting fires, moving boundary markers, or hunting without license. The romantic nature of the scene was underlined by the presence of sacred grottoes and the ruin of a mouldering Toltec pyramid left from the almost unremembered past. The section of this parkland where later were to be located the villas and pleasure gardens of famous Aztec kings was known as Cuauhyacac, "forest's edge."[30] As the succeeding Chichimec kings became more and more acclimatized to urban living, the city of Tezcoco nearby would grow up powerful and important, yet never as beloved by the kings as was this sylvan retreat. Beginning with Tlotzin's successor, all the Acolhua rulers were buried in Cuauhyacac.

Who the Aztecs Were

The Aztec peoples came into Anahuac as invaders, they spoke Nahuatl (or at an early period adopted it), and they lived in cities or confederate communities. These are the major hallmarks that identify them and their way of life, but their ethnic background is uncertain. While consideration of its origin is speculative, Aztec culture was to be a most powerful solvent, erasing differences between disparate peoples and blending them easily into its own peculiar mixture. We have already seen Nahuatl-speaking peoples scattering into the south and setting up their urban residences in and around the great Basin. We have seen Xolotl's Chichimecs also enter the Valley after passing through the dead and dismembered Toltec state. Tlotzin's son and successor, under heavy Culua influence, ordered all his Chichimec followers to give up forever their wilderness ways and to settle permanently in the Acolhua cities.[31] Tlotzin's grandson went further and ordered his followers to speak Nahuatl, by this action stamping them as fully Aztec, at least as we have defined the word. Needless to say these civilizing measures met violent opposition.

A people whom we know as the Tepaneca had entered the Basin from the Toluca Valley and were granted the Toltec city of Azcapotzalco by the dispensation of Xolotl. Azcapotzalco, one of those cities situated on the western shores of Lake Tezcoco, continued to attract further settlers from the west and soon formed around it a compact Tepaneca kingdom—but they too in time spoke Nahuatl as well as their native Otomí and so entered the Aztec world. The cities of the confederate republic of Chalco on the south side of the lake were likewise composed of contrasting tongues and ethnic backgrounds, but they also adopted Nahuatl.

Aztec civilization appeared also in those parts of Anahuac outside the Basin. In the "Hot Land" just over the mountains to the south—what is today the state of Morelos—lived the Tlahuica; their cities too were part of the Aztec world. But most spectacularly Aztec of all were those impressive urban communities on the other side of the eastern wall of mountains: Tlascala, Cholula, Huexotzinco, Teohuacan, and others. The Chichimec invaders of this countryside were speaking Nahuatl when they first came in.

But something further is needed in the definition of the word Aztec, something that will not only tell us who they were and in what manner they spoke, but will identify the cultural orientation of their cities. This can be briefly indicated. Aztec cities existed for the purposes of warfare.

These cities were indeed each different in their popular base; some specialized in commerce, some were pilgrimage centers, some lived on their plots of maize and maguey, while other were cities of fowlers and fishermen. Nevertheless, in every case control was in the hands of an aristocracy dedicated to the gods on the one hand and to battle and bloodshed on the other. Aztec society was more integrated than most, for goals were never in doubt. Questions that naturally arise in societies offering several directions in which one can move could never arise in the Aztec states or in the Aztec mind. This consensus, while it produced a single way of life, could not produce a common policy.

It was an athletic and contentious world that suddenly appeared in Anahuac, and it turned out to be one of the most remarkable cultural

configurations in history. It was the last indigenous culture Anahuac
was ever to have.

Aztec Agreement on the Past

Having shared in the knowledge of—or participa-
tion in—Tula's fall and then in the subsequent wanderings that led
them into the heart of Anahuac, all the peoples who were to become
Aztec looked back to a common history. A semi-legendary account of
this past became sufficiently standardized so that all could adopt the
tale with certain minor variations or differences in emphasis.[32] It ran
more or less as follows:

In the lands to the north and west of Tula there was once a city and
land named Culhuacan (not to be confused with that neo-Toltec city
already mentioned in this chapter). In that land and by that city was a
lake. In the lake was a magic island called Aztlan. The presence of
seven caves in Aztlan gave rise to its designation as Chicomoztoc,
which means "the place of the seven caves." From each of these caves
came a specific Aztec tribe, each called forth by the promptings of the
god. The list of those seven tribes varied rather widely depending on
which city was trying to squeeze itself and its compeers into the arbi-
trary number seven. The following list however can be taken as representative: the Xochimilca, the Chalca, the Tepaneca, the Culua, the
Tlahuica, the Tlascalteca and the Mexica.[33]

A Promised Land was their common goal. The vicissitudes and
hardships of their wanderings, the names of their leaders and priests,
and the stopping places along the route south all differ according to the
source used. But there is one significant fact upon which most of our
versions agree, and that is either a short residence in or a passing
through the city of Tula. This was to vindicate the wandering and to
confer urbanity and the sanction of the past on that particular Aztec
people offering the version.

Some versions stressed the wilderness wandering, the harshness and
terror of the steppe, the nakedness of the wayfarers—the Chichimec
background. Contrasting ones stressed the *toltecayotl*, the presence and
superiority of Tula, in the journey. But both presences were important in painting in the backgrounds. Though it became one, Aztec cul-

ture in its origination tales proudly displayed the two contrasting ancestral strains.

The list of the seven Aztec peoples presented above is important in
another respect; it ends with the Mexica. Inasmuch as the lists always
pretend to a chronological order, this meant that the Mexica were acknowledged to have been the last of the Aztecs to enter Anahuac.
From this were to flow untoward consequences that are the proper subject of this book.

2. The Mexica Gain a King

On the day in 1519 when Hernando Cortez arrived in Mexico, Moteuczoma was to say to him in their first conversation: "From the records which we have long possessed and which are handed down from our ancestors, it is known that no one, neither I nor the others who inhabit this land of Anahuac, are native to it. We are strangers and we came from far outer parts."[1]

It is surely a curious people who kept until the very end of their history such an acute sense of exteriority. Our contemplation of this fact must concern itself first with the Mexican version of the Tale of Wandering, for in that we should discover the deepest substrate of their national feeling.[2]

The Mexica identified the land from which they came as Teoculhuacan, the "real" or "original" Culhuacan. Close to or within this shadowy country was the place called Aztlan, an island in the midst of a lake.[3] And on this island was a rock and a cave called Chicomoztoc, which was both a religious center and an amphictyonic capital for the semi-nomadic tribes. We are dealing here probably with memories of some diffuse and barbaric client-state contemporary with the old Toltec empire and located beyond its northern and western frontiers. The fact that the Mexica classed themselves as Chichimec tells us a little about this hypothetical state. No doubt they lived at the level of the Tamime Chichimecs. They were certainly not the cultural equals of the Culua, who were to precede them on the long migration into the Basin.

A strong and persistent tradition tells us that the Mexica originally called themselves the Mecitin, which name they took from that of their goddess Mecitli.[4] Later their tribal name came to be pronounced Mexitin, even as the name of the divinity became Mexitli, which is a change neither provable nor improbable. When they founded their great city in Lake Tezcoco, the site perforce became Mexico or "the place where Mexitli is." Thus, they would be for all time known as the Mexica, namely "they of Mexico."

The name Mecitli means "grandmother maguey" and its later variant Mexitli means "heart or navel of the maguey." We know that this goddess was an earth-mother and that Mexico was thus that spot of the earth's surface to which she was to become most singularly attached. Curiously, this goddess disappears from the history of the people at the very time that they take up their wandering at her oracular insistence. Her place is taken by a male demon who is strictly identified as the "luck" of the tribe. This is Huitzilopochtli, who, filling in for the now suppressed Mecitli, is referred to as "the frightful" or "the ominous one," with implications of terrifying visitations and arcane utterances. The place on the trek where Huitzilopochtli appeared to the Mexica and became their god is variously given, but in every case he appears with patently warlike characteristics.

The fetish of Huitzilopochtli, bundled up and screened from profane eyes, now preceded the wandering group, carried on the back of his oracle-priest or sorceror who alone was holy enough to handle safely the numinous object. This sorceror represented one of the most primitive priesthoods of Mesoamerica, for he was known as the *teomama*, "he carries the god." He was himself a simulacrum of the god. His voice was the authentic voice of the deity, and, in the sense of upholding the morale of the people, of cowing them, and directing their path, he was the true leader of the group.

There was also an elected trail captain or war leader about whose powers very little is known. The Mexica of later times compiled lists of the names of these captains as well as the names of each *teomama*. Whatever relationship existed between these two conjoint offices, it was nevertheless just such an informal government as one might imagine for an exposed group taking to the dusty ways intent on either snatch farming, hunting, or raiding.

Taken all together, the Mexica formed what was basically a robber nation on the march, no different perhaps than other Chichimec groups also moving south, except in the particularly infamous name they made for themselves as masters of violence. There is ample testimony from their congeners to the unloved reputation that they bore. A close reading of parts of the Tale of Wandering also confirms it. It is highly probable that they formed a conglomerate of small related clans, perhaps four in number, along with a sprinkling of vagrants and renegades from other societies. This heterogeneity may have underscored their need for an identity, which found its answer when they adopted the god who became more than just the spirit of "luck" of the band— he was also, as Huitzilopochtli, equivalent to victory in battle. "The Mexica maintained themselves solely by their addiction to war and their flouting of death"—so they were later to say of themselves with pride.[5]

From the date of their exit from Aztlan, 1168, miracles marked their route.[6] They appear to have begun their journey in loose company with the other Chicomoztoc tribes but soon broke away from them by command of their god, who spoke to them to this end from out of a broken tree in the wilderness. This was the time when, according to the legend, they adopted the name Mexitin, for before this they had formed merely a part of the larger mass. The broken-tree incident was no doubt invented later as a way of distinguishing their special destiny.

There followed one of the more harrowing episodes of the Wandering, namely the descent from the skies of the *mimixcoa*, who appear to have been primitive titans, cave-born monsters, and gods of long-for-

gotten peoples. They were demonic and commanded the arts of sorcery.

The southward progress of the Mexica led them at last to the vicinity
of the city of Tula. Here they settled long enough to dam the river and
to create a lake magical in its plenty and beautiful in its bordering
woods and singing birds. In the lake's center was an island called Coatepec, "Serpent Hill," and here in this latter-day paradise the Mexica
lingered long, forgetting the imperious call of their destiny.[7]

Needless to say, this account of a halcyon sojourn was later produced
under the spell of Tula's cultural prestige. The reality was that the Mexica found the ruins of Tula at the time inhabited by meager bands of
Otomí and Chichimecs. They therefore settled at the foot of the sacred
mountain of Coatepec nearby and lived here several years before moving on. It was here also where, as most accounts have it, they met the
new avatar of their god, Huitzilopochtli. This god, fully armed, had
sprung into being from the womb of the Earth Goddess Coatlicue or
"Snake Skirt." The tale of this furious birth and the succeeding battle
of the gods is one of the fundamental myths of the Aztec world and
will be expanded upon later.[8] Here it is enough to suggest that, probably under late Toltec influence, the "luck" of this wandering band
had been here reinterpreted and remodeled into a likeness of a cosmic
warrior-god. He did not thereby lose his identification with the Mexica
folk as their peculiar patron, but he now expressed in addition their
increasing combativeness.

But no paradise lasts, and the god's anger at them for their temporizing caused him to break the dams and destroy overnight the verdancy
of the land. Thus when the Mexica did move on, Tula was not only a
city long since emptied of its rightful lords and in ruins but was also a
silent city left alone even by the itinerant peoples of the desert. The
Culua had long since separated from the southward-moving hordes and
had moved on.

From Tula the route of the Mexica now led in the footsteps of the
Culua into the Basin and therefore into the domain Xolotl had just preempted. By the latter part of the thirteenth century they had made their
entry. The numerous camps made by the Mexica in the area speak both

of restlessness and of forced evictions. It was probably while Tlotzin was ruling that the Mexica came to Chapultepec, a memorable stopping place for them and the first one where the historian can judge them as a fully historic people. The exact year of their arrival appears to have been 1319.

The Mexica in Chapultepec

Chapultepec means Grasshopper Hill, a reference to the shape of the rock when seen from the side. In the days when this history begins, Chapultepec was a headland shouldering its way out into the shallow waters of Lake Tezcoco. Reed thickets impeded the approach to it by water, while its steep sides and the rolling country just back of it were covered with giant hemlocks, many of them too ancient and massive for cutting. The great rock was a cynosure attracting all eyes. Because of its bulk it was held in awe by all the lake dwellers, but its real distinction was to be found in the rich waters welling out of its base, a never-failing spring for man's life. This spring poured directly out into the mud and the reed flats where its sweetness was lost in the mild brackishness of that part of the lake.

A *huemac* or ruler of Tula had led in a band of Toltecs and Culua years before the Mexica appeared at Chapultepec and had settled there; the bulk of the Culua had then gone farther down the lake to found Culhuacan.[9] The colonization in Chapultepec had momentarily strengthened an older Toltec settlement, probably ancestral to Azcapotzalco, which had occupied the site, but increasing drought and tribal unrest soon wore the community down. The *huemac* disappeared. Because he represented the ancient wizard kings of Tula, he left at Chapultepec an aura of mystery and danger, and his ghost was destined to reappear at the very end of Mexican history. Some of these neo-Toltecs held on, however, and later joined forces with the incoming Mexica, becoming in a short time indistinguishable from them.[10] To this motley community in the succeeding years were added other footloose Chichimec groups moving through.[11] The rock was firmly held by these composite Mexica and well fortified.

It can be seen that the Mexica were an absorptive people. Besides this—as their stay at the rock was to show—they were a disruptive people and, at the time, little different from a nest of brigands. As a people they were not so much resilient as utterly tough and unyielding. Their peculiar genius for the obdurate was already demonstrated by the intense dislike of them evinced by all their neighbors. In the three decades during which they were to maintain themselves at Chapultepec, they grew stronger and always more predatory, raiding in all directions and offending many.

Thus it was here in Chapultepec where the remarkable ethos of the Mexica first truly manifested itself. To the lacustrine world into which the Mexica had injected themselves, Chapultepec finally seemed to be the very mother of outlaws. To the historian of today, Chapultepec was simply a foreshadowing of the spirit of that greater and later community, the city of Mexico.

At some time during this sojourn the Mexica were able to attract a nobleman—possibly an Otomí—from the northern part of the Basin to be their leader. His name was Huitzilihuitl, "Hummingbird Feather," and because of the presence of a later person of that name in the line of Mexican rulers, he is further distinguished as "the Elder." Under him the Mexican encampment became a crowded community, and piratical forays in search of women and loot were vigorously pushed to the point where finally the lake communities felt themselves so menaced that they took concerted action to destroy the Mexica.[12]

Azcapotzalco, the capital city of the Tepaneca, lay only a few miles to the north of Chapultepec and claimed the shoreline both north and south of the rock as well as all fishing and fowling grounds offshore. This Tepaneca city may in fact be reckoned as the claimant overlord of the Mexica, and they as its pensioners. But the tie was loose, and the Mexica had become as major an irritant to Azcapotzalco as to the rest of the cities around the lake. Possibly also they had become a military threat to Azcapotzalco.

Joining together in an uncommon unity under the leadership of Xaltocan, the major cities of the Basin—excepting only those on the east side of the lake—moved against the Mexica.[13] With skill and great hardihood the Mexica resisted but were finally overwhelmed in 1348 or 1349.

When the final operation was over, many of their fighting men lay dead, the survivors had been trapped in an ambush on a shoal in the lake, their settlement at Chapultepec was overrun, their women seized, and the remnants scattered in all directions, either enslaved or in flight. Huitzilihuitl was captured and he, his wives, and daughters, stripped of their clothing, were marched to Culhuacan, one of the allied cities, to be sacrificed there to Toltec gods. The Mexica leader pleaded in vain with the ruler of Culhuacan that he allow his women some scraps of clothing to cover their nakedness for this was the ultimate and unbearable affront. Naturally this was refused. Huitzilihuitl and his women were quickly dispatched. A son captured by the Tepaneca was sold in the slave market of Azcapotzalco, and the first noble line of the Mexica, just begun, came to its inglorious end. "With shields facing every way we Mexica perished on the rock of Chapultepec. Alas! They carried away our children to the far four regions of the earth. Huitzilihuitl vanished weeping." Thus did the remnants of this luckless people frame their lament.[14]

About two miles out in the lake, easily visible from the rock of Chapultepec, there was a low island known as Tlatilulco with some adjoining mud and sand flats just to the south, all claimed by Azcapotzalco.[15] These half-drowned shoals had been used as splinter settlements by squatters and fishermen from Mexican Chapultepec. Because of the shallowness of the lake in this area, the shoals formed nearly impenetrable cane and willow brakes, abounding in fish and aquatic bird life.

In makeshift canoes a certain group from among the survivors of the Chapultepec massacre, who in happier days had used and even settled in this dim archipelago, now fled out there for sanctuary. They were destitute, and as they lingered in the thickets day after day floundering about in the mud searching for duck eggs, edible roots, and insects, starvation further depleted their numbers. And in those days, whenever the war canoes of their enemies came gliding out into the area persistently searching for further victims, the refugees, with hands clapped over the mouths of their young ones, thrashed out into the denser parts of the covert and sank down to nose level in the bitterly cold water—a people in full flight and oppressed with misery. They dressed in the leaves of water plants for they had few garments left. The torment of their lives comes to us only as a vague and almost meaningless echo, but throughout all the years of their future the Mexica were never to forget their suffering at that time.

History records no example more astounding concerning the foundation of a great city. Yet this is the record of the first firm settlement made on the future site of Mexico, a city still famous, though the lake and the reeds have disappeared long since as well as the founding people.

The Night of the Mexica

It was not long before starvation forced this remnant of the Mexica to emerge from among the willow scrub and the reeds and to cluster in their nakedness and misery on the sands of Tlatilulco. Ululating and casting dirt upon themselves they pleaded for mercy from the Tepaneca, to whom the tiny island belonged. Their abjectness proved them to be no longer dangerous. Contemptuously, therefore, the ruler of the Tepaneca offered them their lives, and in return for that mercy these Tlatilulca Mexica shouldered the crushing burdens that near slaves and tributaries always carry. Some years of privation would stretch ahead of this segment of the dispersed Mexica before they climbed back to a position of power.

Others of the captured Mexica had been carried away by the city of Xaltocan as slaves and were never heard of again. The only other significant remnant was the group that finally surrendered to Culhuacan. It is the story of their tribulations and further displacements which must concern us here.

The death of the leader, Huitzilihuitl, on the sacrificial stone of Culhuacan had cut the nexus that bound the Chapultepec Mexica together. The beggarly group that now offered themselves as subjects of the Culua nevertheless found enough cohesion to elect a caretaker leader named Tenoch to represent them. Tenoch appears to have been a *teomama*; at least his role was to act as the living symbol of the identity between Huitzilopochtli and his people. We can refer to this group of the Mexica henceforth as the Tenochca.

Coxcoxtli at the time was the ruler of Culhuacan. That city was approaching the end of its turbulent but influential history. Its Toltec foundation and the settlement there of magnates claiming the blood

royal of Tula had not guaranteed to it freedom from dissensions within
or troubles without. Xochimilco, the city of the inner lake behind Culhuacan, had from earliest days been hostile; the constant drain of martial excursions resulting from this danger had lately kept Culhuacan
effectively sealed away from the main events in the other parts of the
Basin. Her entry into the league that had been recently formed against
the Mexica had been forced upon her by that people's piracy and rap-
ine but did not represent the exercise of any effective leadership on her
part in valley affairs. She gloried in her Toltec derivation and of course
viewed the Mexica as the most uncouth of all the Chichimec peoples,
in spite of the fact that both peoples had shared a part of the past.
Settled in a place called Contitlan for the first two or three years, these
Mexica served Culhuacan as mercenary warriors.[16]

Coxcoxtli ultimately assigned these Mexica to a section of his domain called Tizaapan which was stony, unproductive, and abounding in
rattlesnakes.[17] Here the Mexica eked out a bare existence serving their
Culua masters in menial tasks, cutting wood, polishing stone, and
shaping dugout canoes for them. Cringing and submissive, they had
even for awhile been forced to hand over their god, who thus became
also a prisoner of Culhuacan. Tizaapan nevertheless was a home of
their own and had come to them at the conclusion of a war between
Xochimilco and Culhuacan when their hard-pressed masters had particularly needed their fighting skills. In that conflict the ferocity of the
Mexican warriors had been vividly demonstrated, and this success gave
them subsequently a more independent role in Culua life. It was not
long in fact before the Mexica went on to win the right to intermarriage, thus binding the Culua and the Mexica closer together. Their
greatest success came however when they were allowed to reclaim their
god and to build a temple to him in Tizaapan. The stormy passions of
the times and the exceptional devotion of the Mexica to their god are
illustrated in the following episode.

Some of the Culua, of the faction bitterly opposed to the Mexica,
had at the time of the dedication of the new temple come and thrown
excrement and rubbish on it, thereby polluting it and necessitating the
construction of a wholly new shrine. When the resanctified site was

finally dedicated, Culhuacan had occasion to wonder and fear, for the Mexica, though a servant people, had been able to produce four human victims for the sacrifices, not only a sign of their growing secular power but also of their favor with the gods.

The Tenochca Mexica were under the domination of Culhuacan for at least fifteen years. In this interval they had fought for the Culua in their wars, had married their women, and were again giving evidence of that genius for audacity and success that had distinguished them at Chapultepec. Culhuacan's perennial unrest had been furthered by the presence of these contentious Mexica within the confines of the state, and two parties of the Culua soon formed regarding policy to be followed toward them. The dedication of the new temple polarized Culua and fighting broke out in the city. When the Mexica saw that the opposition had prevailed, they knew their fate had been sealed and they fled for their lives into the night, leaving behind them all they had created in Tizaapan. Once again they were refugees.

The expulsion involved more than the Mexica alone, for significant numbers of Culua friendly to their cause also were forced out in the brief civil war. Many of these fugitives fled eastward to find asylum at last in Tezcoco. Among one of the bands was a considerable number of Mexica under a leader called Ayocuan.[18] In their long period of apprenticeship under their neo-Toltec masters, these Mexica had acquired valuable skills and crafts, and these they took with them to Tezcoco to the immediate cultural enrichment of that city.

But the largest group of mixed Mexica and Culua were forced out onto the low mud islands of the lake. So sudden had been the fury let loose upon them they had been unable to collect dugout canoes for the flight. In silence and near panic they had moved out into the waters pushing matted clumps of reeds ahead of them, attempting to keep dry their few bundles of shelled maize and other hastily assembled possessions. It is probable that the aged *teomama* Tenoch accompanied this group carrying on his back the sacred appurtenances of the god. Huitzilopochtli swam through the lapping waters with his people in this black night of their despair as unmoved in his deeper parts about them as they were devout beyond duty toward him.

Here in various temporary settlements at the sweet water outlet of Lake Xochimilco the Mexica lived for two or three years, still harassed by Culhuacan and greatly weakened.[19] Their exemplary devotion to their god never wavered, and they continued to erect earthen shrines for him wherever they could. In the coming years one of these sacred communities would be known as Huitzilopochco because of the divine presence there, "the place of Huitzilopochtli." Somehow or other, supported by their strong Culua wives, these Tenochca Mexica survived, still feared and hated by their neighbors and constantly on the move. Their spasmodic progress along the edges of the lake and from one marshy island to another led them up the lake in a generally northerly direction toward the site marked by the god as their final destination.

When at last these bands of Mexica straggled onto shoaling ground not far south of the island of Tlatilulco, the twin founding of Mexico had been completed. This particular thicket of rushes and this patch of sucking mud under the labor of their hands would become dry land and would be called Tenochtitlan.[20] Tlatilulco and Tenochtitlan together were to be Mexico, though they were founded at different times. From this point on, the two would grow in the slime of the lake side by side, each inhabited by a different sector of the Mexican people and each with a different tradition of servitude. This divided Mexico would in a few short decades become for the Aztec world both its paragon and its most hated oppressor.

The Founding Myth of Tenochtitlan

A Mexican of later days is reported to have eulogized his city as follows:

This clump of reeds and cane secreted in a great lake of glaucous water, a dreaded lake where seethes fresh water against salt, a place of fish and of birds flying, the place where the great serpent fearfully writhes and hisses and where the majestic eagle dines, Mexico Tenochtitlan, founded by Aztecs and Chichimecs.[21]

The chronicle of the beginnings of their city always fascinated the Mexica. Its true complexity and the commixture of events and peoples that went into the actual founding, however, were carefully hidden away in a much oversimplified tale. The quotation above refers only in vague and colorful terms to the fuller legend that runs as follows.

In the earliest years of the Wandering, the god of the Mexica had prophesied that the site of the city they were to establish would be revealed to them on that day when they came upon a great *nopalli* or cactus-tree, whereon an eagle would be perched devouring its prey. In the days when the Mexica were living at the foot of the rock of Chapultepec, a sorcerer by the name of Copil from the distantly related people of Malinalco went about creating such animosity against his kinsmen, the Mexica, that many great cities had joined him in a league against them. War and expulsion resulted, as we have seen. Copil's success, however, had made him a marked man. He was soon challenged by the most skillful sorcerer among the Mexica to a magical contest. Copil lost the wager and was consequently sacrificed. Consequent upon the god's oracle his heart was taken out into the lake and hurled into the reeds. Out of this heart grew the famous *nopalli*.[22] Later, when searching for a place in which to settle, a Mexican scout pushed into the thicket and came upon the sacred tableau that had been prophesied. In the eagle's beak was gripped a serpent, and at the base of the *nopalli* was a boggy pool whose waters were of the whiteness of chalk, as were the frogs and fishes within it, while the willows edging the scene were similarly a ghostly white. White was the color of sacrifice. Here the first awed Mexica built a sod altar to Huitzilopochtli and thus identified the site as forever his.

There are many variants to this tale that need not concern us here.[23] For the Mexica it was sacred writ, always told with seemly reverence. That scene became thenceforth the emblem or device of Aztec Mexico, even as it is of the successor Republic of Mexico today—the eagle on the cactus gripping a snake in his beak. Specifically it referred to Tenochtitlan and not to Tlatilulco. On certain festivals celebrated later in their history, the Mexica used to erect in the center of the city a crude reed hut pierced through and through with darts while on the ridgepole was placed a stuffed eagle, crowned with the blue crown of Huitzilopochtli and eating the serpent. Thus they symbolized the pathos of their flight into the marshes pursued by enemy missiles and the succor that had come from the heavens. Tenochtitlan means "among the *tenochtli*" (the *tenochtli* is a kind of cactus). It is more probable that the small island already bore this name and therefore gave rise to the miraculous tale than the reverse, as the legend has it.

There is a gloss on this famed Mexican emblem that is of significance.[24] When the Mexican artist was depicting the scene he showed the eagle with a waving scroll-like sign issuing from its beak which, by the uninformed, could easily have been mistaken for a serpent. The object that was being represented, however, was not a serpent but the complicated Aztec hieroglyph which meant "war," *atl tlachinolli*. This stood for the irrevocable command of the Mexican god (as symbolized by the eagle) to his people that he be served with blood and hearts gained in battle . For it was to this end that he had led his people to that spot.

The date of this foundation was A.D. 1369.[25]

The Early Years of the City

After the first bitter struggle to survive, the Mexica acquired superior skills in exploiting the resources of the lake.[26] In their dugout canoes they netted fish and speared waterfowl along the shore and in the reed beds. The women collected duck eggs and pressed a thick algal scum into a kind of cake or cheese. The eggs and larvae of certain flies were also collected from the stems of the rushes and made into edible preparations. In the marketplaces of Anahuac the Mexica exchanged these foods for items they owed their Tepaneca masters as tribute, and with the little surplus left they acquired for themselves maize, beans, some chile, and occasionally salt. Potable water was a real problem, for the water in the shallows where they lived was faintly brackish, further polluted by wastes from their own settlements. Skillfully controlled canoes put out daily from Chapultepec filled with fresh spring water. The careful organization of this water supply was essential to the maintenance of rapidly growing Mexico.

The Tenochca had burned out extensive stands of willows in the neighborhood of their first tiny settlement and, by piling up refuse and mud scooped from the lake bottom, they gradually accumulated dry land around them. Over the years the billowing clouds of this burning in the waters were watched with wonder and speculation by the Tepaneca along the shores, for the reclamation of such miry parts was a superhuman work—even for a people with no other place to go. But for the fact that it was an imperceptible and often interrupted process, this tenacity in creating a city in the waters would have been heroic.

These first years were harsh discipline for the Tenochca, and it took repeated exhortations from the older ones and their *teomama* to keep the community alive. The more warlike in particular were restive and frustrated. At one crucial point they broke out and declaimed against a fate that had cast them down into bog and slime to seine and net and wade about for their daily food! A woman of the tribe is reputed to have brought reason to these hot spirits by coldly stating, "Mexicans, out of somewhere we must get our food."[27]

Both Tlatilulco and Tenochtitlan were growing now not only by natural increase but also by perceptible additions from the outside. If the newcomers were sufficiently numerous they immediately formed themselves into a distinct quarter or *calpulli* with the shrine of their god in its midst. They were all Mexica however, because they now lived in Mexico and shared in the common worship of Huitzilopochtli.

All the cities of Anahuac were at that time in a period of remarkable population growth, and Mexico also experienced this trend with small foreign groups, both further estranged Culua and new Chichimec arrivals, petitioning constantly for entry and settlement. Because of the unevenness of these accretions of people, as well as because of the differences in their foundings, Tlatilulco and Tenochtitlan became yearly more diverse. The former city was the older, its people were the more expert canoesmen, and the time would come when they would add to their distinctiveness by taking up a highly sophisticated and far-flung commerce in luxury goods. The Tenochca looked upon them with scorn, referring to them as "quackers" and "croakers" because of their long life in the reeds. The Tenochca further considered themselves superior because of their close connections with legitimate Toltec houses from Culhuacan and because of their superior craftsmanship. Tenochtitlan quickly became a more dynamic city than Tlatilulco, for it was divided early into many more precincts, each the residence of a separate group.

Of real significance for the future history of Mexico was the fact that, unlike most other Aztec cities, it possessed originally no cornlands at all. This fact imposed an almost unbearable stringency on its development. In common with all the peoples of Mesoamerica, the Mexica considered maize and beans as staples. They had become fishermen not by choice but because they had only the produce of the lake to exchange for the sacks of shelled maize, amaranth, and other edible seeds they so greatly needed. Much later, a well-organized commerce and the expansion of crafts did give them increased wherewithal to barter for the agricultural staples. But always in clear sight of their settlements in the lake was the Tepaneca shoreline with its neat fields leading back into the hills, plots of amaranth, maize, chile, beans, and squash. The distress of not being fully in command of their own food resources gave to the two Mexica settlements an unappeasable land hunger and a burning envy of those cities possessing their own fields and storage bins. Until the days of Itzcoatl the deliverer, the two Mexicos were to be lean cities.

But the Mexica had, in addition to their craftsmanship and incipient commercial skills, another commodity to sell—toughness and proficiency in war. Just as Culhuacan had called upon the aid of Mexican warriors against Xochimilco, so now Azcapotzalco began to take tribute from them mainly in the form of military service. In fact as time went on this forced levy on the fighting men of a rapidly growing Mexico was to become barely distinguishable from a military alliance.

The Imperial Title and Azcapotzalco

Azcapotzalco's war against Tenayuca opens a decisive chapter in Aztec history and by indirection in the history of the Mexica. Quinatzin, the fourth in the line of Xolotl, is accounted the first resident ruler of the kingdom of Acolhuacan on the east side of the lake. He had been forced to leave the old Chichimec capital of Tenayuca in the possession of an uncle and had taken up his residence in Tezcoco, which thus became the new and permanent imperial residence.[28] He had been the first of his house to recognize the necessity of forcing his Chichimec followers to give up their roving ways and their love of the chase for civilized life and agriculture. As a consequence of this he was also the ruler whose reign was taken up with multiple insurrections on the part of his dissident vassals, many of whom directly challenged his overlordship and his right to the imperial title *chichimeca teuctli*. It had been Quinatzin who had welcomed the fugitive Mexica and Toltecs from Culhuacan; he had also gathered in others from Chalco, settling them all in Tezcoco and turning to great advantage their various skills. He had needed every accession of strength he could secure in maintaining the power of his rump empire.

Quinatzin's first serious challenge had come from Tenayuca, where his uncle, claiming family seniority and actual possession of Xolotl's old imperial seat, announced himself to be the legitimate emperor. It was at this point that Azcapotzalco and her Mexican subjects newly settled out in the reeds became involved. To Azcapotzalco the imperial title seemed worth fighting for, especially at a time when serious insurrections across the lake were preventing the youthful Quinatzin from returning and resolving the issue himself. Tenayuca was accordingly attacked by Azcapotzalco and, after a venomous struggle, reduced.[29] The rebellious uncle of Quinatzin fled back to Godland whence he and his people had come and took up there a life of brigandage and futile harassment. The Tepaneca victor now claimed the title of *chichimeca teuctli* as his by right of conquest, and he installed his son Tezozomoc, soon to become famous, as the new ruler in Tenayuca.

But Quinatzin was not to be surnamed Tlaltecatzin, "he flattens the earth," for nothing.[30] He had come successfully through the great upheaval called the Chichimec War, long to be remembered by Anahuac, and his vassals had now been either reconquered in open conflict or expelled to lands beyond the mountains. In view of this, Azcapotzalco judged it expedient to relinquish the magnificent title so recently acquired. This rectification was performed at a ceremony in Azcapotzalco to which Quinatzin came. After being there formally invested with his rightful imperial title, Quinatzin returned to Tezcoco where he ruled long years in honor.

Never again were the men of Xolotl's line to live in Tenayuca. It is very probable indeed that they gracefully ceded the city to their Tepaneca vassals at this time, leaving the Tepaneca prince Tezozomoc to rule it for them. From this accommodation, the full effects of which could not be foreseen, was to spring the situation in which the Mexica were to become great. Tezozomoc, on the death of his father, moved to Azcapotzalco with the claim that his father had never had the right to divest himself of the imperial title, that it was inalienable in the Tepaneca line, and that he alone could wear it.

The Mexica as Wards of Tezozomoc

Tezozomoc, a grandson of the great Xolotl on the distaff side, was to rule in his city of Azcapotzalco for some sixty years.[31] He succeeded to the throne about 1366. Aztecs of later days looked back on this man with awe.[32] In his own day he was thought to be an evil genius or demon.[33] He is in fact one of those rare figures in human history about whom the historian can say nothing inconsequential and nothing good. Throughout all of our historical sources he is a figure of terror and guile, infinitely frightening. He would be a pivotal figure in any version of the Aztec story. Perhaps his greatness comes from the fact that he was the first who attempted to make the imperial title a reality, to convert the loose feudal suzerainty of Xolotl into an effective sovereignty. His resounding failure to do so reduced the title to meaninglessness and thereby confirmed the fragmentation of Aztec political life. He it was who further fostered the rapacity of his loyal subjects, the Mexica, until they were to become the most feared warriors of their day. The Mexica consequently owed the opportunity for greatness to him. His unusually long life and perverse policy continually acted to prevent any accommodation among the cities of the Basin and ensured, though it did not create, the dominance of the warrior nobility in the Aztec states. He was, in short, the outstanding figure of his age, dangerous, effective, malevolent, and quite obviously beloved of the gods. His greatness became something of a model for future rulers in Anahuac.

The story of the Mexica is inseparably linked with Tezozomoc and his policies. Well after the time when he had come to the throne in Azcapotzalco, an event of importance to all the Aztec states took place. Tezozomoc was to take advantage of this and in the process he succeeded in changing the whole power structure in Anahuac. The flight of the

Mexica from Tizaapan in 1366 or thereabouts had been part of a larger picture in the breakdown of legitimate government in Culhuacan.[34] In 1365 the year before, a usurper had seized the throne after murdering the incumbent and had initiated a period of rapid decline; he seems to have represented the anti-Mexican faction. In their new settlement of Tenochtitlan, the Mexica were preparing a vengeance to be visited upon him and his Culua party whenever the opportunity should arise. To this end, in 1375 they brought to their island, Acamapichtli, a prince claiming true Toltec legitimacy through the previous ruler of Culhuacan. In his veins also ran Mexica blood. He was to be their link with the affairs of Culhuacan.

When disunity did finally overwhelm Culhuacan, the last of the Aztec cities claiming pure Toltec legitimacy was blotted out. Her people dispersed in all directions. A number were admitted to Cuauhtitlan where they effected immediate and far-reaching changes upon the backward Chichimecs who had inherited that city. Some went to Tezcoco, and many went to Mexico where they were welcomed as kinsmen. Grass was to grow for awhile in the streets of Culhuacan and the coyote would hunt undisturbed at night under the steps of her pyramids. Into this vacuum, in 1377, rushed the Tenochca. With ease they subdued the city and installed a military rule. The presence of Acamapichtli in Tenochtitlan and the seizure of Culhuacan are two obviously related steps in the aggressive policy of the Tenochca. They could do this because they were already so deeply involved in Tezozomoc's southern policy.

Tepaneca power, alerted to forestall any attempt on the part of the descendants of Xolotl in Tezcoco to extend their influence into the southern part of the Basin, had also moved down into the void created by the above events. Azcapotzalco did not yet command the military resources to subdue the whole area by force, so she contented herself by fashioning a hegemony—with herself as arbiter and leader—over a loose and uneasy coalition of three kingdoms, Cuauhnahuac, Coatlichan, and Huexotzinco. The military rule established by her Mexican vassals in Culhuacan was the underpinning of this project. By means then of this hegemony, Tezozomoc took a somewhat uneasy command of policy in the southern part of the Basin. Because of her prestige in the past, Culhuacan had for many years blocked the formation of any such alliance in the south. Now with her disappearance, that part of the Basin lost its Toltec polarity and reverted to the shifting world of expedient alliances.

Tezozomoc had earlier called up his satellites, the Mexica, and with their help had crushed the Otomí kingdom of Xaltocan in the north, thus pushing still farther back the frontiers of Acolhuacan and whittling away its influence. Both his military advance in the north and his influence in the southern hegemony were directed in the fashion of a nutcracker against Acolhuacan. Amazingly, this fact was not fully appreciated by the ruler in Tezcoco.

The campaign in the north against Xaltocan had added greatly to the laurels of the Mexica warriors. As a reward they were given several of the smaller communities they had helped to conquer. This increment to their possessions put them on the road to being a land power like the other Aztec cities.

Prestige always calls for a symbol. The admittedly marvelous courage of the Mexica on the field of battle had impressed the world of Anahuac. They had thereby found favor in the sight of their overlord Tezozomoc, and this necessitated some outward sign. It had taken only a short time for this people to climb out of the slime and to acquire respect as the accomplices and the strong right arm of Tepaneca power. Mexico—like other cities that had fully proved themselves—should have a king, a *tlatoani*.

Up until 1375 the leadership of elders along with a *teomama* and other naturally gifted men, had sufficed to maintain the two halves of the Mexican state. When coercion had to be applied to the Mexica, it was applied by Azcapotzalco as their recognized lord. But a structure of rule tailored to a simple life among eely grasses could not long satisfy a people who were taking an increasingly active role in the life of the Aztec states around them. At first the division between Tlatilulco and Tenochtitlan did not seem of enough moment to complicate the question of anointing a *tlatoani* of all the Mexica, and plans went forward to secure a prince from some worthy line. A member of the line of Xolotl was naturally indicated now that the Toltecs of Culhuacan had weakened as a city and a people. Accordingly, both halves of the

Mexica turned to their formidable master Tezozomoc and, with something of their oldtime presumption, petitioned for a son of his to rule over them. Any such person would be a great-grandson of Xolotl through the female line. The only blood purer would have to be taken from the house of Tezcoco, legitimately descended from Xolotl through the male line and thus more celebrated. But the Tepaneca policy with which, by choice and by accident, the Mexica were aligned was consistently anti-Tezcoco, and any move of the Mexica in that direction would have outraged Azcapotzalco.

It is reported that Tezozomoc meditated at length before granting the Mexican request. He needed the Mexica warriors in his plans for the future. Also they were, in a sense, wards of the Tepaneca on whose property they lived by sufferance, and as such he should humor them if it were at all possible. Against these pragmatic considerations there had to be taken into account that ominous aura surrounding the Mexica, which, like the whisps of smoke floating over the summit of Popocatepetl, covered deep fires. So doughty a people must always be considered dangerous. He finally granted their request on condition that a conspicuous palace first be erected in Tlatilulco for whatever son he should designate.[35]

The son who thus became the first fully recognized ruler of Mexico was named Cuacuauhtzin.[36] But even in this matter the sinister father carried his plots forward, for he succeeded in having the prince married to a princess of Coatlichan, a Toltec city within the confines of the kingdom of Acolhuacan and one well suited to become the springboard for close thrusts against Tezcoco. By this marriage he tied Mexico directly into his long-range policy of dominating all of Anahuac and of obliterating the claims made by the descendants of Xolotl in Tezcoco to the dignity of the office of *chichimeca teuctli*. The Mexica were therefore paying a heavy price to appear openly as a people of consequence ruled by a *tlatoani*; they moved knowingly into a vicious political orbit, one in which they would whirl about for many years until vast events would shake them loose. The fact that Cuacuauhtzin would soon be leading the entire Tepaneca host to war as his father's most trusted captain was an earnest of the ever-widening convulsions that would continue to mark Mexican history.

The Mexica had at last been accepted as a people of standing in the Aztec world, but only by virtue of accepting as legitimate ruler a prince of Tepaneca lineage and submitting to the barons he brought in with him as a new caste of masters. The great men of Tlatilulco would always take as much pride in their Tepaneca as in their Mexican blood.[37] Tenochtitlan was not as heavily touched by this Tepaneca infusion and remained loyal to her separate Culua traditions; nevertheless she too paid her tribute to Cuacuauhtzin in labor and in kind and shed her blood for his father.

The Mexica had done more than survive. They had made a mark. The temple of Huitzilopochtli in Tlatilulco, which was dedicated in 1378 by Cuacuauhtzin only a few years after taking office, now housed the mightiest of all war gods in Anahuac. This god sat in dreadful majesty in Mexico and looked out on a world he would some day subdue.

3. Mexico under Tezozomoc

 The youthful Cuacuauhtzin was, in the eyes of his new subjects, a *tlatoani*, their first king. To his close Tepaneca kinsmen, however, his role was seen as akin to that of a governor or military commissar, his duties being to harness the already considerable military might of the Mexica to the course of Tepaneca expansion. This difference in understanding meant little to the Mexica, for their pride in him was immense simply because his investiture magnified them all. After all, it had been only a few years since they had first gone out to their islands, and then they had been a people lost to all honor. In Cuacuauhtzin they discovered their own greatness.

While he was specifically the ruler of Tlatilulco, the Tenochca Mexica acknowledged him also—as indeed they had to. The exact date of his accession is in doubt, but the suggested year of 1375 is surely approximately correct.[1] His was to be an extended reign during which the political foundations of Mexico were laid down. By the time of his death in 1418, Mexico had become one of the three preponderant

powers in the Basin. These three were the Tepaneca,[2] their protégés
the Mexica, and the Acolhua under the emperors of the line of Xolotl
—the first two balanced in uneasy equilibrium against the Acolhua
across the lake.

Cuacuauhtzin's residence among his new island subjects was delayed
a year while there was prepared for him in Tlatilulco 'a palace worthy
of his dignity. With the erection of this edifice, the public life of Mexico can be said to have begun. Close to it there arose also the first state
treasury (where tribute could be stored) and the new pyramid temple
to Tlacahuepantzin, a variant form of Huitzilopochtli, sometimes epi-
thetically referred to as "blue sky," but in any case a war god.[3]
Under the divine auspices of this god and under the earthly leadership
of their Tepaneca king, the islanders now embarked upon that series of
directed aggressions that was shortly to make Mexico again both feared
and hated.

Life in Tlatilulco

Few cities in history have had a more complex and
fascinating origin than Mexico. The interconnected lakes of the Great
Basin had seen earlier Aztec cities founded on low-lying islands or in
marshy areas, cities such as Xaltocan, Cuitlahuac, and Xochimilco. A
lacustrine way of life indeed was a pattern that had been established
long previous to these particular urban communities. None of them,
however, grew so portentously as did Mexico, and certainly none overcame so amazingly the disadvantages of their insularity.

Of the two nuclei of Mexico we have seen that Tlatilulco was, by a
little, the older foundation. In spite of its Mexican settlement there can
be no doubt that it was from the first looked upon as a Tepaneca city
—this not only because of the affiliation of its new royal house but also because it pursued consistently a pro-Tepaneca policy.[4] Tlatilulca
nobles are known to have appeared for ceremonies and in battle in the
war dress of the Otomí, a people who formed a heavy substratum in
the social makeup of the Tepaneca.

If its royal house and its noblemen were to be Tepaneca, its people
were still Mexica—hardy, somber, and patient. They had become ex-
ceedingly skilled canoesmen, far more so than their Tenochca con-

freres. In the chill dawn of their every day, they left their thatched hovels on the island and pushed off in clumsy dugout craft, poling in the shallow sloughs where they could gather duck eggs and frogs, and paddling elsewhere in the deeper waters. They speared ducks, luring them with gourds as decoys; or they scooped up surface growth, which later their women would press into cakes and sell in the mainland markets. They netted many of the migrant birds that rested by night on the surface of the lake, and they seined for the small fish that lived in the fresh-water shallows. Here was a people who had been bred in the dust and thorns of the desert and who had successfully adopted the cold lake as a new mother. Out of necessity they became her most cunning sons, scavenging everywhere in her coverts for their subsistence and for a surplus wherewith to pay their tribute. The great lake was never kind to them, and it was often capricious; nevertheless they endured.

Another skill gradually came to them by reason of their close affiliation with the Tepaneca—that of the merchant. Azcapotzalco, which had been in antiquity a Toltec city, had the enviable reputation of holding one of the notable markets in Anahuac, specializing, so it would seem, in the sale of slaves. Tutored by the merchants of the Tepaneca capital, Tlatilulco rapidly evolved into a mercantile partner of considerable daring.[5] What enabled her to achieve this position so early was the practiced energy of her canoe fleet, for she was able to transport large cargoes by lake speedily and economically, whereas the mainlanders of Azcapotzalco had to bring it in more circuitously, on the backs of porters.

The Tlatilulca canoe fleet had another use. It acted as the amphibious arm of Tezozomoc's host. In the evolution of his aggressive policy, the Mexican flotilla formed the vanguard, or at least the most mobile part, of the Tepaneca army.

Tenochtitlan and Its Culua Blood

Tenochtitlan, less than a mile south of Tlatilulco, was not as advantageously placed, being situated in an area of low muck islands. After strenuous efforts the Tenochca had succeeded in creating a nucleus of dry land and on it had raised a large platform that bore the god's shrine and some attached habitations. Wood at first was rare and hard to get, inasmuch as the forests of oak, hemlock, and pine that stood in the back parts of the mainland belonged to the Tepaneca. Stone from the quarries of Tenayuca also was rare, and in any case the energies of the Tenochca could not be released from the neverending task of securing food merely for the transportation of building blocks. The small city was thus little more than a sprawling hamlet of reed huts, net racks, and canoe anchorages with only the endless smoke from the central shrine of Huitzilopochtli attesting to the fact that in the narrow lives of this people they could still support the god who was their whole being.

They had at first paid tribute to their Tepaneca lords on the mainland, but when Cuacuauhtzin was sent out into the Mexican islands to rule, their obligation was shifted to him. There must have been resentment, however, because he was still not the *tlatoani* of Tenochtitlan however much he might be recognized by the Tlatilulca as their own and legitimate ruler. This difference was intensified by the contrasting cultures of the two communities, Tepaneca in the one case, Culua in the other.

In the very year of Cuacuauhtzin's assumption of rule, the Tenochca, as we have seen, engineered a most curious turn of events, one that was to make certain that soon they would have a history of their own. It came about as a result of Tezozomoc's attempt to open up an attack on the Acolhua across the lake, an attack he planned to direct at them along the southern shores of the lake.

Culhuacan was the city that lay directly across the path of this advance. Thus, if it could not be cajoled into an alliance, it would have to be attacked. Since about 1365 Culhuacan had been suffering a rapid and constant erosion of its prestige. The usurper who had gained the Toltec throne of that city by murdering the legitimate *tlatoani* precipitated a rush of events that finally spelled the extinction of the city. In a long-overdue ethnic cataclysm, the city blew apart. Its demise as an independent state was sealed when the Tenochca took it over on Tezozomoc's sufferance.

At some time during those troubled years a certain noblewoman had fled from Culhuacan in fear for her life.[6] She was eventually to find her way to Tenochtitlan. In her care was a youth by the name of Acamapichtli,[7] in whose veins ran both Mexican blood and the blood of the legitimate house—at that time deposed—of Culhuacan. This youth was thus a claimant to be the last representative of the famous Toltec line of true kings;[8] as such his life was in constant danger at the hands of assassins sent out by the regicide then ruling in his city. The presence of this distinguished young émigré in Tenochtitlan was an open challenge presented by the crude and vigorous Tenochca to their erstwhile masters the Culua.

The place of Acamapichtli in Mexican history is an important one, for the Tenochca were later to claim him as their first *tlatoani*.[9] This is almost certainly incorrect considering that Tenochtitlan paid tribute during part of his lifetime to their Tepaneca overlords through Cuacuauhtzin, *tlatoani* of the Tlatilulca. Nevertheless, by the mere fact of adopting him as one of their own, the Tenochca Mexica had thereby acquired a closer claim on the blood royal of the Toltecs. As a figurehead and the living representative of a regal bloodline, he possessed powers an ordinary war leader did not have. It is possible that he filled the office of *cihuacoatl*, a priestly dignity associated with Culhuacan.[10] The elders and chief men of Tenochtitlan gave him their daughters as wives and concubines and soon in their progeny there appeared an incipient nobility in Tenochtitlan of equal if not greater splendor than the Tepaneca line in Tlatilulco.

The Calpulli

Aztec cities grew spasmodically and by accretion. Typically when a wandering group came into an area where there was a community going back to Toltec times, they would petition it for inclusion in its body politic. This had been the case with the Mexica in Chapultepec. Or the accretion might come about as a result of the subjugation of a people; they would be assigned to an unused part of the city territory and then assessed a heavy tax in labor and kind. This was the case of the Mexica in Culhuacan. Or they might occupy a status midway between that of servitude and alliance, as was the case with the Mexica in Tlatilulco. But in any case a designated group of people entered the city or settled themselves therein as a *calpulli*.[11]

Literally, the word *calpulli* means "great house." It is not known whether this is simply a metaphor for "lineage" or whether it is concretely a reference to the central meetinghouse of a clan-like community. Whatever its secondary meaning and whatever its history, it was used by the Mexica to designate those social bits and pieces that formed the city of Mexico.[12]

The *calpulli* was rather more like a hamlet than a clan, for it had an elected headman called the *tequitlato* or "assigner of tasks."[13] He served for life, was of noble blood, and was apt to be succeeded by a brother or near relative. There was thus a sense of hierarchy in the *calpulli*, but one which was not in any way comparable with the prerogatives of a full-fledged aristocratic state. The headman was still only a member of the group, and if he died without issue the lands allotted to him by the *calpulli* escheated back and were subject to reassignment.

The *calpulli* may be nothing more than a survival of that primitive village of Mesoamerica which began to evolve some two and a half millenia before the appearance of the Mexica, and which here, at this late day, was used as one of the basic building blocks of the Aztec city. We see it therefore as essentially a "ward" or quarter of the city, administratively necessary to the whole of which it was a part, though it need not in all cases have been physically contiguous. A *calpulli*, however, could be an artificial creation; it need not have a history of its own. The city could arbitrarily call one into being, give it a name, a god, a temple, and order the election of its first *tequitlato*. The city of Mexico would finally include some fifteen or twenty of these *calpulli*, some undoubtedly artificial, others originating in small nations or bands and worshipping the ancient deities they had brought with them into the area.

It was a curious arrangement. The typical Aztec city was descended from Teotihuacan, through Tula, and as such had a long history of urbanism behind it. Nevertheless, the grass-roots level of its administrative structure appears not to have been an original urban invention at all but an old crutch from an agrarian past forced into new metropolitan uses.

The case of the contemporary lakeside city of Tezcoco reveals clearly the *calpulli* pattern of development. Under Quinatzin, the Chichimec emperor ruling in that city, two bands of people from lands south of the Great Basin came and petitioned him for protection and rights of residence. These were the Tlailotlaque and the Chimalpaneca, both people at a far higher level of culture than his own still savage Chichimecs.[14] Their request was granted. Four hundred of the former were settled in one designated area, which became therefore the ward of Tlailotlalpan, while the rest were scattered widely about—in clusters as far as ten miles apart—in the kingdom of Acolhuacan. In this fashion were settled some of the first and most famous of Tezcoco's eleven *calpulli*.

We have already noted the unsettled conditions in the city of Culhuacan in the days when the Mexica resided there. These upheavals had cast out not only the Mexica but also native Culua, as well as lesser groups of Tepaneca and Huitznahua blood. These émigrés dispersed and went off, some to found Tenochtitlan, others to petition the ruler of Tezcoco for permission to enter Acolhuacan.[15] They were allotted compact lands and house plots there; these *calpulli* became known thenceforth as Mexicapan, Culhuacan, and Huitznahuac.

Because it was built on a small archipelago in the lake, Mexico differed from the normal Aztec city. In the first place, with the exception of Tlatilulco, none of the small islands or mud flats appear to have been previously inhabited to any great extent, and there was consequently no history to look back on and build on. Tezcoco on the contrary had originally been a city in the Toltec empire,[16] which, while it had been seriously weakened in the general disaster accompanying the collapse of Tula, nevertheless could put a distinctive mark on the new peoples rebuilding its greatness. Like Tezcoco, most other Aztec cities had a Toltec past.

What was of more moment for the early tradition of the Mexica was the jurisdiction Azcapotzalco claimed over that part of the lake where the Mexica had built. Yet while Azcapotzalco exercised lordship over those reed beds and manmade terraces in the lake, she needed none of it herself and was little interested in what others might do with it. Thus the various elements of the Mexica, while acknowledging a Tepanec overlord, were freer than most to build their city-state without reference to a superior power.

What additionally distinguished Mexico was the fact that it grew up, not on the mainland where the logic of agriculture tended to force the *calpulli* to become detached hamlets, but on a chain of flats concentrated in one area of the lake. Once planted, the Tlatilulca and Tenochca settlements invited or tacitly accepted the presence of close *calpulli* neighbors. Strength was in numbers, not in walls. These settled shoal areas inevitably tended to increase in size and to link up with others, the wider waters between them narrowing to become artificially deepened canals that continued to be used not only as waterways but also as *calpulli* boundaries.

The sanction for the *calpulli*—the special symbol that gave it its legitimacy as the basic administrative unit of the city—was the presence in it of the *calpulco*, the local temple.[17] Worship of the particular god or gods in this temple was the common bond between all members of the *calpulli*. When viewed in this manner, the *calpulli* was thus a parish. The Mexican *calpulli* of Huitznahuac, for example, worshipped as its own the Four Hundred, a group of cactus gods, the brothers and sisters of Huitzilopochtli. The ward of Amantlan, inhabited by artisans, feather-workers, and dyers, centered about the shrine of an old Chichimec constellation of deities under the presidency of a god called Coyotlinahual; responsibility for this cult belonged to the inhabitants of Amantlan alone. Again, the ward of Tzonmulco worshipped the fire god under his various titles. It is probable that these *calpulli* gods were in some cases simply assigned by the ruler and his advisers to new wards as they were formed and did not necessarily always represent the ancestral gods of the *calpulli*.

While the religious life of the *calpulli* centered about a distinctive cult, the daily business of the ward was transacted in the so-called *telpochcalli* or "bachelor house." Here the elders in the ward gathered to register births, assign *calpulli* fields, collect tribute, or apportion men and women of the ward for services demanded by the ruler. As the number of *calpulli* in Mexico continued to increase, there was superimposed an additional level of city administration based on the sacred number four. This is the most probable explanation for the division of Mexico into four parts (Moyotlan, Cuepopan, Teopan, and Atzacualco) organized so that the temple of Huitzilopochtli stood in the corner-meeting of all four.[18] Roughly four or five *calpulli* were included in each one of these quarters, and they were often of contrasting nationalities to lessen the possibility of rebellion. And as a final rationalization in the process of growth, Tlatilulco, when it finally fell under the sway of the more powerful Tenochtitlan, became for purposes of administration a part of the second or northwestern quarter of the city. But this was still some time in the future.

Life in the Early City

There would come a day in the life of Mexico when it would be likened by Aztec poets to a jeweled retreat for the greatest lords of the earth, a city that lay enshrouded in the beauty of dawn under a "pink mist of flowers." Such hyperbole certainly gives no picture at all of Mexico in the days of its beginnings.

It was rather a city of Herculean labors and notable for its poverty. The fact that it—of all the cities of the lake region—possessed no corn lands made it envious of all those who did possess lands and the seed to sow the lands. In those formative years one might have stood on the low temple platform in Tlatilulco and peered westward over the intervening beds of reeds and shoaling pools of the lake to the dry land by the rock of Chapultepec, where the Tepaneca had their fields. Over there was to be found all the goodness and richness of living, things lacking in the algal scum of the lake shallows. In times of famine— which was most of the time for the Mexica—one could if necessary gnaw on the roots of rushes, though it was no easy task to tear them up out of the mud. Others possessed more than they did and did not ever need to eat rushes.

Very early the Mexica had begun the making of *chinampas* in the parts of the lake adjacent to their island hovels.[19] *Chinampa* means literally "enclosure," and it was generally a large matted and mud-soaked clump of reed and brush put together in those parts of Lake Tezcoco where the water was fresh. On them vegetable crops and even maize could be grown. The labor that went into the building of each *chinampa* was immense. Great bundles of reeds had to be cut and lashed together to form long soggy rafts. These were then towed and pushed out to the city-side and heaped over with mud brought in by canoe.

This newly created piece of land would then settle onto the shallow bottom. More mud would be scooped up and cast over what had now become a *milli*, a plot or garden, ready for planting and standing well above the surface of the lake. Over the years they would be expanded until they had become artificial islands of moist soil heavy with humus and producing crops all year around. Once they were formed, the only fertilizer needed was the addition of a little extra bottom mud. They generally formed a neatly packed grid of very elongated rectangles separated by sluggish canals.

Chinampa culture however suffered from the often violent fluctuations in the lake level. Once in those early times the Mexican *chinampas* were all drowned in a great flooding of the lake. And some twenty odd years after that there occurred an extended drought that caused the lake level to drop disastrously leaving the *chinampas* stranded on what was dry land.

The problem of the first priority for the Mexica was how to feed and supply the city. Drinking water was the most immediate necessity for, though Mexico stood in a part of Lake Tezcoco only faintly saline, the water around it could hardly be considered potable owing to the offal dumped daily into the canals and lagoons. The water was also turbid from the constant stirring up of the muddy bottom by punting poles or by waders going about their business of netting birds or gathering rushes for matting. Canoes were therefore filled with fresh spring water from Chapultepec and cautiously taken out to the city markets for sale. The spring belonged to Azcapotzalco and any Mexican use of said water was strictly at the sufferance of that city. The Tepaneca had in fact no more effective hold over the Mexica than this control of their drinking water—which probably goes a long way in explaining the aid so unstintingly and loyally given by the Mexica to their Tepaneca masters. Any sudden cessation in this commerce in drinking water would have threatened Mexico with disaster.

Wood was another necessity, and here again Mexico had to move in step with Azcapotzalco, for all the great forests back of that redoubtable city belonged to her. Canoes were hollowed out from the trunks of Tepanec fir trees; ceiling beams for the houses of ruler and nobles had to be hewn from them as well. Firewood for the ever-burning bra-

ziers on the terraces of the gods and in the ruler's palace had to be daily
cut and transported several miles on the backs of woodsmen down to
the Tepanec shore.

The growth of the city of Mexico—in fact its very existence—depended on continuing amity between it and Azcapotzalco. So integrated indeed were their respective policies that Mexico at an early date
was allowed to participate in Tepaneca commerce.[20] For many years
Azcapotzalco had specialized in the slave trade and she therefore had
no objection to allowing Tlatilulco to supplement this commerce with
whatever else its enterprise might acquire. Soon after the installation of
Cuacuauhtzin, two Tlatilulca merchants, whose names were to be recorded for posterity, mounted the first caravans to venture out of the
Great Basin and bring back precious feathers for the new Mexican nobility. Under later rulers this trade was to be greatly expanded to include additional items of luxury goods. The actual business of exchanging the fish and fowl gathered from the lake for such staples as
dried maize, salt, and chile peppers remained, however, in the hands of
the Mexican woman who by canoe continued to visit the markets of
Coyouacan or Xochimilco for these homely ends. Everyday commerce,
the getting and exchanging of food by which to live, was no part of the
luxury commerce then emerging.

Diligently the Mexica moved about in their daily rounds, without
bustle or officiousness and with never a thought that they were laying
the foundations of one of the world's most unique cities.

Azcapotzalco's Fighting Vassal

Mexico was a dual city; its two moieties hated and
feared each other while yet acknowledging a common blood and a
common cult. Tlatilulco and Tenochtitlan were both Mexica settlements, and a fraternal bond thus tied them together. Neither alone was
wholly Mexico, yet each would make that claim. These early days in
the history of the city were thus days of abeyance before the inevitable
trial of strength.

To the world of Anahuac, however, the city of Mexico was one; it
was the home of one people known by all to be dangerous. The uncertain dichotomy of the structure of Mexico and the radical differences in

its two policies—one pro-Tepaneca, the other pro-Culua—these internal tensions would not as yet affect the course of the nation. But it was certain that when conflict would come one policy or the other would perforce win out, for the two were incompatible.

At the moment Tlatilulco was the real power center of the archipelago. Here was the palace of the Mexican ruler, and here was situated the Mexican market, soon to become one of the great emporia in Mesoamerica. Added to this was the fact that the lord of Tlatilulco acted under his father's direction as the generalissimo of all the Tepaneca armies.[21] So loyally did the Tlatilulca support and further the policies of Azcapotzalco that they were even referred to as Tepaneca Mexica. Cuacuauhtzin, in fact, held Mexico as a Tepaneca appanage, a key factor to be used in the advance of those ambitious Tepaneca designs that Tezozomoc had inherited from his father.

The target of Tepaneca policy was the imperial title, the office of *chichimeca teuctli*, which Xolotl had been the first to fill and to which an exceptional prestige was therefore attached. On the death of the third Chichimec ruler to hold that title, division had occurred in the imperial house, and Quinatzin, the son and heir, forced out of Tenayuca by his uncle, took his seat in Tezcoco. The uncle now claimed the imperial title by right of fraternal succession as well as by his possession of Tenayuca, the original Chichimec capital. With the overlordship of the valley thus in dispute, the way was open for Azcapotzalco to press its claim.

Tenayuca was, like Azcapotzalco, a city of the lake shore. It lay just a few miles to the north and, also like Azcapotzalco, had been an early Toltec city. Xolotl had found it much reduced from its former importance but still able to guard the road north to the ruins of Tula and to Godland beyond. The city lay with its feet in the coarse brakes and thickets of the lake and its back up against the harsh stone hills referred to today as the Sierra de Guadalupe. Here, in answer to the irruptive Chichimec presence, had arisen a conglomerate cult that joined the old god Tlaloc, who watered the fields of civilized men, with the new mascot deity of the incoming barbarians, probably a form of Mixcoatl. A small temple terrace had been erected there, bearing on its summit the shrines of both gods side by side, each approached, however, by its own stairway. This was an accommodation, not a fusion, but it at least implied that the two parts of heaven found no particular fault with each other.

This was the city that first had to be disposed of if the Tepaneca were to secure room for future action against the imperial forces of Tezcoco. Here the Mexica performed notably in their capacity as military vassals, for it was they who put to the torch the thatched shrines of the city.[22] When the battle was over, the defenders of Tenayuca had fled back north into the wild country, abandoning to Azcapotzalco their claims to the imperial title. The Tepaneca ruler lost no time in personally assuming the dignity and in putting himself up as emperor in opposition to the lords in Tezcoco. All the cities of Anahuac understood that sooner or later a contest between the two protagonists was inevitable. The question of alliances thus became pressing and dangerous.

Behind Tenayuca, and between it and the kingdom of Acolhuacan, lay the diffuse kingdom of Xaltocan, an Otomí state. The Otomí, though formidable warriors, seem not to have taken much part in the fierce polities being evolved by the Aztecs.[23] In fact they appear to have been a rather bemused and unknowing people, preferring generally to live in scattered *calpulli* among the hills or in thick stands of pine. They spoke a distinctive tongue. Though the Otomí were at heart not a city folk, they had been in the land since the days of the Toltec hegemony, and when that power had dwindled away, a portion of them, more urban than the rest, had formed a primitive kingdom on the northwestern rim of the Basin. At first they had not hindered the entry of either the Xolotl or the Chicomoztoc Aztecs into the Basin, but Xaltocan, their chief city, had been the one to lead the forces that broke up the Mexica settlement at Chapultepec. No doubt this had been done in a clear understanding with the house of Xolotl.

Mexican desire for revenge upon Xaltocan now meshed with Tepaneca need to annex or destroy that Otomí kingdom in order to acquire a position directly confronting the kingdom of Acolhuacan. Details of the joint thrust against Xaltocan, a city that stood in the midst of the northern waters of the lake, are meager, but the kingdom was eventually wholly destroyed.[24] One by one its cities were taken and sacked and the Otomí who did not flee to the east, now sank to the status of a despised people.

In performing this feat, Tezozomoc had succeeded in rounding the lake and now stood face to face with the city of Tezcoco. Probably shortly after this, Tezozomoc managed to insert his influence in Acolman, a city only eight miles from Tezcoco. Tezcoco had not been able to prevent this. Tezozomoc had in fact installed a grandson of his as ruler in Acolman and had made it obvious that it was to be used as a listening post until further plans could be contrived.[25] The storm clouds that often hung over the slopes of Mount Tlaloc behind Tezcoco were not as dark for that city as was this presence from the west.

As a result of this campaign, the wheel of fortune had at last spun round for the Mexica. Their contribution to the victory had been noteworthy, and we have seen Tezozomoc duly rewarding them with booty and lands in the north. Before the reduction of the Otomí, Mexico, under the aegis of Azcapotzalco, had been a vassal state whose tribute had consisted mainly in battalions of skilled fighting men. The subsequent increase in her prestige and wealth and in the population growth that resulted therefrom recast her as an ally, almost an equal.

Marriage Alliances of the Mexican Royal Houses

The years had seen a considerable strengthening of Mexican power in terms of the family alliances her great men had contracted. It is of moment to point these out, for in the several complications of marriage and issue lie clearly revealed the policies of the competing houses.

The two ruling Mexican lines, that of Tlatilulco and that of Tenochtitlan, had little in common. The first stemmed from Tezozomoc, lord of the Tepaneca, and had at first no Mexican blood at all. The second stemmed from Acamapichtli and represented such an intimate union of Culua and Mexica blood that the later Tenochca house could claim without fear of contradiction to be Culua by descent. The division between the two Mexican lineages was thus profound.

At some point in the career of Cuacuauhtzin—probably early—his father's avid policy had dictated that he be allied in marriage with a princess of Coatlichan.[26] Coatlichan was the original urban center of the kingdom of Acolhuacan—Tezcoco being at that time mainly the residence of emperors and the gateway to the hunting parks behind. Coatlichan, "the house of the snake," with its sister city of Huexotla, represented in its social makeup the old pre-Chichimec culture. These two cities stood only three miles apart in the most beautiful part of the Great Basin. Cultivated fields at their feet sloped gently down to the lake's edge. Mount Tlaloc rose behind them, its majestic shoulders covered with a green patina of forests. This was a good land for both farmers and hunters. It was also an old land and held many memories of the past; in the quarries behind Coatlichan still lay, partially carved out of the native rock, a massive goddess from the days of Teotihuacan, blind, recumbent, but still filled with power. Many Otomí continued to live in the far upper reaches of the sheltered valleys as they had done in antiquity, while along the lower slopes ruins of Toltec pyramids were all about.

That Cuacuauhtzin should thus marry into the house of one of the elector lords of Acolhuacan was evidence that Tezozomoc, under the guise of friendship, was planting his influence on the other side of the lake, directly in the heart of Acolhuacan. The son and heir of Cuacuauhtzin was also to marry into the house of Coatlichan, further deepening Tepaneca and Mexican influence there.[27] These marriages signaled the first tentative appearance of a three-nation league, which, after some violent remodeling to come, would eventually dominate all of Aztec political life. Here the cities were Azcapotzalco, Tlatilulco, and Coatlichan, representing respectively the Tepaneca, Mexica, and Acolhua peoples. In the great cataclysms that lay just ahead, the league would reemerge, each of the aforementioned three cities giving way to its rival (Tlacopan, Tenochtitlan, and Tezcoco) but with these rivals still representing the same federation of Tepaneca, Mexica, and Acolhua.

This first and inchoate formulation of the famous Three City League was a political instrument in the hands of one man, Tezozomoc, and thus, while its public face was that of an accommodation among three competing interests for their common good, its hidden purpose was subversion by Anahuac's most accomplished master of intrigue.

The place of Tenochtitlan in this evolving picture is curious. It must be remembered that, while in population it was now at least the equal of Tlatilulco, its orientation had been consistently toward the southern part of the Great Basin. Clearly this did not fit perfectly into Tezozomoc's plans, which had ultimately an eastern objective. If Tezozomoc was to continue to have the use of dedicated Tenochca fighting men in his armies, he would have to raise them approximately to the rank of their brother Mexicans, the Tlatilulca. And, considering the rancor between the two cities, this could be a signally dangerous step to take, one to be performed only with proper safeguards.

Tenochtitlan had been growing not only in population but also in self-confidence. It could not yet match Tlatilulco in prestige, for Tlatilulco had a legitimate *tlatoani* duly elected and stemming from an authentic Aztec seigniory. Tenochtitlan, however, did possess an incipient nobility of her own; this lineage was the fruit of marriages between the descendants of the founding chieftains and the many offspring of Acamapichtli.[28] These latter already considered themselves to be sons of greatness; because of their Culua blood they bowed to none either in pride of descent or renown in war. The exploits of this peerage in the field were already considerable and showed them to be equal in hardiness to the warriors of Tlatilulco.

The presence of Acamapichtli in Tenochtitlan had given that city the mission to conquer for him his ancestral seat, the city of Culhuacan; this had become a cardinal objective of Tenochca policy and had been duly accomplished. What complicated this was the fact that the state of Chalco had already extended its influence over the whole of the south shore, including Culhuacan. The Tenochca found themselves involved therefore in a long series of raids and ambushcades directed against cities in Lakes Chalco and Xochimilco.

The Tenochca finally achieved the desired success in momentarily frustrating the Chalca and bringing down the city of Culhaucan, no great feat considering its recent trials.[29] A panel of Tenochca nobles acting under a military commissar was dispatched to the conquered city, which was now degraded radically from its former status.[30] The imposition of Tenochca suzerainty over this city naturally forced a more serious confrontation with the Chalca people, a confrontation that was to have many vicissitudes and would play an extended role in Mexico's history. With help from Tlatilulca and Tepaneca warriors, the Tenochca did gain a temporary advantage over the kingdom of Chalco, but their arrogance in victory created consternation throughout the whole Basin and even far beyond. Led by Tezcoco, an overwhelming anti-Tenochca coalition was rapidly put together and an ultimatum delivered to them. The mere knowledge of this crushing opposition able to bear down on them forced the Tenochca to redress the wrongs they had committed and to reinstate the Chalca royal house that they had unwisely deposed. The world of Anahuac, thoroughly alarmed, was demanding that Chalco be permitted to stand forever as a barrier to Mexican expansion in that direction. Thus did the initial Chalco thrust abort for the Tenochca. Tezozomoc had unleashed his hounds too soon.

These broils took place under the command of Huitzilihuitl, a son of Acamapichtli. A consideration of the status of this Tenochca leader will throw light on the relationship between the two moieties of the Mexican state.

Acamapichtli had exercised little power in Tenochtitlan beyond that which came to him from his exalted ancestry. The city had no king of its own, as did Tlatilulco, and was ruled only by customary procedures under priests and headmen. Tribute was owed to Cuacuauhtzin, sovereign ruler of all the islands of Mexico. The indefiniteness of this status became in the end insupportable to the Tenochca, and finally the crisis of leadership became acute. A solution finally emerged in 1390, which, in spite of strong opposition from the priesthood, recognized the growing need for leadership.[31] Huitzilihuitl, one of the more accomplished young sons of Acamapichtli, was to be recognized as the civil ruler of Tenochtitlan, while his father no doubt continued as the priestly ruler or *cihuacoatl*.[32] No early source tells us that Huitzilihuitl at that time actually became a *tlatoani*, and we get the impression that this kingmaking on the part of the Tenochca was an internal affair and was looked upon as merely ingenuous by the Aztec world around.[33] Certainly Cuacuauhtzin, to whom the Tenochca owed their tribute, must have viewed the action with misgivings. Perhaps he was placated by the Tenochca action in 1391 in withdrawing from Culhuacan the military government they had first set up there fifteen years previously. It was a delicate

period for the Tenochca, but they successfully weathered it. Huitzilihuitl, so long as he kept a relatively undistinguished place, was allowed
to rule.[34]

In 1403, after continuing close support of Tepaneca and Tlatilulca
policies, Huitzilihuitl celebrated the New Fire Ceremony, which inau-
gurated a new life for the world every fifty-two years. The following
year two events seem to have taken place that were closely connected—
the death of Acamapichtli and Huitzilihuitl's marriage to a Tepaneca
princess, the daughter of Tezozomoc and therefore the sister of Cuacuauhtzin. By this marriage he was certainly raised to the status of *tlatoani*.[35]

It seems clear that this move was brought about by Tezozomoc himself in an attempt to keep his Mexican henchmen from coming to log-
gerheads. Cuacuauhtzin obviously still held a position of superior legitimacy, but the election of Huitzilihuitl, coupled with this new alliance
with the Tepaneca royal house, put Tenochtitlan almost on a footing
of parity with Tlatilulco. Traditionally Acamapichtli is listed as the first
of the Tenochca kings, but this is erroneous. His son is the more likely
candidate. And it was this son, Huitzilihuitl, who immediately launched
Tenochtitlan on the southern adventure described above. Henceforth
Tenochtitlan paid tribute directly to their own *tlatoani*, who was a
vassal, not of Cuacuauhtzin, but of Tezozomoc directly.

Huitzilihuitl contracted another marriage almost as important as that
with the daughter of Tezozomoc. Acting in consonance with the already settled Tenochca southern policy, he managed to secure as a second
wife a princess of the house of Cuauhnahuac. This city of the Tlahuica
people lay over the mountains to the south, and alliance with it represented one of the first Mexican involvements in extra-valley affairs.
Not only was this union a sign of the increasing power of the Mexica,
it would also in time produce a child destined to become the greatest of
all Mexican rulers, Moteuczoma I.

And to support further this picture of an expanding involvement in
the affairs of Anahuac, the tie was established with Tezcoco when Huitzilihuitl gave a daughter of his in marriage to Ixtlilxochitl, the new
young emperor resident in that city.[36] That Tezozomoc could not have
looked favorably on this alliance is easy to guess, but that he could have

at the same time foreseen that the child of that union would become the most famous of all Aztec rulers and the one destined to bring the house of Azcapotzalco crashing down in total ruin—this was hidden even from his vulpine gaze. What was immediately offensive to Tezozomoc about the alliance was that arrangements had previously been made for that young prince to marry one of his own daughters. Ixtlilxochitl upset this prearrangement—which would have won for the Tepaneca overlord his first direct entry into the imperial house of Tezcoco—preferring as he did a daughter of the Tenochca as his legitimate queen.[37] The Tepaneca princess therefore became only a concubine. Tezozomoc's cabal was in that respect temporarily checked.

The Call for a Caesar

The times moved fast. The cities of Anahuac were growing at an increasingly rapid rate. Mexico was only one of them, though one of the most feared. Storm was over the land. The perennial bickering among these Aztec communities was like the low rumble of thunder in summer, the treasons and whiplike sallies were like tongues of lightning and the sound of the sack of cities like the voice of great rains. War in this world was not only an instrument of power but also a cult and could not be dispensed with.

In all this hot tempest the labor of the patient Aztec *macehualli* in the fields, bending all day over his digging stick, produced enough for life in the cities and a surplus in addition. Merchant caravans of porters moved in and out of the valley. Newer and nobler temples to the gods rose everywhere. And instead of coarse garments of maguey fiber, the magnates in the cities now wore soft cottons imported from outside the valley. A civilization was approaching its maturity with astounding suddenness, but as yet there was still a wide diversity of tongues and races. How this developing civilization would order itself could not yet be prophesied. It called for a great-hearted master, if such a Caesar could be found.

Tezozomoc, lord of the Tepaneca, with the Mexica as his strong right arm, now set out in earnest to impose his will on this world of movement and color. This attempt of his closes the middle chapter of Aztec history.

Tezozomoc and the Death of Ixtlilxochitl

A new ruler now sat with all the appurtenances of power in the Mexican islands. Cuacuauhtzin had died after a long rule and had left his son Tlacateotzin in his stead. This Tlatilulca ruler was already a grown man when his father died and accordingly filled the office of the generalissimo of the Tepaneca armies as his father had filled it before him. Also, like his grandfather Tezozomoc, he was ardent in his detestation of the Acolhua and threw himself wholeheartedly into the great drive to crush that kingdom once and for all.

Though he was an old man at the time, Tezozomoc's desire to possess the title of *chichimeca teuctli* had in no wise diminished.[38] If anything, he pursued his ancient objective with a ferocity more pronounced than ever. Against him stood the emperor Ixtlilxochitl, inexperienced but like all his house a most gallant warrior.[39] When his father died, he had been unable to match Tezozomoc's speed in declaring himself the true emperor and a pronounced drift had set in among the imperial vassals in the Basin toward the Tepaneca pretender's camp. Tezozomoc's intrigues indeed seem to have effectively prevented any early election of Ixtlilxochitl to the title rightfully his.

When Tezozomoc felt himself sufficiently prepared, he gathered together an army of vassals and allies and moved on three fronts against Tezcoco.[40] The southern or right wing included the Chinampaneca cities and it opened hostilities by launching a desperate attack on the city of Ixtapaluca. Simultaneously Tezozomoc's own Tepaneca troops moved around the northern end of the lake shielded behind Acolman, which, though an Acolhua city, had earlier gone over to Tezozomoc. From the west, the ominous Mexica threatened by canoe all of the great lakeside sites. Thus outmanned, Tezcoco had to position armies on both northern and southern frontiers as well as stand on the alert in the center. It was an unenviable situation in which to have to fight.

After the southern thrust had been repulsed with difficulty, there was a respite in the fighting during which Ixtlilxochitl called up those of his vassals not guarding the frontiers and had himself formally acknowledged as *chichimeca teuctli*. Previously they had demurred, not wanting to commit themselves until Ixtlilxochitl had shown himself capable of victory. Now the lords of Huexotla and Coatlichan took the public oath of fealty to him as emperor and to Nezahualcoyotl, his twelve-year-old son, as his legitimate successor. This was in the year 1414.[41] A demand at the same time was sent to Tlatilulco and Azcapotzalco to also render homage or accept all the rigors of war. The reception of his embassy was predictable. It was contemptuously dismissed.

Now it was the Mexican turn to move into the attack, and, led by Tlacateotzin, they did so with their usual élan. A large fleet of war canoes under cover of night moved silently out across the lake, at least six men to a vessel, paddlemen with shieldmen for protection against projectiles and others to hurl darts. The shields rustled with fringes and skirts of gaudy feathers, and some bore the devices of Mexican knights already known to belong to the select body of the heroic. The flotilla skirted the insular rock of Tepetzinco looming hugely under the stars and at the first paling in the east swarmed in for a landing in the face of the enemy. The Mexica pressed the attack vigorously but finally, after heavy losses, were forced back into the deeper waters of the lake. Tlacateotzin led the flotilla back into the protected waters of Mexico.

The Acolhua thus had two impressive victories, both defensive, to their credit. This at last gave them the opportunity to mount a counteroffensive by land. With good luck and under superb leaders, the Acolhua and their allies from beyond the mountains gradually fought their way back around the northern side of the lake, city after city falling to their advance. Fierce battles raged as far north as Tula, and in every one the forces of Ixtlilxochitl were invincible. Tepaneca power finally collapsed on the battlefield of Cuauhtitlan, and the Mexican Tlacateotzin fled with his beaten army back to Azcapotzalco.[42] The immediate investment of the capital city of Azcapotzalco was now a certainty, so Tezozomoc sued for a negotiated peace. The war in all had lasted three years.[43]

Out of the magnanimity he displayed in that settlement, Ixtlilxochitl, the perfect knight, forged the instrument of his own downfall. The events that swiftly and ineluctably followed should not have been unexpected.

Tezozomoc offered to perform his homage in person before Ixtlilxo-

chitl, and it was agreed that both sides would immediately disarm. It
was also agreed that the city of Azcapotzalco should remain unscathed
and that the Tepaneca should be treated with respect as true vassals of
the emperor. Such were the terms that chivalry and guile made with
each other. What was to happen to Mexico is not mentioned in the
sources. All of Anahuac had been astounded at Ixtlilxochitl's peace
terms, and many cities must have considered them a sign of weakness.

The war had produced extreme factionalism and a confusion in al-
legiances in the valley. Practically alone of all the states involved, Mexico had loyally carried out her commitment, and her friendship or at
least her understanding with the Tepaneca had remained unbroken.
Elsewhere, ruling and noble families had been radically split as a result of decisions to support either the empire or Azcapotzalco. Treason had become so common as to be almost meaningless. Corruption
walked everywhere and hid behind every smile, while the heroic and
the cunning could hardly be distinguished one from another. Only the
hardiest of the nobles survived. Splendor, pride, and duplicity lit mon-
umental fires in which was being annealed the Aztec soul.

With a speed and a sureness uncanny in one so old, Tezozomoc now
set about to suborn Otumpan and Chalco, which were of prime strategic importance to the empire. These two, situated respectively on the
northern and southern frontiers of the kingdom of Acolhua, were lured
into the net and finally, in a very triumph of conspiracy, Tezozomoc
corrupted some of the leading nobles immediately surrounding Ixtlilxochitl. While the emperor had in candor and good faith disbanded
his armies and dismissed his Tlateputzca allies, Tezozomoc had kept
his squadrons, including the veteran Mexica, intact and ready for action.

The trap was sprung when Tezozomoc came to Chiconauhtla ostensibly to swear fealty to the emperor but actually leading an army of
attack. The true situation—desperate in the extreme—was revealed to
Ixtlilxochitl in the report of a spy; he was taken completely by surprise for he had entertained no suspicions at all of treachery. Tezozomoc had with him, not a straggling body of courtiers in a festive mood,
but ranks of fighting men including the dreaded Mexica. Otumpan
and Chalco were on the move and had already crossed the frontiers.

Ixtlilxochitl attempted to give the appropriate orders to his palace intimates only to find that some had already been removed by murder while others had slipped away leaving him almost bereft of support.[44] Overnight his whole empire had dissolved. Few more sudden reversals have ever been recorded in history. From the time when he received the news of the rebellion to his demise Ixtlilxochitl lived only a desperate fifty days.

Heroically and fruitlessly he threw together a ragged defense, too little and too late. His great cities, Huexotla, Coatlichan, and finally Tezcoco were overrun, and those inhabitants who did not flee over the mountains were brutally exterminated. Surrounded now only by a small body of loyal kinsmen, including his son Nezahualcoyotl, Ixtlilxochitl retired up through the rough timberlands of Mount Tlaloc, intent on crossing the divide into friendly Tlascalan territory. In a deep gorge called "the place of the wolf," he and the few with him were surrounded and cut down.[45] His son, hidden in the thick foliage of a nearby tree, watched the terrible scene being enacted below him. Of persons of consequence, he alone escaped.

The shattering fall of such an empire and the death of such a prince were never to be forgotten. From the terse lines of an Aztec epic that adopts the anticipatory style comes a recollection of what it meant:

> And the dearly beloved Ixtlilxochitl!
> Ah! If he should ever let his guard down
> His kingdom would perish;
> Tezozomoc would stand by and pretend to
>   weep.
> And so again in history there will grow for
>   the Aztecs thorny mesquite and cactus.[46]

The Death of Tezozomoc

At the end of his extraordinarily long life, Tezozomoc had become a wraith. He was carried from place to place in a reed cradle or basket bedded down in teased-out cotton and rabbit furs, and at night for warmth he was carefully placed between two braziers. To the very end he continued to cow all those who knew him. He alone was now the *chichimeca teuctli.*

After the collapse of the kingdom of Acolhuacan, he had himself formally invested with the imperial title in a ceremony held at the entrance of the royal hunting park of Cuauhyacac just behind Tezcoco. All the Aztec states in Anahuac (except the Tlateputzca cities that still belonged to the loyalist party) were present at this repellant ceremony conducted in two languages, Chichimec and Nahuatl.[47] The kingdom was formally broken into two parts, and its important cities given outright to various of Tezozomoc's sons and grandsons who would now hold them as fiefs from their superannuated Tepaneca overlord. In recompense for their iron deeds, the Mexica were favored before all others.[48]

To Tlatilulco fell the rule of Huexotla, to Tenochtitlan that of Tezcoco. Their commissars arrived in those ravaged places to organize the survivors who now were drifting back and to collect the first tribute owed them. Tezozomoc was to preside over this new imperial accretion of territory for exactly nine years, his wickedness and his tyranny openly with him to the end. He died in 1426. That death was to open the floodgates through which poured the torrential waters of a new world.[49]

4. The Tepaneca War

 For some years prior to his death, Tezozomoc had been warned of the potential danger posed by the Mexica. Both moieties of this people now had incipient empires of their own among the northern Otomí, in the Acolhua cities, and on the south shore of the lake. Prominent among those who openly advocated action against Mexico was Tezozomoc's son, Maxtla, the perverse and unstable ruler of Coyouacan.[1] The amazing growth of Mexico had filled Maxtla with forebodings. He had been the victim of a corroding envy aroused by the power and prestige of his brother Cuacuauhtzin, and, after the death of his brother, his envy had been transferred to Cuacuauhtzin's son and successor, Tlacateotzin. There was additionally the insulting fact that it was these Tlatilulca lords and not himself who led the Tepaneca cities in wartime. Nor was Maxtla without grounds for believing that the royal house of Tlatilulco might even succeed to the imperial title when his father died.

Maxtla indiscriminately hated all the Mexica whether Tlatilulca or

Tenochca, but the latter particularly. When Huitzilihuitl of Tenochtitlan had been given one of the daughters of Tezozomoc as a wife Maxtla did all in his power to disrupt the arrangement.[2] Not succeeding in
this, he had finally managed to have the only son of that union, his
own nephew, assassinated. Thus when Huitzilihuitl died in 1414, he
was followed in the rule of Tenochtitlan, not by a fully legitimate son,
but by a person named Chimalpopoca, possibly a son by a concubine or
a lesser wife.[3] Chimalpopoca thus acceded to a position that was plainly under challenge from an impressive sector of the Tepaneca people.
But it appears that Maxtla was not the only one who attempted to block
the Tenochca during the lifetime of Tezozomoc. So also had Tlacateotzin of Tlatilulco. In fact it appears that, as leader of the Tepaneca armies, he had urged a spoiling attack on Tenochtitlan before that city became too presumptuous.[4] But as long as Tezozomoc was alive and
mindful of his empire, such evidences of anti-Tenochca rancor were
not allowed to disrupt Tepaneca stability. It was obvious, however, that
whenever he should pass from the scene these tensions would come out
in the open and demand satisfaction.

Receiving the rents from the city of Tezcoco as well as from other
lesser areas—all won in hard fighting—Chimalpopoca felt himself relatively secure as long as Tezozomoc lived. Under him, the Tenochca
nobles, however, were growing more restive and assertive in proportion as they felt their prestige as warriors increasing. Cities in the north
were now under their aegis as well as ones across the lake, all of them
brought in as a result of Tenochca prowess. Their proud boast was that
they were the only true sons of Tula and that the Toltec empire would
be revived again under their auspices. This could be, and no doubt was,
taken as a threat to seize the imperial title from Azcapotzalco.

The nobles in this group would have been remarkable in any Aztec
city. Advising Chimalpopoca was a bastard brother, Itzcoatl, a distinguished baron. There was the young and demonic Tlacaelel, nephew
of Chimalpopoca. There was also Moteuczoma, a son of Huitzilihuitl,
sober but daring at the same time, perhaps the most impressive of all
the great peers in breadth of experience. These then—and many others
like them—were the Tenochca lords, braggart, tenacious, inflexible,

and all of them absolutely convinced of the perfect quality of their inherited mission to subdue Anahuac. They had recently adopted a transmontane style of courtly life, speech, and apparel, which was distinctive of the men of Huexotzinco, who had long been famous for their bearing and martial deeds. Such superior airs did not please the Tepaneca of the mainland. To these somewhat vague irritants in the relations between the two people was added the concrete insult that the two Mexica queens had successfully interceded with Tezozomoc, petitioning that their nephew Nezahualcoyotl be allowed to reside among them. Nezahualcoyotl, son of the murdered Ixtlilxochitl, was alternating now between Mexico and Tezcoco, a captive prince but dangerous because of his claims to the imperial dignity. It must have seemed to the Tepaneca that the Mexica were harboring him against a day in the future.

It was Tezozomoc who had allowed this formidable warrior caste to consolidate itself so swiftly in Tenochtitlan; his eyes had been fixed on glory elsewhere, and his years had become too many. But his Tepaneca sons and grandsons were aware. The open break finally came in the last days of Tezozomoc, when he was senile and no longer in command of his faculties. A few years earlier the Tenochca had received permission from the Tepaneca to bring out the waters of the Chapultepec spring through a channel cut in a newly constructed but impermanent turf and reed causeway. This had given new life to Tenochtitlan and had been responsible for much of its subsequent amazing growth. Nevertheless, maintenance could not keep up with the perpetual disrepair of the open ditch, and Chimalpopoca, backed by all his nobles, now demanded of the Tepaneca, their nominal masters, that they provide stone, timber, and even labor to help them construct a more lasting masonry flume.[5]

The calculated insult contained in this message was not lost on the Tepaneca leaders. Tezozomoc, now dying, could only weakly support Chimalpopoca; he was no longer able either to initiate or to impede action. His council, responding to Maxtla's passionate denunciation, immediately ordered the cutting off of all Tenochca access to the mainland, whether for wood, water, or commerce. The way out to the island was also blockaded against all those who customarily went in to the

Mexican markets, and armed guards were stationed at every path. The reeds along the shore were filled with ambushes. It was at this juncture, with open warfare about to break out, that Tezozomoc died.

Maxtla's Murders

Decisions of every kind in Anahuac were temporarily shelved, and men paused to gauge the strength of the many currents that had incontinently begun to flow. Even before the obsequies of Tezozomoc had come to an end, however, the storm that had been gathering pealed out its opening thunders.

In the year of his death, 1426, Tezozomoc had left his title and patrimony to a relatively unknown son, Tayatzin, but Maxtla forestalled this brother by seizing the capital city of Azcapotzalco. While the Tepaneca nobles were violently split over the issue, the majority ended by supporting him. To the Mexica of both cities this presented a threat that they dared not disregard.

Tlacateotzin, who had openly supported Tayatzin, could not long put off some sort of action, for Maxtla ordered a crushing increase in the tribute due him from all of Mexico—palpably a challenge. Chimalpopoca likewise, but in other ways, was publicly humiliated. He could not hold the allegiance of his barons for long if he accepted the insults. Thus overnight appeared those circumstances that finally turned Mexico away from its hitherto advantageous alliance with Azcapotzalco.

Forced by his own people to act, Chimalpopoca initiated a conspiracy to destroy Maxtla.[6] Only a few details concerning this plot were handed down to posterity, but that it was widespread and centered in Tenochtitlan is obvious. Chimalpopoca first involved Tayatzin, inviting him out to his palace for discussion of the various courses open to them. Between them they decided on the assassination of Maxtla under the pretense of friendship. Almost certainly Tlacateotzin was privy to this scheme,[7] as was the young Acolhua prince Nezahualcoyotl, who was at the time holding Tezcoco under Tenochca suzerainty. The cabal, however, was carelessly put together and was betrayed to Maxtla by one of the hideously deformed buffoons in Chimalpopoca's court. Thus forewarned, Maxtla easily turned the tables on the conspirators.

Our sources are in serious conflict regarding the details of the events that followed, but it is known that both of the Mexican rulers were taken and destroyed. So also was Tayatzin. Nezahualcoyotl escaped. Chimalpopoca is supposed to have been either murdered at night in his own palace or abducted and taken in a wooden cage to Azcapotzalco, where he later died ignominiously of hunger and thirst.[8] Nezahualcoyotl was to have been killed by a bastard brother but managed in the nick of time to escape. He had opportunity to notify Tlacateotzin in Tlatilulco of his danger, and that ruler, fleeing to Acolhua territory for safety, was either intercepted in the middle of the lake and drowned or cut down by his pursuers near Xaltocan. Tayatzin was killed unsuspecting while banqueting in exactly the manner in which he had planned the murder of Maxtla.

Tezozomoc had originally won his empire with the aid of Mexico, Acolman, Otumpan, and Chalco, and all of these, whether subjects or allies, had been properly rewarded. Maxtla, frightened at the portentous growth in Mexico particularly, reversed his father's alliance policy by thus doing away with the two Mexican rulers. He then turned to the rich constellation of the cities in the Chalca confederation for a coalition strong enough to bring Mexico to a final end. This effort of his was to result in failure, for Anahuac had as little love for the duplicity of the Tepaneca as for the hectoring ways of the Mexica. Huexotzinco, as the leading state of Tlateputzco was also wooed, but again without success, for Nezahualcoyotl was in exile there, engaged in carrying on a campaign of persuasion designed to win the cities of that region to his cause. Nezahualcoyotl in fact represented for Maxtla another imperial problem, also pressing: besides crushing Mexico, Maxtla also had to prevent the revival of the kingdom of Acolhuacan. He was not inevitably doomed to failure in attaining his first objective, for he could always count on internecine strife between the two moieties of Mexico to work to his advantage. The second objective was much more problematical.

In 1428, the year following the assassination of Tlacateotzin, the nobles of Tlatilulco elected a grandson of his to succeed him, another descendant of Tezozomoc.[9] This was Cuauhtlatoa, apparently a young man and certainly untested.[10] In spite of the humiliation Maxtla had already imposed on them, the Tlatilulca nobles were at first somewhat inclined to honor their old friendship and blood ties with the Tepaneca, but as Maxtla in his savage repressions made little distinction between the two Mexican peoples, they soon swung about to follow the more independent example of Tenochtitlan. The steps they finally and reluctantly took, however, and the policies they followed were their own; they had no intention of merging with Tenochtitlan, even in the face of such danger as presently loomed upon them.

Mexico Changes Sides

In 1427 Tenochtitlan had elected a new *tlatoani*, a man under whom the entire course of Mexican history was to be reversed.[11] This was Itzcoatl, "Bladed Serpent," one of those who had believed from the first in the independent destiny of Tenochtitlan. At the time of his election he was already 45 or 46 years old, and he had been eminently successful in war for a long period of time by serving under the two previous rulers of Tenochtitlan. Under Huitzilihuitl, he had held the rank of *tlacateuctli*.[12] Under Chimalpopoca, he had risen to command all of the Tenochca armed forces and was acknowledged to be prudent as well as brave. His sons had likewise distinguished themselves both in their marriages and their deeds.

Itzcoatl's claim to purity of blood was somewhat impeached by the fact that, while his father was the illustrious Acamapichtli, his mother had been a mere slave girl, some said a seller of vegetables. He was thus not legitimate. Nevertheless, at the time of his election his record on the battlefield outweighed his bastardy. His nephew Moteuczoma was a strong contender against him in the election but had been mollified by being straightway raised to the full command of the army and given the promise of becoming the next *tlatoani*. Thus the older man was finally chosen by common consent under the ancient usage of the succession of all available brothers before dropping down into the generation below.

As it turned out, it was the most momentous election ever carried out in Mexico, for it was to impose a wholly new course on the future. The Tepaneca, reading its meaning correctly, immediately tightened up the blockade on the landward side of Mexico and prepared themselves for further involvement. Yet Tenochtitlan was even more concerned with the stance that her sister city, Tlatilulco, was going to take at this critical juncture. If Tlatilulco should continue to honor her Tepaneca ties, then the freedom of navigation on the lake that Tenochtitlan enjoyed, and therefore her advantage over Azcapotzalco, would be lost. Tlatilulco's canoe contingent directed againt Tenochtitlan would be disastrous. Fearfully, Tenochtitlan waited out the period of Tlatilulco's indecision.

Even so, Tenochtitlan knew that the role that she undoubtedly would be forced to play would be one with great odds against her. The suzerainty over Tezcoco she had enjoyed had been withdrawn by Maxtla, who had installed there a pliant Acolhua tool in the place of Nezahualcoyotl, whom he had failed to assassinate. This deprived Tenochtitlan of needed tribute. And about the same time the anti-Mexican party of the Acolhua—always powerful—had organized a sneak attack on the city of Ecatepec to the north, also tributary to Tenochtitlan. These losses, particularly that of Ecatepec, where a nephew of Itzcoatl had been ruling, were serious in a material sense, while at the same time they indicated to the world of Anahuac Mexican inability to hold its own possessions. This situation caused Itzcoatl to summon his council to consider the now desperate situation in which the Tenochca found themselves. In these consultations it was finally decided to abandon all pretense of friendship for the Tepaneca and to seek to involve the city in the alliance being constructed by Nezahualcoyotl among the Tlateputzca cities.

Unfortunately this period in Mexican history—so very interesting to us—is confusingly reported; in some sources it is altogether slighted. Dates, names, and the order of events are jumbled. It is thus unknown whether Tenochtitlan took the lead in proposing an accommodation to Tlatilulco. Itzcoatl was cautious under the circumstances, and we do find that after a year of his rule an unusual meeting of the rulers and councillors of both cities was called to sit in Tlatilulco and to determine whether a joint policy could be constructed. Again, nothing is definitely known of the results of this, but the succeeding events show that the two Mexican peoples did begin to pursue parallel, though independent, courses. Thus we may assume that an alliance of sorts was confirmed. It is probable that Itzcoatl's known marriage to a princess of the royal house of Tlatilulco took place at this time and was considered to be the outward mark of that understanding.[13]

With Mexico at one with itself, the next step necessary to victory over Maxtla could now be taken, namely a firm Mexica-Acolhua alliance. Some of the groundwork for this had been prepared when Tezozomoc had originally given Tezcoco in fief to Tenochtitlan. Nezahualcoyotl, who, consequent upon the death of his father, had barely escaped the pursuing assassins of Tezozomoc, was no born friend of the Mexica, but he had been conciliated and installed as ruler in his native city of Tezcoco under the aegis of the Tenochca, and he had in that interval married into the Tenochca nobility. The reconciliation with Nezahualcoyotl had undoubtedly been made easier by the fact that his mother had been of Mexican royal blood. A severe strain, however, had been imposed on the relations of the two people when it was learned that Nezahualcoyotl, in flight from Maxtla's proscription, had approached the Tlateputzca cities and was there in the process of building a great alliance that would again seat him as an independent ruler on the throne of his fathers. Thus, if the Mexica were to make a pact with Nezahualcoyotl, they would have to give up irrevocably all claims to the Acolhua cities they had formerly controlled. Furthermore, they would have to move with dispatch and declare themselves soon one way or the other, or risk being swept away in a general advance of cities allied against the Tepaneca.

Maxtla was also aware of those deepening clouds in the east, for he had sent an embassy with rich presents to Huexotzinco, hoping thus to forestall Mexico. The possibility even existed that, in exchange for peace with the forming coalition, he would aid them in a general and certainly not unpopular attack upon the two Mexicos. Chalco could easily be presuaded to such a course, for her hatred of Mexico was intense.

Tlatilulco and Tenochtitlan therefore seized the occasion and prepared an outstanding embassy to the great refugee prince Nezahualcoyotl, who was at the time in the very act of negotiating the offensive pact against Maxtla.[14] The city of Cuauhtitlan, an ally of Tlatilulco with strong grievances against Maxtla, was also represented in the joint group of ambassadors. The embassy, as it turned out, was successful.

The evidence they presented convinced first Nezahualcoyotl and then the Huexotzinca of the rightness of their cause and of the need for a common front. As a consequence, all the members of Maxtla's counter-embassy, which also was in Huexotzinco contrary to the diplomatic immunities of the day, were slain by being spitted on stakes. Successful here, Nezahualcoyotl then led the united embassies to Tlascala, where he was again able to summon up allies. Thus was the grand alliance put together.

The Mexican embassy was, as we have seen, a dual and separate effort and represented the policy nuances of both Mexican cities. The Tenochca embassy was led by that preeminent prince, Moteuczoma, whose appearance alone would have made evident the high seriousness of the affair; his illustrious presence had counted heavily with both Nezahualcoyotl and the men of Huexotzinco. As soon as Nezahualcoyotl had agreed to the terms of an alliance with this embassy and with Huexotzinco and Tlascala, he thought it prudent to make an attempt to detach Chalco from Maxtla's cause, and accordingly he dispatched the Mexicans, accompanied by a deputy of his own, to Toteotzin, the old and blind ruler of Chalco. But the Chalca had in the past suffered too much under the Mexica to view the occasion as one demanding diplomatic nicety. Toteotzin, a man known to wear a collar of the dried hearts of his fallen enemies, ordered that the Mexican ambassadors be instantly seized and caged in preparation for sacrifice. But fortunately for Moteuczoma and his fellows, Chalco also was deeply divided on the Tepaneca question, and, with the connivance of one of the dissident Chalco chieftains, the prisoners were allowed to escape in the night. There followed a hair-raising journey down through the deep pine covert, hotly pursued, until the nearly exhausted band of Mexicans located a canoe on the lake edge just over the Chalco frontier, and under the stars of another night made their way back to Mexico.

The offensive pact outlined above had been originally conceived and put together by Nezahualcoyotl.[15] It must be said in any summary of the event that his was the energy, genius, and desire for revenge that created the coalition. He had no reason to love the Mexica, who, as agents of the Tepaneca, had fought his father, had opposed him, and had then reduced him to the status of a tribute-paying prince. It was mutual need that had brought him and the Mexica together here, but it was he, not Mexico, who gave direction to the coalition, for Mexico possessed at that moment neither the influence nor the stature to evoke a new structure in city-state relationships. Had the Mexica been truly one people and not two they would undoubtedly have been the ones to take the lead in forming this pact, with consequences that would undoubtedly have made them the top power in the immediate years ahead.

The Tlacaelel Embassy

The Tepaneca War, which was now about to begin, dragged most of the great cities of Anahuac down into its maelstrom. The core of Maxtla's strength was located in the central Tepaneca cities, Azcapotzalco, Tlacopan, Coyouacan, and Tenayuca; less fervent were the Chinampaneca cities and the formerly Acolhua cities, including Tezcoco, now in the hands of Maxtla's henchmen. Chalco wavered and cannot rightly be counted in either camp, though its partial neutrality tended to disappear whenever the Mexica were prominently in the picture.

Such an alignment of forces presented to the allies a difficult strategic problem. For them to attack Azcapotzalco via the south shore would be risky, for a possibly treacherous Chalco would be at their back. To attack via the north would necessitate a long and arduous detour around Otumpan, followed by a battle before Tenayuca. Such an advance would have to be undertaken by the forces of Tlascala and Huexotzinco, and a defeat of these cities so far from their base would be serious. An attack could be delivered most conveniently and most swiftly along the causeways from Mexico, but this would present all the disadvantages of an excessively narrow front. And inasmuch as the exits of the causeways were held in strength by the Tepaneca, even the redoubtable warriors of Mexico would here need support. Surprise was impossible for a sortie of this kind.

A combination of the last two seemed best. Nezahualcoyotl had recently arrived in Mexico with some loyal Acolhua warriors who had flocked to his standard as soon as he had announced his intention of finally avenging the death of his father. These contingents, few though they were, might be enough to aid the Mexica in forcing a passage to the Tepanec shore.

Before Mexico could once and for all commit herself to the hazard, the confusion of opinion still existing in Mexico demanded a final airing. Itzcoatl accordingly called a council of all the magnates as well as the headmen of the *calpulli* to debate the matter at length.

That this gathering of the nobles was one of the dramatic confrontations in all Mexican history is patent from our sources. A strong peace party appeared and based its argument for coming to an understanding with Maxtla on the largely heterogeneous population of Mexico, the many and diverse nations and groups represented among the commoners, and therefore on the possibly divided loyalties that existed among them.[16] The brunt of the battle would fall largely on them, and at the moment they showed no stomach to make Nezahualcoyotl's cause their own. Some among these commoners were Tepaneca themselves, and fears of their imminent defection were prominent in all minds. It is impossible to learn whether the peace party was predominantly Tlatilulca, but it is a good guess that many Tlatilulca nobles were included in it, as well no doubt as some of the more polyglot *calpulli* of Tenochtitlan.

When the peace party had been heard, the fiery Tlacaelel arose and castigated their spokesmen.[17] His was a warrior's appeal to greatness, and in the upshot Itzcoatl sided with him. Neither side, however, was able at this juncture to sway the other. A compromise of sorts was finally reached when all agreed to send to Maxtla a peace proposal honorable to all parties—including the claims of Nezahualcoyotl—with the threat of war to the death if he should refuse to accept it.

It was now necessary to select an ambassador to deliver such a message. The post would obviously call for a man of high courage as well as eloquence, for the probabilities were that he would not come back. Tlacaelel immediately volunteered. The name Tlacaelel means appropriately "Man of Great Heart."[18] Certainly no Mexican ever surpassed him in that Aztec ideal of virility and scornfulness to which his name bore witness. Already in his early thirties, he was a nephew of Itzcoatl, and since his uncle's election he had held the rank of *atempanecatl*.[19] His claim to noble blood was impeccable, for his father had been Huitzilihuitl and his mother a princess from one of the proudest lineages of Chalco; his progeny would be equally splendid in their connections and abilities.

Shortly after the Tepaneca War, epic lays were composed concerning Tlacaelel and his mighty deeds. The one relating the story of his perilous embassy became particularly well known.[20] The hero, spurning the cowardice of the common people of Mexico, heroically volunteered for the commission and presented himself alone to the Tepaneca frontier guards at the causeway's landward end. He successfully convinced them that his person was sacrosanct because of his ambassadorial office, and he was allowed into the presence of the Tepaneca ruler. Maxtla courteously listened to his message but was too weak at the time to act without his council. He dismissed Tlacaelel, telling him to return the next day for an answer. This was a double jeopardy for Tlacaelel, who, however, adroitly talked himself safely back through the guard post. Because he had given his word to the Tepaneca guards to return, he insisted to Itzcoatl that he be permitted to do so; all knew that the enemy guards would probably kill him when he again tried to exit from their territory. Once again he was ushered into the presence of the Tepaneca ruler, who now after consultation with his magnates refused the offer of peace. Hereupon, in accordance with the ceremony sanctioned by diplomatic custom among the Aztecs, Tlacaelel stepped forward and proceeded to anoint the Tepaneca ruler with the black unction of death, to place upon his head the white feathers of a doomed prisoner and to deposit weapons before him. Thus he symbolically declared war on all the Tepaneca and announced their coming defeat. In the best tradition of chivalry—and certainly not in keeping with Maxtla's character— the ruler then pointed out to him a possible escape route and even gave him the means to defend himself. Tlacaelel cunningly escaped from the city of Azcapotzalco to burst unexpectedly upon the frontier guards with vituperation, taunts, and a flight of well-aimed darts. Leaving some of the enemy guards dead behind him, he returned unharmed to report that war had now come by decision of the enemy.

It is obvious that in terms of its plausibility this account leaves much to be desired. It is reasonable to assume that Tlacaelel did in fact lead an embassy to the court of Azcapotzalco at some time before hostilities commenced, and it is reasonable also to believe that this embassy was considered dangerous for those who participated. That Tlacaelel, however, was the lone voice of patriotic courage in Mexico, that the peace party was comprised of despicable commoners only, that it was his eloquence and honorableness alone that passed him through the frontier posts of the Tepaneca, that Maxtla was a gentlemanly ruler not able to make up his own mind, and that he allowed Tlacaelel to ceremonially dress him as a defeated monarch—all this is the fiction that gathers around a popular hero. Epic is always larger than life.

Nevertheless, the account is of value in revealing divided counsels in Mexico and the grave chances the war party took in operating behind Tlacaelel as their spokesman. It is at any rate the popular understanding of Mexico's decision to play her own role in history, no longer fettered to another people. The lay of Tlacaelel's embassy is thus, in story form, Mexico's declaration of independence.

The Tepaneca War Opens

Under an astute fighting captain named Mazatl, the Tepaneca, hoping to anticipate the enemy, launched a sudden and all-out attack across the causeways against Mexico.[21] This was in the early part of 1428.[22] Nezahualcoyotl had just arrived in the city with his war band, and now the two people, Acolhua and Mexica, shoulder to shoulder, prepared to defend the city. This advance of the enemy brought forth for the time being an unusual cooperation between Tenochtitlan and Tlatilulco; between them they erected turf forts blocking the road that ran along the causeway. Here it was, in the Cuepopan or northwestern quarter, that the fighting began.

In the north, the friendly forces of Huexotzinco had simultaneously begun to exert pressure on those cities that were under Tepaneca domination. Cuauhtitlan, restive under a Tepaneca commissar, was secretly well disposed to the cause of the Mexica, as their joint embassy with them had shown. The presumption that this area north and northeast of Tenayuca would keep the strong Tepaneca garrisons occupied was undoubtedly one of the factors leading to the allied decision to challenge the city of Azcapotzalco directly. For this reason, the sudden advance of the Tepaneca, though it may have caught the Mexica somewhat off balance, was no doubt welcomed. The enemy was to be kept busy on two fronts.

The allied forces were broken up into two bodies. The veteran unit was composed of the nobles and select youth groups, no doubt including the loyal Acolhua under Nezahualcoyotl; the other was the less-disciplined corps of commoners. Tlacaelel, under Itzcoatl, is mentioned as the commander of all the forces, but in reality nothing is known with certainty about the command arrangements. Moteuczoma was standing ready to lead a canoe contingent against Tlacopan; this city, it was hoped, would defect to the allied cause if the fighting came to its gates. Nevertheless, the prospects for the Mexica could not have been very promising, for the Tepaneca seem to have been holding all points of importance close in to Mexico. The only hope lay in an immediate offensive, the signal for which would be a fire in the night on the top of Mount Quauhtepec on the north shore. When this was seen, all available forces were to move.

The name of the canal where the battle reached its peak is remembered as Petlacalco, which, if we are to translate it literally as "grain bins," would indicate that the Tepaneca had pushed out onto the islands of Mexico, for we can assume that the city silos would have been near the palace and thus centrally located.[23] Petlacalco in fact seems to have been right at the city's edge. Here Coltic, the twisted Tepanec god of war, faced Huitzilopochtli, his Mexican counterpart. Between them, an Aztec Armageddon was fought out, with the canals finally stained with blood and the stricken of both sides sinking deep into the mud. Mexico fought as it had never fought before; some of her regiments were so bloodied that they came within an ace of surrendering. In the end it was the indomitable magic of Huitzilopochtli, the Mexican sorcerer, that forced the hunchbacked Tepaneca god to cower first and then to turn and run.[24]

By dusk the Tepaneca had been routed. They fell back along the causeways to the mainland, demoralized by the great endurance and the dull ferocity of the Mexica. During the night they retreated back into Azcapotzalco, which against just such a possibility had been circled by a formidable earth glacis and a screening moat; thus they abandoned the blockade of Mexico and themselves became the beleaguered. This retreat of theirs was necessitated by the great successes being gained by the Huexotzinca and Tlascalan armies moving in from the north. The amphibious thrust led by Moteuczoma had also succeeded beyond expectations in threatening Azcapotzalco's southern defenses. Tlacopan had offered no resistance, and thus Azcapotzalco had no choice but to accept siege.

Azcapotzalco had always been one of the notable cities in the Basin and boasted a Toltec history extending far back beyond the times of Xolotl.[25] Under Tezozomoc it had become the imperial capital and had been beautified and planted with trees in keeping with its grandeur. Behind it was Bird Hill, on which stood a temple of the Great Mother widely known and revered.[26] Well-tended fields all about, *calpulli* communities, as well as adjacent daughter cities such as Tlacopan and Atlacuihuayan attested to the vigor and comfort attained by the Tepaneca capital.[27] Now its splendor was at stake as armies from the east, north, and south, breathing vengeance, closed in for the kill.

The siege, replete with attacks and desperate sallies, lasted over four months.[28] Azcapotzalco had been doomed, however, when it was abandoned by its close neighbor Tlacopan, ruled at that time by one of Maxtla's nephews. This defection of Tlacopan was to have significant results in the world that was to arise out of the ashes of Azcapotzalco, for Tlacopan would be rewarded by a share in the future empire of the Three City League; its loss must have rung in Maxtla's ears like the knell of doom. It may have been at this point in the struggle that Maxtla realized the gravity of his predicament and sent off to Mexico an offer of peace and friendship, which was turned down.

The actual scene of the seizure of Azcapotzalco is only briefly described in our sources. For two and a half terrible days the city was put to the torch and sacked; the houses of its nobles were all razed to the ground. Though the slaughter of the inhabitants was immense and indiscriminate, many managed to escape into the wilds of Mount Zacatepec to the west. A story later circulated by the Mexica had it that Maxtla, one of the most thoroughly hated men in Aztec history, had been found at the last cowering in a sweat-bath house and there had been ingloriously dispatched. In actuality, he and others broke out of the fallen city and moved in good order down to Coyouacan, the Tepaneca

city formerly his and which he now reclaimed. Here he prepared to
carry on the fight.

The collapse of Azcapotzalco in 1428 was a resounding event in the
history of Anahuac. While Tepaneca power was not thereby destroyed,
the claims of the Tepaneca ruler to be *chichimeca teuctli* had come to
an end. Tenayuca, then Tezcoco, and now Azcapotzalco had all laid
hands at one time or another on the distinction of being the imperial
capital of Anahuac. None of the three had succeeded long in maintaining this claim. For years Xolotl's imperial shadow had floated over the
Basin like a great thunderhead, fat with lightning and thunder, but no
rains had fallen from it to nourish the land. Now the cloud had dispersed. The times seem not to have been ripe for the imposition of uni-
tary rule over Anahuac.

Mexico had been badly mauled in the great encounter, and the year
that followed was taken up in organizing the victory and in celebrating
her new freedom. Nezahualcoyotl continued to reside in Mexico while
preparing to regain his own patrimonial cities across the lake still in the
hands of Maxtla's henchmen.[29] He built himself a palace in Mexico
and engineered for the Mexica an improved water supply in the Chapultepec parklands.

The Spoils

Hints in our sources suggest that the Mexican fury
that had finally routed Maxtla was in reality the desperate effort of a
people to break out of a lacustrine prison and to secure sufficient lands
of their own for sowing, along with unhindered access to timberland.
This suggestion commends itself to the historian. It supplements and
does not deny the theory that the attack on Azcapotzalco was primarily
designed by Nezahualcoyotl as part of his vendetta against the murder-
ers of his father. Acolhua vengeance and Mexican land hunger both
joined to produce the great event of 1428. The cities that had formerly
been controlled by Tenochtitlan and Tlatilulco in their role as vassals
of Azcapotzalco had been originally assigned to them as tribute-pro-
ducers only—Mexico had no rights to their lands. The case was vastly
different now with Azcapotzalco, whose rich fields had for so long
tempted Mexico.

The fact that the Mexica during the hostilities had rejected Maxtla's peace proposal must be interpreted as evidence that the Mexica wished not for victory over the enemy army but for the absolute ruin of the city of Azcapotzalco and the commandeering of all its land resources for their own uses. This is, at any rate, what happened. Mexico was at last to have broad maize lands and vegetable plots sufficient to feed herself and to provide manors for the Mexican magnates. Most of the lands of Azcapotzalco now became Mexican domain, *mexicatlalli*.[30]

This was the most fundamental distribution of captured lands ever made by Mexico, for on it was to rest the wealth of a newly honored set of noble houses—those that had backed Tlacaelel and the war party. Of the others—those who had advocated submission to Maxtla—we have no exact knowledge, but we can be sure that at the very least they were excluded from the division of spoils or, more probably, exiled or demoted. Thus, as far as the social implications of the distribution are concerned, it symbolized no less than the emergence of an exclusive Mexican aristocracy whose authority rested on their proven staunchness in the battle against Azcapotzalco. These newly elevated barons were looked upon as the second founders of Mexico.

Itzcoatl, the *tlatoani*, was assigned the choicest of the captured lands to support his dignity. Such estates fell into two well-defined categories. They were either allodial lands, *tlatocatlalli* (ruler's lands), his to dispose of if he so wished, or *tecpantlalli* (palace lands), which were entailed to the office; on the proceeds from this latter class of lands he maintained his court.

Tlacaelel and Moteuczoma were honored almost as greatly with vast baronial grants, both *pillalli*, or outright gifts of allodial lands, and *teuctlalli*, entailed lands which were essentially fiefs. Then came Itzcoatl's brothers, sons of Huitzilihuitl, and finally his nephews. The new aristocracy was primarily familial. Finally, large blocks of land were assigned to the *calpulli* of Mexico, which would in turn be subdivided into family plots and apportioned by the *calpulli* headmen to those commoners who would till them. Some of these lands would be assigned to the upkeep of the temples. Our information on the allotment of lands is limited to the Tenochca case. How Tlatilulco participated in the division is unknown, but it is certain that she also gained lands for her part in the war and no doubt used these, as Tenochtitlan had, to expand her nobility and priesthood.

The scattered remnants of the Azcapotzalca were at last allowed to return to their demolished city and to begin the process of rebuilding. But now, as oppressed and despised tributaries, they worked the lands that had formerly been theirs for the benefit of others. Their market, once so flourishing, was reduced in extent and made strictly secondary to that of Tlatilulco. The city of Azcapotzalco was reorganized under two *tlatoani*, each now ruling what was in effect a moiety. The two parts of the city were known as Tepanecapan and Mexicapan, the latter in reality being a *calpulli* of Mexico and inhabited by Mexica introduced at this time. Never again would Azcapotzalco live under one supreme lord.

The Tepaneca War: Middle Phase

The still unsettled situation across the lake demanded attention. Nezahualcoyotl had masterminded the coalition that had been so successful in knocking out the core of Tepaneca power on the western shore of the lake. This had at last given the Mexica elbowroom. Now it was Mexico's turn to aid Nezahualcoyotl in reestablishing himself in his Acolhua kingdom still stubbornly held by numerous minor Tepaneca despots. This reciprocity was part of the bargain between Mexico and Nezahualcoyotl, and that its terms were rigidly observed is no doubt a tribute as much to that great man's overwhelming personality as to his sagacity. This phase of the Tepaneca War, fought out on the east shore of the lake, was to occupy most of 1429 and part of 1430, and when the operation was completed, Tezcoco, Huexotla, Coatlichan, and Acolman had all been recovered.[31] Acolman was the last holdout, and when its impressive defenses were finally breached the whole of the north was uncovered for Nezahualcoyotl's future campaigning. For their part in these battles the Mexica were rewarded by lands in Teotihuacan.[32]

Meanwhile Maxtla in Coyouacan, though he had been powerless to aid his former vassals in the Acolhua cities, had been active in other ways. He saw correctly that he was now limited to a southern policy and that Chalco held most of the uncommitted strength in that part of the Basin; as a consequence he was assiduous in trying to activate a new Tepaneca-Chalco alliance. At the same time he worked relentlessly to sabotage the consolidation of Mexica power on the western shore. Azcapotzalco, scarcely yet awakened from its recent nightmare of carnage, was secretly approached by Maxtla's emissaries and offered inducements if it would rebel against its new masters; but so thoroughly had this cowed city learned its lesson that the offer was rejected out of hand.[33] Maxtla's plans for Chalco also collapsed, mostly because of the traditional ambivalence of the Chalca leaders.[34] Appeals to other cities for supplies and weapons of war also failed. There was left to Maxtla now only the hope that the Chinampaneca cities would hold for him in the conflict that was surely coming.

By now the Mexica had regrouped their forces and repaired their own war damage. Nezahualcoyotl, with his immense prestige and armed aid, was alerted, and the two allies—no doubt accompanied by Tlacopan—moved into this phase of the Tepaneca War.[35] The fortress city of Atlacuihuayan had first of all to be erased, for it was a strong shield held out in front of Coyouacan. This city and its supporting sites were together crushed. The Chinampaneca cities—Cuitlahuac, Xochimilco, Mizquic, Ixtapalapa, Huitzilopochco, and Culhuacan—represented a different problem: communications between them were easy, they completely controlled the waters of Lake Xochimilco, and all stood historically in basic opposition to Mexico, though not at the moment united against her. Potentially, it was a formidable opposition, and the Acolhua and Mexican armies advanced into the area with caution. In 1430, after three inconclusive engagements, Xochimilco, which had cast its lot against Mexico, had been temporarily countered, and the following year the allies stood before Coyouacan with the end of the war in sight. The struggle was correspondingly fierce.

Heroics on both sides were the order of the day as Coyouacan made its last stand. A celebrated Tepaneca knight named Cuecuex sallied alone from the beleaguered city leaping, ululating, brandishing his darts, and shouting his defiance at the entire host deployed in front of him. On the Mexican side Tlacaelel and three knights from Culhuacan attacked the rear of an enemy contingent and alone cast it into confusion. Such actions by themselves were of little account, but without aid from the outside Coyouacan's lot was known to be hopeless. There came the day when the allied armies burst in, wielding their obsidian-bladed clubs and casting torches into the temples. Large numbers of the enemy moved back up the great mountain of Axochco under Maxtla's command and, fighting a desperate and skillful running battle in the great pine savannas and glades of the pass country, successfully made their way south to Cuauhnahuac.

Coyouacan capitulated and agreed to accept the obligation of an excessively harsh tribute in labor, specifically, heavy construction work connected with the building of a causeway and water channels leading out to Mexico; in addition they had to agree to porter service for the allied armies in the future. As for the defeated Maxtla, he led his remaining loyal contingents south into the Tlahuica country in 1431, harassed by his pursuers. His presence in Cuauhnahuac was apparently thought by that city to be undesirable, and he was forced to move on. His flight took him past the ghostly ruins of Xochicalco and into the hills of Tlachco, where he and the retainers left to him pass forever out of our view into obscurity.[36] Tlachco, "the ball court," was an augurial site. In this sacred community there was played in solemn splendor and with incredible skill the ball game called *tlachtli*, often used in forecasting the future. A tale has it that Maxtla played a game here in the nighttime and lost, this presaging what his fate would be were he to continue the contest with Mexico and Tezcoco. After this he was no longer heard of.

Nezahualcoyotl and the End of the War

Officially the Tepaneca war was not wound up until 1433. The extension of hostilities up to this date was due to a number of causes, prominent among which was the ill-concealed enmity that had long been shown by the Chinampaneca cities toward Mexico and their flirtation with Maxtla. But two other factors weighed at least as heavily. First, the Chinampaneca cities were sweet-water settlements and produced a great abundance of food. Second, they lay athwart the road to the Hot Land, that region just south of the mountains that was dominated by the city of Cuauhnahuac. From this area came cotton garments and other furnishings that Mexico's new nobility greatly coveted. Thus the partial involvement of the Chinampaneca cities in the Tepaneca War made it seem that an attack upon them was not only justified but necessary, a final clearing away, as it were, of the peripheral opposition that had been created by the war. This was to be the closing campaign of that war.

It is equally valid to consider this drive as a new war, connected with the Tepaneca War no doubt, but no longer part of Mexico's great struggle for survival. The volcanic energies of the Mexica, up to now absorbed in the conflict with Maxtla, demanded opportunities for their further exercise. It was natural that, already oriented to the south by the Coyouacan venture, they should continue this directional thrust in terms of pure conquest.

In any case, it was not Mexico alone that moved but the alliance of three that had been forming in the latter years of the war: Mexico, Nezahualcoyotl's forces, and the rump Tepaneca under the lead of the city of Tlacopan. The object of conquest in this instance was to be the strong city of Xochimilco. Because the handwriting on the wall was easy to read, namely the loss of her maize lands as had happened first to Azcapotzalco and then to Coyouacan, Xochimilco saw nothing else possible but resistance to the limit of her resources.

To precipitate hostilities, Mexico had sent an embassy to Xochimilco demanding freedom of access to the pine lands and quarries controlled by that city. This carried the implication of freedom of transit to Cuauhnahuac and the exotic world to the south. The insulting demand was rejected, for to have accepted would have been tantamount to acceptance of an inferior status. However heroic Xochimilco's defiance was it was still unwise, because the new league of three already possessed the machinery for swift action. Xochimilco, the city on the lake's edge, older than Mexico by far and equally proud, fought resolutely for eleven days and then succumbed.[37] As with the other cities overrun by the allies, it too was stripped of its best fields and *chinampas* to satisfy the greater vanity and affluence of the conquering nobles of the league.

Xochimilco was now harnessed to one of the remarkable engineering feats of the day, the building of the Acachinanco causeway. The idea for this seems to have been conceived in the fertile brain of Tlacaelel, projected however as a military desideratum rather than growing

out of the economic necessities of Mexico, which was already linked to
the mainland by two causeways, one to the west and one to the north. It
was without any doubt part of an imperial vision that was now beginning to affect the thinking of the Mexica. Aided by slave labor from
Azcapotzalco and Coyouacan, the hungering hordes of the once pleasant city of Xochimilco now moved out into the waters of Lake Tezcoco, sinking heavy rocks and logs into the black bottom mud to form the
foundations of a road leading straight over the waters and into the
heart of Mexico.

The conquest of the famous city of Xochimilco by the allies sent
shock waves throughout the still unconquered parts of the southern
Basin. The last remaining important lake power there was Cuitlahuac,
a city built like Mexico in the middle of the waters, along with its de-
pendency Mizquic. It was not until 1433 that Mexico and her allies
were to mount a full-scale attack against the City of Sorcerers, as Cuitlahuac was called.[38] Mizquic on the shore had to be reduced first, then
allied forces, with Tlacaelel leading the Mexica fleet of one thousand canoes, moved to the attack. The appalling and magnificent sight
as the armada glided toward the island city under a bright sun, the warriors paddling furiously, shrieking with fierce laughter, and shaking
their feathered shields, was sufficient to unman the defenders. One report has it that Cuitlahuac surrendered bloodlessly and without a fight.

The Tepaneca War ended in 1433 with the defeat of Cuitlahuac, for
the whole lake had now been immunized. But an event had occurred
earlier, in 1431, that was of equal or greater moment—the coronation
of Nezahualcoyotl and the actualization of the Three City League. The
allies had first come together to achieve two things, to free Mexico
from Azcapotzalco and to regain for Nezahualcoyotl his Acolhua kingdom. The first had been achieved early in the war, and by 1431 all the
Tepaneca despots had been driven from the Acolhua cities, although,
because of the chaos on the eastern shore and the beginnings of an ambitious rebuilding program there, Nezahualcoyotl still operated from
Mexico as his base.

Nezahualcoyotl was then about thirty years old, a grandson of the Tenochca leader Huitzilihuitl and by far the greatest man in all Anahuac.

Because of his incredible deeds he was already styled Acolmiztli, "Stalwart Lion." He had been closely associated with all of the major campaigns of the Tepaneca War and had attracted to his banners more and more of the Acolhua nobility that had been scattered to the far corners of Anahuac by the proscriptions of Tezozomoc and his son Maxtla. Now, with their aid and that of the Mexica, Nezahualcoyotl had won back the Acolhua cities on the eastern shore and had even staged a memorable triumph in Mexico to celebrate these deeds, for his cities were as yet too ravaged by war to be of much account. It is true that at one time he and all his house had feared and hated the Mexica. But since the dazzling diplomatic stroke that had created the alliance between them, their joint plans had gone well and mutual trust had increased. The Mexica rulers and barons in their soaring arrogance bowed only to Nezahualcoyotl in matters of prestige. In him they recognized not only their own blood but an incontestable right to rule.

Thus, in 1431, Nezahualcoyotl, already the crowned *tlatoani* of Tezcoco, assumed in Mexico the imperial title of his fathers. The rulers of both Tenochtitlan and Tlatilulco in person invested him with this office. As *chichimeca teuctli* he now wore the highest honor in Anahuac, recreating in his person the sublimity of ancient days. At the same time Totoquihuaztli, the grandson of Tezozomoc who had earlier brought the Tepaneca of Tlacopan into the allied camp, was rewarded by being crowned *tlatoani* of that city and overlord of all the Tepaneca. This double coronation[39] formalized the new principle of political order in Anahuac, the League of the Three Cities, which had already been functioning for some time but which was now officially unveiled to the world.

Nezahualcoyotl remained in Mexico for two more years, taking part in the assaults on Xochimilco and Cuitlahuac and in the extensive building then going on in Mexico. By 1433 his scattered people had been with effort relocated back in their old Acolhua homes, and he returned in warlike array across the lake to resume rule in his ancestral city of Tezcoco. The most distinguished part of his long career was about to begin. The twin cities of Mexico were now left alone and secure in the midst of their waters to contemplate the new day that was dawning.

The Aftermath for Tlatilulco

But Tlatilulco continued to be a prisoner of its history. Cuauhtlatoa, the ruler of Tlatilulco who had come on the scene in the year of the outbreak of the war, was a full blooded Tlatilulca. His father, the prince Acolmiztli, briefly succeeded to the leadership in Tlatilulco on the murder of Tlacateotzin but is said also to have been assassinated. One of our sources states that Cuauhtlatoa himself was the murderer, but this is very uncertain. What is certain is that Tlatilulco was undergoing at the time extreme agonies in an attempt to define its basic loyalty, which, until the very end under Tlacateotzin, had always been Tepaneca.[40] Whoever was to be elected to the position of *tlatoani* would quite obviously in his own professed allegiance show forth the allegiance of the state. The fact that Acolmiztli was not allowed to permanently occupy the *icpalli*, the royal cushion, but had to cede it to his son is a sign that these two stood for opposite policies. Cuauhtlatoa seemingly backed the party that was willing to fight by the side of Tenochtitlan against Azcapotzalco—that at any rate is his record, for, from the end of 1427 through the coronation of Nezahualcoyotl in 1431, the Tlatilulca fought shoulder to shoulder with the Tenochca through the most dangerous years of the war.[41]

But something happened at the end of 1431, following the fall of Coyouacan, that suddenly and awfully revived the hostility between the two cities. We are not told the reason for this, but we would expect to find it in some maldivision of the spoils or a slighting of the prowess of the Tlatilulca knights by their Tenochca peers. In that year, with the Acolhua allies no longer among them, the old magmas of hatred burst up out of the Mexican earth; Cuauhtlatoa led a foolish cabal against Tenochtitlan but was forced to back down.[42] Whether fighting erupted in this confrontation is uncertain, but it probably did.

However unclearly this event is delineated to us—for it was later a source of historical embarrassment to all the Mexica—what eventuated was the retention by Cuauhtlatoa of his seat but now in a tributary role.[43] Commerce between the two cities continued, but a frontier of sorts, perhaps a barricade, was erected between them. Finally, in 1435 a stable settlement was arranged. A new temple to the national god was jointly dedicated in Tizaapan, the historic site of Mexica tribulation when they were under the heel of the Culua.[44] Here a newly founded *calpulli*, its members drawn from both Tenochtitlan and Tlatilulco, was provided with a place in the sun.[45] In addition, a pact affirmed the division of the *mexicatlalli* between the two cities in the area just seized from their former ally Cuauhtitlan;[46] it also specified fishing rights in the waters of the lake.

Henceforth for a period of thirty-eight years, Tlatilulco was to be tied to the support of the Tenochca war machine, at first straitly but later with increasing independence. The state can now fairly be called Mexico Tenochtitlan, with Tlatilulco classed as a superior *calpulli*.

The Source of Dynastic Greatness

When Cortez first came to Mexico in 1519, Moteuczoma II proudly mentioned the great dynasty of which he was a member and noted that it began not with Acamapichtli but with Itzcoatl. This is impressive evidence of the importance of the Tepaneca War in the history of the Mexica. Itzcoatl, along with his brother ruler in Tlatilulco, stood as it were in the foaming headwaters of Mexican independence. Theirs had been the enormous decisions that were to make Mexico preeminent in such a short period of time. And if any outside attestation to this fact is needed, we can refer to the Chalca statement that Mexican greatness was the product of the military genius and acumen of Itzcoatl and of Tlacaelel.

5. The Composition of Heaven and Earth

Huitzilopochtli, The Tribal God

After the superlative victories of the Tepaneca War, some five or six years elapsed during which Mexico devoted herself to large building and engineering works as well as to the reorganization of her society. Both Itzcoatl and Cuauhtlatoa engaged the unprecedented tribute labor now available to them to erect palaces worthy of their new fortunes, while the Mexican nobles built brightly painted, two-story town houses on terraces raised well above the commoners' huts. The rock of Chapultepec, ringed about with its wonderful old cypress trees, was, under Nezahualcoyotl's direction, walled in at the base as a pleasure park, and the unfailing spring at the foot was led out through the reeds to both Tenochtitlan and Tlatilulco in an aqueduct of well-dressed stone. Mud shoals and *chinampas* out near the two cities were increasingly joined to the nuclear islands to provide more living space, while the arterial canals leading inward were broadened and deepened to take care of the daily traffic in dugout canoes. Most importantly, the gods, to whose benefactions all this was due, were honored by the erection of shrines proportionate to their greatness.

Huitzilopochtli was not the greatest of the gods, but he was the genius of the Mexican people and their mentor in war. It had been his warnings and his oracles that had given them the tactics of victory, and now he was to be recompensed. We know that an imposing new shrine to him called Tlacatecco was erected in the section of Tenochtitlan that had become the acknowledged center of that island city, the point where the four quarters met.[1] We may presume that there was also erected a new temple to Huitzilopochtli's avatar Tlacauepan in Tlatilulco, equally great and following more or less the same plan. Like the central temples in other Aztec cities, these two were undoubtedly double; each of the truncate pyramids carried two shrines on the leveled top, that of Huitzilopochtli (or Tlacauepan) on the left and that of Tlaloc on the right. Separate stairways emphasized this duality.

It is necessary to understand this duplex building style if we are to grasp how Mexico positioned itself in the world. Huitzilopochtli was the trail god of a people who had recently invaded the land, a being from the untamed world of the hunter, the warrior, and the raider. Tlaloc was the mighty one of storms and fertilizing waters, as ancient as agricultural man in Mesoamerica. Tlaloc was a priestly god and looked far back into a pre-Aztec past rich with cultivated fields and long-lived cities. Huitzilopochtli, on the contrary, was a sorcerer and a tribal god. The juxtaposition of their two shrines symbolized the equilibrium of two traditions that made up Aztec culture.[2]

But whereas Tlaloc was majestically single, Huitzilopochtli was a shape shifter; he was kinetic and indiscriminately stood for many things. Sometimes he was identified with the sky, poetically likened to a blue heron spreading his wings out over the city of Mexico. Sometimes he was Tonatiuh, the sun. He was an omen-giving skull, a magician, or the berserker patron of war—a blood-luster. He could even be identified with the creator and sustainer of all life, a high god, though this was probably unusual.

No one could question the antecedents of Tlaloc, of his right to represent the civilized ages of the Mesoamerican past going back into early Teotihuacan times at least, but there is a certain amount of suspicion

attached to Huitzilopochtli. One questions whether in fact the Mexica
did not steal or invent this god during some stage in their wandering,
and their stay in Coatepec can easily be so interpreted. The historian
can indeed make a plausible theory based on the sources that the original fetish of the Mexica who left Aztlan was referred to as Tetzauhteotl, who, himself an omen of horror and disaster, chilled one with
overpowering fear.[3] The name means "omen god."

Near Culhuacan there were two smaller communities, Mexicaltzinco, "the holy temple of Mexitli" and Huitzilopochco, "the place of
Huitzilopochtli." The importance of this area to the Mexican theogony
is more than attested by the fact that here also, on the hill of Huixachtlan (today the Hill of the Star), was performed the ceremony that
every fifty-two years brought renewed life to the world and to Mexico.
Whatever the truth may be, we can see that this southern shore of the
lake was the scene of early Mexican temple building and possibly the
addition of new deities to the Mexican cult. The worship of the goddess Mexitli lasted at least down to this time, while our suspicion that
Huitzilopochtli, the god of the Mexica, is connected with the Mexica's
sojourn among the Culua remains a legitimate if unproved assumption.
We know that for a part of the Mexican residence in the territory of
Culhuacan, Huitzilopochtli was actually in the possession of their masters—the Culua having demanded him as a hostage at one point.

But this has a curious corollary. If true, it would mean that the final
shaping of the tribal god of the Mexica was a late affair, and therefore
one that could have been easily remembered. And there could have
been little prestige in this. The consequence was a god who, while he
clearly symbolized the destiny of this remarkable people, was nevertheless embarrassed by his lack of legitimacy and great age. Thus he had
to share his seat on the pyramid top with the more ancient god Tlaloc,
the fructifier of the land. The Mexica, in this dual religious structure,
achieved more a polarity between old and new than a conflation of the
two—and this marked it as Aztec.

Cihuacoatl, the Goddess

A most notable religious building from the reign of
Itzcoatl was the temple of Cihuacoatl, "Snake Woman," which had

been started some time after the reduction of Cuitlahuac.[4] Cihuacoatl was a form of Tonantzin, the Sacred Mother, but in this case specifically related to death and evil omens. She had been a goddess greatly venerated in Xochimilco,[5] and her cult may have been introduced into Mexico as a result of the defeat of that city. In the pantheon she shared honors equally with Huitzilopochtli and demanded as many or more sacrificial victims as he did.[6] Her temple did not have a full pyramid base but was a single extended building called Tlillan, "the place of darkness," with only one small hole—symbolizing the entrance to a mountain cave—leading into its fetid interior.[7] Here in this simulacrum of the black interior of the earth was placed her statue, gapemouthed, horrid and invisible to the outside world, so holy in fact that even her own priests crawling on hands and knees into her presence were not allowed to thoughtlessly touch it. Around her in the semidarkness were grouped the crude stone images of the various mountains of Anahuac, for as these mountains rested on the mother's capacious breast, so were they conceived to pay their court to her here. Also, the gods of captured peoples were incarcerated here. Cihuacoatl was the land itself, cavernous and hungry for hearts and blood.[8]

The Mexica were wise to propitiate and worship Cihuacoatl in this careful manner. If one stood on any of the pyramid terraces in the city to gaze across the open waters and reed beds of the vast lake to the encircling mountains, one had to believe in the umbilical centrality of Mexico in the land, and then, by extension, one had to revere the environing power of Anahuac explicit in its mountains.

To the south was Mount Xictli and the higher rolling lands behind. Westward was Mount Zacatepec, a piny and broken rim of mountains referred to by the Mexica as their mother, the scene of sacred hunts. North of the city and closer by were the rocky hills of Tepeyacac that most particularly stood for the Earth Mother. To the east and reflected in the lake was Mount Tlaloc, bringing up the rear of an even greater southern range of mountains. Ahead of Tlaloc came Iztaccihuatl, "white woman," jagged and capped with snows, and then the great volcanic southerner, Popocatepetl, first and tallest of them all leading the way. This was a world without parallel in its array of mountains of all varieties, of all colors, and of all verdancies, some of them arising as islands out of the sheeted surface of the lake, some white with snows, some barren and mouse-colored, many green and inviting—and all of them sacred.

Unlike Tlaloc, who was a god greatly to be petitioned for his heavenly waters that alone supported life, unlike Huitzilopochtli, whose admonition to war provided the Mexica with the pattern of their corporate life, Cihuacoatl the earth was pitiless and inhuman; she stood in a sense beyond effective petition. Her will was to bring men, beasts, and all growing things out of her womb, to make them feel her hollow and echoing power and her otherness, to feed them, to frighten them, and then to call them, lurching and falling, back into the heart of her darkness. Mexitli may have been, indeed probably was, an early form of Cihuacoatl.

In Aztec theory both earth and sky—sky conceived of either as the vault of heaven or as the sun—most particularly drank the blood of humans. Yet the other gods did likewise. It was indisputably their proper nourishment. This Aztec opinion explaining the necessity of sacrifice was interwoven with and complimentary to another theory, that of the divine origin of war. The Mexica were already in the days of Itzcoatl well along in the process of expanding and elaborating upon this theory as a central fact in their lives. The erection of new temples to Huitzilopochtli and Cihuacoatl bear witness to this. Thus a digression on warfare and its sacrificial objectives in the life of Mexico is necessary if we are to further understand the history of the city.

The Meaning of War

That war among the Aztecs—and therefore among the Mexica—had a very immediate side, that it was fought for survival, for loot, for women, for personal glory and adventure, is unquestionable. These were certainly among the dominant motives that drove the Mexica, even from their early residence in distant Aztlan, to make war on others. Their tribal god Tetzauhteotl sanctioned these common uses of conflict. The Nahuatl word for war, *yaoyotl*, is derived from the root *yaotl* meaning "enemy." War is thus "that for which the enemy stands, his business."

But beyond this description of war as a mere confrontation for purposes of gain or prestige, the Mexica were leading the way to an even more distinctive understanding of its nature. The phrase that indicates this distinction was *teoatl tlachinolli*, commonly (and badly) translated as "war."[9] A wealth of meanings, however, lies hidden in this phrase. It literally means "divine liquid and ashes." The first element signifies "blood," and the second is a shorthand statement for the practice of cremating dead warriors on the battlefield, a Toltec custom that released the fortunate soul like a sunburst to ascend into the heavens. War meant the spilling of human blood, which was by definition a liquor destined for the support of the gods; war, in other words, was an act of sacrifice carried out voluntarily by those who killed as well as by those who were killed. In this sense it had a cultic meaning. The element of the ascent of the warrior's soul to achieve nobility in the entourage of the sun god was an added eschatology and described the recompense to the warrior for his sublime action in venturing his life in war. In the well-known emblem of the city of Mexico, the eagle seated on the cactus represented the sun god, here identified with Huitzilopochtli, while the curious device issuing from his beak was the hieroglyphic sign to be read *teoatl tlachinolli*. The whole device thus depicted the god of Mexico commanding the people to instigate wars as a sacred duty.

That the shedding of one's own blood on the battlefield followed by the shedding of the blood of one's captive on the stone of sacrifice was of divine origin is attested in numerous myths of which perhaps the most suggestive is found in the myth of creation. Here the Great Mother, in her person as the night sky, bore from her womb the first recorded thing, *tecpatl*, the stone knife of sacrifice that fell down upon the earth and there initiated the race of gods who, in turn, produced men;[10] men were created to support the gods by the sacrifice of themselves as symbolized in the *tecpatl*. Another tale tied the origin of war to Tula, even giving the year for this occurrence as 13-Reed. In this year Yaoyotl, god of carnage, decreed that war exist.[11] Tula thereupon assaulted Nextlalpan and for the first time took captives for sacrifice. Another myth told how the four creator gods had first to create war before they could create the sun, for his meat and drink had to be at hand as he came into existence.[12] It took the gods two years to create war—so com-

plex and rich a thing it was. Quecholli, the thirteenth month of the Aztec calendar, was especially devoted to its practice.[13]

Other myths put it differently, but the purport is always the same—
the gods are nourished on the hearts of men and drink their blood.
These are their ambrosia and nectar, without which they would weaken
and die. War is created therefore to provide an adequate supply of this
nourishment.

By understanding its divine origin, one can grasp clearly the real nature of Aztec war. It was first and foremost a religious act, part of a
cosmic cult where the warrior was both the officiating priest and the victim for sacrifice. The highest attainable virtue known to the Aztec was
to offer himself courageously on the field of battle, for the food of the
gods was more nourishing when the blood effused came from a heroic
heart.[14] He who so died, whether of wounds received on the field, or
later on the *techcatl*, the sacrificial stone, received the reward of virtue
and lived thereafter in a warrior's paradise.

The implications of this religious act for the state were astounding.
Mexico, even more than most of the other Aztec states, considered that
its main duty was to survive in order to provide a continuing opportunity for war; to this end it proclaimed with all due pomp those wars
it had decided on for the year, choosing the festival day of Xiuhteuctli,
"the lord of the year," for this auspicious action.[15] The paramount edu-
cational aim of the state was therefore to train as the superior product
of its society the warrior-priest. The wealth of the state consequently
had to be devoted to the display of this person and to the iteration of
his worth. Indeed, the faithfulness of the state was evident only when
it nurtured such men, and the pride of these men lay in the fact that the
extreme act of their own faithfulness entailed their death.

This curiously cyclical thinking was never clearly formulated by the
Mexica; it is simply evident in their way of life. It had the virtue of
providing a fully developed rationale for the existence of the class of
warrior-priests, but, by failing to tie the commoners into this overarching concept, it failed to integrate the state. By conscious exclusion from
the concept of the higher sacrifice, the *macehualtin* became nothings,
negatives, a class with no explanation and living only a pale slave-like
existence. In times of stress the commoners, men and women alike,

fought for the survival of the state but without even the dignity that is generally attached to a citizen militia.

In their poetic allusions the Aztecs made especially clear the perfection of their martial virtue. Yaoyotl, the god who personified war, was said to adorn himself with flowers made as offerings to him; these were the lives of fallen warriors who were said to resemble "red roses." Death on the battlefield or on the *techcatl* was a "flower-death" and had been invented by semidivine beings in a never-never land called Tlapallan. Battle itself was exotically compared to a "rain of flowers," referring to the swift dropping of dead warriors to the ground like blossoms in all their evanescence and in the beauty of their sacrifice.[16] The true warrior was said to be always restless and unhappy because of his intense longing for death in battle.[17]

If war was indeed a cultic banquet for the gods, then its proper observance had to be considered an activity of grace and beauty.[18] The most telling instance of this perverse understanding is to be seen in the institution known as the *xochiyaoyotl,* or "flower war."

The Flower War

The Great Mother, Cihuacoatl, who bore as her first child the sacrificial stone knife,[19] was popularly thought of as a woman clad in chalky white and wandering luminously about in the night, carrying on her back—in true Indian style—a bundle within which the grisly blade was swaddled like a child. This object's cult name was "the son of Cihuacoatl" and symbolized her persistent hunger for hearts and blood.

At certain times when her priesthood judged that a reduction in human sacrifice or fatalities in war had left the gods hungry, the sacrificial blade, caked with its accumulation of dried blood, would be reverently bundled up to imitate an infant and carried by an ordinary woman to the marketplace. Here the object would be surreptitiously left with someone among the market women who had come there at dawn to barter. At the end of the day the maternal feelings of the women would be aroused by the presence of a seemingly abandoned child among them, whereupon, opening the papoose, they would discover the repulsive *tecpatl* left there by the goddess as an earnest of her cruel hunger. The news would spread like wildfire throughout the city and rapidly reach the lords in their palaces who, thus admonished, moved instantly to appease the gods. With wailing and deep piety the priests would then reclaim the son of Cihuacoatl and escort him back to his proper habitation. If at that moment the lords did not have sufficient prisoners or purchased slaves to offer in sacrifice, they would thereupon hastily arrange a flower war.

The *xochiyaoyotl* can be glossed as a "war for sacrificial victims." It had some of the characteristics of a tournament, for it was essentially a chivalric enterprise; in legend it went back to the Toltecs. An Aztec city would enter upon a flower war for two reasons. One was practical and had to do with the exercise and perfecting of their men in actual combat whenever wars for empire were lacking. The other reason was religious and has already been explained in the passages on the hunger of the gods. The Aztec cities that took part in these tournaments had designated special fields on their frontiers where such encounters could take place. These were the *teoatempan*, literally "on the shores of sacrificial blood." These fields were sacred, for they were the meadows of Earth Lady (Tlalteuctli) on which the offered blood first fell.[20]

Once agreement on the time and place of combat had been reached between two cities—a preferred time was on the opening day of the Aztec month—the chosen groups assembled and faced each other. Courtesies were exchanged and the images of the appropriate gods were set up nearby by their *teomamas*, who acted in a sense as umpires.[21] The affair opened when a certain number of knights advanced, perhaps two hundred, to be met by an opposing contingent. Additional companies were fed in as the fury of the contest increased or as replacements were needed. The object was to capture an enemy rather than to kill him, but when hopelessly surrounded the truly intrepid warrior often chose to be hacked to death on the battlefield, thus dying a "rosy death" and earning additional laurels and fame.[22] A specially selected panel of higher officers roved through the press of battle, not attempting to take captives, but redressing the battle whenever it threatened in some part of the field to go against them. When exhaustion or an incapacitating loss of men radically weakened one side, the battle would be broken off by mutual consent. Victory was accredited to the side that had taken appreciably more of the enemy captive than they themselves had lost. A flower war could be an isolated engagement or it could be a long series of contests extending over many years and hardly distinguished from a sustained campaign of conquest or attrition. There are recorded instances where the hatred and ferocity engendered succeeded in eventually drowning the chivalric element entirely.

When the Tepaneca in the days of Tezozomoc were fighting flower wars with Chalco, the Mexica took part in them. Nezahualcoyotl organized a series of flower wars with the Tlateputzca cities once he had re-established himself in Tezcoco.[23] In fact, agreement on the desirability of flower wars seems to have been an integral part of the whole settlement between the allies on the conclusion of the Tepaneca War. Tlacaelel, under Izcoatl's successor in Tenochtitlan, appears to have had a great deal to do with expanding the flower wars fought by Mexico, using them as a means of testing and steeling the younger knights, as a source of additional honors for the more experienced ones, and as a pious duty as well. The prisoners taken on both sides were often kept for sacrifice at special festivals. It was as heroic to die under the sacrificial knife as in the press of battle, for in either case the gods dined fatly.

Human Sacrifice among the Mexica

Human sacrifice dedicated to cosmic purposes was a state activity and could not be carried out by individuals alone. Thus the state was a functioning part of the cosmos. The patron god of an Aztec city, whether it was Quetzalcoatl of the city of Cholula, Mixcoatl of Cuauhtitlan, or Huitzilopochtli of Mexico, was the divine personage who stood for the uniqueness of that nation and for its special responsibilities. To that deity great numbers of victims were necessarily sacrificed; the other gods were never forgotten, however, for every city-state had a most vivid perception of its duties and its role in maintaining the functioning of all parts of the universe. Mexico was the most toiling, obedient, and devout of them all.

Our sources state that human sacrifice as practiced by Mexico was not derived from Chichimec custom but had rather been taken from the Toltecs, who were a state-oriented people.[24] The sources also agree that the Mexica carried the morbid tradition to a point far surpassing anything that Tula may have achieved. It is possible that the Mexica began this trend toward excess at the instigation of Culhuacan, the neo-Toltec city under whose tutelage they had lived for a number of years. We do know that religious questions and cult differences were significant in that city and had in fact led to the dispersion of its peoples and to its subsequent destruction.

Our first believable references to human sacrifice among the Mexica correspondingly come from the time of their subordination to Culhuacan. Indeed, the Mexican fervor in this area of cult was what finally excited their masters to expel them from the vicinity. A tale about this particular affair, which may have a grain of truth in it, tells us of the Mexican request for a virgin of royal blood from the Culua.[25] The *tlatoani* of Culhuacan granted this request with the understanding that she would become a person of consequence among his Mexican subjects. This the Mexica intended also, for they cast her in the role of the representative of the Great Mother, sacrificed and skinned her, and then ingenuously invited her royal father to attend the solemn ceremony where a priest danced about wearing her skin. The result was the violent expulsion of the Mexica from Culua territory.

But one can see things in this other than the shock to the victim's father and the insult to the Culua. The avatar of the Great Mother worshipped by the Mexica was Yaocihuatl, "Warrior Woman," the goddess or patron of discord and hostility. She was said to be the grandmother of Huitzilopochtli, and we have already met her as Cihuacoatl. The terrible intensity of the Mexica in their religious observances, most luridly set forth in this incident, could only be understood as aberrant. The Culua were very properly frightened.

The Act of Sacrifice

The style of human sacrifice finally evolved by the Mexica was significant in its variety and its omnipresence. As Mexico conquered one people after another, foreign gods were brought back captive and their cults established in the city on a permanent and servile footing. The gods of allies or otherwise friendly nations were also domiciled in Mexico, though in a more honorable guise. But in any case the manner of sacrifice appropriate to that particular cult—no matter how exotic—was carefully maintained. The style followed in the cult of Huitzilopochtli, however, was standard, and in the vast civil festivals that were occasionally celebrated this method of sacrifice could be used to nourish all the gods.

The captive taken in war and sacrificed was called *xochimicqui*, "who died beautifully," or *teomicqui*, "who died as a god."[26] An intimate and loving relationship was believed to exist between this captive and the warrior who had taken him, the former becoming the latter's "son."[27] Indeed, in the event that it was the ruler who took a prisoner in battle, this captive was treated with the greatest reverence and affection and brought back to Mexico in the royal litter. On arrival he was tumultuously greeted by the populace even before they paid their respects to the ruler, his captor. He was the "son" of the *tlatoani* and was kept in the palace, "his own house," until his death on the *techcatl*. The ruler, like all captors of victims about to be sacrificed, had to fast the night previous to the sacrifice, for here he would be sending his own "son" to become one of the sun god's retinue.

After the sacrifice had taken place, the captor treated a select body of his friends to a commemorative meal where all but the host himself partook of a dish of cooked portions of the victim mixed with squash flowers.[28] By the splendor of his ascension into the heavens, the captive had become a godlike being, a demigod in fact, and this cannibal meal had been designed to establish the identity between him and the select body of knights, all of whom were involved in the same cult of shedding blood in the service of the gods.

Among the many forms of sacrifice in Mexico, two were reserved for those taken prisoner in war, death on the *techcatl* at the top of the temple steps, and death in the Cuauhxicalco. The first was more common and took place at all times of the year. For the *techcatl* sacrifice the prisoners were painted a chalky white—the color symbolizing death —and in guarded queues led up to the foot of the great temple. The steep pitch of the stone stairway leading to the pyramid's summit was intentional, for it symbolized ascent into the heavens. A person placed here at the lowest step could then look upward and see silhouetted against the sky the figures of six awaiting priests and the top of the conical stone of sacrifice, which was placed very close to the near edge of the temple terrace. The victim, whether reluctantly or proudly, was led slowly up the appropriate staircase. This symbolized the sun rising from the earth up to the zenith. At the summit the victim was handed over to the priests; his legs and arms were seized, and he was thrown backward over the *techcatl*, the priests each bearing powerfully down (including the one assigned to the head) so that the victim's back was bowed backward to near the breaking point. Hereupon the priest holding the flint knife, the son of Cihuacoatl, plunged it into the taut belly of the victim and, reaching into the terrible wound, ripped out the still-beating heart. Turning, the high priest then held the heart heavenward in offering before he threw it into the sacred receptacle with the other hearts that had accumulated. These hearts were now the sweet food of the gods and as such were called "precious eagle-cactus fruit," a reference to the emblem of the city of Mexico.[29] At this point the victim was identified with the sun at midday; he was now an "eagle man." The body, spilling blood, was then flung off the stone and went tumbling and bumping down the steep slope to come to rest on the flat space near the base called *apetlac*, "the blood mat."[30] This symbolized the sun falling from the zenith to his final resting place in the dark earth. The body was quickly dismembered by expert priests and the proper pieces claimed by the one who had captured him. The head, however, had to be turned back to the state, for it was to be threaded onto the poles of the skull rack where already many thousands of skulls, jowl by jowl, attested to the hearty appetites of the Aztec gods.

The second type of sacrifice took place in the Cuauhxicalco, which was a rectangular whitewashed courtyard containing the temple pyramid of the sun. On the apron fronting it stood the *temalacatl*, "the stone spindle whorl," so named because of its resemblance to the round pierced weight attached to the lower part of a spindle.[31] Whereas the great double temple of Huitzilopochtli and Tlaloc nearby was the city's center of worship, this enclosed area was the cult center reserved for the sun-knights, the most elite of all warriors, heroes who undertook the task of carrying on the cult of Tonatiuh, the sun.

The name Tonatiuh can be best translated as "he who goes to cast his rays about," where the concepts of motion and splendor are uppermost.[32] Tonatiuh is unique in Mexican religion because he was hardly thought of in anthropomorphic terms at all. He was, rather, the sun disk itself and had only the most meager mythology.[33] He did not have an idol as did the other gods, though he could be likened to a majestic eagle and could be worshipped as Nauholin, "four movement."[34] At- tached to the wall of his small shrine at the top of his pyramid was simply a wheel emitting rays with the hieroglyphic symbols for his name in the center. Nauholin identified the sun as that one illumining the world in our own particular aeon, four other suns having run their courses ahead of this one and having then perished along with all the gods of those aeons.

It was under the patronage of this present manipulator of time and courser of the heavens that the lodges of warriors and eagle and jaguar knights lived their lives and carried on their activities. Here in the Cuauhxicalco they were at home exactly as were priests in a religious order. Here they sacrificed to the sun those whom they had captured in battle. Here in a cult rich in solar symbolism, which we first hear about in the reign of Chimalpopoca but which goes back to Toltec times, the knights served not the god of the Mexica but their own god. The cult was centered about the two stone wheels, the *temalacatl* and the *cuauh-xicalli*, "the sun vessel."[35]

The *temalacatl* was a heavy stone wheel lying horizontally on a low square platform to which access was gained on each side by a low flight of four steps. The victim to be sacrificed was provided with a wooden sword-club, edged not with sharp obsidian blades as was customary, but with feathers or puffs of cotton. He was tied by a short cord to the center of the stone and forced to defend himself against four knights, two jaguar and two eagle knights, each armed with their usual weap- ons. In the ensuing duel the victim, no matter how well he defended himself, was finally wounded, whereupon he was untied and dragged still living up the temple steps to be thrown onto the *cuauhxicalli*, similar to the stone below but carved on its upper surface with the face of the sun and other calendrical signs. Here he was decapitated, his blood flowing across the surface of the stone in a groove and spilling over the edge. His heart was ripped out and offered to the sun while the trophy head was held aloft in a frenzied dance around the *temala-*

catl. The corpse was then skinned, and a young priest ceremonially wore it for many days until it cracked and otherwise became too offensive.

In this ceremony Mexico had telescoped two sets of meanings, one of which was connected with the god Xipe, "the Flayed One."[36] Xipe was an ancient Mesoamerican deity revered by almost every nation. He was a god of battles with very probably solar connections. His shrine in Mexico is even thought by some to have been within the compound mentioned above, the Cuauhxicalco. Tonatiuh was explicitly the sun, whereas Xipe was an inherited, foreign, and complex god whose solar symbolism fused with the symbolism of battle.

The *temalacatl* stood for the round earth oriented in its four directions as we know from the presence of the four priests called the four "dawns." The captive tethered to the center was the personification of the knight involved in battle, exercising and honoring his brothers (the opposing knights), whose display of energy increased the glory of the battlefield. The wounding of the victim led to his sacrifice on the sun stone. But that stone was the sun itself, and the blood it drank from the headless body restored it to vigor; the wearing of the dead warrior's skin symbolized his resurrection. In short, this sacred drama displayed the role of the true knight.

The eagle symbolism is quite clear. The temple of the sun was called "the house of the eagles" (eagle and jaguar knights together). The warriors were the eagles and their father was the superior eagle, the sun. The eagle was taken to be the favorite masquerade of the sun, and the whole cult performance was spelled out in terms of this high-flying raptor.

Repellent as the rite may be to us, we must not condemn the meaning in it. During his fateful climb and descent of the temple of Huitzilopochtli, as well as in gladiatorial combat at the *temalacatl*, the victim was a surrogate of the shining sun, the *teotl*.[37] This fact of substitution sanctified the blood and heart of the victim, making them worthy food for the gods.

The human side of this terrible rite is evident and it need not be lingered on, for fear of death is a heritage common to us all—even to the heroic. There was a prayer offered to Tezcatlipoca that he, the god, might give courage to the victim as he made his ascent up the fatal steps: "Show him the marvel. May his heart not falter in fear. May he savor the fragrance, the sweetness of death by the obsidian blade."[38]

Mexico Rewrites its History

In the heady days following their victory over the Tepaneca, the Mexica were made into a new people. A revised order of nobility and a new tariff of honors were instituted. Tlacaelel stood at the head of that order and was primarily responsible for its definition. He worked in conjunction with Itzcoatl and the Council of the Four Princes; it was they who created various new titles of nobility, assigned them, and distributed newly captured lands to support them.[39]

This transformation of the society of old Mexico had two aspects. The common people were removed even farther from the seats of power;[40] those who had shown insufficient vigor in the struggle just over were exiled, while such commoners as had shown exceptional hardihood were advanced into the ranks of the *teuctli*, though there could not have been more than a handful of these. A conscious hardening of the antiplebeian tendency is to be seen in the decision of Itzcoatl and the princes in council to burn the folded books in which were painted the history of the race.[41] The reasons for this are obvious. Having been the mainstay of Tepaneca power and having been hated and feared for it throughout Anahuac, the ruling Mexica felt it now advisable to smudge this unpopular record and to present rather the picture of a people oppressed and enslaved against their will. Additionally, the record of Mexican predation at the time when they were resident in Chapultepec had to be suppressed and a statement of origins brought forward that would reveal legitimate descent from the Chicomoztoc peoples as well as from the Culua. Itzcoatl himself composed heroic songs celebrating the new past, and no doubt the Mexica chroniclers were ordered to compose and paint novel versions of the annals.

This could not be a thoroughgoing reworking of the past, but its intent is clear. The part of the Mexican nobility that had made its spectacular leap into history during the Tepaneca War had to be celebrated, and any caveats as to their place in the sun had to be removed. The common people were not allowed to object to the wealth and the tyrannous power of this newly elevated aristocracy, nor could they ever be allowed to think that its claims might be historically unfounded. We can easily understand that the natural insecurity felt by a novice nobility made imperative for the Mexica either a new record of the past or one that had been carefully blurred. Indeed, the most reliable of our chroniclers insists that Itzcoatl took this step out of a fear of the heterogeneous masses of Mexico, and we are forced to believe this. Itzcoatl himself was the first ruler of Mexico to order his likeness carved in stone[42]—no doubt on the rock of Chapultepec—and to order similar representations of those of his ancestors whom he wished to honor and through whom he wished to attest his own legitimacy. This realignment of the Mexican annals is one of the most striking aspects of the elevation to power of the postwar nobility as it now took over all instruments of rule in Mexico.

The names of these new men were once very famous. Moteuczoma and Tlacaelel are already known to us. There was Cahualtzin, a brother of Moteuczoma and a fierce fighter raised to the rank of *acolnahuacatl* by Itzcoatl. Cuatlecoatl, another brother and hero, became one of the inner Council of Princes in reward for his great services in battle. Tlacauepan, Ueuezacan, Aztacoatl, Citlalcoatl, Cuauhtzitzimitl, and others —these were the men given broad acres and new titles in the great celebrations marking the downfall of Coyouacan and the end of Maxtla's power.

The Teuctli

There are two words used for the ruling classes in Nahuatl, *teuctli* and *pilli*.[43] For *teuctli* we have used the medieval "baron" because it expresses a similar quality of valor contained in the Nahuatl word. No etymology has been accepted by all scholars.[44] *Teuctli* is a word basic to any understanding of Aztec history. It serves to designate the quality of a great ruler, as witness the imperial title *chichimeca teuctli*, and in these exalted cases we can translate it as "lord." At a level below this the term groups into a class all those of noble lineage who have proved their manliness in war, and here it is fitting to translate it as "baron" or "knight." To be born into a noble family did not of itself give one the right to assume the title. The title had to be won again in every generation.

The word *pilli* is best translated "noble" or "nobleman," for it describes the members of a class who inherit the designation by right of blood.[45] A noblewoman is a *cihuapilli*;[46] the word *cihuateuctli* does not give exactly this sense. *Pilli* has as its primary meaning "son" or "boy." This follows a universal pattern in early societies where the term "the boys" is commonly used for a band or gang. *Pilli* is a familial term and any son of a baron was automatically put in this class, but he did not automatically inherit his father's *teucyotl* or knightliness. *Pilli*, in fact, is almost the equivalent of *tecpantlacatl*, "courtier"—literally "personage of the palace."

The Mexican baronage was a part of a larger aristocracy of warriors common to the whole Aztec world—an international order in fact. Admiration for outstanding warriors of other cities and knowledge that the marks distinguishing a *teuctli* from a commoner were the same in one city as another bound the members of the class together internationally. So also did the custom of marriage between members of noble families resident in different, sometimes even hostile, cities. There was also a set of fashions in speech, apparel, and style of living consciously followed by members of the class. We know, for instance, that the Mexica *pilli* imitated the Huexotzinca in these respects.

Once a *teuctli* had been created, he passed his potential for aristocratic status down through his sons, thus setting up a *mecayotl* or lineage. But just as the noble house had originated in a warrior's bravery, so one act of cowardice could reduce it overnight to plebeian status. After Teuctlehuacatzin, one of the leading Tenochca nobles, poisoned himself out of fear of Maxtla, his peers gathered to discuss the scandal and, in a consensus, attainted his whole house in perpetuity.[47] All members of the family were cast down into the commons, and, even though the male members fought desperately and valiantly in later wars, the stain was never erased. Cowardice indeed was worse than treason.

The making of a *teuctli* was a grave and ceremonious rite.[48] When a young *pilli* had revealed himself to be either courageous or astute, his father would begin the long process of amassing the necessary wealth for the knighting. The young man fasted rigorously for forty days, piercing himself continuously with maguey thorns and abstaining from all pleasures. His nose and lower lip were drilled with an eagle's talon or a jaguar's claw to ready him to wear in those apertures the distinctive jewels that marked the *teuctli*. All the while he was subjected to blows, continuous insults, and opprobrium to harden him and test his serenity. The climax of his proving came when he was kept awake for four nights preceding the final rites. When this was over, his hair was finally tied up in a topknot and he was formally invested with his weapons and his distinctive armorial bearings by a priest in one of the temples. Here he was harangued on the virtues of his noble estate and enjoined to keep himself distinct from the common people by the observance of these virtues. At this point he could add the title *teuctli* to his name and demand all of its privileges. His father and he now offered a set of banquets and rich gifts to other nobles celebrating the occasion with them.

As a *teuctli* he could wear cotton garments. He could enter the palace with his peers and eat from the royal munificence. Particularly he could now eat human flesh, hitherto forbidden. He could drink chocolate and strong drink. He could possess as many women as he desired and act in public life like one of the elite, smoking cigars in tubes and sniffing bouquets of flowers as he sauntered along. He could now own and inhabit a house of two stories. He could cast a vote and be heard in the war council of the *pilli*.

The Mexican baronage, the *teucyotl,* was divided into lodges; little is known about the numbers, composition, and procedures of these societies. The two top and coequal orders were the sun knights—either eagle knights, *cuauhtin*, or jaguar knights, *ocelotin*.[49] These two orders had added a gloss to the myth of the creation of the present sun to sanction their social primacy; this part of the myth told how the eagle followed by the jaguar had thrown themselves into the sacrificial flames and how out of that immolation had emerged the two great celestial bodies. The eagle, totally consumed, became the sun, and the jaguar, only singed in spots, became the moon.[50] We have already seen that these two orders had their own cult in the Cuauhxicalco. Under them was an order of

puma knights[51] and another called the Otomí knights (possibly limited
to the Tlatilulca).[52] These orders each had their own meeting hall in
the royal palace.[53] Their members additionally could take an oath that
—once committed to a place on the battleground—they would never
give back but would first die; these men, the great veterans with several captures to their credit, formed a separate group called *cuachictin*,
"shaved heads."

Each order was under a commander, but only the two classes of sun
knights were privileged to celebrate a feast of such importance that it
became an integral part of the celebration of the Mexican calendar.[54]
This was the feast of Nauholin wherein the eagles and jaguars dispatched to the sun a special sacrificial messenger who carried their pleas
of intercession and their protestations of gratitude to the sun, their father.

The right of these Mexican barons to rule the lands could not be put
to question, for it had been Huitzilopochtli who had first commanded
them to make war, to capture men in war, to sacrifice them, and to eat
them. They were the *oquichtin*, "the braves," or "the real men." Historically they claimed to be sons and servants of Quetzalcoatl, holding
and aggrandizing the land against his return. They and the related *pi-
piltin* were the real Mexica.[55] Showy and arrogant, they likened themselves to trees whose overarching boughs provided shade and protection for those below. The farmer, the fisherman, the fowler, and the
porter were excluded from their colorful and exacting world, for the
shedding of the blood of the commons would have had little effect on
the cosmic forces. The *teuctli* had won the right to honors and to great
wealth by delivering himself up to the violent and solemn cult of war.

Mexico was a parenthesis between heaven and earth, and the clarification of this concept was powerfully promoted in the reign of Itzcoatl.
The city, obsequious and proud at the same time, slaved for the wel-
fare of the gods. The baseborn commons toiled to maintain the *teucyotl* in all its splendor and tragedy so that these magnates, through their
sacrifice, could maintain the cosmos. This was the way of every Aztec
state, but none surpassed Mexico in the zeal with which it pursued that
way.

6. Moteuczoma I and the State

 By the end of Itzcoatl's reign, Mexico had achieved stability and was ready for further adventures. Cuauhtitlan, the former ally and proven friend of Mexico, was attacked and reduced, presumably because it was becoming dangerously competitive.[1] Along with neighboring Toltitlan, this city to the north thereupon entered the Mexican protectorate. More important for the future of Mexico's empire was to be the subjugation by the Three City League of the lands of the Tlahuica south of the Valley.[2]

The opportunity for this was presented when a disgruntled vassal of the formidable city of Cuauhnahuac invited the Three Cities to come down from their aerie to help him in paying off a grudge. This invitation came at a time when Mexico had just patched up a temporary peace with its archenemy Chalco and was purchasing from it vast quantities of darts, arrows, sword clubs, drums, and other materiel of war. Nezahualcoyotl had been doing the same for his city of Tezcoco, and we may suspect that one of the unspoken arguments used by the Three

Cities in pressing Chalco for this delivery of arms was that, if she complied, any possibility of military action against her would be diverted away to the lands of the Tlahuica farther to the south and west. But if this was a factor in Chalco's compliance, she was indeed ill-advised, as the sequel will show.

Situated among ravines, Cuauhnahuac was a city easy to defend, but alone it could do little with enemies closing in from all four sides. Mexico came in from the west, Tlacopan came down from the high pass country to the north, Tezcoco from the east bore along the base of the mountains, while the Tlahuica city of Xiuhtepec held the south closed against possible escape or the entry of reinforcements. It was a well-conceived plan of strangulation based on overwhelming power. Cuauhnahuac fell in 1439, and the Three Cities could now for the first time claim to be conquerors in lands outside the Valley. In the future, instead of haggling in the marketplaces for cotton cloths and fruits, Mexico could claim them as tribute with no loss to herself. The city of Cuauhnahuac and its attached settlements were adjudged to Nezahualcoyotl, for his had been the superior effort, but Mexico acquired for her empire Tepoztlan and Huaxtepec, and from them she drew booty in exotic gold and jade work, woven goods, and paper. Tlacopan received its share.

Moteuczoma and the Council of Four

At the end of the important year of 1439, after having ruled for the most eventful thirteen years in the history of Mexico, Itzcoatl, the *tlatoani* of Tenochtitlan, died. He was well along in years at the time and held many honors. His obsequies lasted eighty days, or a full four months of the Aztec year, and were made resplendent by the attendance of lords from distant parts of Anahuac. No one could now doubt the greatness of Mexico.

The personage elected to fill his place was his nephew Moteuczoma, a man at the time some forty-three years of age. With him the golden age of the Mexica was to begin, and in him they were to serve their most notable ruler. He was the only Mexican ever said to have had a miraculous birth.[3] The popular tale had it that his father Huitzilihuitl fell in love with Miahuaxihuitl, "Jewelled Maize Flower," the beautiful daughter of the ruler of Cuauhnahuac. But this ruler was also a sorcerer who protected his beloved daughter from all suitors by means of powerful enchantments. But Huitzilihuitl, with the help of the god of night, made a magic dart in which was concealed a talismanic stone. This he shot over the great mountains rimming the Basin so that it fell accurately into the center of the girl's courtyard. Miahuaxihuitl took the stone from the dart, put it in her mouth, and swallowed it. In this way she conceived her famous son Moteuczoma.

The name Moteuczoma called forth old tribal memories, for one of the Mexica rulers back in Aztlan had been so named.[4] It means "he becomes wrathful like a lord," and it refers to that quality of impulsive anger deemed to be characteristic of the truly great ruler. His other name, Ilhuicamina, "he shoots at the heavens," appears to have been given to him later in recognition of his personal valor—the reference is possibly to the demigod Citli, who in myth shot arrows at the sun when it refused to begin its proper course in the dawning east.[5]

Moteuczoma had been connected with all phases of the Tepaneca War and, after a spectacular performance before Coyouacan, had been given the high rank of *tlacateccatl* and a seat on the Council of the Four Princes under Itzcoatl. He had been instrumental in setting up with Nezahualcoyotl the original alliance that had flowered into the Three City League. The fact that his mother was a legitimate princess of Cuauhnahuac while his father had been the ruler of Tenochtitlan gave him a legitimacy Itzcoatl had lacked. With his older half-brother Tlacaelel, he was one of the two most distinguished men of Tenochtitlan.

About his election there was no contest, for there were no more brothers of previous kings alive to whom the office of *tlatoani* would first have been offered; Tlacaelel himself preferred to play the role of kingmaker and thus was not a candidate. The mode of election is worth commenting on, for it was to provide thenceforth for Mexico the central organ in her constitution.

Previously there had been in Mexican history—as in the history of other Aztec cities—certain ranks that conferred high dignity as well as responsibilities. Four of these were now grouped around the *tlatoani* to make up what we have already styled as the Council of the Four Princes.[6] Its members were war chiefs, while the attached fifth, the *ci-*

huacoatl, held a priestly as well as a viceregal office. The *tlacateccatl* appears to have been the highest of the military grades; the word itself is translated "he of the Tlacatecco," where the reference is to the great temple of Huitzilopochtli and underlines the office's duty to defend this crucial seat in the heart of the city. Equal to him in rank was the ruler's administrative assistant called the *tlacochcalcatl*, "he of the armory," with the *ezuauacatl*, "the blood clawer" or constable, next. The fourth member was the *tlillancalqui*, "he of the House of Darkness," where the refernce is to the temple of the goddess Cihuacoatl.

It is probable that this fourfold executive adjunct to the ruler was of venerable age as an institution. We see it constantly in use in other Aztec states, which points to a Toltec background. Here in Mexico, it was further modified to take care of the competing claims of the two ruling classes, the *teuctli* and the *pilli*.[7] Two of the offices were classed as "commanders" (*quauhtlatoque*) and two were classed as "dignitaries" (*teuctlatoque*). In each category one of the incumbents was a baron, the other a noble, thus giving equal representation at both state levels to the *teuctli* and the *pilli*. This suggests a real clash of interests between the two upper classes, the men of the military orders and those of good family, whose talents were generally more magisterial. The "commanders," as the name would indicate, had prime responsibility in advising the *tlatoani* in all matters of war, while the "dignitaries" were supreme in all matters of policy and administration.

This consistory, inclusive of the *tlatoani* and the *cihuacoatl* formed a governing college of six in Mexico. Eminent as the ruler's position was in appearance and in reality, he shared his powers of decision and responsibility with the other four princes and the *cihuacoatl*. They were always close kinsmen, either brothers or cousins, and only from the College of Four would be chosen the succeeding *tlatoani*, either the incumbent *tlacateccatl* or the *tlacochcalcatl*. Moteuczoma had been the *tlacateccatl* under Itzcoatl, and this, plus his undoubted capabilities, had preempted for him the top position.

Looked at in this fashion, the executive of Tenochtitlan was a collegiate body limited to members of the lineage of Acamapichtli, each member of which was charged with great responsibilities. We can speculate that the four princes were each assigned to one of the four quarters into which Mexico was divided, thus symbolizing rule over the whole and its parts.

The corporate quality of Mexican rule is further evidenced by the fact that the election of the *tlatoani* had to be accompanied by the election of a full set of members to a new Council of Four. We have vague hints that Tlatilulco may have produced much the same sort of corporate rule but used a slightly differing set of titles, and we know that among the Matlatzinca, who lived over the mountains to the west, a similar executive body existed.

The person who bore the title of *cihuacoatl* was the high priest of the goddess of the same name and on ceremonial occasions wore her garments. His power was based on this close association with the goddess plus his control of all her oracles. Though the *tlatoani* was the head of state, the *cihuacoatl* was a regent or prime minister and, indeed, in the case of Tlacaelel, a veritable second ruler. Tlacaelel was allowed, like Moteuczoma, to wear the royal regalia including the *copilli* or crown; both of them were equally kings and collaborated so closely on all important affairs of state that some of our sources even ended by believing them to be one person referred to under two different names.

In summary, the executive of the new state that had first arisen under Itzcoatl was a consistory of five fraternal kinsmen all elected at the same time and sitting with the *cihuacoatl*, an office that was to be permanently held in the family of Tlacaelel. The *tlatoani* acted as the powerful president of the body. Beside him stood his potential successor, either the *tlacateccatl* or the *tlacochcalcatl*. Taken all together, the Council of Four Princes acted as a body of advisers to the *tlatoani* while he was alive and as an electoral college at his demise.

One can see that such a system was quite fluid depending on the personality and policies of the *tlatoani* in relation to the prestige of the Council. That Moteuczoma was a great man in his own right meant that the *tlatoani* of the Mexica would be from that time on an officer with very real powers and not simply the creature of the Council.

The electoral process was not complete, however, until the rulers of Tezcoco and Tlacopan had each given their assent. In this particular election, the choice of the Council was enthusiastically endorsed by Nezahualcoyotl and by Totoquihuaztli as well. This interesting procedure, whereby there were seven electors in all necessary for the creation of a Tenochca *tlatoani*, meant that the growth and the political life of Mexico were to be thenceforth mortgaged to the success of that consortium of three city-states of which it was one.

The Three City League Proclaimed

As the de facto *tlatoani*, Moteuczoma did not immediately proceed to his coronation but took the advice of Tlacaelel and postponed it until he could acquire—through war—a number of sacrificial victims for the installation ceremonies sufficient to attest his worthiness and the worthiness of the newly elected Council of Four Princes.[8] A flower war was accordingly arranged with Chalco, and, out of the melee that followed, there were to finally march up to the various Mexican temples several files of captured Chalca knights.

The coronation ceremonies in Tenochtitlan were new and baroque. Tlacaelel had expended his imagination on elaborating and redefining the customary symbols of the ruler's majesty, his high morality, and his responsibility toward the gods. Lords from all over Anahuac, many of them enemies, were invited to the affair and many came. The rulers of Tezcoco and Tlacopan participated prominently, while leaders from all the cities subject to Tenochtitlan came in to perform obeisance and to be reconfirmed in their holdings. The *tlatoani* and the attendant four princes endured the required four-day fast and were then ritually presented to Huitzilopochtli, following which they were installed in their offices.

By his participation in the election and later by explicit pronouncement, Nezahualcoyotl rededicated himself to the friendship that had so far obtained among the Three Cities.[9] Moteuczoma followed this up by formally proclaiming the Three City League to be a permanent feature of Mexican policy. There can be no doubt that Anahuac listened carefully to this public commitment, for in the turbulent life of the Aztec states it foreshadowed the possibility of a vast and successful empire differing from all previous attempts. Accompanying these statements was a formal ratification by the magnates of the Three Cities.

To commemorate this great act of concordance there was composed a "summer-song," which for years thereafter and throughout the length and breadth of the empire was sung by the subject peoples in the language of the conquerors.[10] It invoked the high god Ipalnemoani as the source of the wisdom of the three kings, and it spoke of the whole earth and of glory.

The Three City League

In the short history of the Aztecs there is no more interesting institution than the Three City League. It has not hitherto been given the centrality it deserves in scholarly literature, probably because it has not been studied historically. Certainly the statecraft that brought it into existence has not been duly appreciated.

In 1431, following the fall of Coyouacan and the flight of Maxtla, Nezahualcoyotl was crowned in Mexico with the imperial crown of his fathers.[11] At the same time Totoquihuaztli, that Tepaneca lord who had early swung over to the side of the allies, was crowned lord of the city of Tlacopan with the allies' full approval and invested with sovereignty over many parts of the former Tepaneca kingdom, including its Otomí and Mazahuaca backlands.[12] The Three City League, therefore, had its inception in that year of victory.[13]

The coronations and the agreement appeared to reestablish the situation as it had existed at the time of the death of the Chichimec emperor Techotlalla in the beginning years of the century. At that time the whole Basin and some of the surrounding lands had been an empire in theory, united under the *chichimeca teuctli*, whose own personal patrimony had been the kingdom of Acolhuacan. Included in that greater empire had been the Tepaneca and their underlings the Mexica. Now in 1431 harmony once again obtained among Acolhua, Tepaneca, and Mexica, and the empire had reappeared—but with a difference. The empire was now split three ways.

This came about because Nezahualcoyotl clearly realized that he could not hope to revive the Xolotl version of the empire, which had only one overlord. The ferment and carnage that Tezozomoc and Maxtla had brought about showed that such a centralization of power and

prestige in one office and one man would merely incite to constant rebellions and usurpations. Therefore, let the empire be rather a confederate empire of the peoples most capable of maintaining it. The Acolhua and Mexica had proved their capability, and, by the very fact of
their still overwhelming presence on the western shores of the lake,
the Tepaneca could not be left out—even though they had been the rebellious vassals who had so recently disrupted the empire. Nezahualcoyotl argued convincingly for the retention of the Tepaneca state but
only under the branch of its ruling house that could be trusted. Totoquihuaztli had proved himself a staunch friend and had abjured the
ways of his grandfather Tezozomoc while still carrying in his veins all
of his terrible ancestor's royalty.

In brief, it was accepted that the times had changed and in changing had proved that the writ of no one city or no one man could run
throughout Mesoamerica. But, at the same time, empire itself could and
must obtain. This part of Xolotl's vision was to be retained. During
the latter part of Itzcoatl's reign, the alliance had been tested; in the
attacks on the Chinampaneca cities and especially in the great Cuauhnahuac venture, it had held firm, working almost effortlessly. By 1441,
at the installation of Moteuczoma, it was known to be permanent, and
it was accordingly so proclaimed.

The Three City League existed essentially for the purpose of aggrandizement, though it was also a mutual aid pact. By amicably unit-
ing the forces of three important Aztec kingdoms, it confronted the
entire Mesoamerican world with the threat of subjugation. The conquests that had so far been made and that were still to come were to
create what we must call, in order to accord with the facts, the Empire
of the Three City League—what has been often carelessly called the
Aztec Empire. When viewed from the outside it appeared to be indeed
a single corporate empire. But in terms of its inner structure it was
three mutually supporting empires, interlocked and interspersed, but
each quite separate and each sovereign.[14] It was a confederation of
three coequal empires, and its executive was a college of three sover-
eigns: the *culua teuctli*, as the Tenochca lord was called in reference to
his claims of Toltec lineage, the *tepaneca teuctli* of Tlacopan, and the

acolhua teuctli, who additionally wore the older title, now purely hon-
orary, of *chichimeca teuctli.*

The conjoint empires were tied together in several ways. Election of
a ruler to any one of the three kingdoms had to be generally agreeable
to the other two; we have already seen this operating in the ratification
of Moteuczoma's election. The kingdoms were bound together by continuous and contrived intermarriage of the royal lines and thus, as the
generations passed, by increasingly close ties of kinship.[15] In the case
of contesting claimants to one of the vacant thrones, he would be elected whose mother had been a princess from one of the other two cities.
The capital cities were further joined by an exchange of each other's
gods and cults, thus forming a kind of amphictyony. They were bound
together also by the stationing of ambassadors in the others' courts,
ready for instant consultation or ritual presences.[16] Nezahualcoyotl, in
fact, ordered that there be constructed in his palace a triple throne
room, somber and sumptuous in its heraldic decorations, where the
three rulers might transact their business in state. Because of his greatly distinguished past and the fact that he had been the principle archi-
tect of the League, Nezahualcoyotl enjoyed from the other two certain
priorities and courtesies such as speaking and voting first in these meetings. There was, finally, a free flow of information among the three
capitals, which appears to have been unusual in Anahuac where secrecy
and suspicion were endemic.

The machinery by which the Three Cities fought their wars and divided up their spoils was simple and effective. Each city reserved the
sovereign right to declare and fight a war on its own or to chastize by
itself a rebellious subject-state, and to therefore take all the booty that
might be gained therefrom. But when the Three Cities were involved,
they handled the booty from a successful campaign in two ways.[17] A
city captured could be adjudged in its entirety to one of the imperial
cities, in which case the holding power installed in that city its own *calpixqui* to collect and forward the imposed tribute with an accompanying bill of lading. Or the tribute from a captured city could be sent directly to Mexico, where it would be divided up in a 2:2:1 ratio—Tlacopan receiving the smallest lot—and each separate lot then taken up by

agents for the respective rulers. Tribute came in periodically through-out the year according to arrangement, usually every eighty days, which was a standard four-month period in the Aztec calendar.

The effect of the above was to create from each conquered province three currents of tribute flowing annually back to the three Aztec capitals, each a separate exaction. Thus the Three Cities had separate jurisdictions but a common policy; each was sovereign but involved in an indissoluble league with the other two.

All this was to have incalculable effects upon Mesoamerica, and there was to be formally no end of the League until 1525 when Hernando Cortez hanged the kings of all three cities from the same tree. But in the time of its greatness the League was a compelling political creation.

> The splendor of a bracelet weighted down with
>   jade stones
> Is your word and your thought,
> O you kings, Moteuczoma and Nezahualcoyotl.[18]

The Tlatoani

Moteuczoma Ilhuicamina was the very perfection of the Aztec *tlatoani*. The title *tlatoani*, "he who speaks," could alternate with *altepetl*, "realm," and thus bore evidence that the office subsumed the powers and effects of the whole state.[19] The title indicates a true head of state.[20] In his warrior or knightly capacity the ruler was equally a *tlacateuctli* or "lord of men."[21] In the earliest period of the history of the Mexica, we naturally do not hear of the title of *tlatoani*, nor would we have expected to find it back then; a people straggling through the defiles and upheaved bare rock of Godland was not a people of sufficient stature or resources to carry with them *tlatocayotl*, "government" or "speakership."[22]

The *tlatoani* of Mexico was a simulacrum on earth of the god Huitzilopochtli. Thus his orders were almost the equivalent of oracular utterances, and, when for certain occasions he was dressed for ritual purposes in the regalia and war paint of the god, he was then the very god in person. Should he personally take a captive in war, this captive, his "son," was dressed for sacrifice as Huitzilopochtli. Upon the *tla-toani* depended the prosperity of the state. Sun and rain and the generosity of the soil would be in part an emanation of his being, and, if he should fail in the favor of the gods, then the Mexica were lost indeed. One of the significant words in Nahuatl for ruling or governing is *mama* (or *meme*), which means quite simply "to carry on one's back," as a parent carries a child. This reveals one of the basic concepts behind the office of *tlatoani*. Plainly the burden of the office had become immense by the time of Moteuczoma I.[23] This ruler in fact was the first to be cast fully in the role of the semidivine;[24] we cannot be far wrong in seeing this as still another formulation out of the baroque invention of Tlacaelel.

In the short years of its history the Mexican state had evolved amazingly. In the period of the Wandering, the *teomama*—the sorcerer who had carried the idol or fetish of the tribe on his back—ruled the march through his possession of the god. Later, as in Chapultepec, there was added a recognized headman who was neither priest nor *tlatoani*. The disasters that followed Chapultepec seem to have fragmented this incipient chieftainship and to have returned rule to a grouping of elders, any one of whom might be the *teomama*. This was followed, in the period of the split between the Tlatilulca and the Tenochca, by the creation of a true but subordinate *tlatoani* for the former; Tenochtitlan retained for awhile its system of elders but soon added the pregnant idea of descent from Quetzalcoatl in the line of Acamapichtli and his successors.[25] With Itzcoatl, the Tenochca set up their first wholly independent *tlatoani*; Moteuczoma then added to the office a part of the sacred duties of the earlier *teomama* and thus could legitimately become the impersonator of the god. In Tlatilulco meanwhile, the *tlatoani*, because of that city's indecision in the Tepaneca War and its hostility, had been degraded to a status almost that of a client king.

Mexico on the Tarascan Frontier

The early years of Moteuczoma's reign were busy ones. The transmontane conquests among the Tlahuica had to be organized and garrisoned, ceremonials and instruments of government had to be devised and dignities increased for the rapidly expanding Mexican nobility. In addition, Huitzilopochtli, the *genius* of the state, called from out his aerie for an accretion to his majesty as well—namely a more splendid temple. Though we have few details of this important period in the life of Mexico, we can be certain that it was centered around the construction and dedication of the new temple.[26]

The first movement of the armies of the Three Cities was made in a quite predictable direction; it continued the direction of advance that had already subdued the land of the Tlahuica. A drive was initiated south of Cuauhnahuac to the hot lands of the Balsas River. Tlachco, which had been the place of exile of the fugitive Maxtla, was acquired first. Following this, a stance on the Tarascan frontier was taken at Oztoma, soon to become a famous fortress, while an additional forward post was set up at Chilapan, across the deep trench of the Balsas and directly on the Yopi frontier. At these two places Mexican arms came to a full stop and indeed never did succeed in penetrating much farther.[27] The Tarascan borders with the Aztec world ran generally northward from Oztoma up to Xilotepec. Moteuczoma also advanced his armies to Xilotepec, and here Mexican power ground to a halt.

The relationship of Mexico with the great homogeneous block of Tarascan people to the west is a most curious one. There was something about those vast expanses of volcanic slopes, rolling pineland, and plateaus covered with hills and lakes to the west and northwest of Anahuac that perennially beckoned the covetous Mexica. The northern part of the Tarascan country was called Michoacan, "land that has fish," and resembled in many ways descriptions of the legendary Aztlan; the numerous and fruitless Mexican attempts to break into the area can be viewed as their attempt to recover an ill-remembered homeland. The Tarascans were not Nahuas but were a distinctive people, heavily seeded with Chichimec customs and fiercely independent. Like the Aztecs they believed that they had originated in Aztlan.[28]

Because of this new pressure from the Mexica, the Tarascans had begun to patrol their eastern frontiers more regularly and assumed there a permanent defensive posture. The onus for the wars and altercations on this frontier certainly falls on the Mexica. The Tarascans seem to have felt no real need to attack the Aztec world, though they were, like the Aztecs, under a supreme lord whose main occupation was to organize wars to secure captives for sacrifice.

While these moves were being made to the west in the early part of his reign, Moteuczoma was being advised by Tlacaelel in the art of creating an administration able to give strong direction to Mexico and to its emerging empire.

Organization of the Imperial State

Moteuczoma asserted that Huitzilopochtli had loosed the Mexica upon the world to conquer it and to reduce it to *tenochca-tlalpan*, "manor lands of the Tenochca."[29] While the Mexican concept of empire was thus universal in its claims, it was relatively diffuse and tentative in terms of its administration. No systematic postal system or network of engineered roads bound the parts of the Mexican empire together. This is because it was never a homogeneous block of territory, but rather one that was interspersed with bits and pieces of two other empires. Nor was Nahuatl ever imposed as an imperial language, incumbent upon all of the subject peoples to learn. Only if the three empires had coalesced under one centralized sovereignty could the work of binding together the parts have been taken up.

Whenever a state was conquered and brought into the Mexican ambit, its customs and structure generally remained intact. A resident commissioner was stationed in the capital city of each province; his main duty was the collection and dispatch of the tribute.[30] In cases where a determined hostility and armed opposition had been encountered, however, the legitimate line of rulers in the subjugated city was demoted and a Mexican *cuauhtlatoa*, or military governor, installed in its place; this is probably the closest to a system of direct rule ever instituted by the Mexica.

Regulation of the relationships between the various parts of the empire was unknown. Two subject or allied cities, for instance, could engage in war with each other without ever consulting their overlord in Mexico. Instead of instituting a structure and code of provincial behavior common to all their empire, the Mexica contented themselves with police rule—the placing of garrisons and fortresses at strategic sites among the conquered. Such garrisons appear to have been in instances joint efforts with the other two imperial cities. War was so important to the Mexica that an empire peacefully and minutely organized and integrated seems never to have occurred to them as a desideratum.

Mexico imposed tribute liabilities on the various parts of her empire either in kind, in persons, or in services. From her Tlahuica cities, Hauxtepec and Tepoztlan for instance, she received mantles, loincloths and women's garments, carved and embellished jades as well as some gold and feather work. Tulantzinco sent charcoal. Tlachco sent, besides cottons, honey and copal for incense. The Chinampaneca cities that were subject to Mexico sent as part of their obligation young women to be trained as dancers and public prostitutes. Cuauhtitlan sent war materiel, shields, arrows, and darts. Other cities, like Tepeyaca, which was still to be added to the empire by Moteuczoma, had to provide a yearly quota of prisoners taken in war for sacrifice in the temples of Mexico. This latter provision, needless to say, forced Tepeyaca into a permanent war footing with most of her neighbors, for otherwise she would not have been able to fulfill her tribute obligations. Azcapotzalco and Coyouacan supplied some of the vast number of laborers necessary for Mexico's building enterprises.

Luxury items were demanded in order to satisfy the new lavishness in Mexico, but the standard tribute was always maize and the companion foods, beans and chile peppers. After the long and hard war with Chalco had been brought to a successful conclusion by Moteuczoma, it was decided to destroy the varied nature of that rich kingdom's economy and to reduce her to the role of a corn producer only.[31] Chalco thus delivered each year great quantities of foodstuffs to help maintain Mexico and became in time her indispensable granary.

Tribute exactions were harsh and, for any state that decided to test destiny and rebel against Mexico, the result was a doubling of the tribute once the rebellion had been crushed.[32] By any standards, Mexican demands were excessive, and the overbearing Mexican tribute collector, sauntering about fan in hand, became to the unfortunates of many a conquered state the target of an immense, silent, and undying hatred. We have pointed out that states with such a position in the empire had earned their misfortune by daring to oppose the empire on the battlefield. Those states that submitted upon presentation of an ultimatum from Mexico were granted the status of allies. Though tribute was also imposed on these more pliant cities, it was disguised as voluntary gift-giving and was never quite the savage and backbreaking burden as for a city that had fought for its independence.

The city that fought and succumbed suffered, besides the imposition of tribute, another unenviable fate. Its god was taken off as a captive to Mexico and installed in the Coacalco under guard behind wooden bars. The Coacalco was the prison reserved for hostile divinities in the temple complex of Cihuacoatl, the mother of all the gods.[33] Here these potentially baleful powers were kept and fed with the blood of sacrifices under the surveillance of their mighty mother. A people whose tutelary deity was thus locked away in the coffers of the conqueror had little indeed to hope for. The Mexica had never forgotten that evil day when for a short while their own Huitzilopochtli had been a captive in the hands of the Culua.

The disadvantages of a casually conceived imperial system can be clearly seen in the case of the province of the Matlatzinca just west of Mexico. Moteuczoma's successor on the throne of Tenochtitlan was to subdue that province and to reinstate the conquered ruler in his office as *tlatoani* in the city of Toluca. This ruler thereupon became so anxious to remain in the good graces of his new Mexican suzerain that he filled all the tribute demands made upon him with dispatch and in overly full measure. So excessive was the pressure he put upon his own people, both commoners and nobility, that in desperation they revolted against him, thus necessitating the dispatch of another Mexican army to the province. Had the Mexica themselves kept a proper administration in that province, they would have gauged the extent of the unrest and no doubt would have referred the matter back to Mexico where some mitigation of the burden might have been ordered, thus forestalling the uprising.

Because of the special role they played, the communities in the empire nearer Mexico were organized with greater care. *Calpulli* within Mexico, as well as those established out along the western shores of the lake and those of subject communities nearby such as Coyouacan, were structured under *calpixque* elected by the local *calpulli*, if the *calpulli* had a traditional clan-like structure, or were simply imposed if the ties to Mexico were weak or nonexistent.

These *calpixque* in Mexico and the nearby lake area were summoned into special session whenever the ruler or the Council of Princes took decisions necessitating action.[34] The assembled *calpixque* were informed of the decision and of what was expected of each one of them. If it was a war that had been projected, the contributions of the respective *calpulli* or other communities in fighting men, weapons, lodgment, and food were set forth, whereupon they instantly returned to their baliwicks to set in motion the appropriate procedures. If a public work was in question—the erection of a palace, temple, or causeway, or the cleaning of an aqueduct—each *calpixqui* would know exactly how much labor was expected, and he would then see that it was provided. For ease in assigning work in his *calpulli*, the *calpixqui* appointed subordinate officers who each handled a specified number of households; these offices were apparently arranged in a descending hierarchy terminating with the overseer of twenty households. One of our sources states that this system worked so efficiently that the entire population of Mexico and vicinity could be assembled within one hour, prepared to carry out any work assigned.

Courts and Judges

We have discussed the level of government, both imperial and in Mexico itself, that received and executed orders issued either from the *tlatoani* meeting in council or by the heads of the Three Cities. Jurisdiction and justice, however, were arranged much differently and came from a broader concept of rule than that of tribute and war. Here the central institution was the *nappoallatolli*, "the eighty-(day) parliament."[35]

We know practically nothing about the system of judging cases in cities subject to Mexico. It is assumed that each city retained its autonomy in law except insofar as it might concern disputes over the *mexicatlalli*, the demesne land in that city possessed by the Mexican *tlatoani* or nobles. The judge in such an instance was the *calpixqui*. But if the case involved homicide or if he felt the case to be of unusual significance, the *calpixqui* would set it aside for review in Mexico.

Every eighty days the provincial and *calpulli* judges with cases or with knowledge to impart that affected the state were required to attend the assize held in Mexico. Here they gave an accounting of their current performance and briefed the appropriate Mexican panel on the cases they were passing on up to them. There were two of these courts in Mexico.[36] The *teccalli*, a four-judge court under a nobleman of *tlacateccatl* rank heard and made findings in cases involving commoners.[37] This tribunal was connected to the populace through an officer called simply the *teuctli*, who was annually elected from each *calpulli*; it was he who was responsible for daily liaison with the courts concerning cases to be put on the docket. This lower court could also be known simply as the *tlacateccatl*, after the presiding officer's title. The procedure included the presentation of initial briefs painted on paper, after which there was a calling of witnesses.

If the case were in criminal law, it was sent to the upper court, the *tecxitlan*, for hearing. This was also a court of the first instance in all cases involving nobles. It was presided over by the *cihuacoatl* or, in exceptional cases, by the *tlatoani* himself. Including the *cihuacoatl*, it was composed of thirteen members of the highest ranking nobles in Mexico, sitting for this purpose as *teuctlatoque* or "those who judge as lords."[38] Its meetinghall in the palace was called the *tecxitlan*, from which the tribunal took its name. The type of case coming before it was generally a criminal case, or a dispute between two imperial cities or *calpulli*, or perhaps a matter concerning the royal prerogative. It alone could order an execution or the demotion of a noble to plebeian status. Attached to the court were thirteen marshals who were always commoners and headmen in their respective *calpulli*; it was their charge to carry out the sentences of the court whether it might be an arrest, the summoning of a witness, an execution, an enslavement, or a house razing. They were, needless to say, important officials—along with the elected *teuctli*—in the control of the population. A public crier announced the name of the culprit, the crime, and the sentence, and then called the people together to witness or, if the penalty was stoning, to participate.

Similar judicial systems existed in Tezcoco and Tlacopan. In fact, the high court under Nezahualcoyotl was the most prestigious of the three, occasionally operating as a court of appeals from the other two cities.

The Mexica Define their State

At one point during Moteuczoma's early rule, he called a conclave of all the important tributary rulers for the purpose of setting forth their positions and prerogatives, those of their knights, and the corresponding rights of the Mexica. The hierarchy of rank was minutely reexamined, as was courtly etiquette and forms of obeisance.[39] The cults and rankings of the various gods were all collated and verified, and finally a full formalization of "flower wars" was arrived at, this including a definition of the Tlateputzca cities as those found most acceptable for inclusion in this exercise. Tezcoco remained as always the arbiter of Aztec culture in all its forms, and much of the reexamination of traditional customs was carried out under her aegis. But Mexico now also began to powerfully influence Anahuac, especially in the area of its specializations, war and sacrifice.

The full institutionalization of the Mexican state was accomplished under Moteuczoma and Tlacaelel, and, interestingly, it was brought about without either straining or discarding the overarching structure of the Three City League. No matter what we may think of the ultimate orientation of the Mexican state, the work done in these years by these two individuals was a remarkable exercise in state building.

Flood, Frost, and Famine

The middle years of the rule of Moteuczoma were to be implicated in a phenomenal series of natural disasters, each of which tested the resilience of the new state and the spirit of its rulers. The Huaxtec War had just begun, and a glorious victory was anticipated in Mexico when, in the summer of 1450, heavy rains began to fall that soon raised the surface of the lake to alarming levels. The waters continued to rise unabated until the streets and open patios of Tlatilulco and Tenochtitlan were deep under the surface. The unpretentious houses of the poor were the first to melt away, but finally even the artificial terraces upon which the palaces and houses of the nobles were set became undermined and were in their turn toppled into the flood waters. This damage to Mexico, however, was speedily repaired by a labor levy called up from the subject cities of the lake side, though these communities too had suffered heavily.

Moteuczoma turned to his kinsman and ally, Nezahualcoyotl, for advice. After study of the normal current of the lake and the currents after freshets had poured into it, Nezahualcoyotl proposed that a great north-south dike be erected down the axis of the lake. Such a barrier would effectually separate the generally sweet or western waters from the brackish and salt areas to the north and east. Flooding streams always poured more water into Lake Chalco than any other part of the whole system, and Lake Chalco flowed into the main body of Lake Tezcoco just east of the place where the dike would be anchored up against the already existent Ixtapalapa causeway. The barrier's northern end would abut at the headland of Tepeyaca. Thus, closing the appropriate culverts piercing the causeways would isolate Mexico from the part of the lake to the east of the dike, the part that would be receiving the high waters.

When it was finally completed, the dike was nine miles long, built of earth and rock dumped between two parallel rows of pilings driven into the lake mud; in some places the work was of exceptional difficulty where it crossed deep holes in the lake bottom. It took several years to complete the work.

The winter of 1450–1451 saw an unprecedented freeze. Snow normally does not fall in the Great Basin, but now, unremittingly, for a six-day period, it fell accompanied by plummeting temperatures. When it finally let up, the whole land was white and the lake had partly frozen over—such had never happened before, and the suffering among the lowly was acute. The winter continued to be extreme.

The following spring, late frosts killed the germinating crops, resulting in a record famine.[40] Meanwhile, epidemics of respiratory disease took a toll of the weakened population. The cities around the lake, which were still devoting much of their scarce labor to the work of rebuilding Mexico and extending the dike, petitioned Mexico for some mitigation of the levy in order that they might care for the hunger of their own people. Tumults ensued among the desperate peoples, but Moteuczoma preferred to install garrisons in such cities as Xochimilco, Azcapotzalco, Culhuacan, and Coyouacan rather than to cut back on his building schedule. At one point the Chinampaneca, hoping to soften the heart of the Mexican *tlatoani*, sent two of their most beautiful noble girls to plead and weep before his throne. This without avail.

The entire Valley fell rapidly into disorder as drought set in. For three entire years no rain was to fall. Most of the seed corn had been eaten in the year following the freeze, so there was little to plant in any case. By 1452 the famine was decimating the commoners. People ate the bark of trees, the roots of the reeds in the lake, and gnawed on old hides. Even certain violently purgative roots, which with skillful preparation might have been eaten, dried up. All around the lake and in the silent parts of the larger cities, the living no longer buried their dead but left them to the coyotes and prowling pumas coming down off the crags, themselves starving.

The most terrible of all those terrible years was 1454. Of the *macehualtin* remaining in the Valley, many shouldered their few belongings and set out in a great migration. Moteuczoma had already opened up his own granaries and from them had established a totally insufficient dole of tamales to the Mexican poor. Merchants from Couixco and from Totonacapan on the coast, where maize was plentiful, now came into Mexico and the other cities in the Valley and bought children from their parents for a few handfuls of dried maize apiece. These children were taken back for sacrifice and, in the case of the Couixca, for eating. Older people were sold, and long files of them with wooden yoke collars at their necks moved daily out toward the mountains beyond which lay death. In a desperate and no doubt fruitless effort to control this loss of its population, Mexico set a bottom price on its people who wished to sell themselves into slavery to foreigners: four hundred ears of maize for a Mexican woman, five hundred for a man. This way it was hoped that some food might be kept in the city to feed the dying inhabitants. Of those who left the cities voluntarily, unnumbered thousands left their meager bones on the trailsides with their tumplines still clamped around their skulls. The nobles must have been correspondingly affected by the famine, but we hear nothing of their dying. The Mexican garrisons strategically placed close to the nobles' foreign estates and grain bins no doubt adequately protected their private stores of food.

Among our sources estimates vary from 50 to 80 percent of the population lost through emigration and starvation; no doubt the former is the more correct figure, but even that points to a disaster of exceptional magnitude. In those days only the vultures were fat. The famine was to be remembered ever after as the *necetochhuiloc*, "when people died in one-Rabbit" (1454).

The great lords of Mexico tried every stratagem they could for the relief of their people. They continued the hostilities that had broken out with Chalco, no doubt to provide hearts and blood for the gods. It was known that the gods were raging in their anger at the nations of Anahuac and that before all reliefs must come acts of placation. To this end, especially sumptuous performances of key festivals were performed in Mexico. The numerous shrines to Tlaloc on the various mountain summits round about were enlarged and new ones set up.

One of these rites of placation took place at Pantitlan, a spot out in the middle of Lake Tezcoco just off the eastern side of the rocky island of Tepetzinco.[41] In times of severe drought, the fall in the lake level exposed a deep hole in the mud called "the abyss," out of which there came water welling from a sublacustrine spring. Even when the lake was high there was a strong swirl of currents around the spot that could send canoes twisting and turning dangerously. From time immemorial in the Great Basin—long before the entry of the Aztecs—this natural wonder had been the scene of cults connected with Tlaloc, lord of rain, storm, and water. The whirlpool area had been fenced off from the open water by a circle of timber balks driven into the lake bottom. Moteuczoma now presented to this divine sump hole in the lake a great carved stone *temalacatl*, and on it he had numbers of children sacrificed to please the offended god of water and to plead for the return of the life-giving rain.

All of Anahuac was involved in the famine. So serious did it finally become that the rulers of the Tlateputzca cities and those of the Three City League and its subjects came together to discuss a matter first brought up by the priesthood of Mexico. These priests, under the leadership of the *cihuacoatl* Tlacaelel, had discovered that the awful disasters that had befallen their world had been caused because the gods were angered at the niggardliness of the human sacrifice as practiced

by the Aztec cities. The priests accordingly demanded a greatly expanded sacrificial cult to pacify the gods and to prevent a recurrence of their
wrath in the future. Nezahualcoyotl apparently objected to a straight
across-the-board increase of victims and proposed that any expansion be
limited to war prisoners alone. One of the Tlascalan kings proposed
that Nezahualcoyotl's suggestion be adopted but that the increase in victims be derived in normal times from increased flower wars. When
drought or other natural calamities should intervene, the flower wars
could be curtailed or expanded as the need might be.

In a harangue of great power, Tlacaelel backed up the notion of for-
malizing flower wars on a treaty level and then proceeded to give to
Anahuac a further interpretation of the flower wars. He saw them now
as military "fairs or markets" to which the god would repair surrounded by his earthly troops to purchase his necessary foodstuffs, hot and
savory like tortillas taken from the baking plate. In this mercantile
transaction the warrior bartered in the stalls of battle for the precious
jades and jewels of renown in return for the price of his life. Nevertheless the merchandise had to be worth the purchase. The blood of
most distant peoples, non-Aztecs, was inferior, and the god should
purchase only items of the highest quality. Thus Nahuatl-speaking Aztecs were designated as the choicest of food for the divine beings. This
concept of the military "fair" is certainly one of the most disturbing
and original concepts ever to emerge from the macabre mind of Tlacaelel. His advocacy won the day, and all agreed to participate in the
understanding; this included the Three City League, the lake cities subject to it, and the independent Tlateputzca cities of Tlascala, Huexotzinco, Cholula, Atlixco, and Tliliuhquitepec. Each of the Tlateputzca
cities designated a field on their frontiers where the buying and selling
in these grisly markets could take place. Thus did the Mexica, along
with the other leading Aztec states, pledge themselves to a more vigorous service of the gods.[42]

Reconstruction of the Calendar and the New Year

But more was done than simply this; the calendar itself was altered. When the wandering Aztecs had first penetrated the
Valley after the fall of Tula, they found there already established cal-

endars using the fifty-two–year cycle, the *xiuhtlalpilli* or "bundle of
years."[43] It was believed that when the present age came to an end in a
universal cataclysm, it would do so only at the close of a fifty-two–year
cycle. That hiatus, therefore, between the end of one bundle of years
and the expected beginning of another was of the most extreme crisis.
If, at midnight of the last night of the last year of a fifty-two–year cycle,
the Pleiades succeeded as before in crossing the line of the zenith, then
indeed a new span of time had been given to the world.

Up to the time of the great famine, the first year of any fifty-two–year
period was always called one-Rabbit. But one-Rabbit happened to be
the year 1454, when Apizteotl, the god of starving, was commanding
the land. For such an unlucky year to initiate the new series of years
was unthinkable.

One-Rabbit was always followed by two-Reed, and in this latter year
(1455) the rains came back plentifully. Once again billowing clouds
walked across the land of Anahuac trailing their rains like mantles, and
once again the hills clothed themselves in green. The Mexicans began
to live again.

Because of this amelioration of the gods' wrath in the year two-Reed,
it was decided by the Aztec cities to declare it and not the previous year
to be the opening year of the present cycle and all future ones. In Mexico a stone was erected that pictorially presented the gods as at last exultant and demanding the more ample nourishment men promised them
through war. It is today one of the most poignant monuments out of
the Mexican past commemorating as it does not only the shift in the
calendar but also the rededication of the city to renewed effort in the
cult of war.

So it came time in the last year for Mexico to prepare for the vigil of
the death and the renewal of time.[44] The ceremony celebrating this was
the "tying of the bundle of years," and it took place on the summit of
Huixachtlan, the sacred hill near Culhuacan.[45] In preparation for this
grand climacteric, the peoples of Mexico extinguished their fires, broke
all their cooking utensils, and threw their small household idols into
the water. A procession of priests, each garbed as one of the gods of
Mexico, moved gravely through the appointed night; in their company
was a captive of exceptionally high rank who had been saved for this

sublime occasion. He was sacrificed at the shrine on the hilltop at the very moment when the Pleiades crossed the zenith to continue their movement into the new year. A sacred fireboard and drill was now placed in the gaping wound of the slain man, and from it was made the century's new fire. From this small spark a great bonfire was made, its flames leaping up as a wonderful sign in the night, informing all the inhabitants of the Great Basin that the perils of annihilation had been avoided. Runners took this fire to the central temples of every city roundabout, and from there it was dispensed to the lesser temples and to all households. The dawning day was the *xiuhtzitzquilo*, "the (new)-year is taken."[46] Mexico sacrificed four hundred captives in gratitude to the powers who had kept the demonic hosts at bay for another fifty-two years.

7. The Wars of Moteuczoma

 The importance of the great famine in the life of Mexico can scarcely be exaggerated. It established the warrior-priest class firmly in the control of events —as can be seen in Tlacaelel's use of it as a lever to push the flower war up to an even higher level of priority in the state. It intensified and quickened the imperial thrust outward and—in conjunction with the successful debut of the new fifty-two–year period— convinced the Mexica that they at last had the ear of the gods. We therefore turn now to a consideration of the great wars of Moteuczoma that made the middle and last third of his reign so significant. The thirteen-year war with Chalco was to be the most crucial.

Background of the Chalca War

Chalco was typical of the Aztec state in being organized in a loose confederation of communities of which two, Amaquemecan and Tlalmanalco, eventually became the most important.[1] It was under Xolotl that it had been organized into four baronies, three ruled

by Chichimecs and the fourth by a neo-Toltec family.[2] Each of the
Chichimec groups claimed to have been led out from Aztlan by their
tribal god, and thus they settled in the Chalco area under divine auspices.[3] One of these groups named the community they founded Amaqueme, thus announcing themselves as being from Xolotl's old homeland, which had borne that name. No doubt Amaquemecan was considered in some way to be synonymous with Aztlan.

The earlier and indigenous peoples of the fertile area of Chalco that
lay on the western slopes of the great volcano had been known as Co-
colca;[4] they had worshipped a god called Red Jaguar whose sacred site
was taken over by the Chichimec invaders and made into the central
shrine of their amphictyony. This god they had identified with their
own youthful Tezcatlipoca.

Chalco lay across the easy route leading southward out of the Valley.
She was thus perfectly sited to interdict traffic between the cities of the
lake and the lands of the Mixteca.[5] Her communities were thriving and
celebrated; her territory was compact and easy to defend; her fighting
skills were well-known; her fields were watered by the copious rains
that swept around the skirts of Popocatepetl even when other lands
were dry. Chalco possessed great power (though her exercise of it revealed a somewhat isolationist mentality), and it is not surprising that
bad blood existed between her and Mexico from the earliest days. The
record of the events leading up to the final clash between the two reveals the tangled web in which the cities of Anahuac so constantly and
so fruitlessly struggled.

Chalco had been a member of the coalition that had surprised the
early Mexica in their piratical lair in Chapultepec and had sent them
fleeing in all directions. The Mexica had long memories, and they did
not forget this. Those Mexica who had then lived as forlorn suppliants
under Culhuacan had been used by that city in skirmishes against the
Chalca. But the two were brought into a more permanently hostile confrontation when Tezozomoc, using the Mexica as a spearhead, began
intermittent war on Chalco. The first such move was made about the
time when Acamapichtli was brought to Tenochtitlan. Our sources refer to these encounters as flower wars, but even if true, there was probably a more serious Tepanec policy of conquest behind them.[6]

Under the aggressive leadership of Cuacuauhtzin, ruler of all the Mexica, these attacks were deliberately stepped up and finally eventuated in the conquest of Amaquemecan and the imposition on that part of the Chalca nation of an annual tribute in dried maize. This represented an extraordinary accession of prestige for the rising Mexica, and their arrogance had increased accordingly. In 1407 Mexico had appointed three Chalca commoners in Amaquemecan as their *calpixque* or tribute collectors.[7] These meanly born officials soon after proceeded to bring false witness against the legitimate Chalca rulers, claiming that the *tlatoani* Toteotzin was plotting rebellion against Mexico. Without weighing the truth of the charges, Mexico straightway dispatched executioners to destroy Toteotzin and his colleagues. The proscribed leaders, however, managed to flee in time to save their lives. Most of the Chalca nobility also dispersed before worse could happen.

Chalco was now without her legitimate ruler. To reward the three perjurers, Mexico raised them to positions of high command over the part of the Chalca nation that they had traduced. All of this was too much for Anahuac. It had been bad enough that Tezozomoc had given the Mexica a free hand in Chalco, thus clumsily and stupidly extending the power of that fearsome people. But now the Mexica had weakened the aristocratic basis of political life among Aztecs everywhere by contemptuously raising commoners to positions of rule. A league of states was accordingly formed around Cholula, the holy city of Anahuac. In 1411 this league, supported by the combined sentiment of all the Aztec states, forced Mexico to abjectly retract. Toteotzin was brought back, and Mexico installed him again in his royal office, while the offending commoners were promptly executed. Amaquemecan, however, had been brutally used in the interim period and continued to harbor hatred of all things Mexican. Chalco—or rather the part of it in question—continued under modified Mexican domination, paying tribute as formerly.

In the fateful year when Maxtla ordered the execution of the two *tlatoani* of Mexico and thus made inevitable the Tepaneca War, the Chalca had seized the opportunity to regain their freedom of action. They announced this by arresting the five Mexican officials resident among them and by destroying all Mexican canoes found on their shores.[8] The vindictive Toteotzin issued invitations to cities as far distant as Toluca to come and witness the sacrifice of the five Mexica in an appropriate ceremony. Mexico was too embroiled in other pressing problems to seek revenge at that moment. The fact that around this time Chalco refused Maxtla's offer of an offensive alliance against Mexico was not so much a softening of Chalca hatred for Mexico as it was an attempt to regain the semi-isolation that had characterized her policy in the first place.

The Mexican embassy sent to arrange an alliance with Nezahualcoyotl had been led by Moteuczoma. Having attained its primary obpective, this embassy had then approached the court of Toteotzin, the Chalca ruler whom the Mexica had formerly deposed and then with reluctance had reinstated. Its objective was to bring Chalco into the new alliance if at all possible, for time and weapons were in short supply. Moteuczoma and the other Mexican notables with him were seized by order of Toteotzin and thrown into the cramped wooden cages reserved for victims awaiting sacrifice. They later escaped, as related above, but the incident—serious enough in itself because it flouted the diplomatic usages of the day—was to have the most far-reaching effects, for it was this Moteuczoma who would succeed Itzcoatl in the rule of Mexico and who would immediately turn baleful eyes upon Chalco.

Moteuczoma, accordingly, attacked Chalco as a preface to his rule—this was to secure victims with which to dignify the ceremonies of his coronation.[9] No doubt the Chalca could clearly read the meaning behind this, the first official act of the reign, and they must certainly have prepared themselves for what, at the very best, was a dubious national future.

In the early part of his reign, Moteuczoma ordered attacks on the more exposed portions of the state of Chalco, but the attacks were not undertaken in force because of the campaigns he had already mounted against the Tarascans to the south and west. But Moteuczoma had not forgotten, and when he undertook the building of the new temple of Huitzilopochtli, in preparation for the ceremony introducing the approaching fifty-two–year period, he used the opportunity to humiliate the Chalca towns that had already been driven behind their defenses. It seems that he had ordered the cities allied to Mexico on the south shores

of the lake—Coyouacan, Xochimilco, Cuitlahuac, and others—to provide him with stated lots of timber, stone, lime, and workers. At the
same time he asked the Chalca rulers to also contribute to the glory of
Huitzilopochtli, certainly a presumption but not a rare one for the
times.[10]

It was now well into the time of the series of great calamities that included the famine, and the burdens placed by Mexico so callously on
her vassals soon became unbearable. They threatened revolt and con-
spired to place themselves under the aegis of Chalco, in whose protection they could repose some confidence, so great was that nation's hostility to Mexico. Our sources are unclear about this passage of history, but
we may consider that this event initiates what we will call the Chalca
War, which, beginning in 1452—the first year of the famine—was not
to end till 1465.[11]

The Chalca War

The Chalca War began not as a challenge on the part of
one great Aztec power to another for control of the richest part of the
Valley, but as a defection of cities held by one power into the protection of another. The actual pretext for the wars was given when, according to the tradition, a party of Acolhua and Mexica noblemen,
ranging the hills south of Coatepec after deer, strayed inadvertently
over the frontiers into Chalco. They were summarily seized by the Chalca guards stationed in the area and taken south to the court of Toteotzin.[12] Here they were judged to be spies and ignominiously destroyed,
their bodies dried and—according to the scandalized report—used as
flaming torches at the nocturnal carousals of the Chalca court. Toteotzin gave further evidence of his derision; he had the hearts dried and
then threaded on a gold collar around his neck. What made this affront
so unforgivable was the rank of the victims; two of them were sons of
the great Nezahualcoyotl and three were ranking members of the royal
house of Mexico.

It seems, then, that Chalco forced war upon the Three City League;
no doubt Chalco wished to take advantage of the awkward predicament
in which Mexico found herself at the time.[13] Mexico, allied with Tezcoco, had just successfully finished a great campaign against the Huax-

teca, but the cost had not been cheap, and the necessity of planting new garrisons in that part of the world had thinned Mexican reserves. Added to this was the damage done to Mexico by the great flood and the subsequent dislocation of a significant portion of the working population. Possibly disease also was a part of the picture, for Mexico's water supply from Chapultepec had become polluted, and a new aqueduct of more adequate masonry had to be planned. Work on the temple of Huitzilopochtli had been radically slowed also by the loss of labor when the southern cities had rebelled. And now, in addition, the great famine was beginning to have an effect. Thus it could not have been too surprising when the attacking forces of the Three Cities were hurled back from the Chalca frontier in a heavy engagement fought at Techichco. Mexico was able to hold on to Ixtapalapa, but with the worsening of the drought little more was done against Chalco except to conduct feints and alarms along the border.

After the rains returned and the new era opened in 1455, the Three Cities had the opportunity to resume their pressure on Chalco but were once again diverted by the sudden challenge from the Mixtecs in that year. The resultant three-year war so effectively occupied her forces that Mexico, which made the mistake of launching a poorly supported attack on Amaquemecan in 1456, was repulsed. Nevertheless, in spite of the heavy commitments of the Mixtec War, the Three Cities did manage to maintain some kind of pressure on Chalco simply from their new presence in her rear. Slowly, the Chalca began to lose territory now to the Three Cities, one community after another, though the great centers continued strong.

The slow attrition began to have an effect when certain Chalca thought they saw their god Tezcatlipoca, the dark master of destiny, wandering eerily through the maguey fields as if no longer desiring to live among them. It was in fact soon after this when a party of Chalca nobles entered into secret correspondence with Mexico to bring about a surrender, but they were discovered and, as an example to others, all were mutilated before the god on top of the holy hill of Amaquemecan. In any event, suggestions that the members of the conspiracy had made to Mexico had been rejected out of hand by Moteuczoma. Mexico was known to be always a vicious enemy; when in addition she became implacable, then the nation that had earned her enmity might well give serious thought to its future survival.

The unaided Mexica had fought Chalco in many of the early clashes, but the time finally came when the stubborn resistance of that realm made necessary the committing of all of the resources of the Three Cities. At Cocotitlan, "among the doves," this great combined force in a supreme effort now met the Chalca, who were probably inferior to them in numbers. Cocotitlan lay in the nearly level country just behind the likeside city of Chalco Atenco. It was in fact an outlying *calpulli* of that city and was a key point, for it in effect protected Chalco's rear. Its fall would uncover that city and more or less separate it from the two large centers in the hinterland, Tlalmanalco and Amaquemecan.

Here was fought out a protracted and fierce engagement; when the day was done the Chalca had fled the field, leaving many of their knights as captives in the hands of the three allies and leaving uncovered their cities of the interior. Back in Mexico three hundred Chalca warriors were sacrificed by fire in a triumph of splendid proportions arranged personally by Tlacaelel. Cocotitlan was for the Chalca a disaster of major proportions but they still held their three leading cities and for a while longer might securely hold the part of their country that lay on the slopes of the volcano and that commanded the high road over to Atlixco and Huexotzinco.

At this juncture the allied push, so successfully begun, was stalled by the outbreak in 1463 of the Totonac War and the diversion of Mexican energies down into the low country along the Gulf. When in the succeeding year Mexican armies could again align themselves against the Chalca, the latter had to some extent firmed up their defenses, though still unable themselves to take the initiative. Incautiously, the overconfident Mexica now advanced beyond Cocotitlan but were thrown back from Amaquemecan, their ultimate goal, with heavy losses in high-ranking knights. This was an unexpected repulse.

One of the captured Mexica was Tlacahuepan, a brother of Moteuczoma, an almost legendary warrior and one of the ruling four princes. He had fought shoulder to shoulder with Moteuczoma in the bitter struggles of the Tepaneca War and had been closely associated with him ever since. Though past middle age at the time, he had no lack of confidence in his skill in war. It is probable that his exceptional eminence caused the Chalca, desperate now for relief from the intolerable pressure of the Mexica, to offer to settle him along with those other knights who had been captured in a new Mexican *calpulli* in Chalco.[14] He was to be given title and wealth and would rule over what in essence was to be a Mexican government-in-exile under Chalca protection. Such a move, if successfully carried out, would put Mexico in some peril, for it would be a standing invitation to division and treachery. Tlacahuepan feigned acceptance of this offer and demanded that the Chalca erect for him an excessively high platform so that he could face his new subjects in an exalted fashion. Once having climbed up to his dizzying perch, he began to taunt the Chalca and, on a note of high patriotic sentiment, leaped to his death below. The Chalca, appalled at such defiance, killed all those captives around him who were to have formed the nucleus of the new Mexican branch of the Chalca people. The Chalca are reputed to have said of the Mexica that "a people of such courage, a people as terrible as that, should die."[15]

The news of the loss of his beloved brother and of the other notables threw the aging Moteuczoma into a grief no less deep for being elaborately and ceremonially displayed. When the appropriate obsequies were over, rage stepped into the place of sorrow, and out from Tenochtitlan now sped the orders that would dispatch converging armies for the last time against Chalco. Fires flared up from the top of Chapultepec during these nights of decision, signaling the release of frightfulness and terror such as perhaps none but the Mexica themselves could contemplate. These golden points pricking in the Mexican night must have been viewed by the Chalca with the deepest anxiety, for while they could not read the specific meaning in the messages that were passing among the Three Cities, they could at least sense the unchanging purpose displayed.

Tezcoco moved by land directly against the city of Chalco Atenco on the lake, the city that had so long defied them. Tlacopan and the Mexica came over the lake in an armada of war canoes. Toteotzin, old both in years and in his hatred of the Mexica, placed himself in the center of

his army, thinking to meet his Acolhua enemies first before repulsing
the Mexica on the shore. His general Contecatl had to make all the dispositions, for the Chalca ruler was completely blind. Though unable
to engage personally in battle, he still wore around his neck the terrible
necklace of dried hearts. In magnificent array the army of Tezcoco
moved up to the attack; it was led by the sons of Nezahualcoyotl, who
had long been thirsting for the glory of this the greatest victory likely
ever to be offered to them. The Mexica warriors and their vassals had
meanwhile bent to their paddles and were rapidly closing the shore.

When the fighting was over, the Chalca army had been decisively
broken and the blind old king taken captive. With none left to defend
it, the city of Chalco Atenco threw open its entryways and awaited the
inevitable massacre. Its fall was followed by that of the cities in the center of the realm, and at last the sacred city of Amaquemecan was vulnerable to a frontal assault.

While gathering up the loot in Chalco Atenco and binding up their
own wounds, the Mexica and their allies were still able to send a heavy
probing raid into the back country. They knew that the people of Amaquemecan were preparing for a last-ditch stand and that the struggle
there would be intense. Therefore, while they prepared for this final
essay, they launched a preliminary thrust against the sacred hill of
Amaquemecan. This was successful, and the shrine, so central in the
lives of all the Chalca, was razed to the ground. The capture and humiliation of the god must have had adverse effects upon the morale of
the remaining Chalca.

This occurred during a year of suffocating heat and attendant drought
that were serious enough to impose a halt upon the advance, but finally,
at the beginning of the succeeding year, 1465, the long-expected attack
upon Amaquemecan was delivered. A furious defense, also expected,
was encountered. While the final outcome was never in doubt, casualties on the side of the Three Cities were still severe. As the power of
Amaquemecan to resist weakened, the people began to break away and
flee, streaming back along the well-worn road around the southern
flank of Popocatepetl that led to Atlixco and Huexotzinco.[16] The collapse of this last remnant of the Chalca state had been hastened by the
treachery of three of the sons of the ruler of Amaquemecan, one of

whom was later given a Mexican princess as recompense for his perfidy and to keep him thenceforth tied to Mexican policy.

The victors allowed themselves no respite. This was for Mexico the sweet day of revenge; a hot pursuit was ordered. The slaughter of the fugitives went on relentlessly, day and night; parties of heavily armed allied warriors would break away from the main body on the high road to probe high up in the ravines and jumbled rocks of the great volcano, seeking out for destruction those attempting the shortcut over the mountains. Many of the fugitives who did succeed in escaping the swift darts and sword clubs of the avengers nevertheless died soon of exhaustion or starvation in the dark pine coverts. The terror unleashed by the Three Cities was so devastating that what had once been a richly populated Aztec kingdom was now silent and desolated—the only movement to be seen in the land was the lazy curling of the smoke from the burning communities.[17] It was said that some sixteen thousand of the common people from Amaquemecan did, however, finally secure refuge in the territory of Huexotzinco.

In the end the Mexica and their two allies became concerned about the spectacle of obliteration and the utter ruin they had created. If there were no Chalca left to tend the fields, the produce of which was to fill the granaries of the victors, then, while revenge would have been served, interest would have been neglected. Moteuczoma hereupon declared a general amnesty for all Chalca who had fled abroad.

As for the state of Chalco, its independence was gone. Commissars were now sent out from the Three Cities to rule the various Chalca cities and strong garrisons were sited throughout the area. This harsh military occupation was to last in the Chalca cities for more than twenty years. There were few males left among the Chalca after thirteen years of warfare, so the cruel burdens of service imposed upon them fell mainly upon the women, to whose lot it fell to erect in Mexico, Tezcoco, and Tlacopan new houses for the nobles and more magnificent palaces for the kings; the hauling of the great beams was done by women and children as well as the quarrying and working of stone and the burning of lime. The lack of men meant also that what few maize lands had been left to the Chalca after the division of spoils went in part unplanted and untended. The resultant starvation so thinned the ranks of the wretched people for at least four years after the cessation of hostilities that many chose to flee by night over the mountains never to return. The best of the Chalca lands had been partitioned among the three allied states in the agreed ratio. The *tlatoani* and great nobles of each of the three who had acquired these lands saw to it that they at least did not suffer from lack of labor.

Victory over Chalco had taken years and the combined efforts of the Three Cities. Mexico could not alone have challenged the well-peopled realm of Chalco. The success of the conflict not only multiplied the resources of the Three Cities but also solidified their allegiance to the principles of the League. What Quinatzin and Tezozomoc as individual rulers of empires had been unable to attain, namely undisputed sway over the whole of the Aztec world, was now a real possibility for the emergent League. It had proved its right to exist; it could now exult. Drowning out the laments of the conquered came now the sound of the revels of the three victors:[18]

> The drum has been placed in the center,
> The circle of singers has closed up
> Here in Chalco
> In the meadows of Cocotitlan.
> There is dancing here on the terraces of the heroes,
> The lords,
> Moteuczoma, Nezahualcoyotl,
> and Chimalpopocatzin—
> On the dancing grounds of Cocotitlan
> Your hearts are bursting with pleasure.[19]

Tlascala and the Three Cities

We have mentioned in the course of the narrative on the Chalca War three other campaigns of the League, all of them victories. These campaigns were, in chronological order, directed against the Huaxteca, the Mixteca, and the Totonaca. A common thread unites these three military expeditions, which otherwise would be unconnected, and that is the machinations of the state of Tlascala. This state was to play a role in the life of Mexico that was to first baffle her, then to frustrate her, and finally to help in bringing about her fall. The Tlascalans, a sinewy people, seem to have much in common with the Mexica but to have lacked their exaggerated aggressiveness.

As an Aztec people they claimed to have come from Aztlan but to have preceded the Mexica on their trek south. Their early career in the Basin has similarities with the tale of the Mexica, though their activities were centered on the east side of the lake whereas the Mexica were on the west side. Originally they too were footloose Teochichimecs, hunters with the bow and arrow, and for a while they claimed and held the slopes of Mount Tlaloc as their hunting grounds, where they were loosely tied in with Xolotl's empire. Like the Mexica they grew in numbers; they also became arrogant and often dangerous neighbors, and they ended by defying the emperor Quinatzin when he insisted that all Chichimecs under his rule settle down and adopt the ways of civilization. Tezozomoc, overlord of the Mexica at that time, had not yet disowned allegiance to the imperial crown in Tezcoco and accordingly had answered Quinatzin's request for help against the Tlascalans. Cuacuauhtzin and his Mexicans were thus in the forefront of the imperial army that met the Tlascalans under the peaks and defeated them. It was this episode that gave the early Mexica an interest in the area of Coatlichan, a community near the battle site.

The Tlascalan bands were forced to scatter. Most of them moved eastward over the mountains to emerge into "the land behind," Tlateputzco.[20] Here their wild ways and vigor finally won them lands of their own, and they gradually settled into the life of cultivators of the soil that they had previously rejected. They seized the ancient Toltec religious center of Cholula, they founded Huexotzinco, and, a bit farther on to the north, they founded that confederacy of four tribal princedoms that was most particularly theirs—Texcalla, "the crags" as it was known before the Spaniards altered the name in error to Tlascala.[21]

Their princely families soon had close connections with the house of Xolotl, and, despite the fact that they had been put down by Quinatzin's army and expelled from the Basin, they continued communication with Tezcoco, even going to the extent of modeling their early laws on those of that city.[22] But their relations with their kinsmen who were now ruling and occupying nearby Huexotzinco and Cholula degenerated rapidly into a touchy series of disputes and, on occasions, into bloody contests. In at least one of these affairs Mexico was called in by Huexotzinco for support against Tlascala. So Tlascala's relations with Mexico continued hostile, though still remote.

Mexico was becoming increasingly involved in the affairs of Tlateputzco and, as destiny would have it, always as an adversary of Tlascala. As time went on, this enmity became polarized, and peoples like the Otomí or the Chalca, fleeing from the wrath of the Mexica, could always find a ready welcome in Tlascala, where they were generally settled as frontier communities guarding her northern and southern borders.[23] By the time of Moteuczoma, Tlascala felt the need to defend herself behind extensive but discontinuous walls and ditches.

War against Huaxtecs and Mixtecs

To understand the events that follow, one has to be aware of the amazing efflorescence of Mexican trade that had been taking place ever since the conclusion of the Tepaneca War. The most distant parts of Mesoamerica were within the Mexican ken. By now, Mexican merchants, mainly Tlatilulca, were common visitors to the coastal regions along the Gulf and were bringing back small quantities of cacao, jaguar skins, rare colored feathers, and rubber balls for *tlachtli* and other cult purposes. The hunger of the new Mexican nobility for these luxury items was insatiable; it was one of the important drives behind the advance of their terrible armies.

The Gulf coast was divided between two peoples, the Huaxteca in the north and the Totonaca in the center. Taken together, their territories surrounded Tlascala on her northern and eastern sides. Inasmuch as Tlascala fronted directly on those subtropical lowlands, she had been able in the past to enrich herself through barter with their more exotic products. Even more importantly, she received the staple salt from areas along the coast.

Mexico was drawn northward into Huaxtec territory by great ease of communication, for this was the area in which Tezcoco had a historic interest, having campaigned there on her own for some time, thus blazing the way for her ally. Mexico's objectives in the area were twofold and related: first to expand her own commercial penetration there and second to interdict the trade of Tlascala with those regions.[24] And the fact that empire could also ride on the backpacks of the *tlamama*, the lowly bearer of merchandise, was not forgotten. It is difficult to see anything fortuitous in the Mexican move against the Hauxteca. It speaks rather of a settled policy of aggression.

The advance by the Three Cities and their vassals began about 1450 and was the first major military undertaking of Moteuczoma's reign. This was still a good time for the Mexica, for the series of natural calamities of which we have already spoken had barely begun. The *casus belli* was the decision taken by the Huaxtec princes to kill all the merchants of the Three Cities found in their territory and to prevent any further entrances; these merchant forays were now recognized as being for the purpose of espionage as well as for trade. Tezcoco already held the important center of Tulantzinco, which was placed where travelers debouched off the highlands down into the coastal plain, and it was from this point that the allied armies advanced against the strongly fortified cities of the Huaxteca. The Huaxteca were renowned for their fighting qualities but could not compete with the highlanders in their organization for battle. They were decisively defeated, and numbers of their warriors were driven back up the great escarpment, arms pinioned behind their backs, their necks held in heavy wooden yokes. Their shuffling lines, wailing and chanting as they moved along, lamented the fate that was awaiting them on the stone of sacrifice.

Mexico had never before celebrated such an imposing triumph, and Tlacaelel, to bring honor to the occasion, advised that a special *temalacatl* for the coming gladiatorial sacrifice be erected. All Anahuac was invited to come and witness the unprecedented number of sacrifices and to feel the splendor and horror of the event.[25]

To Tlascala the event had brought injury, for it meant that more than half of her passageways into the lowlands had been closed; Mexican and Acolhua garrisons were now situated in the lower parts of the valleys through which her merchants had been accustomed to exit into the coastal plain. Tlascala had, therefore, to take a more active part in the affairs of the Mesoamerican world if she was not to be thrown completely on the defensive. It is for this reason that she became involved in the war between the Mixtecs and the Three City League.

For the traveler going south, Mixtecapan, "the land of the cloud people," began at Acatlan southeast of Popocatepetl. Here began the rugged terrain, often misted over with clouds, which was the immemorial homeland of the Mixteca. These people were grouped into principalities, some of which extended down to the shores of the Pacific. While it is clear that they had an important collective history, they had never coalesced into a single realm.[26] They were the cleverest metal workers and carvers of Mesoamerica, they boasted important commercial centers, they engaged in internecine wars, and they bore a close resemblance to the Aztec world of Anahuac in all but the fact that they spoke a non-Nahuatl tongue and had no traditions of wandering.

Ever since Mexico had shared the province of the Tlahuica with her allies, the hot lands to the south drained by the headwaters of the Balsas and the Mexcala Rivers had drawn her interest. Around 1455 the Mixtec state called Tlachquiauhco submitted to Mexico and received a Mexican garrison. The other Mixtec principalities immediately recognized this threat, which resulted in a challenge from Coaixtlahuacan, the richest market city of Mixtecapan.

Coaixtlahuacan was the highland entrepôt for the rubber balls, gold, pelts, quetzal feathers, and cacao beans of the countryside watered by the Papaloapan River over the mountains. Atonal, the ruler of that city, was known to the Aztecs to have been a Toltec, though what this signified is not clear. His kingdom had for some time been penetrated by merchant caravans from the Three Cities and their tributary states. Convinced of the deception behind this traffic, Atonal finally ordered the massacre of all such merchant groups found within his borders. The news of the affront was brought back to Moteuczoma by a few merchants of Toltitlan who had managed to escape. War was instantly decided upon, and orders were sent to certain of the Mexican vassal states to prepare their squadrons.[27]

The Three Cities almost certainly marched south through Tlahuica territory, because, still locked in war with the Chalca, they could not exit from the Basin at that end. They found the enemy standing on his frontier. The resulting clash was a serious defeat for the Aztec forces, something of a new experience.

Shocked at the unexpected reversal and indeed badly hurt, Mexico and her allies spent the next two years preparing for a return encounter. Mexico had deliberately chosen to play the role of the invincible world conqueror, and after such a setback revenge was a necessity if her prestige was to be maintained. The ominous lull spoke eloquently to Atonal, and he looked about for allies to shore up his prospects. It was almost a foregone conclusion that he should turn to the cities of Tlascala and Huexotzinco for assistance, for all of Mesoamerica was aware of the growing threat to them posed by the Three City League. Tlascala indeed had no option in the matter; it was imperative for her to seize any and every opportunity to injure or obstruct Mexico.

Aided by his new Tlateputzca allies, Atonal was able in a preliminary clearing operation to attack and destroy the Mexican garrison in Tlachquiauhco, which otherwise might have harried his flank as he awaited at Itzucan the main attack. The fury of the onset may well be imagined. The Mixteca and their allies had prepared every imaginable kind of defense and at the last moment even received some aid from the Zapotecs, their neighbors to the south. They were nevertheless overwhelmed and finally broke, the survivors fleeing back to Coaixtlahuacan. Here Atonal set about preparing a last stand but was assassinated by a peace party of his nobles who took over the reins of government and, as a first act, tendered their submission to the Three Cities.

The victory was even more momentous than at first appeared, for peoples east of the mountains and along the banks of the Papaloapan came in to pay homage and to accept tributary status. Among these communities was Tochtepec, soon to become the most active market in the whole of the Aztec empire. The role of Coaixtlahuacan in the empire henceforth was to pass on the goods of Tochtepec to the Great Basin, pouring out before the nobles of Mexico a veritable flood of luxuries never dreamed of by their ancestors. To commemorate the triumph, another great stone *temalacatl* was ordered by Moteuczoma and on it were sacrificed the most heroic of the Mixteca taken in battle.[28] And to add to the joy of the Mexica was the defeat of the Tlascalans, who had—along with the Huexotzinca—supported the enemy.

It was clear by now that the Three Cities, with Mexico in the lead, were embarked on a calculated policy of aggression menacing every city and princedom in Mesoamerica, no matter how distant or inoffensive they might seem to be.

The Taking of Totonacapan

Tlascala now had real cause for apprehension. Through the seizure of Itzucan the way by which Tlascala might be flanked on the south had been flung open for the Mexica, a move which, if successfully made, would effectively seal the ring around her. That such a move was under contemplation in Mexico with the ending of the Mixtec War is evident. Again the chronology is confused and we cannot give a precise year to the first direct move against Totonacapan, the Gulf lowlands south of the Huaxteca.

All the while, however, contingents of the Three Cities from their Hauxtec garrisons had been exerting pressure against Totonacapan from the north. This was one blade of a remarkable pincers movement being directed against the area. The other blade was represented by a strong party of the Three Cities that had gone down the Papaloapan River to attack and seize Cosamaloapan well below Tochtepec.[29] Thus a third thrust, directly aimed at Totonacapan from the west, would have an excellent chance of success, supported as it would be by these flanking movements, though admittedly the latter appear not to have been in great strength. This plan became the order of the day.

But the Tenochca Mexica were at the moment involved in the final stages of the Chalco War, from which neither pride nor hunger for revenge would at the moment allow them to withdraw. It was at this point that Tlatilulco seized the center of the stage and entered on her brief and brilliant political renaissance.

The aged Cuauhtlatoa was still ruling Tlatilulco under Tenochca license. We recall that he had once represented a real threat to the Tenochca but had been forced to back up and accept a status for his city more or less dependent on Tenochtitlan. The grandeur and the power of Moteuczoma aided by the august presence of Tlacaelel had effectively worked to continue this relationship of patronage. It had been the great famine that had softened the asperity of the two Mexicos and had drawn them close together. Around 1453 work on a new and improved aqueduct from Chapultepec was begun, symbolizing this union.[30] It was from this point on that Tlatilulco had been given a greater part to play in the external affairs of Mexico, though Cuauhtlatoa still continued to rule more or less as a client king. Tlatilulco participated increasingly in the growth of Mexico, and, though she was not as populous as Tenochtitlan, the energy of her merchants and the splendor of her market gave real weight to her counsels.

A new star had arisen among the knights of Tlatilulco, a personage called Moquiuix, who, because of merit and connections had been installed as *tzompanteuctli,* "lord of the skull rack." His outstanding feats of arms had commended him to Moteuczoma, and he had been entrusted with increasingly important roles in Mexico's continuing series of wars. Moteuczoma selected him now to lead the Tlatilulca squadrons on the campaign projected against Totonacapan. This appointment was to have fateful effects not only for this campaign but also for the future relations between the two Mexicos.

The central city in Totonacapan was Cuetlaxtlan, "leather land," today Cotastla. It lay in the hot scrubby country on the main road leading down from the highlands through the coastal plain to the Gulf. West of it was the great escarpment of Mexico looming through the clouds, and beyond that the armies of the hinterland. On the very edge of that rampart stood the most august of all the mountains of Mesoamerica, Poyauhtecatl, today called the Pico de Orizaba.[31] The commonly used road from the plateau led down over the broken southern skirts of that massif in a tortuous descent, debouching into the lowlands in a pleasant bay of hills wherein stood the important frontier city of Ahuilizapan (Orizaba).[32] This place was the key to Totonacapan and was accordingly well provided with defenses. Travelers of all kinds, armies, caravans of merchants, ambassadors, all had to file past the fortress sited at that spot. Ahuilizapan, a loyal vassal of Cuetlaxtlan, had long been aware of the predatory Aztec world gestating in the lands back of the clouds, and it knew that sooner or later it would be called upon to defend the pass against the Aztec armies.

Mexico arranged the coming campaign in the approved fashion. Moteuczoma dispatched ambassadors to Ahuilizapan to demand quantities of the great conch shells of the coast that were used as trumpets in the priestly cults. Submission to this demand would be an acceptance by the realm of Cuetlaxtlan of the role of a vassal state. Refusal could mean only war. The Tlascalans, however, had already placed their agents down in the capital city of Cuetlaxtlan, inciting the Totonacs to resistance. What finally convinced Cuetlaxtlan to defy the Three City League was that the two other great cities of Tlateputzco, Huexotzinco and Cholula, stood solidly with Tlascala in offering aid. At the time, any rational analysis of the situation would have predicted victory for Cuetlaxtlan in any contest with the Three City League, since the latter force would have to attack in strength through the pass of Ahuilizapan and of necessity would thus leave its rear open to attack from Tlascala.

Moteuczoma seems to have intended that the Tlatilulca under Moquiuix would carry the brunt of the fighting for Mexico; a number of Tenochca squadrons still heavily committed in the Chalco War made this a logical move. Mexico was in any case totally in the dark as to the dispositions that Tlascala was readying for the event.

It was certainly one of the most illustrious Aztec armies ever to take the field. The commander was Axayacatl, a grandson of both Moteuczoma and Itzcoatl, and already destined to become *tlatoani* when Moteuczoma should die. Assisting him were his two brothers, Tizoc and Ahuitzotl, both also in line to become rulers of Mexico. Along with them came the lords of Culhuacan and Tenayuca, each leading their respective contingents.[33]

The host set out and undoubtedly passed through the territory of Cholula, of whose impending treachery it could not have heard. Cholula was the greatest pilgrimage center in Mesoamerica of the day and, because of that fact, had preempted a status approaching neutrality. It was behind this customary camouflage that she allowed or at least did not contest the passage of the allied advance. In the meantime, certain forces from each of the Tlateputzca cities had slipped secretly down into Totonacapan to take up their stand beside Cuetlaxtlan.

The alarming news of the ambush being prepared reached Moteuczoma in Mexico just as his army had arrived at the top of the declivity leading down to Ahuilizapan. Swift runners sped out from Mexico to warn Axayacatl that he was outnumbered and that he might be trapped by auxiliary forces coming up on his rear. Immediately on receipt of the news, Axayacatl called a council of war to consider the options open to the army. Caution seemed about to win the day, and the major voices were prepared to vote for a speedy withdrawal before the enemy could, theoretically, assemble in the rear. At this juncture Moquiuix arose and demanded a pressing of the attack. He pointed out that such was their assignment and that he, as a Mexican knight, could consider no other alternative. He backed up his bravado by offering to lead his Tlatilulca knights alone against the enemy and boasted that they alone would break the enemy. Such quixotic vaunting was not uncommon among the Aztecs. Succumbing to his superb and contemptuous confidence, the other leaders voted to give him his chance.

It was considered in later years to be one of the great feats of arms in Mexican annals. The small Tlatilulca army, inspired to berserker heights by the knowledge of the odds against them, without a pause carried the day and unaided broke into Ahuilizapan's defenses. The rest of the army streamed in after them. The unexpected suddenness with which this door to the realm of Cuetlaxtlan was hurled open seems to have taken the main Totonac armies and their allies completely by surprise. Like a jaguar springing on its prey, Mexico then leapt from the carcass of Ahuilizapan upon the astounded Cuetlaxtlan and overpowered it too in one fierce assault.

Immense booty and a satisfactory number of captured Totonac and Tlateputzca warriors were gathered in from these two victories, and Moteuczoma's knights from there marched unopposed down to the shores of the Gulf. Any threat that might have menaced the rear of the invaders dissolved when the completeness and suddenness of their victories became apparent. Totonacapan and many of its cities had now fallen into the hands of the Three Cities. The year was 1463, and the new skull rack just erected in Tenochtitlan could be dedicated properly by threading on its poles the skulls of 6,200 additional victims. Tlascala was now surrounded on all sides and at last cut off from all access to the staples and luxuries of the coast. Her last chance to contest the unrolling of the Aztec empire had gone.

Of all the knights who had earned fame in the press of those assaults, Moquiuix was the acknowledged champion.[34] He and his fellow Tlatilulca had themselves personally taken 410 captives. A heroic lay was soon composed about his exploits.[35] This new honor was particularly welcomed by his Tlatilulca peers because of the long eclipse under which they had suffered and which now, because of their demonstrated

prowess, was to be forgotten. Moteuczoma honored Moquiuix by giving him a wife of royal blood, the sister of the commander Axayacatl.
By this act Tlatilulco regained its full identity as an integral part of
Mexico. Cuauhtlatoa, the old ruler, lived only a few years after this
sudden rise in the prestige of his Mexicans, and when he died in 1467
Moteuczoma installed Moquiuix in his place, even though Moquiuix
appears to have been unrelated to the old Tepaneca house that had
ruled so long in Tlatilulco.[36]

Oaxaca and the Road of the Caravans

The years of the great Moteuczoma were drawing to an
end. The armies of the Three Cities continued annually to march out of
Anahuac to distant parts, and the Mexican boast to conquer the world
seemed ready for fulfillment. Tepeyacac was taken by the Three Cities,
and secure communications with the newly acquired Gulf lowlands
were thus established.[37] Trading ventures now probed regularly down
into Tabasco. One of these led to the last great enterprise of the reign,
the seizure by the Three Cities of the strategic valley of Oaxaca.[38]

Mexico had dispatched a merchant caravan down to the emporium
of Coatzacoalcos. It had returned laden with riches traded from as far
away as the lands of the Maya. But as it came over the mountain at the
sacred city of Mictlan (Mitla) the Zapotecs destroyed it, leaving the
bodies where they had fallen among the pines and boulders of the hillsides. Retribution inevitably followed. The Zapotec capital was not
simply taken; it was literally razed to the ground and all its inhabitants
massacred. In a strategic site in the valley, the Mexica founded a new
garrison city that they named Uaxyacac (Oaxaca), its various new *cal-
pultin* being comprised of Aztecs who had been moved down there
from the Great Basin. This was one of the two Aztec colonies ever
placed in foreign parts of whose founding we are explicitly told. It was
ruled by a *tlatoani* who was appointed from one of Mexico's noble
families. The care the Mexica had for this strategic province is clear.

Because of the accession of treasure rolling in, the Three Cities were
now in a period of intensive building activity.[39] In 1467 Tezcoco finished her great temple of Huitzilopochtli. The previous year Tlatilulco
had dedicated a temple to house a growing number of vassal gods and

had erected a new skull rack,[40] all this in the same year when the great aqueduct—thirteen years in the building—began to function and when work on the dike to control floods was completed. Tezcoco was still the most luxurious city in all of Anahuac due to the high imagination and building skill of its *tlatoani*, Nezahualcoyotl, but Mexico now arose out of the wash of her waters with a splendor almost comparable. As for the Mexican knights, none were their superiors and their names were known in every corner of Anahuac.

To celebrate their joint reign the two old men, Moteuczoma and Tlacaelel, had their likenesses carved in the rock of Chapultepec.[41] Moteuczoma could achieve no greater renown—he was one of the very few, a *tlalpoloani*, a conqueror, "one who wipes out nations."[42]

8. The Sacred Nature of the Mexican State

By this time Mexico had become an articulated state, purposeful and grave. She had courts and judges, marshals and runners to carry the will of the courts to distant parts. She had armies and training schools for war and command. She had a treasury organized under diligent officials, she had archives and a system for collecting tribute. She had markets, merchant guilds, and regulations that defined the proper exchange of goods. She had a central decision-making body, a chief of state, and a strong principle of succession. Out of the irregular bands of wandering Mexica in the days following the fall of Tula there had emerged a state.

This state, however, had been born in the womb of war. The various stages of its growth, first the acquisition of a ruler, then tutelage under the Tepaneca, then independence, and finally the creation of a college of four princes under the *tlatoani*—each of these had been a response made in war or to war. The historian is thus confronted with what appears to be the simple actions of a bellicose nation, and on one level this may indeed be accepted. But the historic picture is brought into a different focus when we realize that, to the Aztecs in general and to the Mexica in particular, war was a rite. Our assessment in that case becomes more complicated, and the Mexican state is then seen to be a special political configuration created to maintain a religious cult. Whatever else the Mexican state may have been, it basically existed for a sacerdotal purpose. The usual historic situation wherein states finally become ends in themselves is muted in the instance of Mexico, or only partially developed. Mexico resembles more a consistory within the greater *ecclesia* of the Aztec world than a true state in today's terminology. The inordinate quality that Mexico's history evinces is the product of this powerful and pious orientation; it does not come from mere bellicosity.

It follows, if this interpretation is correct, that the Mexican nation can be thought of as a sacred nation and the *tlatoani* as a pontiff of sorts. The religion that the state professed was centered on the cult of war, and the warrior was thus the indispensible officiant who maintained that cult. The gods were those supernatural powers who were to be pleased or placated by the right performance of this cult.

Masks

According to the Mexica, the gods were not collected together in a pantheon nor were they related to each other in family structures. Thus the gods, unlike men, did not live under a Jovian *tlatoani* who dignified all things under him and ordered them into a harmony. This jumbling of the supernaturals into a hodgepodge of scarcely related beings is curious until we reflect upon the one bond they all did have in common and which the Mexica considered sufficient to identify them as members of one society—they all subsisted on the hearts and the blood of humans.

Nor was any one of the gods the uncontested creator of all things. Particularly in Tezcoco, which was far in advance of Mexico in intellectual concerns, the lords under Nezahualcoyotl did feel a vague need for some such spiritual concept. They referred to the invisible god under several names: he was Tloque Nahuaque, loosely translated as "the immanent," Ipalnemoani, "he through whom all things live," or Youalli

Ehecatl, literally "night and wind," but better translated as "the un-
fathomable."[1] These designations appear to have been theological concepts rather than names of specific gods; they certainly did not belong
to popular religion, for there was no cult of any such being.

Lacking a single creator god around whom to group all other supernatural beings, the Mexica world view was bound to produce for them
a vision not of unity but of variety. This unconnectedness of powers,
however, did not imply for them a chaos in the heavens, since a single
cult principle sufficed for the worship of all deities.

Godhead to the Mexica, as in the rest of the Aztec world, was evident under two rubrics, one direct, as under the appearance of *teotl*,
and the other indirect, as *ixiptlatl*. *Teotl* is the word we ordinarily translate as "god" or "divine," though an eminent man on death can be said
to become *teotl*. The other word is derived from the verb *ixiptlati*, "to
play a role, to impersonate," and its ramifications go deep into Mesoamerican religious life. The verb itself is made up of *ixtli*, "face," and
the verb *iptla*, "to substitute," and thus meant literally "to wear a
mask," or "to feign an appearance." The magical ability of the wearer
of a mask to become one with the person or thing represented will surprise no one. What is of interest is the length to which the concept was
carried in Mexico.[2]

The mask or face paint, the regalia, weapons, jewels, and distinguishing colors of each god were specific and inalienable. We can think of
them all together as the mask. But in Aztec thought, inasmuch as a
specific divinity was acquired by the appropriation of his mask, it is obvious that the mask itself was the equivalent of divinity. Thus, it is erroneous, or at least meaningless, to call the Aztec religion anthropomorphic, rather it was—to coin an ugly word—"prosopomorphic."

Except for the priest of Huitzilopochtli, only the *tlatoani* had the
right to wear the face paint and regalia of that god. This is attested as
far back as Chimalpopoca, who, during the crisis preceding the Tepaneca War, had the intention of sacrificing himself while dressed in the
garb of Huitzilopochtli. On the other hand Tlacaelel is presented to us
as the surrogate or "mask" of the great goddess Cihuacoatl; accordingly, he dressed for ceremonial occasions in her well-known white robe.
Thus the two conjoined and fraternal monarchs, Moteuczoma and Tla-

caelel, ruled not only as themselves, but also as the two greatest deities of Mexico, who were sometimes thought in mythology to be siblings.

Huitzilopochtli we already know as the conceptualization of the Mexica themselves in their role as warriors. The figure of the goddess Cihuacoatl is far more complex, for under this name was subsumed numerous other goddesses who were either epithetical divine beings or special facets of her nature. She was either Tonantzin, "the mother," or Toci, "grandmother," or Teteoinnan, "the mother of the gods." As Quilaztli she was the patroness of birth and bore on her back the sacred papoose, which in Mexico was the swaddled sacrificial knife, her first child. As a divine matriarch she was the one in whose temple, the House of Darkness, all the captured gods of the empire were deposited. Seen as the summa of terror in war, she was Yaocihuatl, "enemy woman." As Tzitzimicihuatl she was a gruesome monster who supported the heavens and who threatened to send it crashing down on the land at the end of the aeon. She was of course Mother Earth also, a giant frog who had grinding mouths at every joint, all of them dripping blood. She was spectacularly known to the Mexica as Iztaccihuatl, "white woman," the stately and snowy mountain lying stretched out along the eastern rim of the Great Basin and believed to preside as a queen over all other consecrated mountains. She was thus "the land" itself.

The creation of an office taking its powers directly from the mythology of Cihuacoatl was clearly designed to institutionalize imperialism as an aspect of the state. We know that Tezcoco also had this office, though whether it was a model for Mexico or a derivative from it we do not know.[3] He who—like Tlacaelel and his successors—possessed the office had the duty of interpreting and publishing Cihuacoatl's oracles of blood hunger and of thus setting the state into motion.[4] As mistress of all the lands and of all the gods, Cihuacoatl was the sanction for the state that would ultimately possess all the lands and subdue their gods. The office of *cihuacoatl* was complementary to that of the *tlatoani*, who was as we know the surrogate for Huitzilopochtli. The *cihuacoatl* counseled and urged the ruler by oracles to extend the sweep of empire and therefore to increase the divine consumption of hearts. The *tlatoani*, as surrogate for executive godhead, duly performed such actions as were enjoined.

God and man were inextricably fused in the actions of this state. It was not a theocracy in the accepted sense of the term, for the principle contained in the verb *ixiptlati* insisted that "the mask" ruled, whether it was worn by gods or men. Thus the Mexica thought to avoid the onerous question that arises to plague most governments: by what right do men act as if they were gods?

Priests

There was an elaborate priesthood in Mexico similar in many ways to that in other Aztec cities. At the highest level, the principle of *ixiptlati* also obtained, for in every important temple there served as *texiptla* or "impersonator" a ranking priest or priestess, adorned as was the deity in question.[5] We have seen that Tlacaelel had taken for himself this office as it belonged to the Great Mother, but the two state gods whose shrines were situated on the terrace top of the great pyramid each had his impersonator-priest. Together and equal in status, they were known as "the *quetzalcoatls*," where the word *quetzalcoatl* is the equivalent of "high priest."[6] By identifying these two high offices with the god Quetzalcoatl, Mexico assured its filiation to the Toltec past. These two personages had other functions than those of substitution. They selected the *mexicatl teohuatzin*, "priest of the Mexican god," to act as the administrative superior of the entire priestly order; under him was a *tepan teohuatzin*, "priest of the other gods."[7]

The state thus possessed not only existential contact with the gods through the individual *texiptla* but a continuing, daily, and formal contact through the priest, the *tlamacazqui*. But on the level of crucial and individual action instead of daily service, there was another priestly figure, the *teuctli*.

In addition to his position as "lord" or "baron," the *teuctli* was also a priest. The connection between the *teuctli* as warrior and the *teuctli* as priest is made by his participation in the cult of war. Not only did he participate in this cult, he did it as a member of a formal association, an order—he was an eagle, a jaguar, a puma, or an Otomí knight. Like the medieval Knight Templar of European history, he was a lay priest. But unlike his medieval counterpart, he was not a mere adjunct of the priesthood serving at its altars. Simply put, the gods would go hungry without him, and the universe would decay.

The quasi-priestly warrior associations, each no doubt with its lodge and its venerable rites, came from the distant past, and there probably had never been a time when the Mexica were not so organized—at least into the two higher orders. It is even possible that the two knightly orders had formed the nucleus of the emerging state of Mexico in the early days. If this is correct, it would indubitably place Mexico in the category of a rich and complexly organized cult rather than in the category of states where the state itself is the overriding organization in a society and operates for its own ends exclusively. Mexico, being a state of sorts, did of course operate in the usual way, blindly aggrandizing itself and itself alone. But on another level, it kneeled unquestioningly to greater powers, and it accepted the ends of those powers as the reason for its being. When Tlacaelel and Moteuczoma confirmed Mexican policy to be that of unremitting warfare—regardless of the injury to the state or to the classes of *teuctli* most exposed—they were conducting themselves as priests would who were vowed to strange but very real gods.

The *teuctli* as warrior was involved in the most dangerous of all acts —the cult of sacrifice. The priest, however, was the one who volunteered for the prolonged cruelties of auto-sacrifice.[8] Herein the Mexica were merely carrying out a practice common to all Mesoamerica. Even in the years of the Wandering, the Mexica had with them holy men who could avert the anger of the supernaturals by tormenting themselves with lengthy and bloody penances. The severity of even the common penitential acts in the Aztec world is astounding. Priests would pass long wands, sometimes as many as four hundred, though holes freshly drilled in their tongues, after which they would attempt to loudly sing the praises of the god. Others would wade out into the bitterly cold waters of the lake at night, remain there until exhausted, and then return naked to sleep on the floors of their priestly quarters. An exercise of particular holiness was to run knotted cords through their genitals or to split the penis down to the base, thus achieving the chastity so desired by the god.

In such exercises the Mexican priests were certainly not remiss, but in fame they were surpassed by the four penitential priests of Teohuacan, "the place of the priests," an Aztec province southeast of Cholula.[9] In honor of Quetzalcoatl, these priests held vigil every other night for a full four years, systematically starved themselves, slept on the bare ground summer and winter clad only in skimpy garments, and continually drew blood from their bodies. Many—perhaps most of them—died before their time was up, but their crazed and degenerate oracles were eagerly sought after by the Aztec rulers.

Quetzalcoatl, Patron of the Calmecac

The Mexican state under Moteuczoma was not only articulated and purposeful but, through the *telpochcalli* and the *calmecac*, it was also institutionally self-perpetuating. While in no way remarkable as schools for the young, these two institutions played a strong supporting role in the workings of the state.

The *telpochcalli*, "bachelors' house," was an institution closely connected with the *calpulli*; it is no doubt almost as ancient an urban institution as the *calpulli*, though we know nothing of its past.[10] To this training school located in or near the *calpulli* temple all youths, both commoners and lower nobility, were sent. By the time they were nine years old, they had been entered into these schools, sleeping in the austere dormitories by night but eating in the parental home by day. At dawn they would be assembled from all parts of the city to await in a certain section of the palace for whatever work order the *tlatoani* cared to issue. When the day's labor was over, the youths trooped to the dancing grounds attached to the *telpochcalli* and there under careful supervision danced until midnight the many and intricate dances in which all adult Mexica were expected to become adept.[11]

A captain of the youth was appointed as master in each of the *telpochcalli* with total power over his charges; he stood to them *in loco parentis*.[12] It was he who organized the younger ones into labor gangs to fell trees, dig canals, build houses, till the maize plots of the temples, or clean the aqueducts. The older youths were organized into corps of cadets and rigorously trained in handling weapons. At a certain stage of their training they were allowed to accompany the veteran armies onto the field to observe battle at first hand. In the city they formed police or guard stations on a basis of permanent alert.[13]

The youths were constantly harangued on the need for virtue and obedience. For minor infractions, punishments were cruel in the extreme, for drunkenness, death. As a reward for his initial performance in war, a youth was allowed to keep a concubine; sexual restrictions as they concerned the respectable daughters of the Mexica were harsh. When he was about twenty, already tested in battle and in obedience, this youth could be released from the *telpochcalli* by petition of his parents in order to marry a girl of their choice. By that time he had been thoroughly inducted into the highly masculine society of the Mexica, and he could give his assent to the objectives of the state. He had graduated under the guidance of Yaotl, "the warrior," who was the patron god of the *telpochcalli* and an avatar of the god Tezcatlipoca.[14] He was now a man who, whatever his place in Mexican society, was first of all a warrior and thus convinced of the correctness of the role of the state.

The *calmecac* was a corresponding system reserved for the sons of the highest noble houses.[15] Here was insured the dominance of the Mexican *teuctli* and his continued mastery of the state. Here he received his training for high responsibility; here he was disciplined as cruelly as was his counterpart in the *telpochcalli*. Here he had access to the keys that unlocked the secrets of his culture, for only here, not in the *telpochcalli*, were taught the reading of the sacred books, the arts of painting, of counting the days and years, of placing the festivals of the gods, of chanting the hymns, and of understanding the demands made by the supernaturals. Doubtless, not all the youths who entered the *calmecac* were interested or even adept in these fine arts, in which case they concentrated on the arts of war or on the dispensing of justice, or on dancing, poetry, or exhortation. Nevertheless, all the youths here possessed the rights to this knowledge because of their high status. Such knowledge was dispensed nowhere else. There were at least seven *calmecac* centers in Mexico; the primary one was connected with the temple of the two divinities Huitzilopochtli and Tlaloc. The second ranking one was the Tlillan *calmecac* connected with the temple of Cihuacoatl and training only the great princes.[16] The rest were located in the *calpulli* that represented the original foundations of the city and which were therefore purely Mexican.[17]

In the *calmecac* lived the priests attached to the various temples as well as the youths undergoing training there. This training can be looked upon as a true novitiate, for the youths brought in wood for the sacred braziers, cut penitential thorns, swept the sanctuary and environs, kept night vigils, and sounded the flutes and conch trumpets during the watches of the night. Disobedience or slackness was punished by tying the hands and feet of the boy, sticking his body with thorns, and then rolling him down a series of stone steps.

Being essentially a house of priests, the *calmecac* and all that was in it was devoted to the god Quetzalcoatl, the archetypal priest.[18] When the great barons brought their small sons to be matriculated here, the act was accompanied by gifts to that god and by the formal dedication of the boy himself to Quetzalcoatl. This is one of the more striking features of the Mexican state, for it meant that the man-god Quetzalcoatl of Tula, the epitome of the just ruler and the perfect priest, stood as the mentor of every Mexica *teuctli*. They were as a consequence to be thought of as Toltec knights solidly aligned under the world's only legitimate ruler and heirs of his historic priesthood. It is true that the Mexica, along with the other Aztecs, had the intellectual concept, which they derived from the Toltecs, of a high god who was the author of all life, but, since this god had no priesthood and no mythology, he therefore had no institutional connections with the state and no influence on it. The whole dynamic of Mexico had been irrevocably tied to Quetzalcoatl.

Chichimec Titans

While the Mexican state looked back to Quetzalcoatl and a formalized religion, the Mexica, as a people with a Chichimec tradition, could not forget the demonism of their past. It was this past that dictated the bulk of their popular beliefs. The *teuctli* may well have been an advocate of Quetzalcoatl first and foremost—in this confirming his own sophistication—yet as a Mexican he was not without fearful memories of those ogres known to his ancestors as the *mimix-*

coa.[19] The mythology enshrining them harks back to the period of the Wandering and is revelatory of a substrate in Mexican thought.[20]

The name *mimixcoa* is a plural form and means literally "cloud serpents"; our word "dragons" is a fair approximation. They were the titans, the early supernaturals who had been first experienced by the Mexica hunters when they roamed the *teotlalli*. They were the gods of the lonesome land, mountain gods, earthquake gods, wolves and coyotes appearing as *nahuals* or familiars, spirits of the water courses, of trees, spiny plants and rocks; because of their omnipresence they were called "the innumerable ones," literally "the Four Hundred." They were inauspicious and used sorcery and apparition to affright or destroy people.

The myth relates that they were born of the Earth Mother and they first lived, not inappropriately, in Chicomoztoc, the Seven Caves. They coursed violently over the Godland, and they indulged themselves everywhere arrogantly and immoderately. In this situation of danger from her own sons, the Earth brought forth five more titans who were delegated to tame their bestial brothers. These five probably represented the five directions, for one of them—Mixcoatl (a singular or perhaps a collective form)—represented the center or nether parts of the earth.[21] One of them was a specific landmark, Hawk Mountain. Eagle Serpent was a dryad, a spirit inhabiting the sacred mesquite tree. Another, "Lord of Ditches," had something to do with irrigation, while Wolf Woman was the spirit of the ball game *tlachtli* played out on marked courts in the desert.

These five succeeded in their mission of subduing the Innumerable Ones and in seizing their stronghold, Chicomoztoc. Mixcoatl, who is thenceforth distinguished as the White Mixcoatl, is the personification of all the cloud serpents and is attested to be, through his possession of Chicomoztoc, the special god of the Aztec tribes of Aztlan. He was a sorcerer, a warrior, and a wandering hunter, and he lived inside the great mountain home in the north. He could be worshipped under the form of an arrow.

Viewed as a divine Chichimec chieftain, Mixcoatl is said to have possessed a personal god that he customarily carried about with him in a package on his back. We have seen that this god was in the form of a white knife and was called Itzpapalotl. Quite clearly this was the fetish

—as well as the instrument—of sacrifice, and, as a god of power, it could speak through oracles. In the long Aztec trek to the south, where Mixcoatl was viewed as the personification of all the Aztec tribes, it was Itzpapalotl who guided the people through bodings and presages.[22]

Being Aztecs, the Mexica shared this myth with their fellow tribes; it depicts the Chichimec part of their background. When the Mexica, during the Wandering, broke away from the other Aztlan peoples, Mixcoatl's place as their tribal deity was assumed, as we have seen, by Huitzilopochtli.

But the Mexica used the myth of Mixcoatl now for an ulterior purpose. As self-appointed heirs of Tula, they looked to Quetzalcoatl, the master of civilized life, as their patron. It was necessary, therefore, to connect the Chichimec part of their legend with that patron. So the myth was made to speak further. The titan, Mixcoatl, in his wandering toward the south, came to the lands of the Huitznahuac, which were presumably near Tula. Here the Earth Mother, Cihuacoatl, appeared to him as a naked woman with whom he copulated. The child of that union was Quetzalcoatl.

This Aztec version of the birth of Quetzalcoatl quite apparently does violence to the most important feature of his story, namely that he was a Toltec and a legitimate ruler of Tula. But it did connect the two disparate features of Mexican history—their savage beginnings and their claims to universal dominion. However gauche, that part of the myth was still a necessity. Their Chichimec background had to be shown to be premonitory of and consistent with their Toltec descent.

Quetzalcoatl in Myth and History

Quetzalcoatl played a signal role in the history of Mexican thought. He was, in a sense, both its alpha and its omega. There were five Quetzalcoatls: the ancient sky dragon, the wind god, the morning star, the Toltec culture hero, and the reforming and revolutionary high priest of Tula who was expelled from the city at the end of its history. These transfigurations are never given to us separately, but they intermingle like the play of colors on watered silk in a manner at once both wonderful and frustrating.

The name Quetzalcoatl is best translated as "precious or gala dragon." He is generally thought to have been Huaxtec, and therefore lowland, in origin.²³ He is depicted as a great rattlesnake in the sky whose
writhing body is covered with the brilliant emerald tail feathers of the
quetzal bird. His day sign was one-Reed, Ce Acatl, which also acted as
his name. He was, by extension, the violent wind that precedes the
coming of rain and, as such, he was said to be the harbinger of Tlaloc,
his ambassador or outrunner. Here he was Ehecatl, the Wind; the Nahuatl word for whirlwind or waterspout was *ehecoatl*, literally "wind
snake."²⁴ The twisting, whipping motion of the tornado probably also
explains the "wind jewel," which was Quetzalcoatl's device and which
he wore on his breast as identification; it was a transversely sectioned
cut of a marine conch shell emphasizing the whorl.²⁵

That the feathered dragon who hurtled through the skies was an old
god is attested by his appearance in the culture of Teotihuacan. He was
old enough at any rate to have been split up into several avatars. As the
wind that roams the world, he became the god of far-traveling merchants, Yacateuctli, "the Lord of the nose." Again in reference to his
many peregrinations he could be called Nacxitl, "the traveler." He was
also lord of the dawn, namely the morning star, who, in the splendor
of his rising, demanded the tribute of human sacrifice.

But it is his connections with Tula that particularly interest us. What
seems to emerge from a study of the fragments of legend that are left is
that the ruler of Tula was by that fact considered to be the *texiptla* of
the god Quetzalcoatl. Thus the figure of Quetzalcoatl as a culture hero
of the Toltecs, the master of civilized arts, of the calendar and of divi-
nation, is probably a composite being—all of the historic rulers of Tula
fused into one benevolent being.

But one of these rulers was undoubtedly exceptional, and it was he
who made the myth memorable. This was Topiltzin. The legend about
him and its probable meaning are as follows. In Toltec times a renowned priest of Quetzalcoatl named Topiltzin left his home south of
the Great Basin along with a great following and wandered north to
Tulantzinco, where for four years he settled, this city no doubt being
included at that time within the confines of the Toltec empire. So wide-

spread was this sage's fame that he was insistently petitioned by the Toltecs to come and rule over them in Tula and to reform or renew the cult of Quetzalcoatl already there. We can suspect that the ruling house in Tula must at the time have been radically weakened to allow such a petition from its subjects. Topiltzin Quetzalcoatl agreed, and he established in Tula a revived and reformed version of the cult.

The presence of this great preacher and the astonishing new features in his penitential cult proved to be divisive. In Tula the cult of the young warrior god Tezcatlipoca was also prominent, as one would have expected in an imperial state, and it centered about the act of human sacrifice. Now the newcomer Topiltzin viewed with horror the shedding of blood on the *techcatl*, and he proclaimed for his god only the sacrifice of butterflies, snakes, and birds. He proclaimed the full majesty of his god and announced him to be the high god who needed not men's blood but their services and the chastity of their bodies. The new cult was thus more humane than any of the other Toltec cults, while at the same time it appears to have been severely penitential. The other cults, however, were more congenial to the warriors' lodges of Tula, and they strongly opposed the influence of Topiltzin. Religious tension increased as well as political unrest in the outlying parts of the empire. A fanatic priest-king seldom makes a good and careful administrator.

The turmoil came finally to a head and, in the fury that followed, Topiltzin and his many followers were cast out of the city. This expulsion depleted the population and resources of the city to such an extent as to leave it racked and leaderless for almost a decade. Nonetheless, the priests of Tezcatlipoca had won. Legend has it that a great sorcerer named Huemac soon took over and set up a new Toltec line; in him we can surely see the high priest of Tezcatlipoca and leader of the victorious faction.

The tale of Topiltzin's exile is the core of the legend and its most colorful part. It related how his departure magically and instantly ruined the splendor of the great city. The groves of rich pod-bearing cacao trees turned into spiny mesquite, and the exquisite birds that had fluttered through those halcyon groves flew away before him, down to the coastal lowlands never to return. The treasures Topiltzin had gathered for the city were swallowed up underground, and his wondrously jeweled house was burned to ashes.

At the head of his band, following a route that previous Toltecs had over the centuries pioneered, Topiltzin moved east and south, performing miracles on the way and naming the great mountains on his route. At last he emerged out on the beaches of the Gulf coast where, old and saddened, he built a great pyre and threw himself into the flames. Out of that conflagration his heart flew upward as a golden spark to become the morning star.

Normally the legend would have ended on that climactic note, but historically more had to be explained. Viking-like companies of Toltec warriors, cast out of Tula in times past by reasons of love of adventure or treachery, had fanned out into far parts of Mesoamerica carrying their arms and their arts with them. One important group, carrying with them the original Toltec cult of Quetzalcoatl, had stormed down to the coast and from Coatzacoalcos—the reputed scene of Quetzalcoatl's self-immolation—had left in a fleet of canoes for Tlapallan, the land over the eastern waters (today Yucatan).[26] They had fought and pillaged among the Mayan centers and had finally succeeded in seizing one of them, Chichén Itzá, which they remade into the likeness of Tula, their former home. This far-off land, misty and romantic to the Aztecs, was now brought into a reworked version of the exile legend. Quetzalcoatl had indeed not immolated himself on the shores of the Gulf but rather, stepping onto a raft of serpents, had flown across the foaming waves to Tlapallan. As he left he prophesied that he or his sons would return on some future year designated one-Reed, for that would round out his destiny. In that auspicious year he would again take up the rule of which he had been so wrongfully dispossessed.

We now turn to the other Quetzalcoatl, also named Topiltzin, who was the last ruler of Tula. Whereas the first Topiltzin whom we have just considered flourished in the second half of the ninth century, this the last *tlatoani* of Tula presumably disappeared during the collapse of the Toltec state, traditionally in A.D. 1051. He also was a Ce Acatl Quetzalcoatl. But though he was swept away in the flood of final events, he left a son, Pochotl, and it was this son, as we have seen previously, who carried the blood royal into Culhuacan, whence the Tenochca Mexica derived their own ruling dynasty.

Quetzalcoatl as an Omen to Mexico

When the state which the Mexica were building came to its *floruit* under Moteuczoma and Tlacaelel it was in part supported by this corpus of myth and legend. Mexico believed that its ruling house was of Culua blood, therefore Toltec and therefore imperial. Its priesthood was Toltec, and therefore episcopally descended from Quetzalcoatl. The anti-sacrificial policy of the reformer priest of Tula was discarded by the Mexica as an embarrassment to them—and had it not been discredited by the powers in Tula itself?—wherefore, with all due piety, Mexico continued to wield the sacrificial knife. And the tale of the exile had become for Mexico the prophecy that the long unrolling of the ages would finally produce a year one-Reed when their true sovereign would return from the land of his exile to reclaim his empire.

But the Mexica by the end of their history had altered the tale a bit, tailoring it to fit their uses.[27] It ran in its finally accepted form as affirming that the Mexica were led into the Great Basin in the first instance by a great overlord (Quetzalcoatl) who had soon thereafter returned to his homeland in the sky. Left to themselves, the Mexica had proceeded to marry the women of the land and to build cities. At some time in this initial period, the mysterious ruler had returned to take them back with him to the land of their origin, but they had refused and even repudiated his leadership. In their guilt, they were aware that one of his descendants in time would appear among them and bring them back under the yoke. Mexico by right belonged to him and would have to be relinquished when he appeared. The line of Acamapichtli was a lineage of place-holders until he should come.

The official Mexican version of the prophecy is curious, for it openly admits the truth of Mexica intrusion into the area. We would have expected an attempt to gloss over the fact that they had been invaders and that, like any vagabond people, they had ingressed without women and without the techniques of city life—that in fact they had been nothing more than adventurers. But apparently their past was all too recent for such obvious historical facts to be expunged. The overlord who, in their version, had led them into the land and who claimed vassals far and wide sounds like a smudged conflation of Xolotl, Huitzilopochtli, and Quetzalcoatl. The prophecy of return was apparently too integral a part of the whole Quetzalcoatl story to be omitted. For better or for worse it stood there, an unfinished end to the story. Like a dragon on the mountainside, it loomed portentously over the state below.

As with all Aztec states, Mexico was given to aeonic thinking. Four aeons in the past, each of many thousands of years duration, had cataclysmically ended; vast and agonizing works of rebuilding had then to be performed by the supernaturals after each event. Time itself was ominous even if imperceptible. Whether or not the prophecy of the return of Quetzalcoatl was viewed by the Mexica in the same light as the end of an aeon, it must have in any case signified a present weakness in the state, for it described its coming demise.

9. The Reign of Axayacatl

The last years of Moteuczoma's life had witnessed a significant increase in the power and prestige of Tlatilulco. The brilliant deeds of the Tlatilulca knights led by Moquiuix, plus the energy of the merchants of that city, had produced this efflorescence. In 1466 the Tlatilulca had built a new shrine to house the gods of the people whom, now in alliance with the Three Cities, they were annually subduing.[1] An expanded skull rack stood in their central plaza, built also in that year. More significant was the vast new temple pyramid they were erecting for Huitzilopochtli and Tlaloc, probably in size and sumptuousness even superior to the temple in Tenochtitlan.[2]

This new temple was certain evidence of a rivalry with Tenochtitlan, but not until after the death of Cuauhtlatoa, the client *tlatoani* in Tlatilulco, in 1467 and his replacement by Moquiuix did it become apparent that to this rivalry was to be added a truly malign hostility.[3] We can only assume that, when the aged Moteuczoma installed Moquiuix as *tlatoani* in Tlatilulco, admiration of his war record had obscured for

Moteuczoma the meaning of his dangerous arrogance. In 1468, as one of the very last acts of his life, Moteuczoma invested Moquiuix with the regalia, quite unaware of the omens pointing to the convulsive events ahead.

Axayacatl Succeeds Moteuczoma

Moteuczoma Ilhuicamina Chalchiuhtlatonac died in 1468, probably late in the year. His ashes were buried, along with those of many of his retainers, in the patio of his palace. His death brought to an end the great period of state building in Mexico. The rulers to follow had no reason to appreciably change the structure he had contrived, for the instrument they inherited remained, in terms of Aztec expectations, resilient and sophisticated enough to be enduring. Furthermore, this state now had an intensity of purpose almost unmatched in human history, and this fact lent to it an inner strength as well. Added to this was a masterful principle of succession. The stability of a state is always most crucially tested by the way it passes on power and high office after the lapse of years and the appearance of new generations. Mexico was now to be so tested and to reveal the skill of her makers.

Unaccountably, Moteuczoma had produced only one son, Iquehuac, who was in a position to claim the legitimacy; this son is known to have borne the title *tlacateccatl* at the time of his father's death.[4] According to the rule of succession, the supreme power would normally have passed to a surviving brother, who, in this instance, would have been Tlacaelel. But Tlacaelel had always worn the regalia and he needed nothing more in the way of honors or influence. He therefore refused. This refusal should have cleared the way for Iquehuac.

But Iquehuac was passed over for a reason unknown to us, and Tlacaelel settled on another line of issue from Moteuczoma, one coming down through a legitimate daughter of his. This daughter had married a son of Itzcoatl called Huehue Tezozomoc, and she had produced three sons who were all to become capable warriors and eventually rulers. These sons were, in descending order of age, Tizoc, Ahuitzotl, and Axayacatl. By shifting to this line, certain advantages were to be gained, the first being the assurance that, for the foreseeable future, Mexico would have an assured supply of rulers, all properly descended. A second advantage was that Itzcoatl's blood was directly brought back into the lineage, with all that that implied of added prestige and solidarity. The three brothers were grandsons of both Moteuczoma and Itzcoatl.[5]

There was another reason of almost equal importance. Chalchiuhne-netl, who was a legitimate sister of the three above-mentioned princes and therefore the most prized princess among the Mexica, had been given in guerdon to Moquiuix, the hero of Tlatilulco and now its ruler.[6] Thus the ruler of Tlatilulco would be related to each of the next three *tlatoani* in Tenochtitlan as brother-in-law, supposing that he lived that long. The two Mexicos were now to be tied much more closely together and perhaps even to be fused into one. Tepaneca dignity would be added to Culua splendor in a combined coat of arms.

The selection of the line of Huehue Tezozomoc also smoothed over a still vexing sore spot among the magnates of Mexico, namely the resentment that Itzcoatl's descendency had always felt against Moteuczoma's line for having snatched the office of *tlatoani* from them on the death of Itzcoatl. The advantages of this present settlement were thus numerous and were to fail expectations in only one notable instance.

But the decision to drop down to the three brothers did not end the necessity of making hard choices. Axayacatl was acknowledged to be the leading contender if prowess in war was the criterion of selection; he had been, among other things, commander of the army of the Three Cities, which had moved so successfully against Cuetlaxtlan. But if primogeniture were to dictate the choice, then Tizoc would have to be elected, for he was the eldest of the three. The choice of Axayacatl would be a particular insult to Tizoc since, of the three, Axayacatl was the youngest.

Violent passions there must have been, but they do not seem to have significantly clouded the selection. The office of *tlatoani* was finally adjudged to Axayacatl.[7] This indeed had been adumbrated in the days of Moteuczoma, when that ruler had moved his grandson Axayacatl into that position of honor on the council considered preliminary to such a choice. Finally, the presence of Tlacaelel on the scene and the enormous weight of his influence made certain the peaceful acceptance of the selection. Iquehuac was presumably pacified by being installed as regent for Axayacatl in the interim period while his palace was being built and while he campaigned to acquire victims for sacrifice.

The election was made by Tlacaelel and the princes; the results were agreed to by Nezahualcoyotl and Chimalpopoca of Tlacopan. It was an election made with due regard to custom, to the constitution of the new state, to treaty agreement, and to a balancing of factions. It seems to have been wisely done. There is no doubt—though there is no direct evidence to support this—that Tlacaelel promised the following rule to the disappointed and vindictive Tizoc should Axayacatl's demise precede his; this must have prevented the convulsions that normally would have been expected at this juncture. Tizoc was accordingly advanced to the rank of *tlacochcalcatl* and became one of the four princes.

Axayacatl chose a particularly daring feat to perform as a prelude to his formal installation. Using the new Aztec colony of Oaxaca as a springboard, he thrust across the Sierra Madre del Sur, down to the shores of the Pacific.[8] No Aztec army had penetrated this far before and indeed long strips of this coast were never to submit to the Aztec yoke. But here the vigor and dash of the new *tlatoani* leading his raiders in person effected a complete surprise. A large number of captives was taken from the Tehuantepeca, and the port of Coatulco was visited. Then the army returned northward through a wild and difficult area to Oaxaca and thence home. Though it was only a raid in force and in no sense a conquest, the campaign effectively proved the right of the new *tlatoani* to rule, and he was accordingly invested with his office with all the proper solemnity in 1469. He was now securely occupying the *icpalli*, the royal cushion.

We know little about Axayacatl except that he was a warrior king of some brilliance and that of the three brothers he most exemplified the ideal of the ruler. The name he bore was a common one, generally considered to mean "water face" or "water mask."[9] It was a word used to designate a certain lake insect whose eggs were collected and eaten by the Mexica. Axayacatl had married a princess of Tula in whose veins ran the blood of that legendary city's first king.[10] One son of this union was to be the fabled warrior Tlacahuepantzin, second of that name, and the other was Ixtlilcuechahuac, the latter being sent up to Tula at this time to become its legitimate ruler. Both of these were destined to die heroic deaths later in a tragic and famous flower war with Atlixco. These connections with Tula, the ancient Toltec capital, could not have been fortuitous, and we must believe that policy lay behind them. So interpreted, we can see it as a part of the continuing Tenochca effort to strengthen the ties that bound them to the Toltec past. Nevertheless, Axayacatl's marriage departed from the custom of the Three Cities whereby the legitimate queen in each should be from one of the other two cities. In all other things Axayacatl carried on the laws established by his predecessor and grandfather Moteuczoma.

The Approach of Civil War

But the reign had begun on a discordant note, one that gave cause for grave forebodings among the Tenochca. The coronation ceremonies had been attended by many of the magnates of Anahuac. All was decorous and grave, but one of the great men present was heard to refer slightingly to Axayacatl's manliness. This person was Moquiuix. With the departure from the scene of the redoubtable Moteuczoma, Moquiuix had begun openly to contemn the Tenochca.

The parentage of Moquiuix is unclear, but it is reasonably certain that he was connected with the Tepaneca-Mexica bloodline—a brother of the first Tepaneca ruler in Tlatilulco in fact had been a person called Moquiuix.[11] The valor of this present Moquiuix was unequaled, as his performances in subduing Cuetlaxtlan and Tepeyacac proved. He had held the confidence of Motcuczoma, who had raised him to the rule of Tlatilulco and brought him, by marriage alliance, into intimate relationship with the Tenochca.

None of this was designed to make an already aggressive person such as Moquiuix any less overbearing, and his insults against Axayacatl and the Tenochca were heard more and more openly as time went on. Actual trouble began in the very year of Axayacatl's installation, when Moquiuix put out feelers among the Chalca as to where they would stand if Tlatilulco should challenge Tenochtitlan.[12] The Chalca were in no mood to at that time court disaster, and they turned the secret emmisaries of Moquiuix over to the Tenochca for execution. Our sources are silent on the outcome of this treachery, but relations must have been smoothed over, because in the following year, 1470, we find the knights of Tlatilulco again supporting their Tenochca peers in a campaign down in the coastal lowlands.

The occasion for this latter campaign was a rebellion of Cuetlaxtlan incited by the Tlascala.[13] This rebellion took the usual form of the sudden seizure of all Mexican officials stationed in the province and their execution by torture—in this instance the Mexica had been suspended by their heels over smouldering fires of hot chile peppers and thus horribly strangled. Mexico threw in an army with such expedition as to forestall Tlascalan aid and crush the rebellion. Punishment was extreme. The entire nobility of Cuetlaxtlan was rooted out, and a whole new one created by fiat; the tribute was doubled. Other cities in Totonacapan that had participated were similarly crushed and prisoners brought back to fatten the gods. Tlatilulco sacrificed her share of these victims.

The year 1472 saw many events beginning to converge on a situation of confrontation between the two moieties of Mexico. A restraining hand was removed when the venerable Nezahualcoyotl, lord of the Acolhua, died.[14] His demise indeed marked a watershed in the history of all Anahuac, for he had been a figure of more than heroic proportions, greater even than Moteuczoma. He was the perfect Aztec knight and had received, in reference to his great personal strength, the additional name Acolmiztli, "lion paw." While a loyal member of the Three City League ever since its formulation, he had still pursued a brilliant and independent policy of his own. Besides his unmatched military career and his avenging of his father, he was a poet of renown, a builder and engineer of original genius, and a lawgiver. Even the Mexica had considered him the most estimable of men and the greatest of emperors. He left the young prince Nezahualpilli as his successor under the tutelage of a regent.

Tenochtitlan must have had difficulty in trying to divine the exact course events would take from this point on, but it certainly could expect that Tlatilulco might attempt something of advantage to itself during this hiatus in rule. Whether 1472 was also the year when Iquehuac, the disgruntled uncle of Axayacatl, tried to put together his own conspiracy and seize power in Mexico, is not known, but it certainly occurred no later than this. In some fashion or other the completion of the temple by Tlatilulco previously mentioned (1472) is said to have also exacerbated feelings. This was a shrine to the goddess Chantico, which is said to have been an answer to the completion of a shrine the Tenochca had built to Coatlicue.[15] The reference is unclear but the rivalry is evident.

The conspiracy now beginning to form in Tlatilulco had its roots in the past. It was as if an ineluctable fate had decreed that the two branches of the Mexica should finally meet in an ultimate contest. But it was ironic that it should have come at the very time when the Tenochca were on the point of allowing the Tlatilulca once again to resume their former places as free Mexica. The two cities had been cooperating reasonably well, and Moquiuix had even been reconfirmed in his office by Axayacatl in spite of the crude insinuations Moquiuix was known to have cast against him. This Tenochca laxness—or amiability—is as difficult for us to analyze as Tlatilulca intransigence.

There were two factions in Tlatilulco, one desiring war with Tenochtitlan, the other fearful of her vast power. The former party was led by a son-in-law of Moquiuix called Teconal, a man as impulsive and fire-breathing as Moquiuix. In addition to him there was Poyahuitl, the high priest in Tlatilulco, who also favored immediate hostilities.[16] It was difficult for the party of caution to get a proper hearing, and, when Teconal was raised to the dignity of *huitznahuatl*, the voices for peace sank glumly away. That it would be a civil war, a slaughter of brother by brother, was of little account. The weight of the past, when they had been all one people out in Aztlan, seems to have been nothing as compared to the supposed weight of their present grievances.

It was obvious to all the magnates secretly debating the enterprise in Tlatilulco that allies would be needed though, by approaching and concerting with them, the advantages of complete surprise would thereby have to be waived.[17] After some discussion in their conclaves of the night, the Tlatilulca decided to approach first the Tlateputzca communities—Tlascala, Huexotzinco, and Cholula especially—all of them known to be strongly anti-Mexican. The plan was sound, though what Tlatilulco was prepared to offer to Tlascala to entice her into the alliance is unknown. In any event, the approach failed, for a reason that

Tlatilulco had not considered. The Tlascalans—permanently suspicious of all things Mexican—could not believe that Mexico was indeed split to that extent; consequently they could only surmise a plot to lure them to their own destruction. Huexotzinco was favorably inclined but sent no aid.

The war party turned then to an area where historic attachments and antipathies seemed more likely to produce allies; these were the Otomí and Tepaneca communities on the western shoreline—Azcapotzalco, Tenayuca, Xilotepec, Toltitlan, Cuahuacan, Chiapan, and Cuauhtitlan. With these cities of the old Tepaneca empire Tlatilulco traditionally had close ties. Though we are told that Tlacopan was approached, it is most unlikely that this was so, for the allegiance of this city to the Three City League was well known. Matlatzinca and Mazahuaca cities in the Toluca Basin over the mountain appear to have been vitally interested and offered themselves as allies against Tenochtitlan—with significant consequences for their own future as free cities. Cuauhtitlan, on the contrary, stood firmly with the empire, so Moquiuix offered that city to the nearby Otomí as their share of the postwar spoils if they would guarantee to pin it down for the duration of hostilities.

But the most important communities expected to adhere to this alliance were the Chinampaneca cities. Their bitterness toward Mexico was enduring, and it was fully expected that they would not hesitate should any rational plan be devised to destroy Tenochtitlan. Their response, however, was mixed. Eventually, Cuitlahuac under its two governors as well as the cities of Huitzilopochco and Culhuacan committed themselves. Xochimilco was more cautious and preferred to have a foot in both camps—or rather in none.

Tenochtitlan was not unaware of this powder keg being laid at its door; in fact the sounds of Tlatilulca contempt directed against her were growing increasingly more strident. In her turn, Tenochtitlan must have gone among her allies and subjects informing them of what was afoot, intimidating them where necessary, or offering concessions. Like the forerunning winds of Quetzalcoatl, these gusts of harsh feeling chilled and dampened the hearths of all Anahuac, but from the brunt of the great storm itself Tenochtitlan felt relatively secure.

There was still commerce between the two Mexicos, for the great

market in Tlatilulco was almost a necessity to the ongoing life of Tenochtitlan. But incidents were becoming almost a daily occurrence as
Tenochca braves continued to swagger defiantly through the stalls, re-
viling and molesting the women.[18] In retaliation, harlots from Tlatilulco ranged about the streets of Tenochtitlan shrieking prophesies of disaster on that city. An important access canal leading into the central
lagoon of Tlatilulco was found blocked one morning, and again, more
seriously, one of the aqueducts bringing potable water in to the center
of Tlatilulco was broken; this happened perhaps more than once. As the
tension mounted among the populace, Moquiuix ordered the stepped-
up training of an additional two thousand cadet warriors, young
men normally classed as novices and never committed to battle. The
shoal waters off the northern and western approaches to the city now
began to witness in the first glimmering of the dawn the maneuvers
of these youths as they attempted to bring down marsh birds and even
swallows in full flight with darts hurled by the *atlatl*. Tlatilulco was
outnumbered and knew it. She needed all of her men, and they would
need all of their cunning.

The full effects of this tragedy of deteriorating relations were visited
upon Chalchiuhnenetl, Moquiuix's queen. She had borne her husband
two sons, one of them named after her brother Axayacatl. This was the
progeny intended to be a firm family bridge between the two cities and
an earnest of their amicable future. Later tales had it that this queen
was ugly and that Moquiuix—to whom were attributed various and
lurid sexual scandals—finally abandoned her in the harem to the insults
and harassments of the other wives and concubines. Portents are nevertheless supposed to have warned him of the onrushing danger; a mask
on the wall uttered words that impelled him to blindly smash it, and
the lips of his queen's vulva are said to have spoken dark words of woe
to him.[19] There is probably truth in at least some of the stories of ill
treatment suffered by this woman of the Aztec past caught up as she
was in the disastrous politics of two of the great cities of Anahuac.

So serious did the provocations become that Chalchiuhnenetl, with
her sons, was finally reclaimed by her royal brothers in Tenochtitlan. It
is reported that she brought information with her concerning the conspiracy then being evolved in Tlatilulco. In the Aztec world no family

of standing could offer a daughter or sister to another family in marriage and not be insulted in its every member to the same degree that she was. The time had now obviously come for one or the other side to make its opening move.

Culhuacan is the only city that guaranteed to begin hostilities against Tenochtitlan by the side of Tlatilulco. The Matlatzinca were too far away to be in at the opening gambit, but they and some of the Chinampaneca cities were to come in as soon as practicable. On these somewhat shaky promises of aid, Teconal convinced his peers in Tlatilulco that they need wait no longer, that in fact they could win even if they fought alone.

The War of Defilement

The brief and deadly war that broke out in 1473 between Tenochtitlan and Tlatilulco was in one sense a civil war between the two moieties of the Mexican state and in another sense the final act of the Tepaneca War long delayed. The tragic flaw in the history of the Mexica had been their separation into two camps after their defeat at Chapultepec, one group given a Culua coloring after years of servile residence in the territory of Culhuacan, the other to undergo a policy integration into the imperial plans of Azcapotzalco and the remaking of its aristocracy on a Tepaneca model. And then fate had added to the tension between these fraternal peoples by placing their cities cheek by jowl in the reeds of the same lake. It appeared to be fortuitous and nothing more that they should hate each other now, for they both worshipped the same ancestral god, though with slight variations, and they looked back to the same origins. There are strong hints that certain of the strategically placed *calpulli* in Tenochtitlan actually went over to Tlatilulco and were to be involved in the final disaster.[20]

Speaking from his office of high priest in Tlatilulco, Poyahuitl now demanded the full commitment of all the knights of that city to the cause.[21] Breathing fire, he officiated at a ceremony where water was poured over the *techcatl*, encrusted as it was with the dried blood of years of human sacrifice, from the putrid offscourings of which was brewed a war potion. Each of the leading warriors partook of it in order to attain the full measure of ferocity. A consummating oath accompanied by sacrifice was then taken, in secret and at night, on the holy mount of Tepeyac, home of the great goddess, its bare rock face looming just to the north of their island. It was now recognized that the inevitable struggle would be against great odds, and Moquiuix knew he would need from every one of his knights the ultimate in courage. Thus the powerful incantations.

Tenochtitlan seems to have awaited the impending onslaught with a mixture of confidence and care. More cunning than Moquiuix, Axayacatl apparently preferred not to show his hand until the event should occur, for it was probably still not clear what parts of the Tenochca empire might defect under pressure. City against city and man against man, Axayacatl knew that he could win. Numbers were on his side, but there was always the worry that, with the recent death of Nezahualcoyotl, the Acolhua might not provide sufficient aid to counterbalance a massive upheaval in the empire should it occur. Therefore, with confidence but perhaps also with some trepidation, the great Tenochca barons stood to their arms, men of valor like Tizoc, Ahuitzotl, Tlilpotonqui, Xippille, Totomatzin, Tzontemoc, Tenamatzin. The lesser knights and the commoners of the *calpulli* were similarly prepared and no less tense.

A last attempt was made by Axayacatl and the princes to avoid the disaster. They dispatched Cueyatzin, a highly esteemed nobleman, to Tlatilulco with words of reason.[22] He was summarily returned to them with taunts and insults. On receiving news of this treatment, the aged Tlacaelel was beside himself with rage, and in an address before the magnates expressed his opinion that no other recourse was left to Tenochtitlan but to formally declare war on Tlatilulco. Cueyatzin was sent back to Tlatilulco with the demand that it surrender. The embassy was rejected out of hand. Cueyatzin was cut down and killed by the fiery Teconal, and his headless body thrown into the ditch that separated the two cities.

Moquiuix seems to have made a serious error in allowing events to get out of hand, for he now had to throw his forces against Tenochtitlan before the time agreed upon with his secret ally, Xiloman of Culhuacan. Because of this impetuosity on the part of the enemy, Tenochtitlan was not forced to the difficult posture of withstanding attack from two sides at once. Even so, the situation was critical, and for a period the outcome was in doubt.

The course of events in this brief civil war is unclear, and its exact duration even more so. There are two contrasting versions, that of the victors and that of the vanquished. We are probably not far wrong if we accept the fact that the actual hostilities lasted merely a few days—perhaps only two days of intense fighting. This at least is consistent with the fact that Culhuacan, which finally did move in and block some of the passages on the southern causeway, nevertheless did not ever significantly come to grips with Tenochtitlan or press an all-out attack. The other Chinampaneca cities fervently hoped, of course, that the hated Tenochca would be crushed, but in their semi-paralysis they too failed to make determined moves. In fact, by the time a few of them had begun to send their men into battle, it was already too late and Tlatilulco had been crushed.

The peoples of the Toluca Basin appear to have been also partially immobilized by the suddenness of events and sent aid to Tlatilulco too late. Cuauhtitlan in the north was standing siege from Otomí neighbors and could send only 160 archers to the aid of Tenochtitlan, but Tezcoco sent the expected contingents. Tlacopan, true to her place in the Three City League, stood loyally by Tenochtitlan and was an important factor blocking the advance of the Toluca peoples from the west.

Thus the *tlazolyaoyotl*, "the war of defilement" as it was later called, was essentially a duel between two cities where heavy reinforcements were available to one side only.[23] It is surely an understatement to say that all of Anahuac watched the event very closely; a victory for Tlatilulco would have had immense repercussions for all of Mesoamerica.

Tlatilulco attacked at dawn.[24] Because of the disparity in numbers, all her warriors and even her cadets in training where thrown in. There were no reserves, and even the women of Tlatilulco took an active part in the fighting. That day's contest was unprecedented in fury. The canal separating the cities had been easily crossed, and a penetration of some depth had early been made into Tenochtitlan. The Tenochca in fact were forced to burn some of the houses in that area to prevent them from being used as shelters for the invaders.

But treason had been at work. Five nobles of Tlatilulco led by Ehecatzitzimitl, "Wind Demon," had previously been in touch with a certain Tenochca who had used them as paid spies. Thus, while the impe-
tus of the initial attack carried the Tlatilulca a short way into the target
area, the attack itself was expected and possibly even known in detail.
By nightfall Tenochca power had begun to tell; the Tlatilulca had
been brought to a full halt, and it was apparent to Moquiuix and Teconal that they had failed miserably to achieve the tactical surprise they
had counted on. Furthermore, Culhuacan, which had guaranteed to
advance from the south, was now seen to be half-hearted at best. During that night, Tlatilulco sacrificed some twenty Tenochca warriors
captured in the initial rush, but that was the extent of their success.

With the following dawn, the whole weight of the Tenochca counterattack struck the Tlatilulca warriors desperately clinging to their
beachhead in the northern suburbs of Tenochtitlan. An allied canoe
fleet had gained control of the water and now moved out of the darkness
to threaten Tlatilulco on the flanks, while Axayacatl's army poured vic-
toriously over the canal to begin the work of fraternal killing in earnest. There was no lack of heroism on the part of the now greatly outnumbered Tlatilulca, and the women took their places beside the men.
But there was no hope. The chance had been taken, and there was
nothing left to wager.

Because a working alliance between Tlatilulco, Culhuacan and the
Matlatzinca had failed to materialize in time, Axayacatl was now able
to send his greatest captains against Tlatilulco from all sides at once.
All day the din of war filled the streets of Tlatilulco. The hoarse shouts
of veteran knights and the screams of the women and children mingled
with the occasional crash of falling walls as they were toppled in on defenders within or spilled over to give a clear way for the showering
darts of those on the advance. The dust early became choking and even
billowed slowly out beyond the outermost houses to hang in a pall over
the lake. The heavy thud of canoes striking each other in this nebulous
exhalation from a dying city would be followed by an instant's silence
and then by violent splashing and tumult and always the cursing and
cries of men.

The Tlatilulca fought now because there was nothing else to do. The weak and the wounded floundered out into the adjoining reed beds for a few hours of safety before death from exhaustion or bleeding overtook them. The slaughter increased in tempo as the blood-maddened Tenochca pressed in toward the great marketplace and the towering temple next to it. Here the closing scene was enacted when Moquiuix, with only a handful of warriors left, retreated fighting up the temple steps to make a last stand on the summit. The denouement was in the nature of things not long delayed. The loyal knights of Tlatilulco died with their obsidian-bladed clubs in their hands surrounding their *tlatoani*. When there were too few left to matter, Moquiuix brought resistance to an end by leaping off the terrace top to tumble to an instant death below. His corpse was seized by the exultant Tenochca warriors and dragged back to Copulco, the closest *calpulli* in Tenochtitlan, and there delivered to Axayacatl, who sacrificed it in the customary style to the god of battles. Effective resistance then ceased. The body of Teconal was located among the piles of dead and impaled on a stake beside the bridge that connected the two cities. There the grisly relic—eventually nothing but clanking bones—would be seen forever by all inhabitants of Tlatilulco crossing the canal on their way to Tenochtitlan. As for the disorganized remainder of the people, most tried to flee up the northern causeway to Tepeyac but were met by Tenochtitlan's allies at Coyonocazco and forced off the causeway into the water. Here they drowned by the hundreds.

The Tenochca, considering themselves the aggrieved party, were now engaged in the butchery of every inhabitant of Tlatilulco whom they could locate and, given another full day, they might well have attained a genocide of mammoth proportions. Only the personal intercession and tearful pleading of a Tlatilulca nobleman, who was an uncle of Axayacatl, stood between his city and total destruction. His plea was successful, and Axayacatl gave the order to his knights to halt the massacre. This they did, but the city of Tlatilulco itself was given up to total pillage, while the survivors were scorned and mocked by being forced to quack like ducks and tumble about in the slime flailing their arms as if simulating flight. Four hundred and sixty Tlatilulca magnates had died, all famous warriors. There is no record of the numbers of the lower *teuctli*, merchants, or *macehualtin* killed; there could have been no accurate count. Ironically, some contingents of fighters from Tlatilulco's most distant allies—possibly the Matlatzinca—arrived when the city was already being put to the sack.

Tlatilulco Defeated

The aftermath of the War of Defilement reveals that Tenochtitlan was little disposed to offer mercy to those who had disturbed her peace. While her allies in the Three City League had indeed stood firm, the Chinampaneca cities had wavered, and had the Matlatzinca moved with more expedition, the affray might well have become protracted enough to have spawned a mighty storm of vengeance called into being by all the oppressed peoples of Anahuac. This had not happened, but it was enough that it might have. Tenochtitlan began methodically to punish the perpetrators, proven or suspected.

Heretofore Tlatilulco's foreign policy had been subordinated to Tenochtitlan, but its independence had been relatively untouched. A treaty arrangement had regulated the joint affairs of the two Mexicos. It had been recognized that whenever she was in need of support, Tlatilulco would turn to Tenochtitlan first. Tlatilulco had been more an allied state than a subject. Moquiuix and Teconal, his son-in-law, had altered all of this.

Root and branch, the sovereignty of Tlatilulco was destroyed, bringing to an end the princely house that had begun with Cuacuauhtzin, son of the old Tepaneca dynast Tezozomoc.[25] The palace in Tlatilulco was condemned and left unoccupied to become a depository of trash and human offal. Huitzilopochtli's image was seized and carried off as a prisoner to become no doubt a minor demon in a dark cell in Cihuacoatl's house, while the sumptuous pyramid temple he had inhabited was abandoned to wreckage and became a public latrine. The high priest Poyahuitl, who had so actively encouraged the war party, along with the traitor Ehecatzitzimitl, were pointed out in the market place and punished appropriately. It appears that their faces were mutilated and they were left to become—till the time of their death—walking and breathing mementoes in Tlatilulco of the dangerous game they had once played against the majesty of the Tenochca state. Without their tribal god and without his high priest, the people of Tlatilulco thenceforth had to worship the Huitzilopochtli of the Tenochcas. There was no more effective way of sterilizing an Aztec people.

The members of the *teuctli* class in Tlatilulco who had survived the slaughter were subjected to a permanent disability, for they were now required to provide Huitzilopochtli with a stated number of prisoners of war on each of the eighty-day tribute periods. If these were not forthcoming the nobles were condemned to sit at home with their women and not to appear carrying their arms or wearing those distinctive devices and costumes that announced their manly status and that were as dear to them as life itself. To escape this ultimate humiliation, parties of Tlatilulca knights were thenceforth continually on the prowl, roaming foreign countrysides, raiding and searching out victims, or engaging in flower wars with Huexotzinco or Atlixco. The aging Tlacaelel, who in his great nostalgia during the conflict had accoutered himself as formerly in full warrior's garb, viewed this new success of his life-long policy with satisfaction. The effect of all this on the Tlatilulca baronage was to bring it powerfully back into the sacrificial cult while at the same time clipping its wings against any further bid for supremacy.

The tribute imposed on Tlatilulco included more than the delivery of a stated number of sacrificial victims. It also included labor service, and a part of this was the obligation to repair annually certain temples. And as with any other conquered nation, some of the corn lands belonging to Tlatilulco on the mainland were stripped away and assigned to deserving Tenochca knights. The lower classes became hewers of wood, sweepers and cleaners of temples and porters for the army in time of war—in all they became almost a servile class. The wealth of the important merchant class, the *pochteca*, was taken over as plunder, and the great market place was split into its respective commodity sections with each section being assigned to either Axayacatl or to one of his magnates. A tax of 20 percent on all sales was levied and delivered over to the Tenochca noble holding that particular market franchise.

With the loss of its sovereignty Tlatilulco also had to accept the military government commonly imposed on twice-offending states.[26] As far as we can see, this involved the imposition of a *cuauhtlatoa*, literally "eagle-speaker," who appears to have held proconsular power.

The office in Tlatilulco was dual, consisting of the *cuauhtlatoa* himself, who was of the rank of *tlacochcalcatl* and was a Tenochca appointee, while at his side there ruled his counterpart, of *tlacateccatl* rank, elected by the nobles of Tlatilulco. It seems probable that it was this latter who saw to it that the Tenochca policies, filtered from Tenochtitlan through the *cuauhtlatoa*, were carried out by his people. He was elected from among the members of the formerly ruling house of Tlatilulco and possessed, because of that fact, the dignity necessary to one who gave orders. This dual institution was a remarkably serviceable office, for it removed from the conquering power the responsibilities of direct rule while allowing it to keep a constant check on the policy of the conquered.

In prestige the office of *cuauhtlatoa* was lesser than the office of *tlatoani*, for the incumbent did not wear the *copilli* or crown. Nevertheless, the imposition of this office did not uproot or demean the *teucyotl* or baronial system so fundamental to the Aztec state. While Tenochtitlan mocked and all but enslaved their conquered brothers, they never contemplated inducing among them a revolution that would in any way attack the concept of knighthood, for this would have brought in question their own social structure.

Whereas before this time the term "Mexico" had denoted only a center of power in the lake, now by an act of war it had come to denote a single integrated state. In the process Tlatilulco was to become little more than another *calpulli* in Mexico, though indeed a large one . Yet over the years Tlatilulco would slowly regain its standing and most of its former wealth. This development was based upon the fading of the old Tepaneca arrogance and the acceptance by the Tlatilulca nobility of the essentially corporate quality of all of the Mexica. This unity, which the Mexica had lost after Chapultepec, they had by the ordeal of arms somewhat regained. Yet it would not be permanent.

The Wrath of Mexico

It was now the turn of those who had offered aid to Tlatilulco to suffer retribution.[27] Mexico moved with speed and thoroughness. Of all the imperial cities, the Chinampaneca had appeared on the eve of battle to be the most threatening, and, though they had not succeeded in delivering a heavy strike against Tenochtitlan, their complicity had been open for all to see.

Xiloman, the powerful ruler of Culhuacan who had agreed to come to the aid of Tlatilulco but who had backed off when Moquiuix sprang his trap too soon, was taken and killed along with twenty of his barons. The tribute obligation was revised, and new *calpixque* installed there to see that the increased and undoubtedly crushing imposition was collected. The ruler installed lasted only some two months and had to be replaced. Culhuacan, source of all of Tenochtitlan's claims to greatness and legitimacy, shuddered now under the iron hand of her former ward. Cuitlahuac had been under military government of the Three Cities but nevertheless had also wavered. Its two governors were executed, as was also the ruler of Huitzilopochco.

Xochimilco had sided with Tenochtitlan and for the moment had nothing to fear, but Mexico, ever alert to spectral presences, was still not satisfied and kept searching for evidence of treachery. Whatever the basis of his suspicions—and it might have been simply a general Mexican envy of Xochimilco's claim to Toltec legitimacy—Axayacatl had occasion not long after the war to invite Xihuiltemoc, ruler of that city, to play at *tlachtli* with him in Mexico. Needless to say, such an invitation was a command. The tale runs that Xihuiltemoc, or the particular champion whom he had selected to play for him, incautiously won the match. Axayacatl had wagered to return all of the recently collected tribute from Xochimilco against some additional lien on Xochimilco—perhaps the outright possession of all their corn lands. In any event, Axayacatl's plans had gone awry when his player lost the game to Xochimilco. He felt the indignity sufficiently to secretly command that Xihuiltemoc be done away with. Accordingly, the latter was invited to a banquet where, after the festivities, he was ostensibly honored by having a garland of flowers thrown about his neck—but hidden in the garland was a rope with which he was incontinently strangled. Xochimilco, the largest and most beautiful of all the Chinampaneca cities and a center of the ancient Toltec art of jade working, selected as its next ruler a person totally acceptable to Mexico.

A more far-reaching act of vengeance was being taken under consideration by Mexico against the several peoples of the Toluca Basin.

These, the Matlatzinca, Mazahuaca, Ocuilteca, and others, had been among those who had heeded Tlatilulco's siren song; therefore they had invited condign punishment upon themselves. None of these peoples were Aztec, the major component among them being Otomí, but all had formed important provinces in the old Toltec empire and therefore had strong links with that illustrious past. Between them and the Aztecs lay high terrain and ghostly forests of fir and oak; the time had come—in the opinion of the Mexica—to leap this barrier and satisfy the continuing need for conquest as well as the desire for revenge. The civil war in Mexico thus had the result of turning Mexico's armies to the west and northwest, and this was to be the direction of Mexican interest for the remainder of Axayacatl's reign.

Like the Great Basin next to it, the Toluca area stood on the edge of the Southern Escarpment and was presided over by the stately and isolated volcano Tolotzin.[28] It too contained in those days a central lake that drained away to the northwest through the Lerma River. Numerous industrious communities and temples lay scattered about in the area, which was not only rich agriculturally but was politically important, for it served as a buffer between the Aztecs and the Tarascans farther to the west. Should the Three Cities succeed in annexing the Toluca Basin, their influence would immediately abut on the homeland of the Tarascans, a part of Mesoamerica of considerable extent and defended by able warriors.

The Advance to the Tarascan Frontier

Totoquihuaztli, ruler of Tlacopan and the Tepaneca, had died at an advanced age either just before or during the civil war in Mexico.[29] Thus had departed the last *tlatoani* from the initial days of the Three City League. A new generation now ruled: Axayacatl in a united and therefore strengthened Mexico, Nezahualpilli in Tezcoco, and Chimalpopoca, legitimate heir to the throne in Tlacopan. These three potentates saw eye to eye on all matters of common policy, and the future of their conjoint empire looked bright indeed.

Mexico's plans for retribution against the cities of the Toluca Basin coincided with Chimalpopoca's own orientation; the empire of Tlacopan extended well back into the mountains and forests that separated it from the Toluca area, and it had long looked to breaking out of this cloud land and swarming down to acquire additional holdings in the richly settled corn lands beyond.

The occasion for war was not long in coming.[30] Toluca, the main city of the Matlatzinca, had a falling out with Tenantzinco, a city that guarded the pass down into the lands to the south. The lord of Tenantzinco came in person to Mexico to request assistance in this quarrel. Axayacatl responded immediately in the affirmative and dispatched ambassadors to the Matlatzinca, demanding that they provide Huitzilopochtli with stone and timber for the renovation and enlargement of his temple, at that time in progress. This was the usual summons either to war or to submission. Toluca refused the request and set about girding herself with allies against the inevitable onslaught.

The Matlatzinca army advanced eastward to the marshy banks of the Lerma River in order to oppose the invaders on their own frontier. In so doing, however, it had to expose its right flank to the forces of Tenantzinco coming up from the south. A battle was fought here that ended in victory for the Three Cities. The shattered warriors of Toluca fell rapidly back upon their city but were unable to organize a defense in time and were straightway overrun. Their god was seized and taken in captivity to Mexico and his shrine burned. With this Mexico considered herself avenged; the year was either 1474 or 1475.

Chimalteuctli, the *tlatoani* of Toluca, was left in his office and made responsible for the delivery of a heavy tribute. However, the two Matlatzinca lords ruling under him were killed, thus leaving him alone responsible for pleasing the victors. The Three Cities divided the booty and lands taken in their usual fashion, installed *calpixque* as their resident agents for tribute, and then returned to celebrate their respective triumphs.

The ceremonies ordered for Mexico were outstanding, for, with the numerous prisoners taken, Axayacatl was able to dedicate adequately the enlarged central temple, as well as a new gladiatorial stone and a *cuauhxicalli*, "sun vessel."[31] Tlacaelel—his thirst for blood in no wise abated by his advancing age—at this point advised that Cempoalla and Quiauiztlan, two as yet unincorporated provinces on the Gulf coast, be invited to witness the festive slaughter. His contention was that if they accepted they would be intimidated by the splendor and ferocity of the event, while their refusal would allow the Mexica legitimately to consider them as unfriendly and to make war upon them. The peremptory invitations were accepted.

In 1476 the alliance with Tenantzinco led to further involvement in the area of the Southern Escarpment. Ocuilan was conquered, Mexican influence was exercised in Malinalco, and Cuauhnahuac further punished for some reason unknown to us.

In the short time that Chimalteuctli had ruled as vassal lord of the Mexica over the conquered Matlatzinca, he had managed to sow the seeds of a further disaster for his people. To curry favor with his new Aztec masters he had ruled so oppressively—exacting from his people the last ounce of their energies and their last handful of dried maize—that in 1477 they rose up and, in a volcanic explosion of popular resentment, swept him and all vestiges of Aztec rule from the scene. Almost all of the communities of the Toluca Basin took part in the revolt.

The sequel could have been foreseen. The Mexica and their allies returned and this time made sure of the area. After a truly desperate but ineffectual opposition, the recalcitrant people subsided. Numbers of them fled westward to seek refuge among the Tarascans of Michoacan, their neighbors in that direction. The Matlatzinca who remained in the basin were subjected to all the rigors and miseries of military government under alien commissars.

Exhilarated by this second victory over the unfortunate Matlatzinca, Axayacatl was now led to commit Mexico to a venture that was dubious at best and at worst a thorough disaster. This was to be an attack upon the Tarascan nation in its homeland, the vast stretches of lands rolling west to Lake Chapala.

In this giant land lying between the Balsas and the Tepalcatepec Rivers on the south and the Lerma on the north the Tarascans were kings. Vast shallow basins scattered throughout this area were separated by low mountains, their upper slopes thickly forested. In the north, the lower parts of the ranges and the valley floors were semiarid and produced mainly cactus and mesquite where jackrabbits and the white-tailed deer made their runs. Farther south were dense forests.

Lakes were numerous up on this plateau country—thus the name of a center that was later given to the whole land, Michoacan, "the place of those with fish"; some of the lakes were of great extent. Here fishing and fowling was a way of life, very much as with the peoples living in and around Lake Tezcoco. The Tarascans had over the centuries been spilling off these cool steppes, down over the lip of the Southern Escarpment, into the hot and labyrinthine *barranca* country below. They were a people of all seasons, far ranging within their territory, accurate and dreaded bowmen. They showed strong affinities with the Chichimecs, who had heavily infiltrated their land. However, unlike the Chichimecs, they were ruled in all their diverse communities by one overlord. He resided on the shores of Lake Pátzcuaro and from his capital, today called Tzintzuntzan, he held sway over his people. In some curious way the Mexica seemed to have felt a relationship between themselves and the Tarascans, though their languages were dissimilar.[32] It is as good a guess as any that Aztlan, the legendary home of the Aztecs, was located somewhere in this part of the Mesa Central or just to the north of it.

Mexico Defeated at Zamacoyahuac

Mesoamerica is a land of travelers and, though its distances are formidable, splendid vistas open up everywhere to visually draw one onward. In those days its northern parts were crossed only by lonesome parties of merchants, by bands of mercenary Teochichimecs, and very occasionally by clusters of pilgrims, the dust from their feet lifting lazily into the air and announcing their approach to the sharp-eyed scout a long day in advance. In the middle parts, green and broken with high hills and lonely lakes, were the villages and ceremonial centers of the Tarascan enemy. Now the dust of Michoacan was to be stirred for the first time by an Aztec army.

Twenty-four thousand warriors of the Three Cities and their subjects, having first rendezvoused in the Toluca Basin, marched through the low hills past Ixtlahuaca and out toward the settlement of those Matlatzinca who had just previously fled their own country. At a certain high place farther on, Axayacatl called a halt and prepared a base.

Here in the daytime, for almost as far as the eye could see over the hillsides, stretched a sea of mat shelters, the tents of the warriors, while at night the campfires and pine torches of the officers twinkled like a carpet of fireflies laid down over the land. Below them in a deep valley was Tlaximaloyan, the first strong Tarascan community, settled and defended by Otomí and ruled by a great marcher lord of the Tarascans.[33]

The military confrontation that ensued was to be—until 1521—the crowning disaster in Mexican military history.[34] Tlaximaloyan was taken in the first rush and thoroughly destroyed, but then the bulk of the Tarascan host put in its appearance, greatly outnumbering even the numerous Aztecs. Chichicha, the Tarascan ruler who had succeeded in luring the Aztecs well out beyond their capabilities, now undertook to drive them back.[35] Reluctantly evacuating the Otomí center, the Mexican army began the long and hazardous retreat. In harsh and sometimes dessicated terrain they moved eastward, continuously pursued by the enemy. There was no relief from the pressure and finally, at a place called Zamacoyahuac, Axayacatl was brought to bay.[36] He arranged his army for attack.

Axayacatl threw rank after rank of reserves into the melee on that ill-omened day, though he had been cautioned against it. Quantities of *yolatl*, "the broth of bravery," made of water and ground maize, were taken out into the press of battle by the squires, but the heat and the exertion had turned Axayacatl's veteran eagles and jaguars into automatons, and they lost ground steadily. Night fell over the terrible scene, and new supplies of darts and lances were rushed into the Aztec camp. With the appearance of dawn, Axayacatl ordered an all-or-nothing charge that his warriors were ill-prepared to deliver. One of Mexico's four princes was killed on the field; thousands of other warriors simply wilted away and were eventually captured or destroyed almost without contest.

Then came the point of open rout, and what was left of Axayacatl's resplendent army broke and fled the field, only a few able to carry wounded comrades away on their backs. The Tarascans pursued relentlessly by day and night right up to the frontier, dispatching most of the stragglers, who were in any case dying of thirst. As the wretched few retreated across the frontier into Matlatzinca territory, they were followed by the exultant shrieks and obscene catcalls of the victors. The Tarascan had earned the right to boast, for he had bested some of the greatest warriors in Mesoamerica.

At Ecatepec the pitiable Aztec remnant was assembled for a roll call. Out of the twenty-four thousand only four thousand came back! If these numbers are correctly reported, few disasters in military history can have exceeded that at Zamacoyahuac or "Big Mouth."

Axayacatl sent a messenger ahead with the news of the wreckage of his army. Tlacaelel received the news, ordered the Mexica into deep mourning, and posted guards on all the approaches to the city lest the slumbering hatred of Mexico's subjects awaken at that critical moment and overwhelm her. At Chapultepec groups of priests and dignitaries, as was the custom, met Axayacatl and the two hundred Mexican knights who had escaped along with him out of the Tarascan vortex. To the lowing sounds of conch-shell trumpets and the deadened shuffle of feet, the battered ones were escorted back into the city. Axayacatl resorted immediately to the temple of Huitzilopochtli to perform there a penitential act of auto-sacrifice. After this he went to the palace and reported to Tlacaelel. That great shadow out of Mexico's past heard the younger ruler out and then spoke as follows: "Take heart, for your vassals did not die comfortably at home spinning like women but on the battlefield, fighting to gain glory for you and honor for your country. They have gained the same fame dying there as formerly they gained in victories. I am thankful to the Lord of All that he has allowed me to see these many deaths of my brothers and nephews. I cannot restrain myself."[37] Whereupon he wept bitterly and long.

The year 1478 was also, as one of the annals has it, the year of phantasms that roamed the dark night ways and of familiar spirits croaking out auguries of doom.[38] From the webby forests and gullies of the encircling mountains, evil airs slid down into the cities of the Basin, shriveling and bringing horrors and diseases.

It is difficult to assess the impact of this defeat on Mexico, but the above speech imputed to Tlacaelel would lead us to believe that Mexica morale was hardly touched. Win or lose, fierce combat had been provoked, and the gods were accordingly pleased. Blood had been copiously poured out and the gods had banqueted. The families of those abandoned in the dust eastward of Tlaximaloyan might lament their own personal losses, but Mexico had lost nothing. On the contrary, she had carried out to perfection her historic role in the world. According to this understanding of the nature of civilized life, to which Tlacaelel had dedicated his entire career, victory and defeat stood on the same plane as long as one had fought truly. A warrior's honor was inviolate in either camp. The fact that Mexico was again at war the same year is evidence that the defeat had only a temporary impact.

The Wounding of Axayacatl

Xiquipilco had formerly been an ally of the Matlatzinca but up to this point had been able to avoid the enmity of the Three Cities. No doubt in a calculated move to recover some of his lost prestige, Axayacatl now moved against this Mazahua site situated not far to the north of Toluca. "Black Lizard," its ruler, was accounted a famous warrior.[39]

On that field Axayacatl distinguished himself in a record display of bravery and skill; he is reported to have already taken three prisoners —a nearly superhuman feat—when his daring overreached itself. Seeking out more victims in the heat of battle, he had dashed into a plantation of maguey, outstripping the Mexican knights who were fighting at his side as well as a small Acolhua company led by the ruler of Teotihuacan, Quetzalmamalitzin. Axayacatl had failed to see the possibility of an ambush in the labyrinthine passageways of the vast maguey field, and too late became aware that he was surrounded and cut off by several of the enemy. As they closed in, Axayacatl fought like a lion but finally fell in the dust, grappling with one of the enemy. Here he received a terrible wound in the hip that, bleeding profusely, rapidly weakened him. The enemy succeeded in subduing him and in fact were already transporting him off the field, when Quetzalmamalitzin, at the head of a few of his men, burst upon the scene, overpowered the enemy, and rescued their fallen leader. The battle at large continued until the Mazahua were routed with the capture of many of their knights, including Black Lizard himself, who had delivered the blow that had felled the Mexican *tlatoani*.

Axayacatl received preliminary first aid as he lay bloody and bedraggled in the dust. He was then lifted into the royal litter and borne swiftly at the head of his victorious army back to Mexico, where he was received with the most splendid ovation ever given to a *tlatoani* returning from battle. The priests carrying the idol of Huitzilopochtli chanted their standard welcome as the royal litter came swiftly down to the causeway: "Welcome to the court-city, Mexico-Tenochtitlan, in the eddyless water where the eagle cried and the serpent hissed, where fish leap and where, among the reeds and rushes, the clear water gushes out to join the muddy—here where Huitzilopochtli holds command."[40]

First into the city came the prisoners in lines with their arms pinioned behind them. They came as honored guests, the captor in every case walking beside his captive. The prisoners taken by Axayacatl in person headed the majestic procession and had been adorned as kings in order to properly greet the god to whom they would soon be sacrificed. Mexica veterans too old for combat, dressed in all their martial finery, lined both sides of the causeway acclaiming the captives and holding out to them cigars and flowers. Then followed the victorious army ceremoniously lamenting its losses. The dead had been cremated on the field and were now represented by the darts they had used in battle. These would be turned over to the bereaved families, who would then dress the weapon in the clothing of the deceased and immolate him properly in the person of this effigy.[41] In the bestowal of awards that followed, Quetzalmamalitzin was greatly honored for his deed of rescue and was given the right to wear on his shield a device commemorating the event.

This was the last act of Axayacatl's reign. In Aztec terms he had been a notable ruler, courageous and much favored by the gods. He never recovered from his injury and died in 1481, not much more than a year later. Serious earthquakes that caused avalanches in the mountains and knocked down houses in the cities had marked much of his rule,[42] and in the year of his death the sun was eclipsed and the stars shone in full daytime. But these evidences of divine displeasure had always been counteracted by Axayacatl's devotion. He had been a fortunate king, and his effigy was chiseled in the rock of Chapultepec beside that of his great predecessor.[43]

10. Two Kings of the Middle Period

The Reign of Tizoc[1]

The death of Axayacatl in 1481 precipitated an electoral storm in Mexico. Tizoc, his older brother, had been passed over by the magnates when, some thirteen years before, they had selected Axayacatl. At that time, in order to prevent a war between brothers, Tlacaelel had guaranteed the succeeding reign to Tizoc. Accordingly, Tizoc had been raised to the rank of *tlacateccatl* and installed as one of the four princes, but unfortunately the passage of the years had witnessed no growth in the popularity of Tizoc, who continued to remain unacceptable to the nobility at large.

What alone prevented a dangerous rift in the state was the veneration the Mexicans of all factions accorded to Tlacaelel, now well into his seventies. Tlacaelel, who wore the *copilli* as his right and could thus address the Mexica as an acknowledged ruler, insisted that Tizoc be elected to the office of *tlatoani*. When the electors demurred, pointing out Tizoc's weaknesses, Tlacaelel brought them around by pointing out that he himself would be the adviser and guardian of the next ruler, whoever he might be. None could gainsay this greatest of all Mexican princes, and he had his way. Tizoc was elected.[2]

Following the practice of the past, the new ruler selected a city to go against in the initiatory war that was to test his leadership and gain victims for his coronation ceremonies. With the concurrence of Tlacaelel, the city of Metztitlan was chosen as a battleground. This formidable Huaxtec city, as yet unconquered, lay to the north in a deep valley in the fall of the Escarpment.

The result was something of a disaster for the Mexica *tlatoani* just beginning his reign.[3] Far from being intimidated by the approaching allied army, Metztitlan met it with great spirit and, in company with other Huaxtec allies from the lowlands, hurled it back. So severe was the blow that Mexico was forced finally to throw in her regiment of neophytes. While these raw young warriors gave a good account of themselves, as was to be expected, they served merely to gain precious time while a more orderly retreat was being organized. Most of these young heroes who survived the rearguard action were knighted on the road back—not only in recognition of their valor but as a practical matter to fill the gaps in the Mexican contingent caused by the heavy casualties. It appears that the Mexica came away from the affair bringing only some dozen captives—a paltry amount and one not likely to placate the grim god of battles.

It was an inauspicious beginning for an Aztec reign and faced Tlacaelel with a serious problem. As the senior partner in the rule he had to move with vigor to shore up what was left of Tizoc's prestige. His own prestige was of course indestructable. Ahuitzotl, the third brother, was impatiently standing in the wings, ready at any favorable moment to seize Tizoc's power. Tlacaelel managed to hold him off; the strategem he used is interesting.

Through Tizoc, he issued a call for an imperial convocation.[4] The rulers and governors of all the provinces of the Mexican empire thereupon came together in a vast levy and heard Tizoc proclaim an extraordinary enlargement of the pyramid of Huitzilopochtli; the various cities were assigned appropriate roles in the great enterprise.[5] Piety such as this was at least temporarily immune from criticism. Certainly the gods would not lightly abandon a ruler who so honored them. The cornerstone would be laid in the following year, 1483. Tizoc now had a second chance to secure a large quantity of sacrificial victims and earn his right to rule.

He was fortunate in the fact that the fires of rebellion had at that moment broken out in some of the cities in the Toluca Basin.[6] Chimalteuctli, the sycophant lord of the Matlatzinca, again was involved in some way in the matter—at least he was closely connected with the punitive forces Tizoc sent into the area, and he and his warriors are even said to have themselves cast fire into the temples of their rebellious kinfolk. Chimalteuctli was finally recognized by the Mexica as a weak reed to lean on, and they soon ordered him into custody in Mexico where he was forced to reside for the next four years while the work of pacification and terror went on in his homeland. The captives taken in these continuing attacks on Matlatzinca centers were sacrificed in the costly ceremonies connected with the renovation of the temple.

The brief reign of Tizoc is the most obscure and puzzling in our entire chronology. Our uncertainty extends even to the correct form of his name, which is variously spelled and is only once translated, where it is said to mean "the pierced one," referring to the pierced nose of the Aztec knight. One of the few facts recorded of his reign is the decision to abandon military government over Chalco.[7] For some twenty-two years the Chalca cities had had no *tlatoani* of their own, each being under a *cuauhtlatoa* or consul sent out from one of the Three Cities. It had been the fate of the Chalca cities to suffer all these years under a total tyranny, and they had finally submitted to their lot, a people who could no longer dare. Their pride and their capacity to resist had been broken. Mexico therefore felt safe in sloughing off the responsibility of direct rule over those Chalca cities alloted to her by the League. She now took up the matter of the Chalca petitions that had been over the years asking for the reinstatement of the four interrupted and legitimate royal houses and the return to each of them of the *copilli*. Tizoc called the scions of those houses to Mexico where they were first given status by being knighted. Each was then formally installed in his respective office and dispatched in an impressive flotilla of canoes down to their ancestral lands under the volcano. Chalca was being raised from the footing of a subjugated state to the more honorable one of ally.

But even as this showy event was taking place Tizoc died; the year was 1486. There is a mystery here that we are unable to penetrate.[8] Several versions have come down to us as to the manner of his death. He is variously said to have been poisoned by the Mexica themselves, murdered by evil witchcraft instigated by the rulers of Ixtapalapan and Tlachco, or to have fallen dead of a massive hemorrhaging at the mouth and nose. There is no way of choosing which is the true account. Some chroniclers refer to him as a good and wise ruler, others as cowardly and do-nothing. As one accepts one or the other of these assessments, one can correspondingly accept the apposite account of his death. From the fact that there was some interest in his reign on the part of the chroniclers, we may at least state that, while he was an unpopular ruler, he was not so unpopular that his name was erased from the canonical list of kings.

Tlacaelel and the Election of Ahuitzotl

Ahuitzotl, the third of the grandsons of the great Moteuczoma was already in position to succeed, holding as he did the rank of *tlacateccatl*.[9] That any opposition to him would be overridden was foreordained, for he possessed all the requisite qualifications: he was a redoubtable warrior, he was next in the fraternal line of succession, and he had the backing of Tlacaelel. Axayacatl's progeny were also aspirants to the office of *tlatoani* and were already beginning to make names for themselves. The oldest, Tlacahuepantzin was a knight of unusual prowess, while another in his teens bore the revered name of his great grandfather Moteuczoma (he was therefore designated as Xocoyotzin, "the younger") and was also looked to as a potential ruler.

In the debates that attended the election, it was again Tlacaelel who ultimately prevailed. Nezahualpilli of Tezcoco had argued as a compromise position that Tlacaelel himself should take the office of *tlatoani* with Ahuitzotl as a Caesarian second. To this the Mexica had assented, but Tlacaelel, in an oration of which the sense has come down to us, rejected it out of hand.

He argued, as he had at Tizoc's election, that he had promised the great Moteuczoma that he would see to it that all three of his grandsons and heirs would succeed to the rule. Therefore he could not allow even the halfway suggestion of Nezahualpilli. Furthermore, he continued, he himself had always been a ruler anyway and he would continue as such until he died; he wore the royal *copilli* and was carried in a litter as only rulers were. Thus nothing would be changed even if they did elect him *tlatoani*. His earlier promise to Moteuczoma was in conformity with the Mexican principle of succession, namely that brother should succeed brother until there remained no more. Mexico must honor that principle. As usual, any position strongly argued by Tlacaelel prevailed, and Ahuitzotl was elected, pointing the way to the election of Tlacahuepantzin next and Moteuczoma the Younger to follow him in the lordships to succeed.

This was Tlacaelel's last great public decision, for not long after, weighted down with years and honors, he died. A comparison of his influence with that of the equally great Nezahualcoyotl would be invidious. While each was the perfect model and ideal of his own nation, they were in other characteristics distinct. Nezahualcoyotl had been born an emperor and his mind was ecumenical and far-ranging. He led his people, the Acolhua, into a renaissance of Toltec splendor without in the least being either unconscious of or embarrassed by his Chichimec background. The whole world was his oyster. Tlacaelel, like his Mexican followers, had been more single-minded. His strength of character, his charisma, was torrential because it was circumscribed by such narrow banks. The mighty things of the unseen world, so elegantly and urbanely handled by Nezahualcoyotl, were seen by Tlacaelel as everlasting fountains of demands poured out upon him. To him piety and ferocity were one. The making of Mexico had been the fulfillment of a prophecy by the god of war, and war therefore had been ordained for the Mexica as the consummation of piety. Tlacaelel was not ambitious for himself except as the increase in his power would give him more leverage to hoist higher the state of Mexico upon the holy pedestal of duty.

It is impossible to say whether Tlacaelel was first a priest or first a warrior. As *cihuacoatl* he would have acknowledged no dichotomy, as indeed in Mexico there was none. If Itzcoatl had been the father of Mexico's sovereignty and Moteuczoma had been its shaper and perfecter, Tlacaelel was its implacable genius, the incarnate spirit of its fever-ish role in history.[10]

One of our sources says he was born in 1397. Assuming that he died a few years after the election of Ahuitzotl in 1486, he would have then lived into his late eighties.[11] He had borne the titles of *tlailotlac*,[12] *atem-panecatl*,[13] *tlacochcalcatl*, *cihuacoatl*, and *tlatoque*. The title of *cihua-coatl* had become so intimately his that it was thereafter never worn by any person not of his lineage.[14] His name adorned all the members of his family. One son was a *tlacochcalcatl*. His daughter Five Flower, so named after the god of pleasure, was a famous poetess. His grandson Tlacotzin would be the last *cihuacoatl* in Mexican history and, as *cuauh-tlatoa*, would be appointed by Cortez to rule over the ruined Mexica.

Tlacaelel's funeral was more magnificent than those of any of the previous kings. All realized that with him an era had ended.

The Personality of Ahuitzotl[15]

The era that was to begin under Ahuitzotl was the product of a robust personality.[16] Typically Aztec in his predilection for war, Ahuitzotl was still a person of open and sometimes careless bon-homie and was never to be constrained wholly into the grave pattern of the ideal *tlatoani*. As he happened upon them, men became a part of his circle. It was in fact something of a scandal during his reign that he used commoners in high positions where only nobles had been used be-fore; he was constantly creating new knights, sometimes in reward for heroism in the field but often out of mere favoritism.

He was fond of the choral theater and of the song and dance so in-tricately and elegantly performed by Aztec professional troupes, and he spent many hours within earshot of the contrasting voices of the drums. The *mixcoacalli*, "apartment of the cloud serpents," the palace com-pound where gathered the singers, song composers, and dance masters of Mexico and where were stored the multitudes of showy costumes, was in his reign more than usually active. His harem was understand-ably large and the *ahuiani*, public women who painted their faces in brilliant reds and yellows and chewed gum, were much in evidence in his day. He was both cruel and good-humored, vengeful and capricious; his generosity was munificent and foolish at the same time. He identified himself with Totec, "our lord," a god of youth and pleasures,[17] and at heart he was always a hater of peace and a troubler.

A Colonial Foundation and a Temple Dedication

Ahuitzotl's reign was introduced by a rebellion among the Mazahua, which was a continuation of the unrest in the Toluca Basin left unfinished by Tizoc.[18] The campaign netted Ahuitzotl a number of sacrificial victims sufficient to dignify his coronation, which thereupon followed with great splendor. But every change of ruler in the Mexican line was the signal—not unwelcome to the Mexican warrior—for a revolt of their more desperate subjects. That imperial salient on the Tarascan frontier, the province of Teloloapan, which contained the great guard city of Oztoman, had attempted in its agony to wrench itself free from the Mexica grasp.[19] It suffered an almost unprecedented fate. In a truly satanic massacre almost all of the adults, both male and female, were obliterated and the children, some 40,200, were allotted as slaves to all the cities that had aided in the reconquest.

However total and therefore efficient this historic slaughter was, it was a patent error in one sense, for it left the great fortress of Oztoman undermanned and the frontier consequently open to enemy forays. To rectify the sad results of their fury, the Three Cities were now forced to a new and most interesting experiment, one that would have held the seeds of a different future for Anahuac had it been followed up. Each sizable city in the Aztec empire was required to send up to twenty families under a headman, all volunteers, to form a frontier population to be settled in Teloloapan. Mexico, Tezcoco, and Tlacopan themselves provided two hundred families apiece. This mass of settlers was broken up into three lots, while over each lot was placed in temporary leadership four Mexican nobles. Their duty was to bring the three newly organized colonies safely over the long hills to their assigned homes and to remain in charge of them until the first harvest was in—reckoned to be the second year after settlement. With the withdrawal of these Mexican commissioners, each of the three settlements, Teloloapan, Oztoman, and Alahuiztlan, would then elect its own ruler.

This vast and heterogeneous population—in all some nine thousand families—was initially gathered together in Mexico where it was addressed by Ahuitzotl and then ceremoniously sent on its way. It must have been a remarkable movement of peoples. When the three sites were reached, maize plots and hearths were assigned to each family, all arranged no doubt under the *calpulli* system. The families from the Three Cities received the most favorable assignments, for they had been designated as a new nobility. When the rulers of the three communities were finally elected, they were brought back into the Basin to be ordained in their offices and granted armorial bearings by the lords of the Three Cities. The Teloloapan cities were now considered to be allies.

The points of interest in this foundation are many, but the most striking to the casual observer is that here the Three Cities had created overnight a mechanism that could have been artificially used to leaven all three empires with a single imperial concept. If similar colonies had been placed strategically throughout the three empires and made answerable to a consortium of the Three Cities, there would then have been introduced a true allegiance to the center. A single empire instead of three contingent empires would have begun to appear.

It is equally interesting that this promising start was not repeated. It was not repeated because in the Three Cities the concept of empire was primitive at the best; empire was tied to tribute only and not to unity and conformity. The incidence of rebellion was not seen as necessarily a bad thing, inasmuch as it provided an occasion for war, and there was therefore no impulse toward finding a political formula for peaceful coexistence that would bind the many parts of the empires together. Suzerainty, not sovereignty, was enough. War, not internal peace, was the ultimate desideratum. Empire was a mere situation, not a whole way of life.

Up through 1487 the Three Cities had been actively on campaign in another part of Anahuac. The northern lowlands of the Huaxteca along the Gulf coast had been reserved in the main for Tezcoco's exploitation, and Tezcoco now decided to push the imperial domain up to the Pánuco River. In this fierce campaign against as yet unconquered Huaxtec communities which were led by the city of Xiuhcoac, the Mexica gained three thousand victims for sacrifice.[20] Prominent among the heroes of this distant melee was Axayacatl's son Moteuczoma Xocoyotzin, already one of the leading princes of Mexico.

Masses of prisoners gathered in this and the forays of the preceding four years had been saved for the dedication of Huitzilopochtli's temple.[21] This occurred in 1487 and was considered by the peoples of Anahuac to be the single greatest event of Aztec history, which—granting the basic importance of the rite of human sacrifice in their cultures—it was. The number of victims sacrificed is variously given, some sources ranging as high as 80,400, some contenting themselves with 10,600. Inasmuch as the slaughter of victims in this ceremony went on without intermission for four consecutive days from sunup to sundown, we may opt for the lower number as the more reliable, it being inconceivable, what with the difficulty of disposing of the bodies and the exhaustion of the sacrificing crews, that more than three thousand a day could have been disposed of. Some of the victims had been offered to Mexico as extraordinary items of tribute by the subject cities, and some were gifts of Nezahualpilli and Chimalpopoca. But in any event all had been taken in war.

Not only were the lords of all the tributary cities in the three empires commanded to appear for the occasion, but invitations were sent to even the most inveterate enemies of Mexico to attend under safe conduct. Nothing in Aztec history reveals so clearly the chivalric core of their society and the preeminence of the cultic over the political. The lords of Tlascala, Huexotzinco, Metztitlan, Yopitzinco, Michoacan, and others are said to have come in person or to have sent ambassadors; these representatives from enemy nations were introduced secretly and under cover of darkness into Mexico so that they would not be molested by the populace. They were assigned to the royal quarters and were guarded by picked men. They viewed all of the proceedings from special viewing pavilions forbidden to the Mexica themselves, and in some cases they watched their own knights and near relatives, captured in previous battles, led to the divine shambles. At the end of the four days they were given sumptuous gifts and, again in deepest secrecy, escorted safely back to their own frontiers.

Four files of prisoners were positioned along the four ways leading into the sacred center of Tenochtitlan, the lines stretching far back along the causeways. At the first light of the first day there awaited them, clad in full regalia, the four rulers, Ahuitzotl, Tlacaelel (still alive at the time), Nezahualpilli, and Chimalpopoca. These four most distinguished men of Anahuac personally sacrificed the first victim after which they yielded to the various high priests, each garbed in the habiliments of his god. The pace of the killings was fast, and soon it became difficult to get the victims up to the *techcatl*, for blood flowed in streams down the steep temple steps making the ascent slippery and hazardous in the extreme. Priests were overworked, rushing bowls of blood to various parts of the city, painting the walls of sacred buildings with it, and smearing all the idols. Gouts of blood clotted and hardened horribly over everything connected with the event, and by the second day the stench had become almost unbearable throughout the city. The heads, which were severed from the corpses at the bottom of the steps, were placed in piles that kept tumbling down and scattering their trophies about like sodden footballs. The bodies were too many to be used in the customary cannibal feasts and were dumped into canoes working continuously to take them away for disposal. Vultures swarmed in clouds over the calm expanse of the lake, gliding and swooping here and there over those slow-moving purveyors of human trash. Those four days may well be reckoned among the most lugubrious in all human history.

When it was all over, Ahuitzotl ordered all the skulls that, up to then, had been threaded on the poles of the *tzompantli* to be removed and burned. The new accretion of skulls was to take their place. The rains that fell over the succeeding months gradually washed away the black scab of blood that had formed over the city, and less frenetic days returned. But it had been a spiritual horror of unparalleled scope, inhuman and never to be forgotten, an offering as monstrous as the god himself.

Mexico, which had conceived and carried out the holocaust, acquired from it a notable accretion of prestige. Reports of the event flew out into every corner of Mesoamerica. Everywhere Huitzilopochtli was honored. His voice, which was the howlings of thousands of Mexican warriors, mellow and ghastly as the voice of the storm, was now fearfully listened for in every land, even in remote Cuauhtemallan.

Imperial Tyranny under Ahuitzotl

It was in the direction of Cuauhtemallan (Guatemala) that Mexico was now directing herself. Michoacan and that part of the west beyond the Toluca Basin was locked against her. North of her was Godland, worthless because it was without cities and inhabited only by wayfaring Chichimecs. In company with her two allies, Mexico had touched upon the Pánuco River far up the Gulf coast; and she had similarly in the south reached Coatzacoalcos and the country of the swamps where easy land travel came to an end. But beyond Oaxaca lay the commercially important Isthmian lands of Tehuantepec and beyond that was Xoconochco, Cuauhtemallan, and the Plutonian land of Atlpopoca, little known but reputed to be rich and populous.

Before swinging his armies definitely in this direction, Ahuitzotl had a care to those subject cities of his empire which, when his armies were deep in the distant selva, might give him trouble at home. But this was not the sole reason for the upheaval he engineered in the ruling houses of Mexico's neighbors immediately following the dedication of the temple. Behind most of these moves was the need to strengthen himself by putting members of his family and partisans in positions of power.[22]

Cuitlahuac, his nephew, he installed as ruler in Ixtapalapan. Another nephew, Ixtlilcuechahuac, was confirmed in the rule of Tula. A relative, Tezozomoc, was given Azcapotzalco, which had at last been forgiven and allowed to appear again in the sun. These men, though classed each as a *tlatoani*, were nevertheless *cuauhtlatoa* or commissars, and their appointment reveals the oppressive nature of Ahuitzotl's policy. The cities of Culhuacan and Xochimilco were also given rulers, as was Coyouacan. Over the mountains the Tlahuica cities of Cuauhnahuac, Tepoztlan, and Huaxtepec had forced upon them new lords about whose loyalty there would be no question. When the *tlatoani* of the important city of Cuauhtitlan died in 1495, his line too was blocked and a military governor installed in his stead. Chalco, which in the last days of Tizoc had been in the process of recovering some freedom of action, was abruptly pulled back and only later allowed a reduced role. One of the regions of Chalco, Huixtoco Tecuanipan, was allowed a ruler of its old royal house, but one descended only through the distaff side—the father of this ruler was Tlilpotonqui, son of the great Tlacaelel.[23] Mexican interests would obviously be safe there.

This tightening of the bonds of empire was also an increase in tyranny from the center. While it was not unexpected, it was nevertheless a sign of fear and perhaps something akin to political bankruptcy. From Mexico's point of view, however, the ill effects to be expected from this increasing heavy-handedness could easily be counteracted by the continued assurances of stability provided by the Three City League. That great instrument was counted on to protect as well as to expand Mexico, and the misery of hundreds of thousands of subjects was reckoned as of little account when placed beside it.

The Great Penetration of the Southeast

The military drive now about to begin into Ayotlan, the land of the far southeast, had been preceded by a remarkable commercial penetration into that same territory by the merchants of Tlatilulco.[24]

About 1492 these merchants, having by that date recovered their former prosperity, undertook to push two caravans as far down into the Isthmus as possible, both attempting to tap directly the springs of Mayan commerce.[25] One turned off to the Gulf coast and trafficked in Coatzacoalcos. Whether it penetrated to the mixed Nahua-Mayan trading state of Acallan is unknown. The other, which was the one to make history, got as far as Tehuantepec along the shores of the Pacific and even went beyond.

This was a multi-purpose undertaking. Ahuitzotl had no doubt conceived of it on a larger scale than any of the previous ventures in barter. He entrusted to the merchants a large supply of his own mantles and slaves to be offered to the foreign rulers among whom they should pass in exchange for gold, jade, feathers, and jaguar skins. The merchants also carried their own trade goods, and thus the caravan became a joint state and private enterprise. Equally important as an objective was espionage; at least some of the party had learned the language, dress, and face paint of the Mayan people of Tzinacantlan.[26] These were part of the merchant class called *nahualoztomeca*, "disguised or guileful merchants," skilled linguists and trained observers who played a dangerous game and were everywhere feared and hated. Merchants from the Mesa Central had been down in those parts before but never in such strength, and it must have been common knowledge that their business was not only traffic in goods but the gathering of intelligence; they were in a sense the heralds of war.

The caravan was made up of merchants of the Mexican empire only, specifically those of the cities of Tlatilulco, Tenochtitlan, Huitzilopochco, Azcapotzalco, and Cuauhtitlan; these were the Mexican members of a more extensive twelve-city merchants' guild representing all three of the empires in the League. The party was composed of large numbers of porters and was under the absolute command of a trail captain, the most experienced of all the merchants. The tutelary god of such ancient voyagers was Yacateuctli, "lord of the vanguard." He was resident magically in the stout black staves of these traveling tradesfolk, and whenever nightfall overtook them on the cold slopes or down in the windless *barrancas* they would bind these staves together, drape some sacred paper upon the bundle, and therein worship Yacateuctli, their luck and their safety.

Custom made it mandatory to exit from Mexico by night in their canoes. Passing through the Aztec city of Tepeyacac, they finally reached the well-known depot of Tochtepec where the twelve cities of the merchants' guild possessed in common a temple to Yacateuctli as well as warehouses for their goods. Here the group split into two parts, one making for Coatzacoalcos, the other for Ayotlan.

"Desolate, ferocious, cruel, and peopled by evil men, spreads the wasteland," so entoned the veteran merchants, giving their charges warnings and advice of the dangers ahead. "You shall go wearied by heat, spent by winds. Your face will become dust covered and deathly white. Your forehead will burn. You shall wipe the sweat off with your hand; indeed you shall be bathed in it. In the corner by the wall, behind the door, you shall hang your head. Your stomach will stick to you from hunger."[27] Centuries of pride in accomplishment, full knowl

edge of the many dangers of the trail, the acquisition of skills in avoid-
ing them, a pervasive fatalism—all these had made the Mesoamerican
merchant a man apart, a Ulysses incomparable in his cunning. As the
Aztec nobility had grown in its pretensions and its demands for luxury,
the merchants had come into increasing prominence. They were now
entering upon the period of their greatest prestige.

The caravan successfully passed through the cities of the Isthmus,
penetrated into the province of Xoconochco, and finally, crossing the
Xochiatl River, entered into the hot and rainy land of Ayotlan. Mexico
at last stood at the gates of Cuauhtemallan, a land of many warring
tribal states, a land rich in topaz and cacao beans and the target of many
commercial enterprises.

This reconnaissance-in-force that was also a trading venture aroused
the inevitable suspicions and ultimately produced difficulties for the
group. They had begun their return from Ayotlan when they found the
road back blocked by a coalition of Isthmian and Xoconochco cities.
The caravan, sufficiently strong in men, went to ground in a place called
Cuauhtenanco, six hundred miles from home. Here for a period of possibly two years, in a site far removed from the nearest large Mexican
garrison in Oaxaca, they withstood a determined siege. In the various
assaults made upon their positions by the enemy, the merchants bested
the flower of the Isthmian knights and took their devices as booty. The
siege finally collapsed, and the caravan slipped safely away loaded down
with plunder of war as well as the legitimate gains of trade.

Ahuitzotl had been informed of the situation too late to be of real
assistance. On receipt of the news, however, he had immediately dispatched to the relief of the threatened party a column under the command of his nephew Moteuczoma. This force, moving southeast under
forced march, to its surprise came upon the insouciant merchants traveling unmolested and obviously well able to take care of themselves. The
year was probably 1495.

It had been a spectacular episode and appealed to the martial Mexica. Because the merchants had brought back with them the arms and bla-
zons of many distinguished foreign knights, they appeared to the *tlatoani* and his nobles in a prestigious light. When the straggling concourse
of porters headed by the Tlatilulca merchants came up the southern

causeway, staves in hand, hair long and matted as was customary, and accompanied by Moteuczoma's splendid regiment, they were accorded a state reception, the first of its kind recorded in Mexican history. Ushered into the palace, they then deposited at Ahuitzotl's feet the banners, regalia, and devices of the knights whom they had taken or killed in foreign lands, to which they added the *tlatoani's* own share of the sumptuous items secured in the trade. In an unexpected and quixotic gesture, Ahuitzotl thereupon rewarded the leading merchants with knightly status and the inestimable privilege of using golden lip plugs and appearing in knightly garb. Such a munificence was of course an invasion of the closed world of the Mexican noble and an insult to his exclusiveness; it was therefore unpopular. The *pochteca* however—except when sitting in their own jurisdictional meetings in Tlatilulco—never thereafter presumed to flaunt these signs of splendor in Mexico lest the latent hostility of the knights break out against them. But the great wealth they brought back into Mexico was welcomed by the knights as they saw now the possibility of ever more and more baroque finery. The feathers of the blue cotinga, the roseate spoonbill, and the regal green of the quetzal now began to appear in profusion in the many festivals of the religious calendar, being worked into armorial bearings on shields or worn in bonnets and tufts on the head. Overnight a new era of elegance had appeared.

As was to be expected, Ahuitzotl, after consulting with his two allies, ordered a vast military parade down into the regions opened up by the *pochteca*.[28] Taking swift advantage of the intelligence gained, it was planned in that year, 1496, to reduce the area to tributary status before it could organize an effective resistance.

This was the most serious undertaking since the attack upon Michoacan and one that was perhaps entered upon in an over-hasty fashion. Nevertheless, it achieved results of a sort. In all, the campaign was to take at least three years, would necessitate at least one replacement army of considerable magnitude, and would not be concluded until 1498 or the year thereafter.

Having reached the Aztec garrison city of Oaxaca, Ahuitzotl halted and summoned a parliament of all the tributary Zapotec rulers to demand from them the supplies and additional fighting men to carry him down to the Isthmus and beyond into Cuauhtemallan. Ahuitzotl had earlier given a daughter to the overlord of the Zapotecs in an overt sign of alliance; this alliance was now directed against the Tehuantepeca. To the great army that finally assembled in the valley of Oaxaca, Ahuitzotl announced a no-prisoners policy because of the difficulty there would be in moving captives the long miles back from the Isthmian battlefields to Mexico. Prisoners could be seized, as was customary, and for the deed the warriors would be appropriately recognized then and there on the battlefield, but the prisoners would have to be dispatched immediately, not as sacrificial victims but as logistical problems.

The campaign began with a defeat of major proportions administered by the enemy coalition led by Tehuantepec. A dispute over booty and a near mutiny on the part of the Aztec contingents began to erode Mexican prestige in the Isthmus. The military stalemate that followed apparently led to some kind of pact between the two coalitions, though our sources are not helpful here. Mexico and her allies did manage to secure the right of transit though the Isthmus with hegemony over certain cities to be used as guard posts on the long Isthmian trek to Xoconochco.

A later thrust succeeded in subduing the province of Xoconochco, which lay on the borders of Cuauhtemallan. This was now reckoned as the most distant of all Aztec provinces, and it appropriately assured to Mexico and her allies the most exotic products of the south. So great had now become the flow of these luxuries into Mexico that even the buffoons, hunchbacks, and dwarfs in Ahuitzotl's court were richly dressed. But the empire had reached its geographical limit. The far recesses of the world of Chiapas and the Petén, the quarries of green and milky jade, the crumbling cities already half lost by travelers, the canopies of cloud forest stretching over that antipodean land with its myriad volcanoes—these purlieus of the Mayan peoples would remain forever untrodden by Aztec armies. Even their merchants had gone as far as they could go.

How the Aztec States Were Bound Together

Apart from the administrative ties of empire, the cities of Anahuac, and to a lesser degree those of the surrounding culture areas, were linked in a network of international (i.e., intercity) confrontations, observances, customs, and expectations. A consideration of these will help to explain the life lived by Mexico as it rose to become the first city of the land.

Aztec society was preoccupied with the *teuctli* and his central role. It was the interests of this class that colored intercity relations at least as much as the purely political concerns of the cities themselves, which we may denominate here as national concerns. The social milieu of the *teuctli* was chivalric and supra-national. These two views of man's ultimate necessities were incompatible and led to such curious intrusions into the settled policy of the state as the disastrous attack upon Michoacan, which had been called forth by an unheeding aristocracy bent on war for its own sake. It is the mixture of the two—of chivalry and self-interest, of knighthood and the state—that goes into the functioning of that international life in which Mexico had been cradled and in which she had grown great.

Considering the nations of Anahuac and of the surrounding areas as states, we find that their view of the whole was not unitarian. They did not see that world as an international continuum of free and equal states, but as conglomerations of various sizes and complexities; these included treaty leagues, federations of *calpulli* based on propinquity, hierarchical arrangements of states either tributary or allied or both, or groupings based on cultic interests, historical background, or commercial affinities—in other words, the larger Aztec world saw in such ill-assorted clusters of states the highest political reality. The concept of the state alone and by itself, isolated ideologically like a god in exile, they did not conceive of. The relationships between states was to them more important than any intellectual concepts used to define them singly.

There are six verbal roots commonly used in classical Nahuatl to present the idea of governing: *itqui, mama,* and *nopaloa* give the idea of burden-bearing and therefore stress the idea of the pain and responsibility of rule; *yacana* gives the idea of guidance, keenness, and forethought; *cuexana* means protecting a child or object while carrying it wrapped up in the folds of a garment; *pachoa* means literally "to compress, squeeze, cause to bow or bend," this bringing in the ideas of punishment, fear, coercion, and majesty. Certainly all the necessary qualities of rule were clearly comprehended by speakers of Nahuatl, yet no one word exists that even remotely approaches our intellectually isolated concept of "the state." We assume that the Aztecs saw no need to so classify that complex of institutions that we today call the state. They saw not an institution but *tlatocayotl*, "lordship."

To this concrete vision of rule was added a knightly class that owed allegiance to a code of war common to all the states. Thus the national self-interest, as summed up in the ruler, was contradicted by the wider moralities and dedication of the *teuctli*. Joining these two opposites created what we call the world of Anahuac; the excessively kinetic quality of this world was generated by the tension between them. The case of Mexican-Tlascalan relations is an example, at first chivalric and tied mainly to the flower war but increasingly changing into a true matter of state with Mexico's growing aggrandizement. In the last years of Ahuitzotl and all the years of the reign of Moteuczoma II, Mexico was to take up—but too late—the project of crushing Tlascala. The Aztec state never really fixed on the fact that it could be primarily an institution where its own self-interest was paramount and where war was a means to that end. Part of the time it saw itself as a school for the international orders of knights and as therefore ancillary to them.

There were two characteristics that especially marked the cities of Anahuac: territoriality and identity. This was true in spite of the fact that many of these states were comprised of scattered and even racially disparate *calpulli* and were not therefore compact urban centers. Borders were defined in all cases with great exactitude and were posted with picked companies of frontier guards on a round-the-clock alert.[29] In certain instances, for example Atlixco, the *quiauatl tlalli*, literally "entrance land," was untilled because of the constant wastage of attack and counterattack in that precarious area. The eastern frontier of Tlascala was so vulnerable that besides the garrisons there, which were changed every eighty days, there had been erected a formidable defensive wall.

The obverse of this coin was the prevalence of espionage, accusations, and associated treacheries. A constant neurosis of fear and suspicion was characteristic of all the cities, and rumor could cause a bloody

pogrom to erupt at a moment's notice. The Tlateputzca cities, for example, had spies placed in and around Mexico whose information, fed
back to parties of raiders waiting at home, caused the ambush and
death of numerous Mexican companies or brought the news of surrep-
titious armies on the march. Azcapotzalco's great victory over Ixtlilxochitl of Tezcoco had been effected by spies and suborners resident in
the court itself. Permanent spy rings in fact were always maintained in
the territories of especially dangerous enemy nations.[30] Informers were
generously rewarded.

A city was identified by its armorial bearings depicted on a banner.[31]
In battle, this was sometimes worn by the commander of the troops on
his back or it was planted in an open spot close to the battlefront.
When attacking, each nation sounded its own battlecry, which was simply the name of the city and served not only to challenge the enemy but
to identify one's own fellows. Thus the battlecry of the Mexica was
simply "Mexico! Mexico! Tenochtitlan!" An army sensing victory
drove directly toward the particular monument that, even more than
the palace, served to identify the people to be conquered, namely their
central temple. When the torch was successfully put to this, all resistance on the part of the losing side ceased, for the identity of the city in
the person of its divine talisman had been obliterated. We have seen
from the early history of the Mexica how tenacious they were of their
identity in both defeat and victory; not all the Aztec cities were that
indomitable.

Because of the many ways in which the Aztec states could be
grouped, they also assumed various postures toward each other.
Though universal empire was known as an ideal, it had so far not come
into existence. The most powerful combination achieved up to this
point was the Three City League, but there were other leagues also in
operation, the best known among which was the Nauhteuctli, "the four
lords," comprising the cities of Ixtapalapa, Culhuacan, Mexicaltzinco,
and Huitzilopochco.[32] The state of Tlascala itself was in reality a league
of four communities permanently attached to each other, as was Chalco. These leagues of four (the sacred number) could constitute either
true states like Tlascala or loose confederations like the Nauhteuctli.

On a formal level, the *altepetl* or city spoke to its contemporaries, whether friendly or hostile, through ambassadors who, in theory at least, possessed inviolability. Aztec history is studded with cases of savage mutilations and killings of envoys, but such actions were always recognized as being egregious. The ambassador was the *titlantli* or the *tlatolitquic*, literally "he who is carrying words."[33] Either ranking warriors or high priests could be used in that capacity. If the communication was in the nature of an order sent from a central source to a subject state, it would go from the *tlatoani* or the council of princes to a commissioner of posts or secretary of state who had under him a corps of messengers and minor ambassadors; these were in constant use. Any major embassy usually comprised three or more specially chosen magnates wearing distinctive dress and carrying each in his hand an arrow held upright by the point. In other ways a complete etiquette surrounded the reception and dismissal of these ambassadors.[34] The language spoken was Nahuatl, the lingua franca of Mesoamerica. "There is no language," wrote Muñoz Camargo, "that is more elastic and rich in words. Not only is it a dignified tongue, it can be at the same time delicate and soft. It is above all lordly and presuming. It flows smoothly and easily but is so concise that there is no end to its subtlety."[35]

In Anahuac the need to dishonor and humiliate other communities as a token of the identity of one's own city was widespread and rendered the whole international situation extremely volatile. In some part this was mitigated by the thick web of royal marriages that had early been spread out over Anahuac.[36] Marriage-politics in fact appears as early as Xolotl, when it was used to graft Chichimec rule onto a neo-Toltec society. The Chichimec custom of exogamous marriages was soon given up in favor of the Toltec custom of marriage with near relatives—cousins and nieces for instance. A swift integration of royal blood lines and an increase in aristocratic solidarity followed.

Marriage soon became an international technique among the separate states, being used for the ends of aggrandizement and self-interest. Tezcoco would often recognize a subject ruler as legitimate only after he had married an Acolhua princess. By the time of Itzcoatl's accession, Mexico had married into the ruling houses of just about every neighboring community. And in the high tide of that city's prominence, Mexican noblewomen were sought after throughout Anahuac to strengthen weaker dynasties or to add additional prestige to a great one. Any woman of the Mexican royal line married to a tributary ruler became automatically the first wife and the one through whose issue therefore that line would trace its future legitimacy.

Not only was a new alliance sealed through a marriage between the participating houses, so also was a victory on the battlefield reinsured by a marriage with either the widow or a princess of the conquered royal house; the issue from such marriages would then be elevated to the rule of the subjugated state. But marriage could be a *casus belli* as well as a bond between cities—the instance of the Tenochca wife of Moquiuix comes to mind. Cases of adultery in foreign courts involving noble or royal women from any of the Three Cities were commonly used as pretexts for war.[37]

Empire, when it was contemplated at all, was seen as a vast system of appanages all bound by filial loyalties to a common center. Empire was thus a familial state where the imperial father and stock of the family, after conquering and suborning adjacent states, installed his own sons and nephews in their seats of rule. Either that or he forced daughters upon the conquered princes, thus legitimately acquiring sons-in-law. There was no other close bond conceivable between cities.

Such ties as bound the political pieces of Anahuac together were heavily buttressed by the networks of markets, by joint commercial ventures, by pilgrimages to holy centers, and by the custom of inviting both hostile and friendly rulers to state funerals of importance. Yet it must be realized that the civilization of Anahuac was of very recent making and still not well integrated. The nobles of the various cities were not patriotic in the sense that they primarily represented their cities; rather they saw themselves first as members of an international order. The *altepetl* was a culture oftentimes different in its objectives from the aristocracy and to some extent subordinate to it. In brief, Anahuac was a brilliant but unstable graft of two potentially sovereign entities, the state and the *teuctli*. Had the state been able to predominate it would quickly have invented the idea of war as an instrument to achieve its own ends, as did the contemporary Inca empire. But the state in Anahuac found itself unable to move beyond the *teuctli*'s concept of warfare as an end in itself, a sacred skirmishing, stately, bloody, and pleasing to the gods. Thus these two societies, one national, the other international, remained basically incompatible, and it was this weakness that finally brought about the fall of Mexico.

The Flood

Ahuitzotl had been fortunate in his reign. True, there had been untoward signs that all was not right in the land. In 1489 a frightful night-wandering phantom created panic in the Basin,[38] and at the same time convulsions shook the earth. Then in 1496 an eclipse of the sun and even more devastating earthquakes occurred, shaking down mountains and many of the works of man.[39] Also at about that time or somewhat earlier the heroic prince Tlacahuepantzin, in a flower war fought in Atlixco, was captured and carried off to Huexotzinco to be sacrificed.[40] Much as this event was bewailed by the Mexica, who had greatly cherished the young warrior, its full fatefulness was obscured to them; from that point on, all looked unquestioningly to Moteuczoma the Younger, the oldest remaining son of Axayacatl and one of the Four Princes, as the ruler who would succeed Ahuitzotl. But all in all, up to 1498, Ahuitzotl's reign had been fortunate.

The politics of the Tlateputzca cities had been getting increasingly more complicated. About 1498 Ahuitzotl decided to take advantage of their disarray and launch a knockout blow against them. This was to be no chivalric flower war, but an effort to at last come to grips with Tlascala. With Tezcoco and Tlacopan in support, he hurled an army against the strategic city of Atlixco, but a sudden snow blizzard buried large numbers on both sides as they were seeking positions on the higher slopes preparing to ambush each other.[41] Then, to add to their ill luck, the Mexica attack was turned into a disaster by the swift and unexpected aid Huexotzinco brought to Atlixco. The eminent warrior, Toltecatl, one of the princes of Huexotzinco, so distinguished himself here that his city in gratitude raised him to the position of ruler. This hasty action brought on a fierce civil war in Huexotzinco, for Toltecatl was opposed by the city priesthood, whose use of magic and the full paraphernalia of cult in the end proved irresistible. Toltecatl and the leading nobles of his party finally fled to Chalco where they asked for asylum. Hereupon Mexico ordered their vassal rulers in Chalco to destroy the entire party of suppliants; this was accordingly done, but for a reason unknown to us Mexico was unable to follow up this act of treachery and move in upon a weakened Huexotzinco. Tlascala, shielded by Huexotzinco, proved as far away as ever, and Ahuitzotl was no nearer to achieving his desire.

An equally significant failure awaited Ahuitzotl in the Basin. The fact that 1498 had been a year of drought had encouraged him to look about for additional supplies of water, not only to raise the now dangerously low lake level around Mexico but also to provide more drinking water for the ever-growing city. To this end he had approached Tzotzoma, lord of Coyouacan and a subject ruler in the Tepaneca empire of Tlacopan. Ahuitzotl coveted the runoff of five springs and freshets in the vicinity, chief among which was the Acuecuexatl, "the river of rapids." The five sources were to be diverted into a common reservoir to be built above the sweet-water part of the lake and from thence taken in a flume along the southern causeway into Mexico.

No doubt with the intention of protecting his own supply of precious water, Tzotzoma temporized and warned Ahuitzotl against the plan, saying that the freshet was erratic and subject to abnormal fluxes. Several times he insisted on this during the negotiations until Ahuitzotl, in a sudden outburst of anger, ordered him killed. Tzotzoma was strangled by executioners dispatched from Mexico to do the work, his son was installed in his place, and the disputed stream was peremptorily seized by Mexico. The incident sheds an ugly light not only on the short temper of imperial Mexico but also on the decidedly inferior position in the Three City League now held by Tlacopan, for Tzotzoma was under the jurisdiction of that city and was furthermore the son of the ruler of Azcapotzalco; Tlacopan had been unable to raise a hand against his killers. The deed occasioned much ill will in Tlacopan and even clouded Mexico's relations with Tezcoco, which saw the killing as a dangerous omen for the future.

A large dam with a six-mile retaining wall and an aqueduct into Mexico were now constructed by forced labor raised in the subject cities roundabout. It was an immense work and pushed through with ruthless efficiency. In 1499 Ahuitzotl, in the presence of his full court, performed the ceremony of welcoming the waters into the imperial city. As lock after lock was opened, the water rushed foaming along its new channel toward the imperial city. It was conceived of as the very person of Acuecueyotl or "Waves," that aspect of the goddess of running water whenever she appeared as imperious motion, tumbling and pouring over the surface of the earth. Clad in her regalia and painted blue, the high priest of the goddess moved at the head of the stately procession, dipping his hand now and then into the water, drinking it, and casting it over the crowds about him; he welcomed the goddess with courtly and flowery speeches into the city. Youths were held over the current and sacrificed so that their blood could fall directly upon the lovely goddess. Ahuitzotl and the people of Mexico shouted in joy and welcome as the head of water at last burst into the tanks and conduits of the city.

At this point the tragedy began. Rain clouds that had been piling up for days past on the peaks surrounding the Basin now unloosed torrential and continuous rains; for a long time Mexico took no notice of the danger ahead and thought of the rain as a mercy from Tlaloc sent to break the drought. Indeed, the rapid rise in the lake level was at first welcomed, for canoes could again operate in the city and the stinking mud flats and crushed reed beds that had spread out from the city on all sides were at last submerged. But the flood grew daily more importunate, and the downpour increased in intensity until the Mexica could no longer believe in their own safety. The waters newly impounded near Coyouacan and Huitzilopochco became uncontrollable and at last burst out with a savage roar; the pounding rain and the far thunder of those waters was all that the stunned inhabitants of the city could hear. In those voices they heard Tlaloc and Acuecueyotl together clamoring their hatred for the peoples of the Basin and for the Mexica in particular.

It was the worst flood in Mexico's history, inundating the causeways, destroying most of the buildings, and turning the temple pyramids into forlorn monuments standing isolated in the lake.[42] All knew that Ahuitzotl had sinned and in sinning had brought this ill event upon the city. He himself in public acknowledged his transgression and made such restitutions as were possible to the royal house of Coyouacan. The year of 1499 was passed by the Mexican nobles in the villas and palaces of others more fortunate who lived on the mainland. The common people reverted to canoes almost as had their ancestors, who in former times had fled out of Chapultepec into the reeds; their maize plots were gone in the washing and gullying of the storms, and they subsisted now on doles from the depleted granaries of the ruler and on the eggs of waterbugs, or on reptiles and small fish.

The year 1500 was one of famine because no planting had been possible in the drenching weather. It was also the year when the stunned Ahuitzotl summoned up his remaining energies to remedy the disaster. He ordered repairs for the dike that separated the salt from the sweet waters of the lake and which had suffered severely. Also, at the insistence of Nezahualpilli, who mediated in this disaster with the gods, Ahuitzotl performed penitential rites at the site where he had originally constrained the waters belonging to the goddess, and in person he oversaw the destruction of the great complex of earthworks so recently and with such labor erected. Divers were sent down into the springs and river pools to deposit jewels on the bottom in the hope of placating the divine wrath.

But the goddess was not yet satisfied. Ahuitzotl had been able to inhabit a part of his palace out in the lake during this time, and here one day he was caught in the sudden collapse of the edifice and partially crushed under the slow settling of the roof beams. Floundering about waist-deep in water and wreckage, he received a severe head injury that from that time on incapacitated him.[43] He performed no more public actions as *tlatoani*. The *cihuacoatl* appears to have acted the part of regent for Ahuitzotl and to have zealously carried out the tasks of restoring Mexico.

The opening of a new *tezontli* quarry in the Basin came at a most opportune time.[44] It was organized into a continuing operation and soon the houses of the nobles and the royal palaces in Mexico, all splendidly built anew of blocks of this handsome reddish stone, rose again over the surface of the quieted waters.

Each magnate was given an allotment of various subject *calpulli* in the area, and with the forced labor of these people he drew the stones out of the quarry and transported lime and timber to the site of his

building. The *cihuacoatl* in turn oversaw the beautification of the reno-
vated city in its entirety, bringing in trees of several varieties to plant
in parks and open areas. In 1501 the ground level of Mexico had been
so far raised by stones, clay, and turf brought in by canoe that, with
the return of normal weather, Mexico again stood on dry land. And in
her outward form she was more beautiful than ever before. Other cities
in the lake like Cuitlahuac, which were not able to command the pro-
digious labor needed to raise themselves out of the mud, had to be
abandoned until the lake level fell sufficiently.

The now helpless Ahuitzotl, in preparation for his demise, commanded the carving of his effigy in the cliffside of Chapultepec, and
here accordingly he was immortalized beside his predecessors. The expected rash of rebellions that had broken out at the first news of Mexico's desolation and Ahuitzotl's injury were put down by the Three
Cities moving together and posed no immediate threat to empire.
Ahuitzotl's condition worsened with the passage of the months, and in
1502 he died—less like a great Aztec ruler than an ignominious commoner, broken by fate.

The Death of a Ruler

His was the last notable state funeral Mexico was
ever to have.[45] Toltec and Chichimec burial customs were fused in this
impressive ceremony. In Chichimec fashion, the corpse was swaddled,
adorned with a turquoise mask, and seated on the royal *icpalli*. Beginning with the two living emperors, Nezahualpilli and Totoquihuaztli
II, magnates from all over Anahuac came to pay their respects at a levee.
The dead ruler was addressed courteously as if alive and merely resting
after some specially heavy exertions. In Toltec fashion, however, the
body was finally cremated along with numbers of retainers and concubines and the ashes interred at the base of Huitzilopochtli's temple.
The sacred number four dictated the number of days during which the
complicated ceremonies lasted. There was preserved of Ahuitzotl only
his warrior's scalp lock, wherein resided the memory of his soul and
the knowledge of his birth date and death date. This memento of his
presence was kept for a while after him.

Thus did the essence of Ahuitzotl, purified in the radiance of the

pyre, depart to Tonatiuhixco, "the place of the sun's appearing," there
to spend four blissful years in the presence of the god whom he had
served as a warrior, at the end of which time his soul was to become a
cloud or a hummingbird.[46] So at least went the Toltec dogma concerning a great one who died. But a less aristocratic fancy, and one perhaps
more in keeping with his Chichimec ancestry, had him descend to Ximohuayan, "where are the unfleshed," a house of shadows under the
earth where he along with all men great and small would lie down forever, crushed by the feet of Tezcatlipoca.[47]

Well might he have recalled then the words that had been spoken to
him years before at his royal installation, words that invoked Tezcatlipoca as the master of all destinies: "Our roads and works are not so
much in our own hands as in the hands of him who gives us life."

11. Moteuczoma II and the Presences

 Anahuac had always been filled with presences. The clarity of its skies and the enchanted quality of its vistas imposed upon the inhabitants an unreflecting submission to its grandeur. The earth under their feet evoked a feeling of awe, of ghostly power, and of oneness. The hills and mountains were in multitudes, as people were in the streets of cities, and the various divinities attributed to them were each carefully noted and scrupulously worshipped. Each mountain had a name. And just because he was a stranger in that land, a newcomer, the Mexican humbled himself and was uneasy in the midst of all such godly and indigenous presences. He tried to tread warily, to meet every demand faithfully—to acknowledge the self-preemption of the land into which he had so recently intruded. What we today would call the scenic beauty of the land he called its holiness, and he trembled at it.

There was one particularly disquieting presence in the land that— unlike the mountains—could not be seen. This was Quetzalcoatl, whose dominion this was by right. His historicity, the belief that he

still lived and would return some day to claim his patrimony, made for
a deep-dwelling anxiety in the Mexican state. The Earth Mother and
the mountains were always there and most palpable, but Quetzalcoatl
brooded in a faraway and patient land, invisible, and known to men
only through omens and prophesies. His mere being kept the present
in a state of expectancy. No one doubted his imperial rights to the
land, and no one doubted his intention to reclaim it. Mexico therefore,
with all its arrogance, was still a self-acknowledged caretaker state.

In Tenochca coronations the new ruler was customarily adjured to
look forward to this divine return: "Remember that this royal seat was
not yours but your predecessors'. It is given to you in trust and will be
returned to its true possessor. You will not last forever and you occupy
this seat on sufferance."[1]

These words had been spoken to both Tizoc and Ahuitzotl and most
probably to the rulers before them as well. They were now to be spoken to Moteuczoma Xocoyotzin, the new *tlatoani*, and were to affect
his actions notably in the future.

The Election of Moteuczoma II

When Ahuitzotl died, Moteuczoma, who held the
rank of *tlacochcalcatl* in the Council of the Four Princes, happened
to be in the Toluca Basin, where he held estates inherited from his
father.[2] He returned to Mexico immediately, prepared to contest any
other contender's claims to the lordship that was now properly his.
Normally, the sons of Tizoc (who had been the oldest of the three
royal brothers) would have been the preferred candidates, but Tizoc's
soiled reputation plus the fact that he had not been the first of the
brothers to rule eliminated his issue. The only other serious contestant
was Moteuczoma's brother (most probably a half-brother) named
Macuilmalinal, who held the high rank of *tlacateccatl*. What gave him
some advantage was the fact that he was a son-in-law of Nezahualpilli,
yet curiously it was Nezahualpilli who undercut him by putting forward the superior candidacy of Moteuczoma. Macuilmalinal thus remained on the Council of Princes and had to content himself with the
prospect of succeeding Moteuczoma should he outlive him.[3] In this

year of his election Moteuczoma was thirty-four or thirty-five years of age.

An anecdote connected with this election was long remembered and several times recorded in our sources. After the preliminary protocol was concluded and the magnates were about to turn to serious discussion of the candidates, Moteuczoma, a pious man, left his place and retired to Huitzilopochtli's shrine where he was afterwards located by the electors who had just chosen him. He was found sweeping the floor before the statue of the god in an act of ultimate humility.[4] He was then escorted back to the royal chamber where he was officially notified of his election. He did not go out to accept the encomiums of his new subjects but instantly retired to take up his interrupted task before the god; nor would he go to claim his new dignity until satisfied that the god had been pleased with his servile sweepings. Finally he accepted the formal acclamation. In the historic moment of his seating one of the magnates exclaimed: "Rejoice now, O happy land! seeing that the Lord of Creation has sent you a prince who will be a strong pillar."[5]

Ironic words!

The Person of Moteuczoma II

The character of the man whom the Mexica had selected to be their next ruler has evoked controversy from the times of the early Spanish chroniclers down to the present day. The decisions he was to make—as well as those he did not make—have tagged him generally as a weakling. We are, however, under the necessity of assessing him again because of the pivotal role he is to play in this history.

There was nothing particularly striking about Moteuczoma's outward appearance according to all accounts. Spare, rather small than large, he in a sense deserved the designation Xocoyotl that distinguished him from his great-grandfather; the name means the cadet, the youngest or the smallest son.

He had been born in 1467 or 1468[6] in Aticpac, a *calpulli* in Tenochtitlan,[7] this event occurring at the very end of the era of Moteuczoma I. Nothing is known about his mother except that she was a woman of high rank from Ixtapalapa.[8] He had received his training in the *calmecac* in the reign of Axayacatl, but he did not begin his career on the field of battle until the reign of Ahuitzotl. In the early years under this latter ruler, he had distinguished himself for bravery in the attack on Cuauhtla, taking several captives. He accompanied numerous campaigns, gaining laurels each time until he finally took his seat as *tlacochcalcatl* among the Four Princes.[9] He was one of the *cuachictin* or "shaved heads," a ranking of knights who had performed exceptional and daring feats.[10] He had latterly been designated as we have seen to take an army down into the Isthmus to relieve the merchants besieged there. After his brother Tlacahuepan was captured and sacrificed by Tlascala, he was acknowledged to be first among his peers.

To support his dignity he had married the daughter of the ruler of Ehecatepec and had then succeeded his father-in-law as *tlatoani* of that city a few years before the death of Ahuitzotl. We find him also married to Miahuaxochitl, a princess of the house of Tula. This second marriage was obviously designed to cement his claims to be not only descended from but presently allied to the Toltec line of Quetzalcoatl. Being a politically strategic marriage, it probably took place at the time of or soon after his coronation. The union, however, that satisfied the requirements of the Three City League was the one he contracted with a daughter of Totoquihuaztli of Tlacopan. Finally, he espoused a daughter of Tlilpotonqui, the *cihuacoatl* and the son of Tlacaelel. His major marriage alliances thus protected him on all fronts and were accounted to be exceptionally splendid.[11]

In the early part of his rule he was to act out the part of an Aztec ruler to perfection. He was grave, even dour, spoke seldom, and then sententiously.[12] He believed that his responsibilities were fulfilled most aptly in the rigor of his sentences, and almost immediately upon taking office his anger was felt by many. He carried the elitist orientation of the state to a peak by instituting a new order of knights (of which he was the commander) even superior to that of the eagles.[13] Commoners were summarily executed for looking at him, as were noble pages when they spilled food or fumbled in his presence. According to one source, he had always counted on ruling, and he desired to be remembered as the most admirable and the most feared of all the Mexican rulers. Few rulers indeed have demanded and had such instant obedience as he. He is said to have been a monster and tyrant, though it is hard for us to judge this; he was certainly cruel.

Underneath these appearances there seems to have been a quite different person.[14] The anxiety that lies in all of us and is our common heritage as men was in Moteuczoma experienced with a singular vividness. His fear of death was pronounced and resulted at the end of his life in the abject surrender of all his outward dignity. His suspicions of himself and fear of failure forced him into the extreme policies and the typical assertiveness of the self-righteous man. He demanded to be treated almost as a god, more so, it would appear, than had been the case with previous Mexica rulers. His pride was gross and indeed abnormal.

A question of his courage arises. There can be no doubt that as an Aztec knight he lacked nothing of courage in the press of battle. It was rather in the realm of the spiritual that he was a craven, so much so that, as he neared the end of his reign, he spent most of his time as a penitent, immured away from men, fasting, praying, and performing auto-sacrifice. Clavigero notes that his superstition was the major cause of the withering of his personality, and he is probably close to the truth in this assertion. Moteuczoma was even for his time notoriously and morbidly religious; like all such persons he was also most zealous in regard to the minutiae of religious works. Sorcerers were among his closest counselors and he himself was learned in, and therefore bedeviled by, astrology. His need to read the secrets of the future became an increasing obsession with him. He was a man who labored under the whips of demons.

But there was something of a saving self-awareness about him. Underneath, he knew that he was no god-man like Quetzalcoatl, but a mortal and frail. He knew that his vassals hated him, but he was their leader and had earned his position by his courage. The fact that his society gave him no higher model to pattern himself upon than that of a stern and angry ruler was no fault of his. That he abandoned these better parts of himself in the last years is the real charge that can be brought against him. Unlike the stereotype of the noble hero who falls into tragedy and who deserves our sympathy, Moteuczoma is an involuted and disturbing person to contemplate, complex and shifting, pathetic rather than tragic.

The coronation took place in 1503 on one-Crocodile, an auspicious day;[15] it had been on this day years before that the great Moteuczoma Ilhuicamina had assumed the office of *tlatoani*. The god who had charge of this day was Tonacateuctli, the Saturnian lord of subsistence who presided over the ruins of that great pyramid at Teotihuacan that had anciently been his. Thus everything possible was done to insure greatness and prosperity in the new reign as Moteuczoma Xocoyotl sat down upon the *icpalli*; he was the ninth lord of Tenochtitlan and the twenty-sixth of Culhuacan.[16]

He began his rule with an unprecedented and shocking action. Previously, while the *tlatoani* had in accordance with custom kept all significant honors for the enjoyment of the barons, he had nevertheless also utilized the services of commoners at court on some of the tribunals and in various other positions of trust. Ahuitzotl in particular had allowed some blurring of class lines, and Mexico to that extent had been under him a state with a certain amount of social elasticity. All this was now swept away in a studied catastrophe ordered from the top.

As he left with his army to crush an uprising in the Isthmian province of Nopallan, Moteuczoma placed the government in the hands of the *cihuacoatl*. Specifically, he had given him the charge of purging the personnel in the palace and the leadership of the various *calpulli* of all persons tainted with common blood.[17] Moteuczoma is reputed to have said, "Those of royal blood do not sufficiently stand out surrounded by people of common birth,"[18] and we may guess this sentiment to have been the reason for his present action. Thus suddenly was revealed his intention to demean the commons and to further divide them from noble and legitimate houses. The *cihuacoatl* is said to have argued with him that such a thoroughgoing obsession with aristocracy would only weaken the state, but he was peremptorily overruled. Of the obsessive character of Moteuczoma's war on bastardy and plebeian blood there can be no doubt. His desire to assert the perfection of his own lineage had made it necessary for him to demote others.

From the precepts of his youth he believed that the *macehualtin* were by nature vicious and lazy, and he consequently saw no renown for himself in being served by such as them.[19] He sincerely believed them to be human rubbish and incurably vulgar. In this he differed to a slight degree from his ancestors, for rulers such as Itzcoatl had sometimes rewarded merit in the lowly as well as in the high. Moteuczoma let it be known that the commoner, man, woman, or child, who looked on him would be instantly killed. He further decreed that their housing continue to be miserable—crowded, dark and airless—and that they should aspire to nothing better. It is perhaps not true that Moteuczoma ordered many of the servants and harem overseers of Ahuitzotl whom he had inherited to be killed out of hand, their fault being that they were base born, but it would not have been inconsistent with his beliefs.

Moteuczoma's presumption even reached out to demean the noble class, for while the nobility was alone worthy when compared to the vulgar, when compared to him it also had to be made to appear lesser. He had decreed that his subject rulers should serve him in person when he appeared among them, washing his hands like menials and serving him at meals. All nobles, whether Mexica or vassals, were informed that their sons were liable for service in his court as pages, sweepers, doorkeepers, and the like. These youths, some of them pulled at an early age out of the *calmecac*, were organized into a hushed and incredibly deft corps of servitors; the least slip as they served the *tlatoani* was punished by instant death. Throughout the empire the *calmecac* system was given new orders. In the past bastard sons of the nobility had had easy entry and through this training had later risen to high positions; all illegitimate youths now training in the *calmecac* were to be expelled and none thereafter admitted.

This was in no sense a social revolution engineered at the top by one man. From the viewpoint of those times it was, rather, a purifying of the state. Though extreme, it was wholly consistent with the cultic orientation of Mexico, for it merely emphasized values already old and accepted. Nevertheless, it came as a complete surprise to the Mexica. They had known Moteuczoma as an honorable knight, brave before men and humble before the gods. Now, with the suddenness of a

thunderclap from the blue, he had changed, appearing before them in
the guise of a high and holy one with a mission. It was the unexpected-
ness of this alteration in the personality of a man that startled them.
But though hatred and fear were to result from the stringency of his
rule, there would never be successful opposition to him, for in the end
he was only guiding Mexico to the goal implicit in all its early history.
Men feared him, not because he was a revolutionary but because he was
so consistent. There was no room in his system for accommodation or
humanity.

Moteuczoma's harsh policies were also to affect Mexico's relations
with the other two members of the Three City League. Here the work-
ing-out of another logic in Mexican history is evident. The League,
upon which Mexico had so heavily depended in her rise to greatness,
had now begun to seem to her anachronistic. It is true that the three
sovereign armies continued to march together, but, increasingly, leadership of these enterprises had been shifted to Mexico. The experienced Chimalpopoca of Tlacopan had died just before Moteuczoma II
came to power, and his son Totoquihuaztli II appears to have come
increasingly under Mexican domination. Of more importance than this
were Mexico's worsening relations with Tezcoco.

Nezahualpilli was closely tied by descent to the royal line of Mexico.
His mother had been a Tenochca, and two of his wives were of the
same *calpulli* as Moteuczoma, being nieces of Tizoc. But it so happened that another royal wife, who was a sister of Moteuczoma, had
become involved in a notorious affair of the Tezcoco harem and had
been executed—along with four hundred other people suspected of
complicity—by order of the outraged husband. Mexico had been invited to send its own executioners over to kill her, but had refused.
What particularly angered the Mexica was perhaps not so much the
accusation that a woman of their royal line had committed adultery as
the publicity attendant upon her execution, for she had been garroted
in the open in the fashion reserved for plebeians. They could only feel
that the vulgarity of her exposure to the public eye was a studied insult
directed at them. This had happened in 1498, five years before Moteuczoma became *tlatoani*, and it had laid the groundwork for an un-
pleasant tension between the two great states.

What perhaps counted for more was the undoubted fact that Neza-hualpilli's prestige among the Mexica was as high if not higher than that of Moteuczoma himself, and this to the Mexican ruler must have been a constant irritant and certainly something of a challenge. Mo-teuczoma is even said to have once insolently declared in Nezahual-pilli's presence that he and he alone was emperor. The hostility had deepened on the occasion of one of Acolhua's great military defeats. An army from Tezcoco was ambushed by Tlascala in a deep ravine on Eagle Mountain near the frontier and almost totally destroyed.[20] Mo-teuczoma had immediately exploited the resulting Acolhua weakness by making inroads on her empire among the Chinampaneca cities. Nezahualpilli strenuously objected to the appropriation of his tribute rights there but was unable to secure redress. Sad, withdrawn and bod-ing evils to come, he had soon after died.

That the bad blood between the two rulers had not come to the point of actual conflict was understandable given Moteuczoma's infatuation with signs and portents.[21] Nezahualpilli was considered to be a necro-mancer of great powers and therefore dangerous. Since his birth he had been known as a shape-shifter, a *nahualli*, and could see into the future. His study of the stars had taken him farther into the esoteric than Moteuczoma himself had gone, and his observatory of the night skies in Tezcoco was famous.

The Failure of Mexico's Tlateputzca Policy

It was to be expected that Moteuczoma's major mili-tary effort should have been directed at the Tlateputzca cities, those in-veterate enemies of the Mexican royal house. His whole reign in fact, while interspersed with varied campaigns, was increasingly occupied with the Tlateputzca question. A memorable series of contests fought on the customary battlegrounds on Atlixco's frontier opened the con-frontation. The historian has the utmost difficulty distinguishing among these tournaments, but one at least was never to be forgotten.[22] Knights from many cities in the Basin in this particular engagement here met their corresponding numbers from Tlateputzco. The ruler of Tula, a half-brother of Moteuczoma, had with his companions in arms seized the initiative and had asked for the honors of first blood. In this

suicidal opening, most of the knights of Tula and their leader were cut
to pieces or captured in a berserker display of bravery before the order
to support them was given. Of those now fed into the battle, other close
kinsmen—including a son—of Moteuczoma were killed while an excessive number of ranking knights, both Mexican and allied, were also
eliminated either by death or capture. Blind fury and audacity had their
day, and the end was a notable disaster for the Mexicans and their fellows. They had taken few prisoners and themselves had lost a great
number of knights. It was said that only one-third returned home.

Moteuczoma pretended to find that the knights from Tlatilulco who
had been engaged in the affair had not been sufficiently intrepid in the
melee. Accusing them of cowardice—the most wounding thing that
could be said of an Aztec warrior—he forbade them to wear their
knightly gear or to enter the palace. He ordered his executioners to enter the house of each of these Tlatilulca veterans to personally cut off
their topknots, the sign of their valor. In an explosion of feeling, Tlatilulco called a meeting of its magnates and seriously debated immediate and all-out rebellion. The cooler heads prevailed, and a year later
the knights were able to return into their sovereign's favor after a fine
showing in a successful flower war against Huexotzinco—here they
lost 370 men but gained a hundred prisoners! These tournaments apparently took place in 1508 and 1509.

Clashes with the cities of Tlateputzco were considered mere contre-
temps, not serious. But the situation changed radically when a rift
appeared in the united front that the Tlateputzca cities had always
presented to the peoples and cities of the Basin. Tlascala and Huexotzinco, as it happened, had fallen out in 1501 and for a number of
years thereafter had repeatedly flung armies at each other. The long
bleeding had an unexpected effect. In 1515 Huexotzinco appealed to
the Three City League for aid. Such an opportunity had never been presented to Mexico before, and Moteuczoma therefore decided that now
was the time to mount a supreme effort and crush Tlascala once and
for all. Should he succeed his fame would equal that of the renowned
ancestor whose name he bore.

The course of the war that followed shows a curious lack of determination on the part of Mexico. Although possessing unequaled ad-

vantages, Mexico did not press the attack home. One suspects a weakness that is hidden from us in the desultory coverage of our sources. A part of the explanation is certainly to be found in the erosion of Acolhua influence in the councils of the Three City League and the growing distrust between that people and the Mexica. The crushing defeat of the Tezcocans on Eagle Mountain, where they had been ambushed by Tlascala, was a part of the tragedy. Tezcoco came to believe that Moteuczoma had lured them into that trap in collusion with Tlascala—they believed in fact that Moteuczoma had gloatingly watched the slaughter of their helpless warriors from a nearby height. This is probably untrue, but in any case we know that there arose bitterness between the two old allies over the setback, and we may presume a lack of cooperation between them from that time forward.

Just as important a factor as this lack of vigor on the part of Mexico in prosecuting the war against Tlascala, however, was Moteuczoma himself, whose personal disorientation at that time had drained away his courage.

The war opened with the evacuation of Huexotzinco in 1515. The war of attrition that Tlascala had been waging against Huexotzinco had forced her to send an urgent appeal for help to Mexico.[23] Their fields, after years of burning, could no longer yield harvests, and they had not the men any longer to hold off the enemy. Along with this appeal went an offer of limited submission to the League.[24] After due consultation, the Three Cities agreed to provide Huexotzinco with protection on the proviso that they could garrison the Huexotzinca territory as they saw fit, this to include their presence right on the Tlascalan frontier. The wretched Huexotzinca, exhausted after more than a decade of fighting, lacked the power to bargain and agreed that a treaty defining such a relationship between them would run for four years.

This understanding provided for what was essentially a population exchange. Most of the Huexotzinca were withdrawn from their homes and farmed out among the Three Cities and their subjects around the lake. Mexico received the most important contingent, which included the *tlatoani* Xayacamachan and his leading nobles. In return, each of the Three Cities sent some of their people as garrison populations, forming three new and separate *calpulli* in Huexotzinco; the Mexica who went appear to have been Tlatilulca. This arrangement scarcely hid the fact that the Huexotzinca in Mexico had now become menials and servants, while their fellows remaining in Huexotzinco were incorporated into the anti-Tlascalan plans of the Three Cities and their plight was not much better.

As Mexico now stood on the very threshold of completing her encirclement of Tlascala, few men could be in doubt as to the end. And yet the Mexica were never able to push on the few remaining miles into the heart of Tlascala. The only success in fact achieved by Mexico was the capture alive of the celebrated and gigantic Otomí warrior Tlahuicole.[25] This was a windfall so unexpected that Moteuczoma in a gesture of high chivalry freed him, endowed him with a Mexican coat of arms, and even sent him off as captain of a Mexican group raiding the Tarascans. The captive accepted all these honors, however, only as a prelude to sacrifice, which he insisted on. He even refused a final offer to be taken into the Mexican nobility with the title of *tlacateccatl*. Only after three years did Moteuczoma finally give in and order Tlahuicole's death on the gladiatorial stone. The incident admirably illustrates the exotic mixture of motives in Aztec warfare.

Not only did Mexico fail to push home her advantage against Tlascala,[26] but she handled the Huexotzinca problem badly. Acting the part of a conqueror rather than that of a treaty ally, Moteuczoma demanded to have Camaxtli, the great god of the Huexotzinca, brought to Mexico and installed along with all the other subjugated idols in the House of Darkness. This was profoundly resented by the Huexotzinca, who resisted strenuously and succeeded at least once in foiling a Mexican attempt to abduct the god.

The events that follow are uncertain, but it can be seen that the Huexotzinca realized that the Mexica were using their former lands beyond Popocatepetl as a permanent military base against the Tlascala and were not seriously defending its fields and productivity. It was further suspected by them that the terms of the four-year treaty would not in fact be honored by the Mexica and their satellites when the time of its expiration came. So the depleted fragments of the Huexotzinca people began to give ear to agents from Tlascala and Cholula urging them to take action to protect themselves before it was too late. The date is not known, but at some time in this four-year period the Huexotzinca still living in their own city rose against the Tlatilulca garrison killing twelve hundred of them and seizing Totozacatzin, their captain, for sacrifice to the god Camaxtli. It was also undoubtedly at this time that the Huexotzinca domiciled in Mexico and the lake communities began a breakaway, heading back to Tlateputzco.[27] Mexico was forced out of Huexotzinco by this sudden revival of the traditional alliance of Tlas-cala, Huexotzinco, and Cholula against her, but in retaliation she was able to ambush large numbers of unfortunate Huexotzinca in Chalca territory as they attempted to leave the Basin. This breakdown of the four-year treaty occurred in 1518.

As the next year came around, the year of the Spanish landing under Cortez, Mexico was back where she had been fifteen years before when Moteuczoma had made the decision to eliminate Tlascala.

War in the Southeast

The other wars fought by Moteuczoma follow no discoverable pattern of conquest and are for the most part crowded into the first six years of his reign—for reasons that will become evident. Besides Tlascala, the parts of Anahuac still unconquered by the Three Cities were those ancient enemies the Huaxtecs along the Pánuco River, Metztitlan, the mountain Totonacs, Michoacan, and parts of Tehuantepec. By the end of his reign Moteuczoma had made no significant advances against any of these. Despite the loss of momentum in conquest resulting from the crisis in the Three City League, we cannot discount a stiffening resistance in all parts of Mesoamerica, as the monstrous pretensions of Mexico created an inevitable desperation by way of reply.

In Moteuczoma's campaign down into Nopallan in 1503,[28] the Tlatilulca warriors took a significant part, owing to their reinstatement as fully accredited Mexica. When Tlatilulco had been defeated in 1473 by Moteuczoma's father, it had been put under tribute. This tribute appears to have been waived by Tizoc and Ahuitzotl because of their increasingly cordial relations with Tlatilulco. In one of the first acts of his reign, however, Moteuczoma had summoned the Tlatilulca barons and demanded the full tribute owing to him, threatening them with a general massacre if they did not immediately comply. Recovering from their shock, the Tlatilulca had not only produced the goods that had formerly been agreed upon, but offered more if it were desired. This so pleased Moteuczoma that he pronounced the Tlatilulca fit to fight by his side in battle and to move about in their own companies under their own officers; they were restored to all their former honors and were at last allowed to renovate their own temple of Huitzilopochtli. Significantly, however, Moteuczoma did not allow them fully independent status, for he never remitted the tribute they owed him. Nor did he return to them their own ruling house with sovereign powers.

Certainly a part of this reconciliation was due to Moteuczoma's interest in the luxury trade carried on by the merchants of Tlatilulco.[29] In carrying on Ahuitzotl's southeastern trade policy, Moteuczoma elevated a certain Tlatilulca merchant to head the entire commercial guild. Greatly increased activity was the result, and state trading ventures now became common. Also—as in the former reign—merchants were used on fact-gathering expeditions preceding conquest. The best excuse for a distant war was always the massacre of a caravan of Mexican merchants.

Tlatilulco was still represented by Itzcuauhtzin, the original *cuauh-tlatoa* appointed by Axayacatl in 1474. He was a legitimate scion of the old ruling house of Tlatilulco, but he did not wear the *copilli* and his powers were limited by three other military appointees who sat as a council with him.

The early war against the Isthmian cities of Icpatepec and Xaltepec was a resounding success. Its impact could be seen in the haste with which the Zapotecs sought accommodation with Mexico, the ruler of Tehuantepec requesting one of Moteuczoma's daughters as his queen. The army escorting its many captives returned in victory, but with a show of royal languor Moteuczoma sent it back into the city without him.[30] He himself stopped off on the small and sequestered island park of Tepepulco where he had a villa. It was unprecedented for a *tlatoani* not to accompany his triumphant army on its entry into Mexico, but Moteuczoma's purpose was to increase his prestige by remoteness and a show of personal whim. Our sources also suggest that he returned under cover of night by canoe to Mexico so that, unknown to the *cihua-*

coatl and the court, he might spy out any infractions of the orders he had left. There are indeed many items similar to this mentioned in our sources where Moteuczoma deceptively or in disguise tested the efficacy of his commands in the daily work of his officials.

He may have been lured by the ease of the Nopallan campaign to believe in the docility of the Isthmian Zapotecs. In 1506 the whole southeastern region of the empire flared into rebellion, cutting off Mexican access to the province of Ayotlan.[31] Tehuantepec was involved first; afterward the contagion of revolt flowed back into the Mixtec highlands. The war, or series of wars, lasted into 1508. The pivotal garrison of Oaxaca was lost and then regained. The lands of the Mixteca were three times invaded by vast allied armies under Cuitlahuac, Moteuczoma's brother, a token of the fierceness of the resistance.[32] Finally Yanhuitlan was taken, Coaixtlahuacan and Tototepec surrendered, and Tzotzolan was burned and deserted by its own inhabitants, who scattered far and wide into the rough hill country rather than submit. Mitla, the holy city, likewise was abandoned to the forces of the League.

Three years of the most savage fighting Mesoamerica had ever seen came to an end with the Three City League triumphant and the whole southeast once again sinking into the deadly silence of the defeated. Cuitlahuac was greatly honored for the thoroughness of the reconquest and multitudes of Mixtec prisoners were sacrificed in spectacular rites.

Years of Omens

The years of Moteuczoma's reign were filled with events much like those recorded of any other Aztec ruler; the Mixtec rebellion and the confrontation with Tlascala have been outlined. A severe two-year famine beginning in 1505 tested the endurance of the Mexican state and found it well able to function.[33] Though Moteuczoma seems to have learned from the past, as when he imported maize from Totonacapan, the relief amounted to little in the face of the widespread starvation. Even some of the lower nobility were forced to sell their children into slavery outside the Basin. The drought broke in 1507 and the fields once again grew green. This was known to be a favorable omen, for 1507 was the year two-Reed, the beginning of a new fifty-two–year cycle.

The New Fire Ceremony of this year was celebrated with the dedication of an enlarged shrine to the god of fire on his hilltop near Culhuacan.[34] A campaign had been launched the previous year for the purpose of acquiring a large number of sacrificial victims for this event, and a total of over eight hundred prime prisoners had been taken there by the warriors of the Three Cities and their subjects. Moteuczoma, in pursuance of his bent for the astrological, gave orders that the noble victim in whose opened breast the new fire was to be kindled should be a man whose name bore some relation to the ceremony. An investigation turned up a prisoner from Huexotzinco named Xiuhtlamin, literally "year's end," and he was accordingly selected for the great honor. His captor, a Tlatilulca warrior named "Dog," had his own name now altered to "he offers Xiuhtlamin (as a victim)" to indicate his own derived prestige.

The New Fire Ceremony on Mount Huixachtecatl had become by this time a pan-Aztec ceremony held under the presidency of Mexico. To it all the subject cities of the empire contributed. The venerable site of the Fire God's cult on Huixachtecatl had in the last few reigns been effectively absorbed into the larger cult of Mexico, which, in her own imperial fashion, she now consented to share with the lesser peoples and cities around her.

The lurid and exaggerated part religion and religious sanctions played in Mexico under Moteuczoma II is of particular importance if we are to understand his failures.[35] The growing paralysis of the state—particularly from 1509 onwards—is reflected in feverish temple building and the appearance of omens. Moteuczoma's well-known and neurotic concern for the cults of the various gods is mentioned in several sources. He assiduously consulted oracles both in Mexico and in more distant centers such as Cholula, Tehuacan, and Achiutla. He insisted on the most meticulous observance of cleanliness in the temples and in the letter-perfect performance of their rites. Increasingly, he associated himself with sorcerers and sought out from the far parts of the empire the most eminent diviners. On coming to power, he had ordered the construction of a temple to Cinteotl, the deity of cultivated crops. In addition he had renewed or rebuilt the round temple of Quetzalcoatl, covering its tall conical roof with new thatch. This edifice was dedicated

in 1504.[36] The concern shown by Moteuczoma for the cult of Quetzalcoatl reveals how seriously he took his royal office, acknowledging it to
be handed down from the ancestral Toltec hero Topiltzin Quetzalcoatl.

It was therefore not only a shock to the state but most particularly to
Moteuczoma himself when, some time after this, lightning demolished the temple of Xiuhteuctli, the god of time.[37] The dire event had
consequences other than the religious terror it inspired, for the sight of
the flames leaping upward from the center of Tenochtitlan caused the
Tlatilulca just to the north to believe that an enemy had broken into the
city. Brandishing their arms and in full battle array, they bore down on
Tenochtitlan thoroughly frightening Moteuczoma, who could only believe that they had planned the fire as an act of arson and were moving
in to destroy Tenochtitlan in the resulting confusion. He ordered the
immediate arrest and removal from high office of all the prominent
Tlatilulca nobles and confined them to their own suburb. After a few
days, when the truth of the matter became evident, he rescinded his too
precipitate orders.

But this did not ease the concern of the state. If the fire had not in
fact been the act of a vengeful Tlatilulco, it could then only be a blow
and a warning from the heavens—perhaps from Tlaloc. This was the
second year of the drought. Did not the event speak of the continuing
wrath of Tlaloc against Mexico and its royal house? Or was the true
meaning that time and the years would indeed come to an end, giving
way to a new aeon? Though Moteuczoma rushed a rebuilding program
through, a feeling of uneasiness about the reign and its prospects was
rising.

Just as the fifty-two–year cycle was coming to its end in 1506, Moteuczoma decided upon the erection of a new Coateocalli, the shrine
that housed the Earth Mother in her avatar as mistress of endings and
death and as the final arbiter of all the gods. A statue of this brute goddess was ordered and in all probability it has survived as that most
striking of pieces now housed in the National Museum in Mexico City
—"she who wears a skirt of serpents," Coatlicue.[38] For the dedication
of this spectacular shrine Moteuczoma needed a holocaust of victims.
He accordingly selected Teutepec, a city in the Oaxaca area that had
just previously massacred a column of Mexican merchants. A wild as-

sault by the armies of the Aztec empire upon the well-fortified city followed, and the prisoners taken, to the number of 2300, were sacrificed
en masse to appease the goddess in whose province was the power to
annihilate time itself. Thus was the cycle of years appropriately ushered
out.

The successful entry into the new fifty-two–year cycle and the simul-
taneous breaking of the drought to some extent alleviated the widespread malaise. Things in fact seemed to be returning to a more normal level of expectation when, about 1509, an event occurred that
could not possibly be explained or wished away. The phenomenon is
variously reported as a cone of light or a tongue of fire in the eastern
sky beginning at midnight and continuing until the rising sun caused it
to fade away. The sources describe it as a luminous banner-like wraith,
as a spindle-shaped cloud, or like smoke and flames ascending. Others
refer to it as a comet. It lasted well into 1510 and was seen in every
corner of Anahuac.[39]

One can say that the descriptions of this phenomenon best fit those
given of the zodiacal light, but beyond that feeble conjecture there is
no certainty. What is indeed evident is the unnerving effect it had on all
the peoples of Anahuac, for it clearly could not be referred to any
known god—except perhaps to Quetzalcoatl, who was still hidden
away in the mysterious east. To Moteuczoma, especially sensitive to
portents and who witnessed the prodigy himself, the reading of its dire
secret was of the highest priority.

Whatever the kennings offered, he could take no satisfaction from
any of them. He called in the young man who that year was the *texiptla*
for Tezcatlipoca and who was to be later sacrificed;[40] though this youth
was the god incarnate, he offered no satisfaction to Moteuczoma, who
finally decided to consult Nezahualpilli, the ruler whose fame in the
land as a reader of the occult was most generally recognized. For Moteuczoma to have taken the decision to seek the aid of the ruler whom
he had so recently scorned is a telling sign of the hazards he believed
were threatening him.

Nezahualpilli came in person to Mexico for the conference. As a
preliminary step it was agreed to by both of them, as well as by the
ruler of Tlacopan, that for the time being offensive wars were to be dis-

continued. The omen itself was read by Nezahualpilli as portending evil. Perhaps he did prophesy, as later accounts have it, that the sign indicated a disastrous invasion of Anahuac and the end of time. Moteuczoma refused to accept this merely on the word of his fellow ruler and insisted on submitting the prophecy to the arbitrament of the gods. A game of *tlachtli* was accordingly arranged between teams of champions representing the two cities. Should the team of Tezcoco win, it would point to the rightness of Nezahualpilli's prophecy. This in fact is what happened. Moteuczoma now spurned Tezcoco with an even more sullen antipathy than before, but he was nevertheless still affected by the gloom of the prophecy. He continued his search, going now more openly in search of more favorable opinions. Sorcerers and astrologers from all over were sent for, and when their readings of the future also hinted at darkness and cabalistic endings, Moteuczoma would sometimes order them dragged through the streets with a rope around their necks till dead, their homes razed, and their kin uprooted. "Where to fly? In what place can I hide myself?" he is reported to have exclaimed. "Would I were a bird!"[41] So desperate was he that he even dispatched an embassy to distant Cuauhtemallan, near the supposed home of Quetzalcoatl, but our source does not state the content of the message carried by this mission.

After the departure of Nezahualpilli, Moteuczoma retired to his hall of meditation for fasting and autosacrifice. From 1510 on, a rash of rebellions broke out across the empire as waves of superstitious unrest attendant upon the malign light erupted among the distraught peoples.

When the prodigy in the east had finally disappeared, Moteuczoma ordered the building of new shrines, concentrating particularly on the Tlamatzinco, which he dedicated with a vast number of victims taken from the Mixtec city of Tlachquiauhco, which had again revolted. Along with this he ordered the quarrying and carving of a new and larger *temalacatl*, one whose massiveness would be sure to please the gods.[42] The great block was taken out of the hills back of Ayotzinco and moved on rollers along the southern edge of the lake. It was then escorted with music and priestly incantation up the causeway toward Mexico. But again the signs were evil, for the great weight of the piece caused it to crash through one of the wooden bridges, carrying many officiants with it to their deaths in the water below. Later in 1511 it was recovered and installed in Tenochtitlan. The popular mind, however, did not forget the recalcitrant stone and many embellishments were added to the bare story of its reluctance to enter the imperial city.

We need not detail the other omens that now began to accumulate as Moteuczoma struggled desperately against the growing hostility of the heavens. It is evident that much of the material in our sources is a reflection of the growing spiritual malaise of Moteuczoma himself. Trying to flee the death he saw ever before him, he continually sought out oracles and prophecies, gathering them up in bewildering variety, yet was always dissatisfied with their answers. It was probably in this state of depression that he ordered his effigy cut in the rock of Chapultepec as all his ancestors had done on feeling the approach of their end. A veritable flood of rumors and speculation now poured out unchecked over the palace and rushed thence, proliferating into the streets of Mexico and out to the farthest corners of the empire. Any unexplained night sound now sent the countryside into spasms of fear. Signs and wonders were everywhere.

Schism in Tezcoco

The year 1515 was crucial for all of Anahuac. In that year Nezahualpilli died under mysterious circumstances without having named a successor.[43] For some time previously, in anticipation of Nezahualpilli's death, factions had been growing up around his potential successors. Of the legitimate sons there were three main contenders, Cacama, Coanacochtzin, and Ixtlilxochitl.[44] The twenty-one–year–old Cacama was favored because his mother was a sister of Moteuczoma—he therefore represented the pro-Mexican party. Ixtlilxochitl, as his name might imply, stood for the recovery of Tezcoco's freedom of action from Mexican domination. Coanacochtzin stood in the middle, though he leaned slightly toward accommodation with Mexico. According to the constitution of the Three City League, Cacama could claim the election, but the strength of patriotic sentiment among the Acolhua knights spoke provisionally for Ixtlilxochitl.

Cacama was finally selected, but not before the Acolhua empire was torn apart. So deep was the chasm dividing the Acolhua nobles and so thorough had been the work of Moteuczoma's agents that the nativist party was unable to prevail in the course of the electoral discussions. The deadlock could not be broken, so an admitted expedient backed by Moteuczoma was tried. This was to offer the rule to a less-distinguished brother whose name was Quetzalacxoyatl. No other solution offering itself, the Acolhua leaders proceeded to elect him.

The temporizing nature of their choice was vividly brought out when, subsequent to the coronation of this prince at the hands of the Mexican *cihuacoatl*, he suddenly disappeared from the scene, whether dying a violent death or not our sources do not say. In the confusion Ixtlilxochitl, still insistent on an uncompromising stand, was forced out and fled with a significant body of followers into the highlands of Metztitlan to the north, an area as yet unconquered by the Mexica. Here, in the style of his eminent grandfather, he began collecting forces with which to return someday into his patrimony; nevertheless he made it abundantly clear that he was not threatening the Acolhua state as such, but that his enmity was reserved for the obsessive *tlatoani* of Mexico.

Though the Acolhua nobility was by now thoroughly disorganized, Cacama still did not have the strength on his own to force the election, so he fled across the lake in an impassioned appeal to his uncle for aid. Moteuczoma viewed those nobles who had accompanied Cacama as constituting a proper electoral group, and he accordingly proclaimed Cacama's election. The situation was not yet favorable for Cacama to return to Tezcoco to take up his office, and he did not do so until 1516. When he did return, he was escorted across the lake by a great fleet of Mexican war canoes with Cuitlahuac, Moteuczoma's spokesman and general, in charge. Backed with this powerful Mexican force, Cacama was officially installed as *tlatoani* in Tezcoco.

By 1517 it was apparent that Acolhuacan was finished as a unified and fully independent state. Ixtlilxochitl had moved as far south as Otumpan, where he held an army poised to strike; he controlled all that part of the former empire of the Acolhua north of Acolman. Coanacochtzin had exacted as the price of his peace the rule of all the Acolhua territory south of Tezcoco. In order, therefore, to be accepted as *tlatoani* in Tezcoco itself, Cacama had been forced to agree to a treaty with his two fraternal rivals validating the territorial status quo.

Mexican machinations had indeed succeeded not only in radically weakening Acolhua but in fragmenting her into three parts. Cacama was patently a puppet ruler belonging to Mexico, and the proof of it was the fact that many cities in Anahuac as far away as Campeche were communicating secretly with Ixtlilxochitl, proffering him aid and informing him of their hatred against Mexico. The vigor of the old and prestigious line of Xolotl could now be recognized only in the hotheaded and energetic Ixtlilxochitl, who was increasingly taking on the stature of Mexico's leading adversary.

The Coming of the Spaniards

That Mexico would have to reply to this challenge was evident, and the world of Anahuac tensely awaited the test. In 1518 Moteuczoma ordered north what armies he could spare from his commitments in Tlateputzco. Here they battled Metztitlan, winning some engagements against that country which was backing Ixtlilxochitl but without lasting effects.

There was a reason for this comparative lack of success. In 1517 rumors, winged with baleful prefigurations of doom, raced up along the Gulf coast and then leaped over the great Escarpment to enter Mexico, the heartland of Anahuac. These rumors were as yet lacking in much substance, but they foreshadowed the return of Quetzalcoatl. They were based on the voyage that Francisco Hernández de Córdova made in that year, a voyage of discovery that carried him along the coast of Yucatan toward Anahuac as far as Champoton. Coasting merchants from Champoton brought in the news of the three ships and the great slaughter made of the strangers on those distant beaches. In its passage through many hands, details of the encounter were garbled, finally coming to Moteuczoma in a frightening and grotesque form.

This portent had happened well beyond the confines of the Aztec empire so Mexico could not authenticate it; as a consequence there were at once a thousand explanations and none. The most that Moteuczoma could do was again to consult the oracles. One of the seers consulted was the ruling lord of Cuitlahuac, who bore the title of *tzompanteuctli*.[45] This house claimed descent directly from the god Iztac Mixcoatl and possessed divinatory powers. Reaching out in his confusion for ways of placating the gods, Moteuczoma now requested of the *tzompanteuctli* his opinion of a plan whereby he would honor Huitzilopochtli by building for him a shrine of colossal proportions. Commanded to reply, this subject king gave out that such a construction would exhaust the people and even offend the heavens—besides, the real lord was on his way! In a tantrum of fear and rage on receiving this prophecy, Moteuczoma directed the execution of the *tzompanteuctli* and the extirpation of his entire line, thus bringing the sacred history of the city of Cuitlahuac to an abrupt and bloody close. But Moteuczoma's need to know continued to be insatiable, and he turned to the demonic mother, Coatlicue, for her favors and began to build for her a vastly more impressive shrine.[46] In her granite bosom she carried the secrets of all things, and Moteuczoma hoped that she could be persuaded by his piety to divulge them.

The following year Juan de Grijalva with four ships completed the previous tragic voyage, touched at Coatzacoalcos, Chalchicuecan, Nauhtla, and only turned away from the coast as he was approaching the mouth of the Pánuco River. It was toward the end of June, 1518, when his ships dropped anchor off Chalchicuecan, the site later to become famous as Vera Cruz.[47] The pressure of the mysterious events caused Mexico to falter in her war with Tlascala, and she was forced to watch the remnant of the Huexotzinca desert to that cause with relative impunity

Mexico had early been alerted to the arrival of Grijalva's ships, and when they touched at Coatzacoalcos, just beyond the effective frontiers of the Aztec empire, Moteuczoma moved to contact the strangers. His embassy, however, did not find them because they had already moved on up the coast.

The ships had passed leisurely along to Chalchicuecan and in that roadstead had come to anchor for a matter of several days. The Mexican *calpixqui* in Cuetlaxtlan, in great alarm, rushed down to the coast to gather information. Here he and his few companions disguised as merchants had their first view of the wallowing conveyances and of the awful beings in them. Through interpreters, the strangers announced that they were there only temporarily but that they would return in a year. They asked for the name of the land and its lord and, having given the Mexica some green and yellow beads, they departed.

Pinotl, the *calpixqui*, and the men who had been with him on this mission returned posthaste to Mexico to report. They were ushered instantly into Moteuczoma's presence—an unheard of breach of protocol —and were told to reveal all that they had seen and heard of the newcomers. The effect of their words on Moteuczoma was ghastly. Stricken with fear, he could barely bring himself to ask his officials whether they thought the intruders were indeed the gods of prophecy. They answered affirmatively, citing the black beards, the glistening accoutrements, and the ponderous vessels of the strangers, which could only be floating temples out of the sea. Furthermore, they had come from the east, and they had said before they left that they would return in the next year and that year would be Ce Acatl, one-Reed, the fateful year of prediction. Moteuczoma dismissed them with the admonition to secrecy lest the news they had brought reach the ear of the people and disturb their ways.

The Council of Four was instantly convened and was joined by the other two emperors of the League and several of the greater magnates. Inasmuch as this was the group that determined Mexico's first policy response to the Spaniards, a full listing of their names may be in order. Cacama we know as callow and already shorn of much of his power. Tlaltecatzin of Tlacopan is to us only a name, nothing more. Besides these two, Cuitlahuac, the brother of Moteuczoma and ruler of Ixtapalapan, was also called in on the deliberations; we have seen his notable accomplishments in war and diplomacy and there is evidence in the sources for believing him to have been the most important figure of his day. Among the princes were Quappiatzin, with the rank of *tlacochcalcatl*; Ecatempatiltzin, with the rank of *huitznahuacatl tlailotlac*; and Quetzalaztatzin, the *tizociahuacatl*. With them sat the *cihuacoatl* Tlilpotonqui. It is not known whether Itzcuauhtzin and Cuauhtemoc, both rulers in Tlatilulco, were present or not, but it is most probable that they were.

To this the most august company in all of Anahuac was given the crucial task of determining the identity of the newcomers; upon this all else hung. It is history's great loss that their opinions and debates are not better attested, for as they sat with eyes downcast for the sake of their gravity, their measured words and equally sententious silences foreshadowed and indeed made inevitable the tragic unfolding of their future. After viewing the beads and hearing the newcomers described, they decided that they were indeed the gods or their followers and that Topiltzin Quetzalcoatl had shown himself through them. The time had therefore come to offer him the kingdom he had returned to claim. They rejected the idea that the newcomers might be apparitions sent by Tezcatlipoca or Tlaloc, possibilities suggested earlier.

An embassy of five ranking magnates was quickly assembled and enjoined to seek out these beings. They were charged to do them homage as vassals, and they were further to discover their intention toward Moteuczoma, whether they wished him to die or to live out his life under them as their *calpixqui*. When this embassy arrived on the coast, however, in spite of the haste they had made, the strange beings in their ships had been wafted away out to sea to be heard from again briefly at Nauhtla and then at Tuxpan and then no more. The embassy returned with the rich gifts it carried unoffered.

Moteuczoma ordered the green and yellow beads buried in the great temple of Huitzilopochtli as being too sacred for the uses of men. Other scraps of things obtained from the intruders were taken in solemn procession to Tula and there deposited for safekeeping in the venerable temple of Quetzalcoatl. Meanwhile, against the predicted return of the gods a special coast watch was set up.[48]

Mexico now relapsed into a state of subdued terror to wait out the time. There still remained, however, certain gnawing doubts. Moteuczoma turned again to the sorcerers, sending agonized questions to the holy city of Cholula and to the great mountain sanctuary and oracle of Achiutla in the land of the Mixteca.[49] Tocual, a famous painter of books, was called in to depict on paper, from Pinotl's description, the story of what had happened and the shapes and numbers of the intruders.[50] This book was then submitted to the custodians of the archives of prophesy in Cuitlahuac but without any positive results. Men from Malinalco and the other Tlahuica cities renowned for their knowledge of the sacred parts of the past were summoned, but they could offer no clarification. In desperation, Moteuczoma consulted a *teomama* of the goddess Quilaztli in Xochimilco. Quilaztli was that avatar of the mother goddess who had borne Quetzalcoatl and was thus indicated as the oracular court of last resort in this particular respect. Tocual's book was submitted to this necromancer, and when he had finished comparing the pictures with those in his own holy books he identified the strangers with certainty as the followers of Quetzalcoatl; they lived, he said, in a place called Tzonapan, and he added that they would certainly return.

Moteuczoma thus gave up his frenzied search for someone who would deny the truth of the ancient prophecy. He pushed the completion of the goddess's shrine in Coatlan, and then, as if to at least prevent future treachery on earth, he instituted a purge of subject rulers in certain of the Basin cities.[51] The lords of such cities as Xochimilco, Azcapotzalco, Ehecatepec, and Tenayuca were ruthlessly dispossesed, and members of Moteuczoma's immediate family installed in their places. Pinotl, down on the coast, was replaced by a new *calpixqui* named Tentlilli. It is doubtful that Moteuczoma knew what it was that he hoped to really achieve by such spasmodic measures, but the net effect was certainly to increase tyranny and confusion in a land already stricken.

In the year Ce Acatl, the year of prophecy—about the middle of March, 1519—all Anahuac shook with the news that the return had occurred. The gods had been seen in Tabasco, and they had brought to that coast death and destruction. On the twenty-first of April, their six ships cast anchor off Tecpantlayacac, a coastal community from which a road led back to Cuetlaxtlan.[52] The following day they came ashore, swarming like black ants, and they carefully planted in the pebbles of the seashore their curious standards, red and black and gold. As those flags flapped sullenly in the cool mist driven down from the north and as the gods strolled casually around them, muskets and pikes at the ready, few could have doubted the greatness of the events that were to follow.

12. The Failure of a Mexican Tlatoani

Two Years and Four Months

Cortez stepped ashore on the twenty-first day of April, 1519. Only two years and four months later the proud and imperial city of Mexico was to lie under his feet, a muddy and fetid wreck awash in the lake. It can truly be said that for the Mexica the heavens and the earth in that short space of time were torn apart in what was a total disaster. Few peoples have fallen from the pinnacle of power so swiftly.

That Moteuczoma was not the leader to confront these events is obvious. There were men around him, notably Cuitlahuac, who advised him to adopt a more courageous and a more consistent stand, but he did not have the heart for it and he ended by vacating every vantage point presented to him. His pride collapsed at the outset, and he dwindled away to become at the end a person of little consequence. Cuitlahuac and Cuauhtemoc, far greater men, followed him in the office of *tlatoani*, but it was then too late. Moteuczoma's abdication of leadership at the beginning of the Spanish invasion—and indeed even before—had erased Mexican influence in Anahuac. Mexico's fall was not a necessary consequence of Moteuczoma's failure, for the power of European culture would sooner or later have reduced Anahuac to submission. Nevertheless, his failure doomed the Mexican fall to be the final act in a drama of pathos, not one of high tragedy. Perhaps because of that it is more human and therefore more understandable.

The Centaurs on the Coast

Tentlilli, the *calpixqui* in Cuetlaxtlan, sent back the first authentic reports of the visitation.[1] On the strength of these Moteuczoma now selected as his personal envoy to the gods the *tlillancalqui* who had on occasions before served him on missions of exceptional delicacy and danger. This highly placed envoy carried with him the full regalia of the god Quetzalcoatl, which he was to offer to the strangers who had come in his name.[2] He was also the bearer of a distracted and temporizing message from Moteuczoma to the effect that the land was indeed the possession of Quetzalcoatl but that it was hoped that he, Quetzalcoatl, would not at the moment advance inland to claim it, for panic had seized Anahuac at his entry and all things were unsettled. Such a reluctant welcome was the fruit of obvious indecision, reflecting Moteuczoma's piety, fears, and insecurity all at the same time, and could not help but further erode the Mexican position.[3]

The *tlillancalqui* returned with firsthand impressions of the newcomers. So sacred was the occasion of his report from the gods that Moteuczoma commanded the sacrifice of several victims and the sprinkling of their blood over the various members of the embassy before the *tlillancalqui* was allowed to speak. The gods, so the ambassador reported, were strangely served by beasts. They could join themselves to great hornless stags to become as if one thing. Nevertheless, their identity with the followers of Topiltzin was decidedly unclear. In fact, if they were gods, they could well be enemy gods, for they carried weapons of fire and thunder. Their own claim was that they were ambassadors from a superhuman *tlatoani* or emperor by the name of Carlos, who ruled lands beyond the sea. With them the newcomers had a divine woman who could speak Nahuatl. She was called Malintzin, and it was she who relayed the strangers' keen desire to learn all they could about Moteuczoma, his name, his wealth, and the location of his realm. They had said that they would certainly ascend the Escarpment and visit him.

This first communication was followed by a spate of others, for Moteuczoma could not rest and kept parties of spies and ambassadors constantly on the road. The anxiety that underlay his personality now came to the surface and turned his thirst for the most current information into an addiction and his fear of the strangers' approach into an illness. He summoned one meeting of the Council after another, and his frequent vacillations resulted in creating among them a deep cleavage of opinion. One party, that led by Cuitlahuac, increasingly came to believe that the newcomers were men, and they therefore favored issuing a harsh proclamation to them to return whence they came. The opposite party, led by Cacama, who was now permanently residing in the Mexican court, was undecided about the nature of the newcomers; they held in any case that, if they were indeed ambassadors, then it did not comport with the dignity of a Mexican *tlatoani* to turn them away. The *tlillancalqui* threw in with this faction and finally went even so far as to state as a fact the friendliness of the invaders. The net result of all these urgings was that Moteuczoma, unable to come to a clear-cut decision, hoping to believe one side and fearing to believe the other, ended by taking both positions at once.

But something more deadly than indecision was at work in that heavy time—treason. Our view of perfidy in the inner councils of the Mexican state is limited by our lack of prime sources; such material seldom comes to light, and all the more so here since the state with all its records was so soon to founder in total ruin. What does appear is that when Tentlilli returned to his station in Cuetlaxtlan, two nobles remained there on the beaches to serve the strangers and to keep track of their intentions. These may be the same two mentioned as nephews of Moteuczoma who were sent down at this time with additional gifts and warnings. At any rate the precariousness of Moteuczoma's situation was at this time betrayed to the Spaniards by members of his own court.

The two disaffected men were Atonal and Tlamapanatzin, the first one claiming direct descent from Acamapichtli and the second either a nephew or a close relative of Moteuczoma himself.[4] They were lords of communities near Otumpan nominally subject to Tezcoco, and their aversion to Moteuczoma may be tied to the hostility so recently engendered in that state by Mexican high-handness. We hear that back in the

Mexican court they had been in some way involved with a famous painted book of prophecies attributed to Acamapichtli, which foretold the arrival of the god. Moteuczoma had ordered the burning of this book, no doubt with the intention of muting the divisive issue of Quetzalcoatl's return, and he had charged these two magnates with the commission. But realizing that the possession of such a manucript would be of advantage to any cabal bent on unseating Moteuczoma, they had not complied with his order, but had retained the manuscript. Once down on the coast they had secretly approached Cortez with the offer to deliver it to him within twelve days, the book being no doubt secreted somewhere in Tenochtitlan. Their terms were that Cortez should move at once to destroy Moteuczoma and the tyranny he represented.

An understanding was reached. Atonal and Tlamapanatzin allowed themselves to be baptized into the religion of Christ somewhere around the twentieth of May as evidence of their good intentions. They turned over to the Spaniards not only the book of the prophecies of Acamapichtli but a great deal of other useful information as well.[5] Moteuczoma was unaware of this treachery and used the two again as ambassadors to Cortez, who was then moving up from the coast. From that point on they played out consistently their role as spies, aided in bringing about the defection of Chalco and were in Mexico when the Spaniards arrived. Their undercover activities and urgings helped to finally bring about the arrest of Moteuczoma. For all this they were later to be amply rewarded by the invaders.

With clouds of suspicion increasingly hemming him in, Moteuczoma at one point made up his mind to turn his back on the problem and flee. The reports he was receiving that the inexorable intruders were reiterating their determination to come and behold him in person worked so upon his imagination that he finally called in his necromancers and demanded that they help him escape. How true this statement is there is no way of knowing. What probably happened is that he left his palace for a period of penance and fasting and that his absence from the seat of rule later gave rise to the fantastic story of the cave of Cincalco.[6] Just back of the rock of Chapultecpec was the cave popularly thought to be the entrance to a divine land under the earth. Its name, "the house of corn," denotes both its chthonic and its elysian features. Into it the last of the Toltec *huemacs* had disappeared upon the collapse of the empire of Tula, and there in a paradise of continual feasting and joy he presided over a court of immortals. Moteuczoma is said to have investigated the possibility of retiring secretly into Cincalco, but shame overcame him and he renounced his intention.

Enough has been said to reveal the source of Mexican confusion in dealing with the Spaniards who were now beginning their move up country. Along with signals of this advance came news of an equally distressing kind—certain parts of the empire that lay in the path of the advancing gods were throwing off their allegiance to the Three Cities. Of the roughly thirty Totonac cities, most had already cast their lot with the invaders and had openly and brazenly proclaimed their independence of Aztec rule.[7] Led by the city of Cempoalla, this rash of rebellions had erupted spontaneously. Cempoalla had seized the resident tribute collectors from Mexico at the same time that they had welcomed the invaders into their midst. But the purport of this news was obscured by the fact, known soon after the news of the rebellion came in, that the invaders had intervened to free two of the Mexican officials, thus giving Moteuczoma, who was eager to believe the best, reason to send them further rich gifts along with words of gratitude.

Some of Moteuczoma's generals strongly advised him to send an army down to stamp out the fires of rebellion before they spread, and he had accordingly allowed his garrison commander in the Totonac hill-fortress of Tizapantzinco to take action against Cempoalla.[8] This had resulted in a setback, for the Spaniards leading the Totonacs now as allies had counterattacked and, with great dash, had taken the fortress. The sequel was without precedent in Aztec warfare, for the Spanish had allowed the Mexican troops to go free but without their arms and insignia. The news of this flashed from one end of the empire to the other. Moteuczoma wanted no more armed confrontations with the intruders and sent secret instructions to Cuauhpopoca, his vassal in the coastal city of Nauhtla, to invade Totonacapan only after the intruders had left.

But he still sought to dissuade or delay the intruders from their an-

nounced intention of moving inland. He accordingly ordered a group
of Tlahuica sorcerers down to the coast, but they failed in their designs,
reporting back that the flesh of the gods was hard and their hearts im-
pervious to enchantment.[9] And still the Spaniards in the exchanges
with Mexican envoys continued to insist that they intended to come to
visit Mexico. To facilitate this, Moteuczoma gave orders to all his garrisons on the difficult route up the Escarpment not to oppose the Spaniards.[10] At the same time he was sending messengers bearing gifts to
the Spaniards, he was continually stressing the perils of the route ahead
and advising that they turn back. He was unaware that all the covert
weaknesses of his regime had been laid bare by informers close to him.

The Lesson of Cholula

The route taken by the Spaniards in their advance up
country, accompanied as they were by a Totonac army, led them around
the north side of Mount Orizaba and therefore was leading them directly to Tlascala. This news appreciably increased the pressure on Mexico. Inasmuch as Mexico was locked in deadly combat with that nation
and had vowed its destruction, the danger loomed that Tlascala would
be tempted to throw in its lot with the invaders and then, in an invincible coalition, pour down over the green slopes of Mount Tlaloc to
threaten Mexico. Mexico dared not make an offer of alliance to the
Spaniards, for by so doing she would tacitly condone the Totonac rebellion, thus inviting the rest of her subjects to do likewise. In any case
such an alliance would have to be followed by an invitation to the invaders to enter Mexico. Thus was Moteuczoma caught in an impossible
strategy. The best he could do, again giving lip service to Cuitlahuac's
more positive stand, was to insist more peremptorily than before to the
Spaniards that they turn around and go back. To perform this embassy,
he appointed the *atempanecatl* with five other barons and a retinue of
porters with gifts.[11] They found the invaders camped on Tlascala's
eastern borders and gave them their message, adding that Moteuczoma
agreed to pay to Carlos, the hidden emperor or god, any amount of
tribute he should care to impose. The envoys, also on instructions,
warned the Spaniards against the perfidy of the Tlascalans. It was at

that very moment when a redoubtable host of Tlascalan warriors advanced against the Spaniards to test their mettle and to discover whether indeed they were gods or men. The result was a defeat of major proportions for Tlascala.

This military debacle along with the disturbing presence of the Mexican ambassadors in the Spanish camp convinced the Tlascalans that they were better off as friends than as enemies of the strangers from overseas. Their fear was the reverse of that of Mexico; they saw as a real possibility a Spanish-Mexican alliance crushing them from two sides like an egg.

It was now September. With the Mexican envoys still in his train, Cortez accepted the submission of Tlascala and took them into his friendship, entering the conquered city in a splendid triumph. This event was felt by all of Anahuac as the opening of a new era, for Mexico was now truly vulnerable for the first time since the early days of Itzcoatl. Huexotzinco, returning to her old Tlascalan orientation, quickly came into the alliance,[12] and, even more importantly, Ixtlilxochitl, from his armed camp in Otumpan, placed himself squarely on the side of the invaders, offering them the aid of his not inconsiderable army.[13]

Moteuczoma must often have rued the day, following the demise of Nezahualpilli, when he had chosen to override the Acolhua and had ended by fragmenting them irrevocably. The resultant weakness of the formerly staunch Acolhua empire had indeed allowed him to put on the throne of Tezcoco his own nominee, Cacama, but his gains had turned out to be illusory; at this crucial juncture Mexico had no longer a strong ally across the lake with whom she could take council and prepare measures. On the contrary, Moteuczoma now had the responsibility of protecting Cacama, the refugee emperor of the Acolhua, whose inexperience and lack of prestige made it certain that no significant body of Acolhua warriors would thenceforth support him, and whose only advice in council was to invite the onrushing invaders into Mexico. What military power Acolhua had left of any immediate consequence was with Ixtlilxochitl in Otumpan and was wholeheartedly anti-Mexican.

It was no doubt the presence of Ixtlilxochitl in Otumpan that in part

moved the Mexica to attempt to divert the invaders southward toward
Cholula. This tactic was to have consequences of the highest importance. Cholula was one of the few cities of Anahuac that was unaligned
and in a real sense truly international. Its privileged position as the center of the Ce Acatl Quetzalcoatl cult counted for more than armies,
with which in any case it was poorly provided. At the present time, because of a recent altercation with Tlascala, the city tended to favor Mexico but was in no sense a part of the Mexican empire. Near it were the
two Mexican garrison cities of Itzucan and Acatzinco with several thousand troops between them; these troops were to play a part in the events
to ensue.

There is no doubt that the Spaniards and their Tlascalan and Totonac
allies were supposed to walk into a trap in Cholula should the signs be
found favorable. We cannot be far wrong in seeing this tentative conspiracy primarily as a testing of the role that the god Quetzalcoatl
would play. The priesthood of Quetzalcoatl in Cholula had long adver-
tised the threat that their god, should his temple ever be so much as
scratched, would let burst from its holy walls torrents of wind and water to drown and sweep away the desecrator. If indeed these particular
invaders were not the sons of Quetzalcoatl, as many of the Mexica
nobles now averred, then surely in Cholula if anywhere the wrath of
the god would visit them with condign destruction. Mexico proposed
to have it both ways. Through her ambassadors, she would lure the invaders into Cholula where a true test of their divinity could be made
and where, in the event of their discovery to be mere mortals, they
might be attacked and done away with. Such an interpretation of the
sources dealing with this passage in Mexican history can alone explain
the subsequent events.

Mexico, therefore, with gifts and promises persuaded Cholula to
friendship and to test the invaders. The troops from Itzucan and Acatzinco were to be on the alert and would be used in the event that a
Cholulan plot seemed about to succeed. As a tactic, it had all the disadvantages that accompany vacillation.

The sequel was to rock the world of Anahuac and to initiate upheavals in its traditional loyalties and systems of belief.[14] In fact it is not too
much to say that in this event Mexico lost her empire. Cholula's double-

dealing had been discovered by the strange men from the east, and they had turned the tables, visiting upon the city a wholesale massacre.

The first news of this came to Mexico in garbled form. It told in brief how the Spaniards and their allies, some six thousand men in all, had entered the city, how Cholula had been in the act of setting up the ruse by which to overpower them when their intended victims turned upon them in the central plaza and cut down their leading men as they milled about in panic fear. Not only had vast numbers of Cholulteca fallen under that sudden storm of swords and darts, but the holy house of Quetzalcoatl, aloft on its artificial mountain, had been forced open, its priests burned to death, and its idol overthrown. For two terrible days destruction was wreaked upon the city, and it was that long before even the vultures dared descend into the embers to find their food.

Ce Acatl Quetzalcoatl had not defended his own! The inundations that, according to his promise, would gush uncontrollably out from the very mortar of his colossal shrine had not occurred. The news spread with the rapidity of wildfire from coast to coast and down even into the regions of the distant Maya, how Quetzalcoatl had proved to be a false god.

It is difficult for us to appreciate the full impact of this event. Cholula represented in spiritual terms the eternal verities of the Toltec past. Cholula was the navel of all religious life in Anahuac, and from her arcane house issued the most authentic oracles. The booming and hollow thunder of her conch shell trumpets sounding by night and by day from the terraces of his pyramid hill were the very voices of the god. He was the alpha and omega of Aztec society—he was associated with the Toltec diaspora that had given birth to the Aztec peoples of Anahuac, and his return was to bring that aeon to an end. If he had indeed returned here in the person of his followers, why then had he in fury destroyed his own shrine? And what was the meaning behind the toppling of his own image? No answers could be given to these questions, and a swift erosion of faith set in.

In Mexico the news was accompanied by a message from the invaders, relayed through one of the Mexican ambassadors who had been resident with them since Tlascala.[15] The message was harsh and completed the consternation among the nobility. The invaders knew of Mexican complicity in the aborted Cholula plot, and they stated again that they intended coming to Mexico adding that, if necessary, they would come with fire and sword. The choice belonged to Moteuczoma, then, whether they came in peace or war. Shattered by the terrible news from Cholula, desperate for his rule, and above all for his own personal safety, Moteuczoma retired again into the house of Cihuacoatl. Here, for eight days of fasting and sacrifice, he complained bitterly to the goddess of his hard fate and continued his pathetic search for a favorable oracle.

It was therefore through the Council that a reply had to be sent to Cortez, accompanied with the usual profusion of rich gifts; it denied Mexican guilt in the alleged Cholula conspiracy and offered for the first time an invitation to the invaders to come to Mexico. In this reversal it can be seen that the Cacama faction had finally won. Cuitlahuac's policy of cautious hostility was abandoned, and Mexico's last feeble attempts to control events crumbled. With her *tlatoani* incommunicado, the affairs of her empire came to a halt; all things now seemed to be awaiting a full revelation of the nature of the calamity.

Spies brought in the word that the Spaniards, accompanied by a strong guard of Tlascalans and Huexotzinca, were now on the move; but instead of taking the easy and dignified route that swept southward around the base of Popocatepetl, they were directing themselves straight up over the pass between that mountain and Iztaccihuatl. This was a hard road and certainly an unexpected one, being only a track winding through the dark forest and over great rocks, most of it lost in thick clouds. Moteuczoma immediately sent Tzihuacpopoca, a close companion and one of his most notable barons, to meet the invaders up on the heights in order to test their intentions; if asked to identify himself he was to reply that he was Moteuczoma and then, supposing he was allowed to live, he was to report back on how they had used him.[16] In this episode Moteuczoma's anxiety—his cowardice in fact—appears clearly. The deceit was easily discovered by the Spaniards. A group of sorcerers sent up into that wild country to work whatever of their arts they could against the newcomers also returned with their objectives unachieved. They claimed that on those slopes, which were the special preserve of Tezcatlipoca the Youth, they had met the god disguised as a drunken commoner lurching about among the maguey plants; he had shouted angrily at them and warned them away. Moteuczoma heard these reports with the finality of a man who fully despairs.

Down from Ithualco, a half-way station that stood at the summit of the pass, came the invaders. They were described by the Aztecs as follows: "Marshaled together, in a concourse, they came stirring up the dust. Their metal lances, their metal halberds glistened from afar and their metal swords moved in a wavy line like running water. Their metal shirts and head gear jingled. And what some wore was all metal; they came turned into metal, gleaming."[17]

Resigned, yet still seeking avoidance of his fate, hopeless but clutching at every straw, Moteuczoma now turned, incredibly, to the Tarascans of the far west for help, proposing to them a mutual defense pact.[18] Though the great lord of Michoacan heard this embassy out, as might have been expected he made no move to extricate his ancient enemies from their dilemma.

The Crumbling of the League

The strong shield that the kingdom of the Acolhua might have been for the Mexica against this visitation was no more. Cacama, almost a prisoner in Mexico and because he could not do otherwise, had ordered his brother Coanacochtzin to rule in his name in Tezcoco and to receive the invaders in peace should they move first into the lands on the east shore of the lake. Thus, unexpectedly possessed of the center of Acolhua power, Coanacochtzin's first move was to make an alliance with the rebel brother Ixtlilxochitl, further isolating Cacama from any influence in Acolhua and deepening the anti-Mexican cast of that vestigial kingdom.[19] Having in the first instance stirred up division in the line of Xolotl, Mexico could now do nothing about the situation beyond continuing to treat Cacama as if he were still in fact the Acolhua emperor.

Mexico had always relied on Acolhua power to help keep Chalco in line; now, as the Spanish invaders moved down toward Amaquemecan, the princes of all the Chalca cities flocked to their standard, doing extravagant homage to them and offering them women and rich gifts.

Though the Chalca cities in no sense openly repudiated their allegiance to Mexico, it was known that they were welcoming the invaders in response to certain weighty oracles given by the gods; this knowledge—plus their own unresolved religious quandary—effectively stymied any action the Mexicans might have taken to restrain Chalco. The best that Moteuczoma could do in the matter was to designate Cuitlahuac—who stood in the eyes of the empire for firmness—to Chalco, where his presence might be thought to do some good in the absence of a specific policy. When Cuitlahuac went out from the city of Chalco on the shore of the lake to greet the Spaniards, he reiterated to them that the city of Mexico was poor, that it lay miserably in a mire, and that it could be reached only in canoes. Along with such garbled and deceptive statements, he made yet another offer from his master to submit to any tribute desired if the invaders would only turn around and leave.

Cuitlahuac brought back the expected answer as well as his no doubt cautious assessment that the leader Cortez was not a god but a man and that he was merely the *tlacateccatl* of a mysterious emperor called Carlos beyond the sea. The failure of this embassy did not prevent Moteuczoma from dispatching Cacama to Cortez a few days later when he had arrived at Mizquic, with again the same dispirited welcome—meeting again with the same rebuff.

As the Spaniards moved leisurely along the reedy lakeside, the Mexican empire in those parts seemed to melt away at their touch. The Chinampa cities along the route, able at last to fully slake their hatred of Mexico, openly and bitterly spoke of the Mexican tyranny to Cortez and asked for his protection. In Ixtapalapan the League of the Four Lords listened to the siren song of the intruders, but nowhere was the demise of the Three City League as an effective institution so clearly revealed as when elements of the southern Tepaneca came in to offer their allegiance, thus putting Tlacopan beside the partially defected Tezcoco as an imperial center shorn of its following. And meanwhile, cities like Tliliuhquitepec and Tepoztlan, diverse in many ways but united in their hatred of Mexico, sent token numbers of warriors to swell the ranks of the Spanish allies.[20] The Mexicans were kept posted of all these desertions and they said to one another, "The time has come when we are to be destroyed; let us await death here."[21] Only a spring and a summer had gone by since the landing of the Spaniards on the coast—no more.

The Arrest of Moteuczoma

On November 9, 1519, Cortez, with three hundred Spaniards and some six thousand Indian warriors, entered Mexico City via the southern causeway.[22] Four outriders galloped ahead, circling and thrusting into the spaces between houses and behind walls to ascertain if the way were safe. Spotted mastiffs raced along beside them. Then came the standard of Castile: "By himself came as guide, going as leader—going ahead alone—one who bore the standard upon his shoulders. He proceeded, waving it back and forth, making it circle, and tossing it from side to side. It would stiffen and raise itself like a man; it would smartly curve, fly up in turning, and billow."[23]

Behind this handsome symbol of power came the infantry and, following them, the body of horse whose sweatings and nervous movements created great apprehension. Then came the crossbowmen, a select feudal group of men who had already adopted Aztec armor and feathered bonnets. "In their arms rested the crossbow. They came wielding and repeatedly testing them, sighting along them. And some bore them upon their shoulders; these came along shouldering the crossbows. And their quivers were hung at their sides or passed under their arms; these went filled, crammed, with arrows—with metal bolts. Their cotton armor reached to the knees; it was very thick, very hard, very dense, like limestone. And their heads were likewise wrapped in cotton armor, and from the top of their heads arose quetzal plumes, dividing and outspread."[24]

Then followed the arquebusiers, and riding behind them came Cortez himself, the *tlacateccatl* of the host. Flowing behind him like a rolling tide came his Indian allies, dressed for war, shrieking, crouching, ululating, and brandishing their weapons at their hated enemies the Mexicans, among whom they now so unexpectedly found themselves.

At Xoloco, the towered gateway on the south side of the city, Moteuczoma, his entire nobility, and the other two emperors stood to greet Cortez. Tlatilulco was represented by its *tlacochcalcatl* and ruler Itzcuauhtzin and by Topantemoc,[25] a Tenochca representative assigned there. The Mexican Council of Princes stood behind them, and with them Cuitlahuac. All were barefooted except Moteuczoma, who alone wore sandals.

Cortez said through Malintzin, his interpreter, "Is this not you? Are you not he? Are you Moteuczoma?"

To which Moteuczoma replied, "It is so. I am he."[26]

The ceremonies of greeting were elaborate.[27] Gourds of lovely flowers were set out in the space between the parties, garlands of flowers were thrown around the necks of Cortez and his captains in great profusion, magnolias, jasmine, and cacao flowers. But around the neck of Cortez as a special sign Moteuczoma placed a necklace from which hung the distinctive wind jewel of Quetzalcoatl—thereby he identified him as the god returning to his rightful patrimony or as his *texiptla*. In his address of greeting, Moteuczoma further so identified Cortez.

Moteuczoma acted the part of the majordomo turning over the properties and insignia of rule to the arriving owner: "O our lord, you have suffered fatigue; you have spent yourself. You have arrived on earth; you have come to your noble city of Mexico. You have come to occupy your noble mat and seat, which for a little time I have guarded and watched for you."[28] And then in the more humble fashion of a servant: "For I dream not, nor start from my sleep, nor see this as in a trance. I do not dream that I see you and look into your face. Lo, I have been troubled for a long time. I have gazed into the unknown whence you have come—the place of mystery. For the rulers of old have gone, saying that you would come to instruct your city, that you would descend to your mat and seat, that you would return. And now it is fulfilled; you have returned."[29]

By this greeting and in all of his later iterations Moteuczoma saddled upon Mexico the requirement of believing that the Spaniards were indeed the sons and ambassadors of Quetzalcoatl. But he did not convince any significant portion of the nobility, certainly not the members of his own Council of Princes. The events of the succeeding days were to greatly strengthen this doubtful party in their opinions.

Moteuczoma ordered that the Spaniards and their allies be given the palaces of Axayacatl and Moteuczoma I and that all their desires be attended to. The problem Moteuczoma faced of maintaining control over his more fractious nobles was complicated by the alarming presence in the very heart of Mexico of an army of Tlascalans equipped for war. The day after his arrival Cortez met with Moteuczoma and his court and demanded that they enter into a pact of friendship with Tlascala.[30] This deepened the anger of the opposition party, which was beginning to recognize fully the impossible situation into which their *tlatoani* had led them.[31] The Council of Princes several times in this interim period insisted on meeting with Moteuczoma to discuss ways and means of destroying the Spaniards, but the dire fate of Cholula loomed too large over these clandestine meetings; the tension and paralysis afflicting the Mexican state continued.[32]

The greed evidenced by the Spaniards in their incessant demands for gold and their senseless destruction of such prized items as quetzal feathers and jade pieces made a deep impression on the Mexica, but it was nothing to the humiliation they suffered at the depreciation of their idol Huitzilopochtli.[33] Not only had the Spaniards scorned the Aztec gods, but they had ordered human sacrifices discontinued in Mexico and the cleansing of all its blood-encrusted and fetid shrines. Also, with Moteuczoma's permission, there was erected on the summit of the great temple terrace a cross of wood, the emblem of a strange religion. It was probably at this point that the party of opposition began to receive strong support from the priesthood, for the prohibition of human sacrifice would not only deprive the barons of their claim to usefulness in the world, but would enfeeble the gods and thus endanger the priesthood.

The storm was slow in gathering, however. It was hindered by the fact that leadership in the person of Moteuczoma was, if not in the camp of the invaders, at least unwilling to take any forthright stand. The opposition struggled in vain against this handicap and, though it was contemplating an armed attack on the enemy installed in the palaces—as was charged by the Tlascalans—nevertheless it still could not bring itself to act.

The situation in Mexico, thus on dead center, was abruptly changed when without warning, only six days after their arrival, the Spaniards arrested Moteuczoma and brought him to the safety of their own quarters under heavy guard. At first sight the deed is almost unbelievable and constitutes an act of unprecedented daring. This is superficially true, but the act becomes easily intelligible when one realizes how far Moteuczoma's power with his own people had slipped away. The rapidly increasing strength of the court party of opposition, if not checked by the Spaniards, promised shortly to force Moteuczoma to do its will or to step down—thus depriving the Spaniards of their leverage. It was to prevent this eventuality that Moteuczoma was taken into custody by Cortez, who could have been no more happy about the move than Moteuczoma himself. For Cortez there was no choice. The Spaniards could reap advantages from Moteuczoma's friendship and declining authority only so long as they could keep him ruling. And to keep him ruling they had to keep him safe. Itzcuauhtzin, Cacama, and Cuitlahuac were seized along with Moteuczoma, but the members of the Council of Princes saved themselves by fleeing.[34] Their opposition now at last could become effective, though from a depleted base.

The occasion for the seizure was connected with Moteuczoma's tepid duplicity. Earlier, as we have seen, he had ordered Cuauhpopoca, his vassal in Nauhtla, to bring the Totonacs back to heel and to do whatever damage he might to the Spaniards left there on the coast. Cuauhpopoca had faithfully carried out his orders and, though unable to reduce the Totonacs, had succeeded in killing nine Spaniards. The Spanish lieutenant left on the coast immediately reported this event to Cortez with the evidence that it had been instigated by Moteuczoma.

With his own plans carefully laid, Cortez requested an audience with Moteuczoma. In the midst of this interview Cortez brought up the Cuauhpopoca affair and accused Moteuczoma of treachery.[35] Moteuczoma denied the accusation and as evidence of his good faith immediately dispatched messengers to Nauhtla to summon Cuauhpopoca to appear in court. But Cortez now carried the matter a step further by unexpectedly insisting that Moteuczoma submit himself to Spanish custody until the affair was cleared up. Intimidated and confused—but only after some hours of repeated objections—Moteuczoma finally agreed to his own arrest and was borne off to the palace of his father where the Spanish were lodged. To conceal his shame at acquiescing in his own arrest—and perhaps still not daring to test the wrath of Quetzalcoatl—he assured his personal retainers that the matter indeed pleased him and that he was accompanying Cortez of his own volition.

This was the end of whatever real prestige Moteuczoma had; only his immediate family and servitors plus some of the nobles continued to give him their trust and their service. While there were no tumults in the city when the news of their *tlatoani*'s capture reached them, the Mexica began at this point to talk pointedly about the illegitimacy of sovereign power when it was unfree. The morning after his capture, Moteuczoma, regally installed in his new quarters, summoned his nobles to meet with him.[36] Most of them refused.

The Deeds of a Captive Tlatoani

From this point on, the person and policies of Moteuczoma become of diminishing importance in the history of the Mexican state. His personal trauma had been up to this point the trauma of the Mexican people, his paralysis theirs. In captivity his position as a mere creature of events was now plain for all to see, and this knowledge now slowly released Mexico to attempt the recovery of her soul and of what remained of her resources. But this could not be accomplished overnight, for the wound of the invasion had cut deep. Remnants of the habit of loyalty to Moteuczoma still remained and had to be exorcised before his people could adopt a policy of self-interest. Mexico was still to receive a series of tremendous shocks, one hard upon another. All of them together would bring her down eventually; nevertheless the story of her attempted resurgence and final defiance are at the very least a tale of partial self-discovery. Moteuczoma II had not truly represented the toughness that was in the foundation of the Mexican character. With his immunization, the wonderful hardness of the Mexica was again—though only briefly—to reappear.

The imprisonment of Moteuczoma began in the middle of November and ended on the last day of the following June, 1520, with his death—a period of something over seven months. The arrival of Cuauhpopoca sometime in December is our first recorded event in this abeyant period. Moteuczoma promptly handed Cuauhpopoca over to Cortez for torturing and burning, a form of execution which to the Mexica was particularly dismaying. Their consternation was increased by the fact that the Spaniards and Tlascalans emptied the *tlacochcalli* of all the darts, arrows, and sword clubs stored there for use in war and heaped them up in a vast mound to provide the pyre upon which the unfortunate Cuauhpopoca was immolated. Under torture he had earlier confessed that it was Moteuczoma who had originally ordered him to attack the Spaniards.

On this evidence Moteuczoma was thrown in chains. His grief was violent and inconsolable, and Cortez shortly gave orders to release him, whereat his joy was equally extravagant. Moteuczoma, however, refused at this point a guileful offer from Cortez for complete freedom.[37] Moteuczoma's explanation for his refusal is revealing, for he said that if he should accept his freedom and return to his own palace his people would then force him to take up arms against the Spaniards. This is unequivocal evidence of Mexico's toughening stand against the invaders and of its growing reluctance to believe that they were sons of Quetzalcoatl. But more can be read from it than that. Moteuczoma was really frightened for his own safety, because he knew that in betraying a loyal vassal, as he had just done in the case of Cuauhpopoca, he had further forfeited the confidence of his people.

Perhaps the ultimate in perfidy was reached by the now degenerate Moteuczoma in the affair of Cacama.[38] The execution of Cuauhpopoca had at last brought this inexperienced puppet ruler to his senses. Hitherto obligated to his uncle Moteuczoma and himself identified with a pro-Spanish policy, he (along with Cuitlahuac, his opponent in that policy) had been forced to remain with the captive ruler. Now he was no longer able to stomach Moteuczoma's actions, and he began to urge upon him the necessity of ejecting the Spaniards and their Tlascalan allies before it was too late. He threatened to lead Tezcoco against them if Moteuczoma refused. Needless to say, Moteuczoma refused.

Cacama then managed to escape and fled to Tezcoco, the city of which he was nominally the ruler but where his brother Coanacochtzin was actually in power. Here, in a series of meetings with the magnates, he began the task of persuading his people to an open declaration against the Spaniards and—as a sop to the moderates of Coanacochtzin's persuasion—to the release of Moteuczoma from captivity. Ixtlilxochitl, the violently anti-Mexican brother, was present at these meetings, but his position had become thoroughly ambiguous because Moteuczoma, his mortal enemy, had identified Mexico with the Spanish cause, which he himself had been supporting.

Ixtlilxochitl solved the dilemma cleverly. At the instigation of Cortez, who wished to punish Cacama, Moteuczoma had alerted those of the Acolhua nobles who were in his pay to abduct Cacama if possible and return him to Mexico. Ixtlilxochitl found himself here able to fall in with his Mexican enemy's designs and so either winked at the plot or actively aided it. At the same time, he was flirting with the idea of seizing the island of Tepetzinco in Lake Tezcoco as an Acolhua base for a massive attack on Mexico. He hoped by handing Cacama over to please the Spaniards, but he could never bring himself to a pro-Mexican stance.

Cacama was treacherously seized, hustled into a canoe, and taken back to Mexico. Moteuczoma refused even to see him and gave orders that he be immediately delivered over to Cortez. Thus did Moteuczoma avert the great and immediate danger that Tezcoco would reunite and pursue an independent, anti-Mexican and anti-Spanish policy. It was an astonishing and indeed a powerful stroke for a captive ruler to engineer, and was predictably followed by the installation in Mexico of a new puppet emperor of the Acolhua, a younger brother of Cacama named Cuicuitzcatl. Moteuczoma had originally raised Cacama, his nephew, to the rule of the Acolhua; now he had betrayed him in favor of another brother who would be more pliant. It is not a pretty record.

Cacama was kept in chains until shortly before the Spaniards exited from the city, at which point he was secretly strangled. Coanacochtzin continued his *de facto* rule in Tezcoco and Cuicuitzcatl, like Cacama before him, ruled in name only—protected by the Spaniards—in Mexico.

Cacama's arrest was immediately followed by an act of homage when Moteuczoma and his rump court, in the presence of a Spanish notary armed with proper European documents, legally delivered the state over to the Emperor Carlos and received it back as vassals under the present occupation.[39] To those unhappy Mexica present Moteuczoma insisted that he was forced to do this because of the tradition of his family, based on the old prophecies, that Quetzalcoatl could and would one day demand back what was his. Carlos he identified as being a son of Quetzalcoatl. The act of fealty was performed by each member of the court individually, all of them weeping. Moteuczoma was not the least of those so affected.

Thus, suddenly and officially, ended the Mexican empire, though by many Mexica on the outside the act was not considered legitimate inasmuch as the Council of Four had not consented. With Mexico now legally in his grasp, Cortez ordered Moteuczoma to turn over all the gold and silver stored in his warehouses and to dispatch messengers to all the provinces with the same object in mind.

Moteuczoma soon regretted his betrayal of Cacama, and there are strong indications that it was the belated but peremptory intervention of the priesthood that brought about his second thoughts.[40] It was known that all the gods were angry at Moteuczoma, particularly Tlaloc, who threatened a prolonged drought if the Spaniards were not ousted. As for the barons, they told Moteuczoma that they were prepared to join the cause of the dissidents and depose him if he did not straightway exercise more effective leadership.

For Moteuczoma there was no other course but to agree. In extreme perturbation, he demanded an audience with Cortez and informed him of the situation, explaining that if he, Cortez, did not leave Mexico, then his own deposition would follow with a resulting attack upon the Spaniards and their allies. Cortez temporized, agreeing to leave but stating that inasmuch as he had no ships down on the coast in which to leave, he would need assistance in building them. At this crucial moment, toward the end of April, 1520, runners from the coast came in with the news that a fleet of ships had just cast anchor in Chalchicuecan. This was the signal announcing the arrival of Pánfilo de Narváez, come from Cuba with a warrant to arrest Cortez.

Moteuczoma was no match for Cortez in cunning. The latter kept a tight grip on Mexico, leaving most of his party under Pedro de Alvarado in the city while he rushed down to the coast at the head of a flying column to meet the new danger. The Mexican court now believed— but without foundation—that Moteuczoma was finally to be counted with them, and they began to lay before him possible plans for the destruction of the Spaniards, who were now divided into two vulnerable camps, one in Mexico and one on the coast. When a secret embassy came from the newly landed Narváez to Moteuczoma informing him that Cortez held no legitimate authority from the great Carlos but was a rebel against him, this information might well have been used by Moteuczoma to rally all factions around him. But he was incapable of true decision, and the opportunity passed.

It was now the middle of May and the festival of the month Toxcatl was upon them. The Mexica were convinced that in any case they would shortly be led in a mass uprising against the Spaniards, and they may have seen in the extended ceremonies of this great festival an opportunity to entice the Spaniards out into the open where they could be easily set upon. But certainly there was no specific plot on the part of the barons to do so at the dance of the Macehualiztli, "good fortune." Instead, they themselves were to be taken unawares in that performance by the men of Alvarado. Some six hundred to a thousand of the ranking magnates of Mexico, probably mostly Tenochca and all unarmed, were butchered in the temple precinct on the night of May 21, caught unaware as had been those of Cholula by the always prescient Spaniards.[41] But here the hurt to Mexico was singularly damaging, for a significant number of her greatest men, all of whom she would need in the perilous days ahead, were in these shambles lost to her. Ecatzin, the *tlacateccatl*, had warned Moteuczoma against the possibility of just such a tragedy occurring, but Moteuczoma had replied, "Are we at war?" and had allowed it to happen.[42]

Open war had come at last, and Moteuczoma's insistence that the intruders were the sons of Quetzalcoatl had for all Mexicans ceased to ring true. The Spaniard, whatever the power of his thundersticks and crossbows, whatever the speed of his horses and the sagacity of his dogs, was at last known by all the Mexica to be a man. The agonized lamentations of the Mexica for their illustrious dead was equalled now only by their determination to end once and for all the situation of humiliation in which they found themselves. The Spaniards became aware of the coming tumults, and, in an effort to calm the scene, they had Moteuczoma and Itzcuauhtzin led up onto the terrace roof of Axayacatl's palace. In the *tlatoani*'s name, Itzcuauhtzin pleaded with the Mexica surging about in the open areas below, informing them that they were already prisoners of destiny. He and Moteuczoma were shouted at and reviled.[43]

The Release of Cuitlahuac

Following the Toxcatl massacre, the Spaniards were straitly besieged in the palaces. The affairs of the great city came to a standstill, and the market was discontinued—a very great deprivation. Mexicans taken who were thought to be provisioning the enemy were instantly torn apart. A panic of hatred filled the streets of Mexico. Organized fighting, however, was sporadic because of the lack of formal leadership, and little damage was in fact inflicted on the Spanish forces holding the vast palace areas.

Cortez had now returned from his dash down to the coast and his defeat of Narváez; he was accompanied by a strong reinforcement of Spaniards, men who had formerly followed Narváez but who had easily transferred their allegiance to the wily Cortez. He was also followed by a contingent from Ixtlilxochitl's army. The Mexica allowed this strong column to enter the city and join the Spaniards under siege, for they were well informed of the hunger and thirst being suffered by the beleaguered, and they were not displeased to see the situation thus aggravated. Once in the improvised fortress, Cortez fully realized the seriousness of the supply situation and immediately demanded of Moteuczoma that the market be reinstituted. Pathetically anxious to please, Moteuczoma replied that he was willing to do so but that only a Mexican of the highest rank could bring it about, and he accordingly asked Cortez to release his brother Cuitlahuac for the performance of that mission.[44] Cortez agreed.

The Death of Moteuczoma

The release of Cuitlahuac transformed the scene. Confusion among the Mexica now gave way to direction. Cuitlahuac was the most highly respected warrior and counselor in Mexico. His hostility toward the Spaniards was well known, and he had of course no intention of carrying out his assignment—one can only wonder at Moteuczoma's naivete in recommending his release.

The Council of Princes, which had reconstituted itself outside the palace pale, promptly elected Cuitlahuac to the office of *tlatoani*.[45] Moteuczoma was removed from the office and would have been executed had he been in their hands. The state lay all about in wreckage, and it is a tribute to Cuitlahuac's ability that he was able to accomplish anything in the short time he had to rule.

Events were racing to a conclusion. It was readily apparent that the enemy would soon starve or be forced to break out of the trap he had thus prepared for himself. Every day strong holding attacks were made against the palace, and at one point the Mexica sent out a party of knights to fortify the strategic summit of the temple of Huitzilopochtli, but this party was destroyed by a sudden sortie of the Spaniards.

Tradition has it that the wound that killed Moteuczoma was received by him on the last day of June. The significance of this famous event has been greatly overstated by most writers, for Moteuczoma was of no account to either the Spaniards or the Mexica at this point. There are two versions of the event, diametrically different.[46] The Spanish version, generally accepted, has it that Moteuczoma feared that Cortez would have him killed if he could not stop the incessant attacks, and so he requested permission to appear before his people on the palace roof and exhort them to submission. Escorted up there, his words were drowned out by the crowd howling curses at him. Arrows and rocks began to fly and, though protected by Spanish shields, he was struck on the head by a slingstone. The wound was serious and he died from it soon after, refusing all food and comfort and finally entrusting his children to Cortez. The Mexican version denies this and states that when the Mexica later took over the palace, following the departure of the Spaniards, they found Moteuczoma dead of strangulation or stabbing. Nearby were the bodies of Itzcuauhtzin and Cacama similarly disposed of. The corpses were found just outside the palace walls on a canal bank at a spot called Teoayoc.

Both versions are to some extent suspect, but the probabilities point to the truth of the Mexican version. What is certain is that the rulers of Tenochtitlan, Tlatilulco, and Tezcoco—all of them in the possession of the Spaniards—were dead when the Spaniards exited Mexico, and that the murder of the latter two is nowhere denied. Itzcuauhtzin's body was taken away by his subjects and properly cremated. Moteuczoma's body, shot full of arrows by his vengeful people, is said to have been finally burned but to the grinding of teeth and the sound of imprecations. The ashes were buried in the ward of Copulco.⁴⁷ Duran memorializes Moteuczoma as "a king so powerful, so feared and served, so obeyed by the whole of this new world, who came nevertheless to an end calamitous and shabby so that even in his last rites there were none who spoke for him or bewailed him."⁴⁸

The Reign of Cuitlahuac

Cuitlahuac had not been *tlatoani* long enough to constitute himself undisputed master of Mexico at this point. Precautionary tactics had only been sketched in against the moment when the enemy should make his breakaway. As it was, the alert was quickly sounded on that memorable night of the death of Moteuczoma when the enemy stole out of the dark shadows of the palaces and began to move with stealth down the causeway to Tlacopan.⁴⁹ A fine drizzling rain was coming down at the time and at first helped to conceal the enemy. But when the vigilant priests on the temple summit shouted out their hoarse warnings in the middle of the night, then the entire body of the Mexica sprang up as one to assault the absconding enemy. Poling their canoes with frenzied speed, the Mexica burst out of the reeds that lined the causeway, attacking from both sides at one. The Noche Triste, as it was to be later known to the Spaniards, was the night of June 30/July 1.

As with all night actions, the affair was desperate and confused. For the Spaniards and their Tlascalan allies it was a comprehensive disaster. The last of the four deep culverts they had to pass over—from which the Mexica had earlier withdrawn the bridges—was crossed only by a remnant who used the drowned and trampled bodies of their companions as a footbridge. Heavy casualties were also suffered by the Mexica, but in terms of prisoners taken they were particularly fortunate, for some hundred of the Spaniards bringing up the rear failed to force their way through and were then pressed back to the temple pyramid where they took refuge on the summit. Without food and water they held out here on this sacred eminence for two or three days, in the end to be taken and sacrificed.

Yet on careful consideration it must be read as a defeat for the Mexica. Though they pursued the exhausted and nearly defenseless enemy up past Tenayuca and then around the north edge of the lake, they were unable to exterminate them. This was mainly because the enemy was befriended along the route by the Otomí, whose hatred of the Mexica was deep and abiding.

Considering the unraveled nature of the Mexican state at this juncture, Cuitlahuac acted with energy and dispatch. He decided that by the time the fleeing enemy reached Otumpan he could arrange to have an army assembled there and stationed so as to block their flight out of the Valley. Inasmuch as most of the troops would have to come from what was left of the Acolhua, command of this scratch army was given to a magnate of that nation still loyal to the alliance, a person named Cihua-catzin. The army gathered together consisted of men from the Acolhua cities in the vicinity, Calpulalpan, Otumpan, and Teotihuacan, as well as an ill-equipped group rushed in from Mexico. On July 7 battle was joined in the draw back of Teotihuacan and under the sacred hill of Tonan.[50] The bravura of the Spanish that day won an amazing victory against a vastly superior antagonist; the Acolhua battle standard fell in the dust, and the morale of an enemy already on the run in the end proved superior to the fresh masses of Mexico and her allies. This, the last army ever assembled from the Three Cities, then broke up and the Spaniards were allowed to limp across the border to a safe welcome among the people of Tlascala. So, within sight of the ruins of Teotihuacan, the mother of cultures, vanished Mexico's chance to destroy the enemy. Whatever the strength of her resolve or the fervor of her fighting men thereafter, Mexico was doomed at Otumpan.

Cuitlahuac was busy at home. He supervised the cleaning and restoration of the temples, the disposal of the bodies, and the recovery of the loot abandoned by the enemy. He reopened the market, began the immediate restocking of the arsenal, deepened certain canals, and in general reconstituted the city's defenses. Ambassadors were sent to the vassal states that had wavered or that had openly abandoned Mexico, offering them a year's remission of tribute in return for their loyalty and for their aid in coercing neighboring states that were still in the camp of the enemy. He imposed Coanacochtzin upon Tezcoco as its legitimate ruler after it had become apparent that the Acolhua themselves could never agree upon a *tlatoani*. A pretentious ten-man embassy was sent to the ruler of Michoacan to reiterate Mexico's request for an alliance. The times called for instant action on many fronts.[51]

The situation just to the south of the Tlateputzca cities, which were now harboring and refitting the Spaniards, was especially serious. The strong Mexican garrisons dominating Tepeyacac, Cuauhquechollan, and Itzucan would be gravely threatened should the enemy concentrate their forces there. Cuitlahuac not only reinforced these garrisons, but sent a memorable embassy to the Tlascalans, the first communication of consequence with these inveterate enemies within the memory of any living Mexican. This embassy offered a pact of perpetual friendship and the immediate cancellation of the commercial blockade. In addition, Mexico guaranteed to turn over to Tlascala certain adjacent vassal states formerly parts of the Acolhua and Mexican empires. Tlascala, in effect, was invited to substitute for Tezcoco in a new Three City League. In return for these far-reaching concessions, Tlascala had merely to destroy the Spaniards resident among them. The offer was considered but rejected after heated discussion among the Tlascalan knights. Tlascala's real and irrevocable answer was given when, in company with the reanimated Spaniards, she moved in force against the Mexican garrisons and forced them to relinquish their hold over the whole strategic area southeast of the Basin. After Itzucan fell, the strong Mixtec city of Coaixtlahuacan voluntarily moved over to the enemy.

All the best efforts of Mexico were thus brought to naught, but it was not simply armies and the regenerative power of the Spaniards that were responsible for this ill success. As they had fled out of Mexico, the Spaniards had left behind them as an ally, in absentia, the *uey zahuatl*—smallpox.[52] This epidemic, new to Mesoamerica, had been introduced by infected members of the Narváez party and in a short few months had effectively weakened not only the Mexica but the rest of Anahuac. The ruler of Michoacan was dead of it before the Mexican embassy could deliver its message to him.

So fierce was the onset of the disease in Mexico that burial and cremation were discarded during the first days, and bodies were simply rolled into the canals for disposal or towed out into the lake. For two months the terrible disease took its toll and then loosened its grip. Among its victims was Cuitlahuac.[53]

13. Of What Advantage Pride?

Mexico Purges the Peace Party

 Inasmuch as Cuitlahuac had ruled only some four months at the most, any assessment of his full stature is not possible. He appears to have represented the best in Tenochca tradition. He had come to rule legitimately elected, being the oldest of the sons of Axayacatl living after the death of Moteuczoma and a man ripe in experience. After his unexpected death, other younger brothers stood ready to claim the office of *tlatoani*, but were prevented by a great upheaval that now shook the Mexican state.

The crisis was two-fold. It was caused primarily by the ineffectiveness of Moteuczoma's rule, which had introduced serious and lasting schisms among his people the Teonchca, but to this was added the undying resentment the Tlatilulca cherished for their brothers. These two disharmonies in the state, one new the other old, interpenetrated each other to a great extent, but it is still possible to distinguish them, although we can see the actual details only darkly. The story appears to be as follows.

With disease still haunting the purlieus of Mexico and with famine lurking in the background, the magnates gathered together in October or November of 1520 to elect and acclaim a new ruler, the eighth since Itzcoatl. These deliberations were taken bearing in mind Moteuczoma's failing as a Tenochca ruler, which the Tlatilulca ascribed to his cowardice. Some drastic change was therefore needed.

The man finally selected by the Tenochca was Cuauhtemoc, a son not of Axayacatl but of Ahuitzotl and moreover a grandson of Moquiuix, the tragic hero of the Tlatilulca. Cuauhtemoc had been one who had earlier cautioned the hotheads as they sought a total confrontation with the Spaniards; he seems in fact to have favored peace. But the situation had changed, and his election turned him to resistance. He certainly owed his elevation to the knights who had been frustrated under Moteuczoma, but he appears to have been strongly supported by the priesthood as well. The priesthood viewed him as a vigorous supporter of the native gods and therefore as opposed to the supine policies of the deceased Moteuczoma. This support cast Cuauhtemoc in the additional role of an antagonist to that small group of nobles and kinsmen who were still bathed in Moteuczoma's pallid mystique. What Cuauhtemoc's election really signified was that Tlatilulco was at last to be represented in Mexico on an even footing;[1] it did not resolve the issue of whether or not war against the Spaniards was to be pursued wholeheartedly, for the small party of surrender, most of them Tenochca, remained amazingly intact. This party was centered about the person of the *cihuacoatl* Tzihuacpopoca, a man who wielded considerable power and who was universally venerated. Through him all important oracles were normally released. Generally speaking, the *tlatoani* and the *cihuacoatl* pursued a common policy in all affairs of state. Such was not the case now.

The problem came to a head soon after the election, for it was now clear that, after months of preliminary sparring, the Spaniards and a huge Aztec army were on their way back into the Basin, seeking an ultimate trial of strength. The ominous resurgence of enemy strength had made it imperative that Mexico declare herself unequivocally on the subject of war or peaceful submission. Cuauhtemoc, who now stood for the party of war, issued a call to as many of Mexico's allies and associates in empire as were left in order to concert the appropriate reponse. Coanacochtzin, emperor of the Acolhua, was present, having abandoned his city of Tezcoco along with some of his nobles in the face of the enemy advance. The emperor of the Tepaneca was also present and likewise shorn of much of his power by defections to the enemy. It was a radically truncated Three City League that was represented.

When the warlike stance that Cuauhtemoc represented was finally ratified by this late gathering of the barons, the Tenochca leaders of the peace party were of necessity proscribed.[2] Tzihuacpopoca, the *cihuacoatl*, was located, treacherously lured into the presence of Cuauhtemoc, and there slaughtred. In quick succession followed certain sons of Moteuczoma, including Axayacatl, a potential claimant to Cuauhtemoc's office and therefore dangerous to the state. These stern and frightful measures were called for if Mexico was to fight at all, but the loss of these men, who were among the last remaining leaders of note among the Tenochca, left bitterness and continued division in the city of Tenochtitlan. While technically Cuauhtemoc had been elected *tlatoani* of Tenochtitlan, the murders served to identify him as the choice par excellence of Tlatilulco, for that city finely relished any humiliation of the Tenochca royal house. Tlacotzin, a man of Tenochtitlan and a nephew of Cuauhtemoc, was installed as *cihuacoatl*. He was a direct descendant of the great Tlacaelel and was thus by custom entitled to the office while at the same time, through his affiliation with the line of Cuauhtemoc, he was acceptable to the war party. The way had now been prepared for an all-out effort on the part of Mexico to test its fate in war.

The War of Position

The crisis was upon them. The great army of invaders had directed themselves over the pass leading from Texmeluca and debouching near the lake at Coatepec. Their progress had been only a little impeded by the felling of trees across their path and by the presence of an Acolhua army hastily thrown together and weakened by divisions in its rear. When the new year of 1521 came around, the enemy —some twenty thousand strong—was in Tezcoco, Nezahualpilli's pal-

ace had been looted and burned by the Tlascalans, the important Acolhua communities of Coatlinchan and Huexotla had gone over to the
enemy, Coanacochtzin had fled to Mexico, and Ixtlilxochitl had been
invited to replace him as puppet emperor under the Spaniards. By this
time, Cuauhtemoc had sent most of the older people out of the city of
Mexico, up into the mountains behind Tlacopan for safety. He drew
into the city as many fighting men as would join his standard, training
and exercising them along with his own Mexica so that on the appointed day they might be fit and ready.[3]

It was to take the enemy until the end of May to close in on Mexico
from his new base in Tezcoco. In this preliminary phase of the confrontation, Mexico fought with great determination to prevent any
closer approach. There were three phases to the encirclement of Mexico and her response. In the first phase, with the enemy still consolidat-
ing his power in Tezcoco, Mexico concentrated on the Acolhua shore,
attempting espionage and incitation to keep the Acolhua cities in the
fight on her side. This ended in failure for Mexico when Cuauhtemoc
became aware that Chalco was becoming restive, forcing him to transfer his attention to that point.[4] The second phase was the effort to defend the western land approaches. This failed lamentably with the fall
of Xaltocan and the taking by the enemy of Cuauhtitlan, Tenayuca,
and Azcapotzalco, none of them adequately defended inasmuch as
many of their fighting men had been drawn into Mexico. This phase
ended with the sacking and burning of Tlacopan by the Spaniards and
Tlascalans. Here in Tlacopan, on the doorsill of Mexico's western approaches, war raged for seven days before the enemy, victorious in every engagement and having proved his ability to take the western shore,
withdrew temporarily. The third phase closed off from Mexico all ave-
nues to the southern parts of what was left of her empire. In this stage
Mexico attacked Chalco, her most ancient and inveterate foe, hurling
at least three sizable armies against her. But in addition to her already
known Spanish allegiance, Chalco had cast her lot with the Tlateputzca
cities, thus successfully detaching herself from her long bondage to
Mexico. While this maneuvering was going on and in support of it,
the enemy swept down south of the Escarpment behind Chalco and
one after another crushed the strong Mexican garrisons in Huaxtepec,

Yacapixtlan, Yauhtepec, and Cuauhnahuac. Then from the rear, Xochimilco, greatest of the lake cities next to Mexico and Tezcoco, was
taken and burned despite the most heroic efforts of contingents from
Mexico. So crumbled the south and so ended Mexico's hold on the last
of her empire. As in her earliest days, Mexico was now only a city
alone in the lake.

We have not entered into the details of this swift war of position
that detached the empire from its metropolitan city. Mexico had in the
beginning optimistically believed that the kingdom of the Acolhua
would support her and had thus received a profound shock on learning
that the greater Tezcoco area had, without a struggle, fallen to the enemy. But what struck her even harder was the defection of Chalco,
strategically the most important part of her empire. This rich and beautiful land had been held by Mexico for so many years that she had
come to view it as hers by prescriptive right. Its loss brought home to
her the extreme peril in which she herself stood. Because of this she
had reacted there with exceptional vigor, but, as we have seen, to no
effect. The loss of Chalco pulled out the underpinning of her empire;
because of it Mexico had been unable to hold the indispensable Xochimilco. Finally, when Chalco unilaterally declared war on the Chinampaneca cities, which at first had been neutral in the contest, she forced
them to seek protection in the Spanish camp and thus to close all possibility of aid to the Mexica. The Matlatzinca of the Toluca Valley had
appeared ready to stand with Mexico, but during the siege were to
switch to the Spanish side when real pressure was applied. Everywhere
the Otomí supported the Spaniards.

Mexico, stripped bare of empire, could count for assistance not on
whole cities formerly hers but only on a few refugee rulers and such of
their barons as they could persuade to follow them. These were individuals tied to Mexico either by family connections or by the *teuctli*'s
sense of honor. If the rulers of Cuitlahuac, Tlacopan, Azcapotzalco,
Cuauhtitlan, and Coyouacan were now in Mexico along with some of
their knights, this only underscored the cruel divisions that had ripped
their cities apart and thrown most of them into the camp of the enemy.

But most revealing is the fact that the only loyalty to Mexico that
stood the acid test was that of the Tepaneca cities—and even here only

in part. This quite comports with what we surmise about the revolution in Mexico wherein Tenochca power had disintegrated to leave Tlatilulco as the sole upholder of the great Mexican tradition. We know Tlatilulco to have been in its origins as much Tepaneca as Mexican. As Tenochca prestige dwindled, Tlatilulco stood forth with her pride strengthened in inverse proportion to the revealed weakness of her Mexica brothers. Tlatilulco remembered that, under Tezozomoc, she had been the first to elect a Mexican *tlatoani*, and this at a time when the Tenochca were at best a disorganized set of neighbors. At that time, in the very inception of Mexican history, Tlatilulco had been Mexico. She was to be Mexico again at the end.

But the rule of Cuauhtemoc is only a postlude to Mexican history, which essentially ends with the death of Cuitlahuac, who was the last to stand for Tenochca ability to rule and to make policy. Mexico as an independent state had been born under Tenochca auspices and had been carried to grandeur by Tenochca skill and vigor. Any regression from Tenochca designs—which is the way we must read Cuauhtemoc's election—could only mean that Mexico was retreating far back into the evil days when the tribe was divided into moieties.

But Cuauhtemoc's election did not really shift the possession of the state from one group of the Mexica to another. Rather, it dissolved what there was of the state and replaced it with the irresponsible *teuctli*; acting together as a stateless caste, the knights chose a course that could only be fatal for Mexico. Had it been the state that called him to power, Cuauhtemoc would have immediately sued for peace, for any other course would have been rationally disastrous. But he was called to the rule by fellow heroes; he was elected to be the chieftain of a band fighting as knights in the service of the gods. Cuauhtemoc's name is literally translated as "falling or swooping eagle"; symbolically it is a specific reference to the setting sun, and therefore a fitting name for the leader of the doomed.

The siege of the city of Mexico is one of the most savage and desperate encounters in all history. It is heroic in the classical mode and hopeless at the same time. The enemy's policy of calculated terror and total destruction caused the city to melt away before the defenders' eyes, so that it became in its desolation much like the original mud flat of the founding days. One source says that 100,000 Mexica and close allies were killed and drowned in the siege, with as many again dying of starvation, dysentery, and other diseases.[5] The Tlatilulca remembered their city at the end in the following terms: "In the streets lay broken bones and torn out hanks of hair. Houses had fallen apart; they lay open with their walls spattered with blood. Worms wriggled in the cluttered streets. Walls were dirtied with bits of brains. The water was dyed with blood. Even so we drank it. We drank it salty with blood."[6]

The Siege

The Chapultepec aqueducts had been cut as early as May 13, 1521; the siege proper began on May 31, and ended August 13.[7] Cuauhtemoc had divided his warriors into four corps, three to hold the crucial causeway approaches and one, a flotilla of canoe warriors, to combat the brigantines that Cortez had assembled in Tezcoco and now had launched out upon the lake.[8] Cuauhtemoc's energy and supervision were exemplary as he passed ceaselessly by canoe from one part of the laboring city to another, weapons in hand as befitted the leader of barons.

Xoloco, the fortress where the southern causeway entered Mexico, was essential to the defense, but the enemy with great skill and the use of artillery unexpectedly broke through. Holding this strong position had been the responsibility of the Tenochca, and their failure here to protect Tenochtitlan, their own city, produced a catastrophic break in their morale.[9] Hurling accusations of cowardice at each other, their captains fell out among themselves. In the resulting civil tumults four of them were killed, two high priests and two of their most outstanding warriors, including the prestigious Cuauhnochtli. This fratricidal strife sealed the fate of Tenochtitlan; after only three days of attack, the enemy siezed the central temple area in spite of all that Cuauhtemoc could do to hold it. A horde of Tenochca refugees—warriors, women, and children—abandoning their city fled north over the bridges to seek safety in Tlatilulco.[10] Organized Tenochca resistance had ended.

The Tenochca had brought Huitzilopochtli with them in their flight, and now they surrendered him to the Tlatilulca. This was the god to whom Cuauhtemoc had appealed not many days previously and who had given his people a clear omen calling for resistance and promising victory. The Tenochca warriors—those who remained—also surrendered to the Tlatilulca, handing over to them their shields, insignia, and standards, after which they publicly cut off their warlocks and, weeping, covered their heads with their mantles. They were a beaten people and they acknowledged it. Those who could fled by night, disguising themselves in the dress of other tribes. Their wives remained, stumbling about in Tlatilulco wailing and begging for food. Everywhere they were mocked by the Tlatilulca who, while they were truly appalled at the disaster that had befallen their sister city, nevertheless could not help gloating over the humbling of its pride.

The Tlatilulca warriors had gone to the aid of Tenochtitlan and had fought valorously to save it. Its collapse now thrust the Tlatilulca back solely upon the defenses of their own city. For an amazing two months the city of Tlatilulco continued to resist, seemingly tireless, able, and indomitable. Her leaders were the most baronial of men.[11] Two of them were jaguar knights and captains, Temilotzin and Coyoueuetzin; another was an Otomí knight, the brilliant fighter Tzilacatzin—all three were Tlatilulca. Ecatzin from Chilapan was also an Otomí knight, famous for his cunning. Mayeuatzin was the ruler of Cuitlahuac, now isolated from the majority of his subjects but still fierce in his pride; he appears to have commanded some warriors from the Chinampa cities. Motelchiuhtzin and Tlacotzin, the *cihuacoatl*, were the only Tenochca of importance at the end except Cuauhtemoc himself. Finally, there were the other two emperors, Coanacochtzin and Tetlepanquetzaltzin, neither of whom commanded significant bodies of men. A fragment of a warrior's chant—pathetic now in its savage pride—comes down to us out of these last days: "You are nobles and lords, O Huanitzin, Mayeuatzin, Coanacochtzin. You are not base commoners. Your fame in Mexico will never perish."[12]

The naval capacity of Tlatilulco, upon which the city had confidently depended, had been radically reduced at the beginning of the siege, when the Spaniards in their brigantines had mounted a successful amphibious attack on Tepetzinco, the Mexican strongpoint out in the open

waters.[13] The brigantines had quickly spotted the canoes setting out
from Tlatilulco to prevent the seizure and, with a favorable wind, had
run them down. Most of the warriors in this flotilla were lost by
drowning. Even with this initial handicap, Tlatilulco was able to cope
with the massive pressure squeezing her from all sides. Well over 200,-
000 Tlateputzca warriors were now aligned against Mexico, exulting at
the approaching end of their foe.

The city managed to score one victory during the siege. This was an
ambush set up toward the end of June on the Tlacopan causeway and
commanded by the wily Ecatzin.[14] Some forty Spaniards and at least a
thousand of their Indian allies were taken when the trap was sprung.
All of those captured were sacrificed and eaten, to the tumultuous joy
of the Tlatilulca. The heads of the horses taken were sent secretly to
certain of Tlahuica cities from which Mexico still believed succor might
come. Starvation, dysentery from the contaminated water of the canals,
the impossibility of disposing of bodies and human offal, the depletion
of the stocks of weapons, exhaustion from the need to maintain a constant alert, and, finally, continual and torrential rains led to the weakening of the defenders. Yet whenever the enemy proffered peace terms,
Tlatilulco as often turned it down.

But the end was near. The Tlatilulca were finally fighting in the marketplace itself—the center of their city. It was at this point that Tlacotzin advised the people that their own human resources were exhausted
and that they must depend now on their tribal god. He ordered that one
of the young warriors be dressed in the war regalia of Ahuitzotl,
Cuauhtemoc's father, and that he be given the two magical darts of
Huitzilopochtli.[15] It was hoped that this epiphany of the god would accomplish what the Tlatilulca as mortals could not. The pathetic hope of
course failed, for though the young warrior strode out in sight of the
enemy and brandished the sacred objects, he accomplished nothing.
The god of the Mexica was no longer with his people.

By now the Tlatilulca were so weakened that the enemy found it relatively easy, right after Cuauhtemoc had turned down another gesture
from Cortez, to move in swiftly and slaughter many thousands of the
starving and now almost helpless people, mainly women and children.

The last large group of Tlatilulca was finally hemmed in so that they occupied only the *calpulli* of Amaxac.

When it was apparent that destruction was to be Tlatilulco's lot, the last auguries were taken.[16] Huitzilopochtli's priest explained that if after four days there was still no hope in sight, they could surrender, for as he had calculated it that many additional days would complete a sacred eighty-day duration for the siege. On this understanding, some of the Tlatilulca continued fighting, but as the rains increased in intensity, flooding the smouldering ruins of the city and rendering it almost impossible to stir, the last miserable remnants of the common people, no longer controlled by their leaders, began to move out. Emerging from their puddles and holes they tottered out into the darkness, most of them to be easily dispatched by the Tlascalans waiting for just such an exodus.[17] Few could move at a pace sufficient to escape their pursuers. Many were toppled and pushed into the canals, where they drowned. Others were struck down by obsidian blades or shot with arrows. Many more killed themselves. These thousands of Mexica had chosen the Tepeyacac causeway as the route of refuge, as if the north were the preferred direction, a homeland from which they had once come and toward which, at the end, they now felt themselves impelled.

A small group of warriors was left manning the few remaining war canoes in the lagoon beside the marketplace. When daylight came they could be seen dimly through the heavy downpour by the Spaniards, who in several brigantines had at last made an entry into the canoe pool. Cuauhtemoc in the command canoe was soon spotted and, as the brigantines turned to close him, he stood up in the stern of the craft ready to offer resistance. Crossbows were leveled at him, and under their silent threat he finally lowered his weapons. Along with his captains he was taken to Cortez and there he formally surrendered.[18] These last heroic Mexicans stood together in a bedraggled group, their regalia, their quetzal feathers, their jades gone. They were wearing rags and even the tattered remnants of women's huipils. This day, August 14, 1521 closed the last chapter of Mexican history.[19]

The city of Mexico lay in total ruin, most of the walls pulled down and all the temples pouring forth dense smoke. Over forty thousand bodies floated in the canals or remained stacked in rain-soaked piles in designated buildings for lack of burial ground. Long after the bodies were finally removed, the stench of death clung about the ruins. There may have been about thirty thousand Mexica left on the day of surrender.[20]

Counting from its founding in the year 1369 to the date of surrender, the city of Mexico had lasted 152 years.

So It Befell Us on Earth

A most remarkable history had closed, abruptly, but with no special surprises. The three emperors would not be hanged from the famous *ceiba* tree in Yucatan for three more years, but the story of Aztec Mexico had in any case ended on the day of the surrender.

There is something most awe inspiring in the tale of Mexico and something that, at variance with its exotic quality, is very common and close to home. The friars may indeed have put the following words into the mouths of the conquered Mexica, but one suspects that they accurately reflect the Mexican experience: "Of what advantage to us were pride and grandeur? Of what advantage to us were riches on earth? Many such things fall confused like the shadows of smoke. They are like the messenger running fast; like the rapidly moving canoe, as if driven by the wind, of which nothing is seen where it goes; like the bird which flies swiftly leaving no trace of its flight; like the arrow quickly reaching its target, nor is it seen where it flew. Behold, so it befell us on earth."[21]

ABBREVIATIONS used in the notes. See References for complete titles.

AA	Sahagún, *Augurios*
AC	Velázquez, *Anales Cuauhtitlan*
ACN	Anonymous Conqueror
ACT	*Anales Conquista Tlatilulco*
AM	Chimalpopoca, *Anales Mexicanos*
ANE	Hernández, *Antigüedades*
AOG	Olmos, *Fragmentos*
ATCT	Berlin, *Anales Tlatelolco*
ATH	Barlow, *Anales Tula*
AZR	Zorita, *Life and Labor*
BF	Barlow, *Triple Alianza*
BRA	Alarcón, *Supersticiones*
BSR	Burland, *Selden Roll*
CAM	Camargo, *Tlascala*
CAS	Las Casas, *Indios*
CCH	Castillo, *Fragmentos*
CDH	García Icazbalceta, *Colección Documentos*
CLA	Clavigero, *Historia*
CM	*Chronicles Michoacan*
CODAUB	*Historia (Códice Aubin)*
CODHALL	Dibble, *Codex Hall*
CODRAM	Tovar, *Códice Ramírez*
CODX	*Códice Xolotl*
COR	Cortez, *Cartas*
CP	Caso, *Calendarios*
DB	Granados, *Diccionario*
DINE	Durán, *Historia*
DS	Bryan Davies, *Señoríos Independentes*
EST	*Estudios Cultura Nahuatl*
GCNE	Gómara, *Cortés*

GHL	Garibay, *Literatura Nahuatl*
GLL	Garibay, *Llave Nahuatl*
GPMX	Garibay, *Poema Mixcoatl*
GPN	Garibay, *Poesía Nahuatl*
HE	Herrera, *Historia*
HM	Ponce de León, *Historia*
HMAI	Wauchope, *Handbook Middle American Indians*
HMP	*Historia Mexicanos Pinturas*
HTC	*Historia Tolteca-Chichimeca*
IXCH	Ixtlilxochitl, *Historia*
IXREL	Ixtlilxochitl, *Relaciones*
JAC	Acosta, *Historia Natural*
JM	Jonghe, *Histoyre Méchique*
LPR	Sahagún, *Ritos*
LPT	León-Portilla, *Trece Poetas*
LS	Velázquez, *Leyenda Soles*
MBG	McAfee and Barlow, *Guerra*
MEN	Mendieta, *Historia Ecclesiástica*
MI	Yáñez, *Mitos*
MOL	Molina, *Vocabulario*
MON	Torquemada, *Monarquía*
MQ	*Mappa Quinatzin*
MTL	*Mappa Tlotzin*
OB	Orozco y Berra, *Historia*
OM	*Origen Mexicanos*
PL	Ponce de León, *Tratado*
POM	Pomar, *Relación Tezcoco*
PP	Ponce de León, *Breve Relacion*
PRM	*Mexicanische Bilderhandschrift*
RB	Sahagún, *Relación Fiestas*
RCAA	*Relato Conquista*
RELA	*Relación Anónima*
RGL	*Relación Geneología*
ROCA	Chimalpahin, *Relaciones*
SAHG	Sahagún, *Historia*
SER	Serna, *Manuel*
SFC	Sahagún, *General History* (Anderson and Dibble, trans.)
SIM	Siméon, *Dictionnaire*
SS	Swadesh and Sancho, *Elementos*
TCM	Tezozomoc, *Crónica Mexicayotl*
TEZ	Tezozomoc, *Crónica Mexicana*
TMH	Motolinía, *History*
TMM	Motolinía, *Memoriales*

TP	*Tira Peregrinación*
TPT	Guzmán, *Manuscrito Boturini*
TTT	*Tlatilulco Través Tiempos*
VE	Vázquez de Espinosa, *Compendio*
VET	Sahagún, *Vida Económica*
VHA	Veytia, *Historia*

NOTES

INTRODUCTION

1. HE, III, 160.
2. SAHG, IV, 130.
3. GPN, II, 135.

1. THE FALL OF TULA

1. A third and also comon use of the term Anahuac was "the coast-lands"; this included all areas of present-day Mexico and Central America along both Gulf and Pacific Coasts as far down as Nicaragua. See IXCH, p. 318; SAHG, I, 289, III, 16f., 28; SFC, IX, 17; TEZ, p. 398; ROCA, p. 228; MON, I, 21; CLA, II, 221; VET, p. 38. It was this latter use that led the Spaniards to equate Anahuac with New Spain.

2. The steppe was referred to also as *huey tlalli* (AC, p. 97; GPN, II, 90), *ixtlahuatl* (VET, p. 53; MOL, I, 74; PRM, pp. 56, 65), or *tlalhuactli* (MOL, II, 124). The term *teotlalli* is almost a synonym for north (SAHG, III, 214; AC, p. 6). The usual translation, which we adopt here, is Godland (SER, p. 313), but it can equally well mean hunger land (SS, pp. 65f.) or rocky land (OB, II, 150n.; SAHG, I, 234). Garibay opts for the last (OB, II, 150n). In Tenochtitlan there was a walled enclosure planted with rocks and cactus, which was attached to the temple of the Chichimec god Mixcoatl and was called Teotlalpan (MON, II, 148; SAHG, I, 234); it commemorated this Aztec place of origin; there was a similar shrine in Tezcoco (IXCH, pp. 185f.). *Teotlalli* as a general topographical designation should not be confused with the specific Teotlalpan, which was a province in southern Hidalgo; see S. F. Cook, *The Historical Demography and Ecology of the Teotlalpan* (Berkeley: University of California Press, 1949).

3. SFC, XI, 256.

4. In this section I have leaned heavily on Howard F. Cline's forthcoming work, pertinent chapters of which he graciously allowed me to read in manu-

script. All the Teotihuacan and Toltec datings here are taken from his MS. One of the latest published attempts by a Mexican scholar to grapple with Toltec dating is R. Piña-Chan, *Una Visión del México prehispánico* (Mexico City: UNAM, 1967), pp. 207f., 221–223.

5. The *huemac* may well have been considered in Tula as an avatar or impersonation of Tezcatlipoca (PRM, pp. 14f.).

6. Dr. Cline accepted 1168 as the date of the final destruction of Tula, which is the same year he assigned to the departure of the Aztecs from Aztlan.

7. This last *huemac* is often confused with a much earlier Toltec ruler and sage filling the same office; see GPN, II, 136; CLA, I, 150; IXREL, pp. 31f.; VHA, I, 139, 168; DINE, II, 7.

8. AC, p. 15; LS, p. 127; HTC, pp. 69f.; TEZ, p. 503; DINE, I, 518f.; PRM, p. 17.

9. TEZ, pp. 503–507, 511–514; DINE, I, 515, 521f.; SAHG, IV, 34f.; SFC, XII, 26; CODRAM, p. 108.

10. HE, IV, 105.

11. The three-fold breakdown of the Chichimec groups belongs to Sahagun; see SFC, X, 171–175; SAHG, III, 190–193.

12. The Nahuatl etymology most commonly accepted for the word *chichimecatl* (pl. *chichimeca*) is "lineage of the dog" or "dog people" (*chichi*, "dog" + *mecatl*, "lineage"), but one source specifically denies that is a Nahuatl word and instead translates it out of an unknown tongue as "eagles" (IXCH, p. 37). Whatever the etymology, the sense is clear. It meant barbarians (CAM, pp. 27f.) who lived by hunting (CODRAM, p. 17; DINE, II, 127) and who were newcomers to the settled lands in and around the Basin (SAHG, III, 76). The element *teo-* in the name Teochichimeca is to be translated as "true, pure, or original"; see SFC, X, 171; SAHG, III, 190; OM, p. 260; GCNE, pp. 157, 299; TMM, p. 218.

13. SFC VI, 34.

14. On Chichimec religion in general, see MTL, p. 62; SAHG, II, 81; III, 207; TEZ, p. 6; AC, pp. 6, 30; MON, I, 39, 147. On Itzpapalotl as the sacrificial knife, see SFC, VI, 14.

15. SAHG III, 193.

16. Tamime is a plural form meaning "shooters (of arrows)"; see SIM, p. 389; SFC, X, 171.

17. It is well attested that a severe drought afflicted Tula at the end; see MON, I, 67; AC, p. 13; LS, p. 126; IXCH, pp. 32f.; IXREL, p. 473; CLA, I, 153.

18. The Culua were definitely more advanced than the hunting Chichimeca (CDH, I, 253). They were a significant part of the Toltec diaspora; see IXREL, p. 476; RGL, pp. 243f., 246; OM, p. 261; TMM, p. 5; JM, p. 19. Led

by Nauhyotl they were one of the three Toltec splinter groups to enter the
Basin; see AC, p. 15; JM, p. 19; HMP, p. 235; AOG, p. 70; MON, I, 97. We
may take it that the Culua came originally from Teoculhuacan ("the original
Culhuacan," not to be confused with the one they founded on Lake Xochimilco), which was apparently a Chichimec province distinct from Aztlan and
either an integral part of the Toltec empire or heavily influenced by it. The
sources sometimes place it adjacent to Aztlan (HMP, p. 218; JAC, p. 321;
ROCA, p. 68; CODRAM, pp. 17f.; AOG, pp. 39f.), or else they confusedly
relate them to each other as is an island in a lake to the mainland; there are
evidently two contrasting traditions here. The name Culua most probably
means "he who has ancestors" (I am unable to understand Garibay's translation of Culua as simply a plural form of *colli*, GLL, p. 339); this is borne
out by CODRAM, p. 18.

19. The undisputed claim of Culhuacan to Toltec legitimacy is well attested;
see RGL, p. 247; IXREL, p. 90; GPN, II, 90; DINE, I, 115f.; AC, p. 17.

20. The date 1179 is arrived at by adding one fifty-two–year round to the
date given in AC, p. 16.

21. IXREL, pp. 98, 270f., 276f.; IXCH, pp. 38f.; CODX, p. 38, plate II;
MON, I, 56f., 62.

22. Xolotl poses one of the main problems in Aztec studies. His real name
appears to have been Amacui (MTL, p. 59; SIM, p. 706), which can mean
in Nahuatl "he takes or has paper," paper being a cult substance and a sign of
holiness; nevertheless, his family did not speak Nahuatl. Garibay believed that
Xolotl and his people spoke an early form of Otomí (GHL, I, 258).

23. Xolotl can also mean "beast" (CAM, p. 174) or "hunchback, page, or
dwarf" (TEZ, pp. 503, 505) or "twin or counterpart," SAHG, II, 261f.; PP,
p. 376. It is used in parallelism to "jaguar" in SER, p. 168. In AC, pp. 40ff.,
it appears to mean "Caesar," "highness" or "greatness." For other meanings,
see SS, p. 75.

24. Unlike the Chicomoztoc groups who came from Aztlan and Teoculhuacan, Xolotl and his people came from Amaqueme (MON, I, 39f., 44, 46),
which is also called Oyome; see IXREL, pp. 78f., 82, 276; VHA, I, 211. Piña-
Chan, *Visión*, p. 223, equates Oyome with the Mezquital. For a genealogy of
Oyome rulers, including Xolotl, see IXREL, pp. 78f.

25. Xolotl's dates vary widely and the attempt to rationalize them is evident
in such sources as VHA, I, 273, where Xolotl is made out as over two hundred
years old. Giving each of the Chichimec rulers back from Ixtlilxochitl approximately a twenty-nine–year rule would place the start of Xolotl's rule about
A.D. 1246. This would render reasonable the hypothesis that the inclusive years
of his reign were 1244–1304, as given by Piña-Chan, *Visión*, p. 224. Sahagún
gives 1246 as the specific year for the beginning of Xolotl's rule; SAHG, II,

291; SFC, VIII, 15. Most sources have earlier dates; Clavijero gives ca. 1170 (CLA, I, 174). Dr. Cline had Xolotl moving through Tula in 1174 (private communication), which to my mind seems too early. The reasons why our sources push him back in time is obvious; it is to connect him with Tula. One of the more interesting of these efforts is found in VHA, I, chapter 35; II, chapter 1.

26. The title of *chichimecatl teuctli* was also borne by one of Xolotl's contemporaries who settled in that part of Chalco to which he gave the name of the tribal homeland, Amaquemecan; see TCM, p. 48.

27. The area claimed by Xolotl, the *chichimecatlalli* (CLA, I, 158), extended from Metztitlan to Cuauhnahuac and from the Nevado de Toluca to Mount Orizaba; CODX, plate I and map; DS, p. 23; VHA, I, 236. This area is excessively extensive and is probably a memory of the territorial limits of the late Toltec empire; Xolotl had no way of actually controlling so much territory. The formal taking of possession began on Mount Xocotl (IXREL, pp. 87f.; CODX, p. 26; VHA, I, 236f.), near modern Jocotitlan in the western part of the state of Mexico.

28. MON, I, 51ff.; CLA, I, 163; IXREL, pp. 94, 269f.; CODX, p. 34.

29. Nopaltzin's most famous exploit was the reduction of Culhuacan; see IXREL, pp. 98, 270f., 276f.; IXCH, pp. 38f.; MON, I, 56ff.; VHA, I, 250; CODX, p. 38, plate II.

30. Cuauhyacac is the modern park in Molina de Flores; it lay on the edge of the hilly area and parkland referred to as Tezcotzinco; see ANE, p. 114; MON, I, 133; CLA, I, 245; II, 308. For information on Cuauhyacac, see IXREL, pp. 96f., 182, 478, 482; IXCH, pp. 46, 55, 100, 209–212; CODX, pp. 20f.; VHA, I, 234; POM, pp. 53, 55.

31. The Chichimec process of acculturation that began with the Tenayuca census (MON, I, 44) is mentioned in CLA, I, 158f., 171; VHA, I, 240f.; CODX, p. 61, plate III; JM, p. 11; MTL, pp. 60ff.; IXCH, pp. 57, 73; IXREL, p. 477; MQ, p. 77; MON, I, 73; ROCA, pp. 74, 78.

32. The Aztec origination myth is a standing invitation to guesswork and boasts a swollen bibliography. A few things stand out clearly. The Xolotl traditions going back to Oyome/Amaquemecan are quite distinct from the Aztlan/Chicomoztoc/Teoculhuacan/Quinehuayan complex of tales, but both traditions stress a location north or west of the Basin of Mexico. The mass of the migrations are coincident with the fall of Tula and its aftermath. All the migrating groups except the Culua are identified as living at a sub-urban level of culture. All groups were led out by a god and the migrations are therefore movements of whole peoples. The migrations, however, were uncoordinated— only in the Xolotl horde is there evidence of some kind of overall leadership.

33. A radically variant list can be found in PRM, p. 41.

2. THE MEXICA GAIN A KING

1. COR, p. 42

2. Source material on the Wanderings is collected in M. Acosta Saignes, "Migraciones de los Mexica." TTT, VII (1946), pp. 177–187.

3. Aztlan is untranslatable. Garibay derives the word from Aaztlan* (from *aaztli*, "wing," SIM, p. 3), which he translates as "the place of the play of wings"; see Garibay's edition of Durán, *Historia de las Indias* (Mexico City: Editorial Porrua, 1967), II, 579, 584. I have found no reading of the famous place name with a reduplicated *a* and therefore do not accept Garibay's interpretation. The word *aztli* is found in the personal name Azcueitl (ATCT, p. 27), but its meaning is unrecorded. Aztlan has often been compared to the island of Janítzeo in Lake Pátzcuaro; in such a case Chicomoztoc would have been the ancient cult area on the island, no doubt attracting wandering tribes to it from great distances around. The Pátzcuaro identification raises problems, for it implies that the Aztecs came from the heart of a Tarascan-speaking territory; see HMAI, VIII, fig. 2, between pp. 728 and 729. The people of Michoacan are always brought into the Tale of Wandering at least peripherally, and to posit a Tarascan site for Aztlan may therefore not be untenable. Most authorities, however, place Aztlan somewhere in Jalisco; see also MON, I, 31.

4. For the original name of the Mexica as Mecitin or Mezitin, see IXCH, p. 62; IXREL, p. 476; SAHG, III, 207f.; SFC, X, 189; LS, pp. 122f.; MEN, I, 163; DINE, I, 19. One tradition has it that Mecitli was the eponymous priest who first led the people out, another that it was the name of the earth goddess (LS, p. 122; TMH, p. 265; MI, p. 20). Both can be correct at the same time but the latter certainly is. *Mecitli* would appear to mean either "maguey hare" (SAHG, III, 207f.) or, better, "grandmother maguey" (MI, p. 20). The name change of the people to Mexitin and (later) to Mexica is well attested (ROCA, pp. 66f.; TCM, 22f.; MON, I, 78f.; CODAUB, p. 22), though the explanation behind it escapes me. A variant and interesting etymology is given in JM, pp. 14, 17. When read as Mexitl, the deity's name can properly be translated as "maguey leaf" (SS, p. 74), which is apparently what Sahagún had in mind when he wrote that the god was born cradled in a maguey leaf (SAHG, III, 207f.). Mexitli was finally replaced by Huitzilopochtli; see GCNE, pp. 158f.; HE, III, 226; CLA, I, 200; II, 76; TMM, p. 143; MON, I, 293; II, 145.

5. ATCT, p. 27.

6. I have omitted the fascinating Malinalxochitl episode (DINE, I, 21ff.; TCM, pp. 13f., 28f.; TEZ, pp. 9–12; VHA, I, 292f.; CODRAM, pp. 25f.; ROCA, p. 65) and the subject of Tarascan connections as being somewhat extraneous to the story of Mexica wanderings. The breaking off of the Malinalca people, however, did represent one of the three major defections from the Mexica in the period before they founded Mexico (DINE, I, 43).

7. Coatepetl was an important stopping place before the Mexica came to Tula, but the two sites were closely connected—it should thus lie to the west or northwest of Tula. It was a shrine of the form of the earth goddess Coatlicue known as Coyolxauhqui.

8. TCM, pp. 34f.; HMP, pp. 220f.; TEZ, pp. 12f.; MON, II, 41f.; CLA, II, 77f.; AOG, pp. 43f.; SAHG, I, 271ff.; SFC, III, 1–5.

9. Chapultepec was called by the Toltecs Cuitlapilco, "the tail or rump"; see LS, pp. 126f.; TCM, p. 46.

10. Veytia gives 1298 as the year of the Mexica entry into Anahuac (VHA, I, 286), whereas Cline assigns the nearly coincidental arrival in Citlaltepetl to 1284. Torquemada assumes a date of 1269 or 1270 for the Mexica entry into Chapultepec (MON, I, 288). Clavigero puts it in 1245 (CLA, I, 194), whereas Cline places it in 1319. I accept the latter.

11. Chapultepec in those days was visited by many peoples. There were resident Neotoltecs; there was a Chichimec group led by a person called Mazatl (AC, p. 17), a Nonohualca group led by a person called Timal (ATCT, pp. 35f.; ROCA, p. 172), a Tlacochcalca group led by Chalchiuhtlatonac (ROCA, p. 156), and a Chichimec group that later went on to Tlateputzco (PRM, p. 59). Some of these groups no doubt assimilated into the Mexica (ROCA, p. 58).

12. There were other groups besides the Xaltocan alliance attacking the Mexica during these years. Attacks came from the Toluca (ROCA, p. 54), from the Tepaneca (AC, p. 21), and earlier from the people of Culhuacan (RGL, p. 248).

13. AC, p. 18; HMP, p. 225; ROCA, pp. 58, 70; AOG, p. 50; ATCT, p. 36; MON, I, 83f.

14. ATCT, p. 49.

15. Tlatilulco was originally called Xaltilulco, "gravel spit" (MON, I, 295; MBG, p. 51) from *xaltetl* + *ololoa* + *co*, literally "the place heaped up with shingle." Thus it meant something like "island or embankment" (TMM, p. 143; GCNE, p. 159; CODRAM, p. 40), but it was not derived from *tlatelli*, "island," as is generally asserted.

16. CODAUB, p. 32; AC, p. 22; MON, I, 91; TCM, p. 81.

17. Tizaapan cannot be the same as present-day Tizapan just west of University City, inasmuch as the Mexica community must have been near Zapotitlan on the south side of the Sierra de Santa Catarina (DINE, I, 31f.). According to Cline, the Mexica were in Tizaapan for about nineteen years; see also ROCA, pp. 60, 148, 153, 176.

18. The Mexica on the southern shore of the lake appear to have broken up into three loosely related groups (HMP, p. 224; AOG, p. 48).

19. From Tizaapan they went to Mexicaltzinco, "the house of the god Mexi," where they built a shrine to the god. They then went to Huitzilopochco.

Neither of these two places was in the jurisdiction of Culhuacan. Inasmuch as they were on opposite sides of the channel through which Lake Xochimilco flowed into Lake Texcoco, it is clear that the Mexica were attempting to hold those strategic narrows to the detriment of Culhuacan. These two sites became holy places to the Mexica (DINE, I, 374) and represented in their histories a renewed dedication to Huitzilopochtli (AOG, p. 48; HMP, p. 224; TCM, pp. 58f.).

20. We cannot assume that the name Tenochtitlan has anything to do with Tenoch the *teomama*. Tenochtitlan can only mean "by the *tenochtli*-cactus"; see GCNE, p. 157; ATCT, p. 35; CAM, pp. 234f.; MON, I, 92; TCM, p. 3. Thus the full name of Mexico Tenochtitlan means "where the god Mexitli is, the place of the *tenochtli*-cactus." Barlow suggests that Tenochtitlan is a shortened form from Teonochtitlan (TTT, I, 25n.). If the name Tenochtitlan refers to the myth of the eagle on the cactus and is not simply a geographical designation, then the name Temixtitan (i.e., Temixtitlan) and its variants, which the first Spaniards used for the city (ACN, pp. 57, 61; CDH, I, 412, 422, 490; II, 175, 187, 204) was probably a like name, as is said by OM, p. 269. Inasmuch as *cuauh* seems to substitute for *te* in the name (AOG, p. 56; HMP, p. 227), the *te* may indeed be a contraction of *teo*; the god is then being identified as the eagle. *Mixtitlan* means "hidden or of unknown origin" (GLL, p. 353), literally "in the mists"—thus Temixtitlan would give the sense "where the god is hidden."

21. TEZ, p. 368.

22. The Copil episode is of great interest. He was said to be a sorceror from Malinalco and to have been instrumental in organizing against the Mexica a strong coalition of the Tepaneca and peoples of Malinalco, Toluca, Texcalte-pec, and others; CODRAM, pp. 28–31; DINE, I, 28f.; ROCA, pp. 54f.; JAC, p. 327. In a shaman's duel on the island of Tepetzinco, he lost to his Mexican counterpart Cuauhtlequetzqui. He was then sacrificed by the Mexica and his heart buried where Tenochtitlan would later be founded. For translated versions of the Copil Story, see GHL, I, 278–280, 322–324. He may well have been a shaman, but he was also certainly a military and political figure as well during the final years of the Mexican residence at Chapultepec. His heart was buried under the first altar (it is called a "terrace," *tepetlatl*, TCM, pp. 42ff.) to Huitzilopochtli out in the lake. Copil worshipped Malinalxochitl, a goddess rejected by the Mexica.

23. One of the more interesting variants of the founding legend relates the accomodation made by Huitzilopochtli on the island to Tlaloc, his predecessor there (GHL, I, 302f.).

24. The emblem of Mexico originally showed the eagle on the nopal with the war-screed issuing from his beak (*atl tlachinolli*) and grasping a bird, not

a serpent, in his claws (CODRAM, pp. 38, 81; JAC, p. 330; HE, IV, 108). Note that the emblem of the eagle issuing the command to war was not exclusive to Mexico; it was also used by the people of Cuauhtinchan (PRM, VII).

25. It is possible that the year of the traditional founding of Mexico (1325) is a confused memory of an early settlement of the Tlatilulca on their island; this, however, is mere speculation. The year 1300 is also given (TMM, p. 150; TMH, p. 271) as well as 1318 (AC, p. 27) and 1322 (AOG, p. 64). There is no reason to doubt that while the Mexica were in Chapultepec they were also using the island later to be known as Tenochtitlan; certainly other small and related groups like the Culua were using the island before 1369 (TMM, p. 6).

26. Groups of Chichimecs related to the Mexica but who did not leave Culhuacan with them continued to harass the new settlement (CODAUB, pp. 41f.). For early life in Tenochtitlan, see TCM, pp. 72f.; AOG, p. 57; CLA, I, 201, 209, 267; II, 326f.; ROCA, pp. 77f., 94f.; DINE, I, 41f., 83, 105; TMM, p. 6; CODRAM, pp. 38f.

27. ROCA, p. 95.

28. Tenancacaltzin, the uncle of Quinatzin, held Tenayuca in fief (MON, I, 84; IXREL, p. 476).

29. IXREL, pp. 119f.

30. For Quinatzin's honorific name Tlaltecatzin, see MON, I, 73, 75; IXREL, pp. 131f., 209; for his birth name, see MQ, pp. 76f.; MTL, pp. 54f.

31. There is no accepted etymology of the name Tezozomoc. Siméon takes it as "he gets angry at people" (SIM, p. 399), which is preferable to "hare lip" (MQ, p. 94). If Siméon is correct, the name is simply a variant of the name Moteuczoma.

32. LPT, p. 147.

33. GPN, II, 136.

34. For the collapse of Culhuacan, see AC, pp. 29–32; RGL, pp. 250ff.; ANE, pp. 122f.; IXCH, pp. 78f.; IXREL, p. 120; SAHG, II, 283; ATCT, p. 46; AOG, p. 57; VE, p. 133.

35. Before Cuacuauhtzin there was a ruler of Tlatilulco called variously Teotlehuac (HMP, p. 228; AOG, p. 58; TTT, I, 28), Mixcoatl (IXREL, pp. 103, 118f., 137, 285, 448; CODX, pp. 69ff., 75, plates IV and V; VHA, I, 318f., 325), or Epcoatzin (IXCH, pp. 54f., 63, 79; VHA, I, 278). It is probable that one person is subsumed under all three names (ATCT, p. 47). He was removed from office after only two Aztec months owing to his incompetence. Another curious figure who is unplaced in the Tlatilulca list of rulers is Matlalilhuitl (CAM, pp. 58f.; MON, I, 265). He is very probably one of those Tepaneca commissars Sahagún called "consuls" who probably ruled Tlatilulco before kingship was instituted (SAHG, III, 16).

36. Cuacuauhtzin is a shortened form of Cuacuauhpitzahuac, "slender horns" (TTT, VI, 36; ATCT, p. 48).

37. CAM, p. 106; MON, I, 99, 260, 265.

3. MEXICO UNDER TEZOZOMOC

1. Barlow tentatively suggests 1375–1418 as the years of Cuacuauhtzin's rule (TTT, VI).

2. Tecpaneca ("People of the Palace, courtiers") is occasionally found in place of Tepaneca; AM in fact uses it consistently. Tepaneca can mean "the superior people," "people of the wall or frontier," or less certainly, "people of the stone bridge" (CODRAM, p. 21).

3. For Tlacauepan as an avatar of Huitzilopochtli, see GPN, II, lxxxviii; CLA, II, 79; MON, II, 281; SAHG, I, 229; SFC, II, 165. For his special worship in Tlatilulco, see HMP, p. 229; AOG, p. 60.

4. On Tlatilulco's Tepaneca connections, see EST, VI, 222; MON, I, 99, 127f.

5. On Tlatilulca expertise in commerce, see GCNE, p. 160; CLA, I, 260f; MON, I, 178; SFC, IX, 23.

6. Illancueitl is variously said to be the mother, nurse, or wife of the young Acamapichtli. All sources agree that she was of noble Culua blood and left Culhuacan to live in Coatlichan. From there the Mexica brought her and her young charge in 1375 (Cline's date based on Codex Telleriano-Remensis), in 1382 (VE, pp. 133ff.), in 1383 (RGL, p. 254), or in 1384 (SFC, VIII, 15; AC, p. 32) to reside in Tenochtitlan.

7. The name Acamapichtli cannot mean "handful of arrows" (CODRAM, p. 42), nor can it mean "reed finger" (SIM, p. 5). The former meaning would produce the spelling Acampachtli, of which there are no known examples.

8. His flight to Mexico was simply one incident in the story of the breakup of the state of Culhuacan. His only claim was to the rule of Culhuacan, not Tenochtitlan, which remained tributary to the Tepaneca in his day (DINE, I, 48; MON, I, 98f.).

9. The implication in CODRAM, p. 47, is that, while Acampichtli was the father of Huitzilihuitl, he was not himself a ruler.

10. It is said that Acamapichtli was the one to first hold the office of *cihuacoatl* (MON, II, 352).

11. Metaphorically, the *calpulli* was the *ima icxi in altepetl* (MOL, II, 38), "the hands and feet (i.e., members) of the city."

12. That the *calpulli* could be conceived as a lineage can be seen from the use of the word to substitute for "clan" or "tribe" (TCM, pp. 15f.). The early Mexica in their wandering period are referred to as *calpulleque*, "those who have *calpulli* [as a social structure]" (TCM, p. 13).

13. For other titles used for the *tequitlato*, see DINE, II, 223; MON, II, 545.

14. MTL, p. 65; MQ, p. 78; CODX, p. 64; IXREL, pp. 123f., 289; IXCH, p. 70.

15. For the Culua refugees admitted to Tezcoco, see MQ, pp. 79f.; CODX, pp. 79f., 97; MTL, p. 65; POM, p. 13; IXCH, pp. 73ff., 78; IXREL, p. 295.

16. IXCH, p. 61.

17. *Calpulli* can also mean specifically the temple of the ward (MON, II, 587; SAHG, I, 113; SFC, II, 179), though generally the temple seems to have been referred to as *calpulco* (SAHG, I, 159, 209).

18. The theory that the four quarters of the city were original and represented the first layout of the city is found in JAC, p. 330; HE, IV, 108; TCM, pp. 74f.; CODAUB, p. 18. The division into four quarters was possibly a standard urban administrative and cultic procedure in Aztec cities and is in Mexico to be also connected with the Council of the Four Princes. Yet if there had indeed been four *calpulli* to settle Tenochtitlan at its foundation, they would have been exclusive of all later ones. But we find that they comprised all the *calpulli*, including later and foreign ones.

19. For *chinampa* agriculture under Cuacuauhtzin, see ATCT, p. 52. Of the *chinampas*, only the small nursery plots floated. These could be dragged about through the shallow canals by ropes. Lake Chalco was pretty well filled up with these *chinampas*.

20. For the growth of Tlatilulca commerce, see SAHG, III, 15; SFC, IX, 1f.; VET, p. 29.

21. IXREL, p. 154.

22. IXREL, pp. 113–116, 283f.; AOG, p. 58.

23. The Otomí were always classed as Chichimecs (AOG, p. 36; PRM, p. 51; SAHG, III, 190; CLA, I, 176; TMM, p. 12).

24. IXCH, pp. 77f.; IXREL, p. 478. Cuacuauhtzin led the Tepaneca forces against Tenayuca, Coacalco, and Xaltocan (SFC, VIII, 7; SAHG, II, 286; ANE, p. 125). The Xaltocan campaign is put in the reign of Quinatzin and also in that of his son (IXREL, pp. 111, 113). The latter reign is to be preferred (IXREL, pp. 137ff.; MON, I, 87; CLA, I, 213).

25. CLA, I, 225.

26. EST, V, 107f.; CODX, p. 75; IXCH, p. 79; ATCT, p. 51.

27. TCM, pp. 99f.; EST, V, 109.

28. TMM, p. 7; TCM, pp. 86ff.; OM, p. 270; TMH, p. 78; RGL, p. 251.

29. IXCH, pp. 78f.; TMH, p. 78; TMM, p. 7; OM, p. 268; HMP, pp. 227f.

30. Some of the sources erroneously give Acamapichtli as the ruler who took over Culhuacan. While he was probably alive at the time (HGL, p. 252), it was his son Nauhyotl who was installed as governor. It may well have been this great event that impelled the Tenochca to set up Huitzilihuitl as some kind of ruler, possibly simply as a war chief at the beginning.

31. VHA, I, 348f.

32. For a three- or four-year period stated to have elapsed between the death of Acamapichtli and the election of Huitzilihuitl, see ROCA, p. 183; ATCT, p. 52; CLA, I, 211; AOG, p. 71; HMP, p. 236. It is my opinion, however, that Acamapichtli died much later, perhaps in 1404. There is a curious reference in CDH, II, 11, to a "tyrant" who ruled between Acamapichtli and Chimalpopoca and who is named Tuztlantli. If this is a trustworthy reference, Tuztlantli may well have filled this three- or four-year period. I know of no other references to him.

33. Huitzilihuitl is said in a late source to have been the ancestral ruler of all Tenochtitlan (VHA, I, 392).

34. Huitzilihuitl is said to have begun his rule in 1390 (MON, I, 106; ATCT, p. 54; ROCA, p. 189), which would put Acamapichtli's death in 1386 or 1387. This agrees fairly well with ROCA, pp. 83, 196, and CLA, I, 210, but not with the 1404 tradition, which I have tentatively accepted, found in DINE, I, 52; ATH, p. 4; AC, p. 35.

35. TCM, p. 89; MON, I, 103; CODX, pp. 73f., plate V.

36. MTL, p. 65; MON, I, 110; ROCA, p. 184; CODX, p. 86; IXCH, p. 82; IXREL, pp. 301, 449.

37. IXCH, pp. 79f.; IXREL, p. 145; CODX, p. 86.

38. IXREL, p. 155.

39. All the Chinampaneca and Tepaneca cities were allies of Azcapotzalco as were Culhuacan, the two Mexicos (MON, I, 114), and the cities of the north (Cuauhtitlan, Tepotzotlan, Xaltepec, Otumpan, and Tula). Tezcoco's allies were the Acolhua cities, most of the Tlateputzco, Tullantzinco, and Teotihuacan. Chalco aided the Tepaneca but with some divisions.

40. For accounts of the inception of the war, see CLA, I, 219; MON, I, 108; CODX, p. 90; IXREL, pp. 146ff., 299f.; IXCH, p. 81.

41. CODX, p. 119; CLA, IV, 73.

42. For Tlacateotzin's part in the war, see VHA, I, 402f.; II, 11. The poem translated in GHL, I, 223, no doubt refers to his activities in this war.

43. The most circumstantial (and too seldom trustworthy) accounts of the war are in IXCH, pp. 81–97, and IXREL, pp. 145–170.

44. For the famous incident of the death of the Acolhua hero Cihuacuecuenotzin, see IXREL, p. 480; EST, V, 105; AC, p. 37; MON, I, 111.

45. ROCA, pp. 89, 189; POM, p. 44; IXREL, pp. 166–169, 306f., 479f.; IXCH, pp. 91–97; CODX, p. 97; CLA, I, 225.

46. GPN, II, 90.

47. IXREL, pp. 179–182; CLA, I, 228.

48. CODX, p. 101; MON, I, 114; AC, p. 37; CLA, I, 227.

49. ATCT, p. 55; CODX, p. 102; IXREL, p. 190; AC, p. 37; MON, I, 117f.; CLA, I, 231; TEZ, 24, 26.

4. THE TEPANECA WAR

1. Maxtla had been ruler of Coyouacan since 1409 or 1410 (ROCA, pp. 186, 190; AM, p. 49).

2. MON, I, 104ff.; CLA, I, 216f.

3. Chimalpopoca is variously said to be either a son or a brother of Huitzilihuitl.

4. AC, pp. 36, 38, 66; AM, pp. 52f.

5. HF, IV, 111; CODRAM, pp. 51f., 55; JAC, pp. 336ff.; DINE, I, 62ff.

6. AC, pp. 37f.; CLA, I, 233–236; IXREL, pp. 197–200, 485–488; IXCH, p. 108.

7. For Tlacateotl's support of Tayatzin, see VHA, II, 57, 63.

8. CLA, I, 239–242; HMP, p. 230; AM, p. 50; DINE, I, 65; CODRAM, p. 55; IXCH, pp. 111f., 119f.; POM, p. 44; MON, I, 106f., 123–126. The accounts of the death are curious and amazingly contradictory. There is probably some substance behind the account where Chimalpopoca garbs himself as the god, preparatory to self-sacrifice.

9. For the date of Cuauhtlatoa's election, see VHA, II, 108; TCM, pp. 108, 110; ROCA, p. 191; TTT, X, 15–19, 35f.; AM, p. 66.

10. Veytia denies that Cuauhtlatoa was of the royal line, VHA, II, 108. Tlacateotl's son (Acolmiztli), who was the father of Cuauhtlatoa, is said to have ruled briefly in Tlatilulco and then have been killed by his son (TCM, pp. 100, 110; ROCA, p. 191; AOG, p. 72; EST, V, 113; TTT, X, 15). The rule was probably only a matter of days.

11. There is near unanimity that Itzcoatl came into office in 1426 or 1427, more probably the latter. For his election and its immediate results, see MON, I, 132; DINE I, 66ff.; JAC, p. 338; CLA, I, 246. A son of Chimalpopoca (Xihuiltemoc) is said to have ruled for three Aztec months before Itzcoatl (TCM, p. 104), after which he died. He was probably a candidate of the Maxtla party in Tenochtitlan, and his swift disappearance from the scene no doubt represents the failure of that party to carry the day for a policy of continuing alliance with Azcapotzalco.

12. For his previous titles and prestige, see ROCA, pp. 83, 89; MON, I, 107, 132, CLA, I, 247.

13. ATCT, p. 54; EST, V, 108.

14. AC, pp. 45f.; AM, pp. 51, 54, 58f.; MON, I, 135–139; CLA, I, 250–253; ROCA, p. 191; IXCH, pp. 146f.; IXREL, pp. 222ff., 314f., 488ff.

15. IXCH, p. 195; AC, p. 46; ANE, p. 113.

16. DINE, I, 69–75; CODRAM, pp. 58, 62; TEZ, pp. 27, 30; CLA, I, 257f.; JAC, p. 340.

17. Clavigero confuses Tlacaelel with Moteuczoma (CLA, I, 250), while Torquemada confuses him with Itzcoatl (MON, I, 171).

18. The name is erroneously spelled Atlacaelel in CODRAM. The name Tlacaelel (correct spelling Tlacaellel) is difficult to define with precision. It was an epithet applied to a deity whose power, cruelty, and unconcern for men was outstanding. *Elli* means "liver or bowels" (MOL, II, 29; GPN, I, 123; GLL, p. 343) with derived meanings of contempt for opponents, scorn, or a display of spirit or valor (SS, p. 49; MOL, II, 115; VHA, II, 108). Torquemada translates the name literally as "man of great heart," but the intent is much more demonic than that.

19. ROCA, pp. 91, 190; TEZ, p. 27.

20. CODRAM, pp. 59–62; DINE, I, 72–75.

21. ROCA, p. 93; AM, p. 61; EST, VII, 214; MON, I, 140f.; IXREL, p. 490; IXCH, pp. 149f.; CLA, I, 258ff.

22. BF, pp. 147f.

23. For the location of Petlacalco, see SAHG, IV, 526.

24. While the fire god was considered the national god of the Tepaneca (AOG, pp. 40f.), their deformed war god was Coltic (ROCA, p. 93).

25. The names of eight or nine rulers of Azcapotzalco are known for the period before the entry of the Mexica (MON, I, 252f.), and yet CODX does not even show the site. This is most curious.

26. The sacred hill of the Tepaneca was called Bird Hill (IXCH, p. 399). For other possible names, see SAHG, I, 204; SFC, II, 25; CAM, p. 225. It is today the shrine of Los Remedios.

27. The Tepaneca fortress city of Atlacuihuayan (MON, I, 144) is the modern Tacubaya near Chapultepec Park.

28. VHA, II, 135.

29. VHA, II, 143.

30. Clavigero's breakdown of the system of landholding into three categories (CLA, II, 210f.; DINE, I, 79f.) is useful: crown lands (*tecpantlalli*), nobles' lands (*pillalli*), and community lands (*altepetlalli*). The latter can also be referred to as *calpullalli* (IXCH, p. 170). Before its distribution land seized as loot in war was classed as *yaotlalli*, "lands of the enemy" (IXCH, pp. 170f.). The estates given to the great nobles to be held in permanent fief and therefore entailed were *tecutlalli* (better, *teuctlalli*) or *tecalli* (CAM, pp. 104f.; AZR, p. 105; VHA, I, 283), while the smaller lands given outright to less eminent nobles or retainers were *pillalli* (here a specific use of the above generic term; see CAM, p. 104; TPT, p. 95; CLA, II, 210). For types of owned lands, see also MON, II, 545. The breakdown of these lands is in any case unclear.

31. BF, p. 149; AC, p. 36; CLA, I, 248ff., 266f.; IXCH, pp. 139ff.; MON, I, 135f.; IXREL, p. 231.

32. TPT, pp. 94f.

33. DINE, I, 80; TEZ, pp. 41–45.

34. AM, p. 62; ROCA, p. 95; CLA, I, 250f.; DINE, I, 88; TEZ, p. 46; AC, p. 45.

35. DINE, I, 89ff., 94f.; BF, pp. 149; 153f.; ROCA, pp. 96, 192; CODRAM, pp. 67, 69–72; TEZ, p. 56; MON, I, 144f.; CLA, I, 267ff.; JAC, p. 344.

36. AM, p. 62; TCM, p. 109; ROCA, pp. 193f.; ATCT, p. 55.

37. For the defeat of Xochimilco and the building of the causeway, see CODRAM, p. 75; EST, VII, 217; TEZ, pp. 62ff., 68; DINE, I, 106ff., 112f.; MON, I, 148; CLA, I, 272f.; ROCA, pp. 95, 192; JAC, p. 346.

38. JAC, p. 346; CODRAM, pp. 76f.; CLA, I, 273f.; TEZ, p. 69; ROCA, p. 194; DINE, I, 117–122; AM, p. 63; AC, pp. 49f.

39. IXCH, pp. 152, 157; IXREL, pp. 317, 492; AC, pp. 48f.; BF, p. 154; MON, I, 145; ATCT, p. 55; VHA, II, 158.

40. Perhaps the most difficult aspect of Mexican history to deal with is that of the relationships between Tenochtitlan and Tlatilulco. Deliberate falsifications occur in the sources as well as grave errors. Worst of all are the omissions. I believe my account to be essentially correct, for it explains much that follows in Mexican history, including the long hiatus in Tlatilulca campaigning from 1431 to 1450; see PRM, pp. 81, 83; HTC, pp. 114f. For Tlatilulca hostility to the Tenochca under Tlacateotzin, see AM, pp 52f.; EST, VIII, 212; AC, pp. 36, 66.

41. ATCT, p. 55; AM, p. 51; ANE, p. 126; EST, VII, 212; TCM, p. 106; ROCA, p. 93.

42. ROCA, pp. 95f., 193; AC, p. 66; MON, I, 156f.; CLA, I, 280; AOG, pp. 60f.; HMP, p. 230.

43. VHA, II, 151.

44. For the 1435 settlement, see AC, p. 50; ATCT, p. 56; TTT, I, 43; X, 20; VHA, II, 159. This arrangement was undoubtedly a part of the larger arrangement of boundaries between Tezcoco and Mexico (IXCH, p. 158; IXREL, p. 491; TEZ, pp. 75f.

45. ATCT, p. 56; AC, p. 50.

46. CLA, I, 275; HMP, p. 230; AOG, p. 61; MON, I, 150; AC, pp. 47f., 50.

5. THE COMPOSITION OF HEAVEN AND EARTH

1. Tlacatecco has three references. Primarily it referred to the central shrine of Tenochtitlan (SAHG, I, 347), secondly to the whole central district, just as *calpulli* were called by the name of their temples (SFC, II, 155; IV, 77; CAM, p. 169), thirdly to a specific building attached to the main temple where all newly elected rulers retired for their four-day fast (MEN, I, 171; TMM, p. 284; CAS, p. 147). The usual translation is "house of magnates" (GPN, I, 228; POM, p. 13), where the central element is from *tlacateuctli*. Siméon,

however, derives it from *tlaca+tequi+co*, which would give a meaning like "place for cutting up men" (SIM, p. 505) or even "place for washing men" (SS, p. 66), both of which would have reference to sacrifice. I believe the usual translation is preferable, but I would amend it somewhat to read "place of the sovereign."

2. The tale of the drowning of Axolohua refers to the welcoming of the new god Huitzilopochtli to Mexico by the older god Tlaloc, who refers to Huitzilopochtli as "my son" (EST, VII, 216f.; GHL, I, 302f.; CODAUB, pp. 39–41; MON, I, 288f.).

3. CCH, pp. 58, 82f.; ROCA, p. 63; SER, pp. 208, 229f.; TCM, pp. 12, 18f.

4. CLA, I, 275.

5. For Cihuacoatl as present also in Culhuacan, see HMP, p. 225; AOG, p. 52.

6. DINE, II, 171, 176; SAHG, I, 46f.

7. SAHG, I, 234; DINE, I, 310, II, 171, 173. Attached to this temple was the Tlillan Calmecac (SAHG, II, 292; MON, I, 235).

8. DINE, II, 172.

9. For the phrase *teoatl tlachinolli*, see HTC, p. 101; GLL, p. 116; CCH, pp. 67, 89; ROCA, p. 173; CAM, p. 113; OM, p. 283; IXREL, p. 130; MOL, I, 67; II, 8, 118. Note that *teoatl* can be shortened to *atl*, which is translated "*the* liquid" (i.e., blood). A poetic synonym of *teoatl* is *xochiatl*, "precious liquid" (GPN, I, 21; II, 61; III, 54). For *tlachinolli* as referring to the dead warrior's pyre, see GPN, I, 79ff. Sahagún's translation, "the sea and the conflagration," is not sufficiently specific (SFC, VI, 11, 67, 244).

10. The flint knife of sacrifice was the *tecpatl ixquauac* (TMM, p. 59; MOL, II, 93; SFC, II, 47; SIM, p. 200). For this knife as the child of the goddess, see SAHG, I, 46f.; DINE, II, 176.

11. AC, p. 14; GHL, I, 461.

12. AOG, p. 34.

13. George Kubler and Charles Gibson, "The Tovar Calendar," *Memoirs of the Connecticut Academy of Arts and Sciences* 11 (January 1951): 32, 41.

14. POM, p. 20; SAHG, II, 83; DINE, I, 298.

15. SER, p. 180.

16. GPN, II, 11.

17. SFC, VI, 23.

18. Both the sun and the earth benefited by drinking the warriors' blood (SFC, VI, 11).

19. SAHG, I, 46f.; DINE, II, 176.

20. TEZ, p. 482; SAHG, II, 109, 111. For poetic designations of the battlefield, see GHL, I, 19f., 76. Less poetically, the designated battlefield was also

known as *yaotlalli* (CLA, II, 240; MON, II, 538) and possibly *cuauhtlalli* (?);
see ANE, p. 66.

21. For the chivalric procedures connected with arranging flower wars, see
IXCH, pp. 207f.; TEZ, p. 462; POM, pp. 46f.; ROCA, pp. 152, 189.

22. DINE, I, 434.

23. The flower war is said to go back to Toltec times (IXREL, pp. 51f.). I
suspect it goes back even farther. Nezahualcoyotl is often given credit for
initiating the concept among the Aztecs (POM, pp. 41f.; IXREL, p. 321), but
this is claimed also for Quinatzin (CLA, I, 172).

24. The Mexica consistently referred human sacrifice back to Tula (HE, IV,
106; GPMX, p. 38; IXREL, p. 39; MON, I, 82; AOG, p. 45; CODRAM, p.
27). The Chichimecs did sacrifice victims in the baroque Toltec style (in spite
of AC, p. 30; see further CM, pp. 15, 17f., 140, 217f., 225f., 228, 230), no
doubt as a result of their contact with the great empire. Their own indigenous
custom of sacrifice was to shoot arrows into a victim stretched out on a wood-
en frame (DINE, I, 147; MON, II, 291; PRM, 65; HTC, plate xv).

25. TCM, p. 54; DINE, I, 32f.; CLA, I, 203f.

26. For *xochimicqui*, see LS, p. 140; MON, II, 160.

27. TMM, p. 301; SFC, II, 52f. The captives were "brothers" to the other
knights of the captor's city (TEZ, p. 254).

28. CLA, II, 114; SFC, II, 47f.; POM, p. 17; MON, II, 118.

29. SAHG, I, 143; SFC, II, 47.

30. For the *apetlac*, see SAHG, I, 188; III, 53ff. Garibay translates it "in the
shining waters," taking *petla-* from *petlani*, "to shine," I prefer the derivation
atl + *petlatl* + *co*, where *atl* is to be translated as "*the* liquid," namely blood.

31. Note that the *temalacatl* could be called the *cuauhtemalac[atl]*, the
"sun wheel" (HTC, p. 102). For the act that took place on the *temalacatl*, see
DINE, I, 177ff., 281; II, 150; SAHG, I, 144ff.; SFC, II, 176; VIII, 84f.;
MON, I, 154; ACN, p. 25; POM, pp. 18ff.

32. For the name Tonatiuh, see MON, II, 55f.; SS, p. 66.

33. SAHG, II, 84.

34. GPN, II, lxxi; III, xxxii; EST, V, 51.

35. For the *cuauhxicalli*, see DINE, I, 86, 310; II, 149, 157.

36. POM, pp. 17ff.; MON, II, 252f. Xipe is generally derived from the
Pacific coastal area (SAHG, I, 65; II, 261; SFC, I, 16; X, 187; LPR, pp.
128f.).

37. For the use of *teotl* to refer specifically to Tonatiuh, see MON, II, 56.

38. SFC, VI, 14.

39. For the distribution of lands and the creation of new noble titles and
houses, see CLA, I, 270; CODRAM, pp. 64, 72f.; TEZ, pp. 36, 41, 52, 57f., 60,
66; ROCA, p. 194; DINE, I, 78, 96f. The patrimonial manor of the *teuctli*
was his *teccalli* (AZR p. 104; MON, I, 277).

40. For the anti-plebian bias, see CLA, I, 263; DINE, II, 287.

41. SAHG, III, 209; SFC, X, 191.

42. DINE, I, 123.

43. For the two classes of nobles, *teuctli* and *pilli,* see CAM, pp. 186f.

44. Vaillant quite erroneously states that *teuctli* means "grandfather" (G. C. Vaillant, *The Aztecs of Mexico*, rev. ed., 1966, p. 127). The word for grandfather is *colli* or *tecol* (MOL, II, 94), i.e., "someone's grandfather." But SS, p. 5, states that there is only one syllable in the stem of *teuctli*, whereas obviously there are two in *tecol*; *teuctli* is still legitimately subject to metathesis, as witness the noun *tecuyotl*. The title is also found spelled *tecuitli* (TMM, pp. 286, 290), and this would give a proper derivation translatable as "he seizes someone, he takes people." The word *tecuitli* indeed is found (SIM, 404) and means "captor," but its main element *cui*, "to take or seize," is also composed of two syllables. In short, there is no certain etymology of *teuctli*.

45. For the social difference between the grandee (*teuctli*) and the caballero (*pilli*), see AZR, p. 105; DINE, II, 162; SAHG, II, 113; MON, II, 361; CAM, p. 103. There are many other words, all of which for lack of specific information we translate simply as "noblemen": *tecpilli, tetlapanca, calpampilli, tlatocapilli, teuctlatoque.*

46. For *cihuapilli* (or *teciuapil*), see MOL, I, 36; II, 23, 93; CAS, p. 138.

47. AC, p. 38. In line with this, note that Moteuczoma I was to send sorcerors up to Coatepec near Tula to try to locate the original site of Chicomoztoc (DINE, I, chap. 27), this being a continuation of the attempt by the Mexica to create a respectable history.

48. For the knighting ceremony, see VHA, I, 269ff.; MEN, I, 172–177; ANE, pp. 42–45; CLA, II, 207f.; CAM, pp. 42, 45ff.; TMM, pp. 286, 288ff.; HE, III, 181.

49. The order of the eagles was the *cuauhyotl*, that of the jaguars, the *oceloyotl* (GPN, II, 23). For more poetic designations of the orders, see GHL, II, 402f. There is a remarkable poem from the time of Moteuczoma I describing Mexico as the center of the eagle and jaguar orders (GHL, I, 211f.).

50. The knightly version of the myth of the creation of the sun and the moon is conveniently found in Garibay, *Epica Nahuatl*, (Mexico: UNAM, 1945), pp. 15f.; see also LS, p. 122.

51. JAC, p. 314; VHA, I, 271; CODRAM, pp. 100f.; MON, I, 565; HE, IV, 132.

52. DINE, I, 169f., 291.

53. LPR, p. 81; DINE, I, 198. Note that among the Tarascan Chichimecs a similar "eagle house" existed (CM, pp. 52, 123).

54. DINE, I, 197; II, 155–159.

55. The plural form of *pilli.*

6. MOTEUCZOMA I AND THE STATE

1. For the expansion of Cuauhtitlan after the war, see, AC, pp. 47f. The conspiracy of silence among our sources regarding the subjection of Cuauhtitlan is striking. The event is barely mentioned in AC, p. 50; MON, I, 150; AOG, p. 61; HMP, p. 230; CLA, I, 275.

2. CODAUB, pp. 43f.; ROCA, p. 195; CLA, I, 274f.; IXCH, p. 196; MON, I, 149.

3. For the legendary birth of Moteuczoma, see AOG, p. 59; TCM, pp. 90–95; HMP, p. 229.

4. The name Moteuczoma goes back into the mists of Aztlan (TCM, p. 15; DB, p. 445). Note that the name is also found as Motlatocazoma where *tlatoca* substitutes for *teuctli* but gives exactly the same sense (GPN, II, lxxxv; IXREL, p. 234; MON, I, 163; MQ, p. 93). In a shortened form the name can appear simply as Mozoma, "he becomes wrathful" (IXREL, p. 136). See also *mozomani* (MOL, I, 7). The references in the above instances are to a ruler who flares up violently at the slightest check to his will (CAM, p. 218). Ilhuicamina is also a fairly common name. Garibay says the latter name refers to the sun, who, as a warrior, shoots his rays throughout the heavens (GHL, II, 404). I do not know his authority for this statement.

5. For the myth of Citli, see CLA, II, 65f.; MEN, I, 85.

6. For the titles of the four princes, see EST, VIII, 33; ROCA, p. 194; JAC, p. 313; CODRAM, p. 73; DINE, I, 102f.; HE, IV, 131; TEZ, p. 159 (note that the last substitutes *cuauhnochtli* for *ezhuahuacatl*). There is a real problem in that Sahagún gives significantly differing titles as follows: *tlacochcalcatl, tiçociuacatl, titlancalqui* (or *pochtecatlailotlac*), and *huitznahuatlailotlac* (SAGH, II, 329; IV, 85; SFC, VIII, 61; XII, 9). The appearance of the third title might give one justification for feeling that Sahagún is here giving a list of the titles in the Council of Four of Tlatilulco and not Tenochtitlan. The connection between the *tlillancalqui* and the *cihuacoatl* presents another problem to which we do not have the answer; that the offices were distinct appears from the fact that Tlacaelel is never designed as the *tlillancalqui*, though he held the office of *cihuacoatl* for life.

7. For the dual military-civil division of the Council of the Four Princes, see SFC, VI, 110; SAHG, II, 113, 122, 311, 140.

8. For the pre-coronation war, see HE, IV, 113; CODRAM, p. 79; CLA, II, 200.

9. DINE, I, 125.

10. IXCH, p. 155. For the *xopancuicatl*, "summer song," see GHL, I, 87, 232f.; IXCH, pp. 235f.

11. For the events of the year 1431, see IXREL, p. 317.

12. CLA, I, 269; IV, 319; IXCH, p. 153f.; IXREL, p. 232; BF, p. 154f.

13. For the full promulgation of the League, see GPN, II, 22f.; IXCH, p. 155; CLA, II, 196. The League had been adumbrated early in the reign of Itzcoatl (CODRAM, p. 78; IXCH, p. 157).

14. For the independent nature of the three confederate empires, see IXCH, p. 154; DINE, I, 409; AZR, p. 89; GCNE, p. 156; CAS, p. 147; TTT, X, 31; CLA, IV, 319; ANE, p. 101.

15. GCNE, p. 156; POM, p. 34.

16. IXCH, p. 178, 241; DINE, I, 362.

17. For the tribute arrangements of the League, see ANE, pp. 65f., 112; MON, I, 146; IXREL, p. 492; TMM, pp. 354ff.; AZR, p. 89; CLA, I, 269f.

18. GPN, II, 3.

19. For the equivalence of *altepetl* and *tlatoani*, see MOL, I, 103; II, 4.

20. *Tlatoqui* is an alternate word for "ruler or king" from the same root as *tlatoani*. Both words were in common usage among the Aztec states. From *tlatoani* we could derive the imperial idea, as in *cemanahuac tlatoani*, "ruler of the entire world," or *nouian tlatoani*, "lord everywhere" (TEZ, p. 459; MOL, I, 99; IXREL, p. 276).

21. SAHG, IV, 84; TEZ, p. 437; SFC, XII, 5; EST, VIII, 32f.

22. GPN, II, 27, 47; ROCA, p. 165; LS, p. 135.

23. Note that Moteuczoma II was styled *tlacateuctli tlatoani in tlacatl*, "lord of men, ruler, master."

24. On the divine nature of the ruler, see AZR, p. 98; ANE, p. 52; CODRAM, pp. 41, 48, 153; GCNE, pp. 210, 213; SAHG, II, 75, 89f., 95; SFC, VI, 52; POM, pp. 12, 36; DINE, I, 55, 192, 217; MEN, I, 178; JAC, p. 229; MON, II, 298.

25. For the ruler as Quetzalcoatl, see TEZ, p. 247; MON, I, 97, 380; RGL, p. 245; CLA, I, 181; ROCA, p. 61; SER, p. 123.

26. We can assume that the new temple of Huitzilopochtli was designed to be ready for the New Fire Ceremony which began the year 1455. In this respect the date 1453 for the inception of the work is probably accurate (AM, pp. 63ff.). This is supported by Tezozomoc's statement that the work was begun right after the Huaxteca war (TEZ, pp. 80, 114). For other references to this temple, see MON, I, 151; AOG, p. 61; CLA, I, 277; DINE, I, 132f.; ATCT, p. 16.

27. IXCH, pp. 201f.; MON, I, 157; EST, VI, 223.

28. A careful reading of CM will make clear the astounding resemblance of the Tarascans to the Aztecs. Only in the difference of language and of the role of urbanization in their culture do they significantly show themselves to be of contrasting cultures.

29. For Huitzilopochtli's command to the Mexica to conquer the world, see DINE, I, 232.

30. For the office of tax collector (*calpixqui*), see CLA, II, 212f; HE, III,

222; ANE, pp. 59, 101; TEZ, p. 112; DINE, I, 131; II, 165; SAHG, II, 308; POM, p. 9; ROCA, p. 107; PL, p. 134; MEN, I, 167; RELA, pp. 15f.

31. DINE, I, 246.

32. IXCH, p. 289.

33. For the Coacalco, see AOG, p. 52; SFC, II, 168; SAHG, I, 233f.; COR, pp. 52f.; MON, II, 146f., 149; ANE, p. 104; GCNE, p. 165; CLA, II, 95; HE, III, 235. Coacalco is probably to be translated as "house of assemblage," where the element *coa-* means, not "snake," but a public gathering; see SIM, p. 102 (*coatlaca*) and MOL, II, 23 (*coatequitl*). It is strange that SS does not note this use of *coatl*.

34. The *calpixque* of Mexico are also referred to as "the lords," *teteuctin* (pl. of *teuctli*); see MON, II, 544f. For other duties of these officers see the following section.

35. MON, I, 168; ANE, p. 59; CLA, II, 132, 217f.; MEN, I, 148f.; AZR, p. 130; POM, p. 39f.; IXCH, p. 193; TMM, p. 307. Eighty days is the equivalent of four (the sacred number) Aztec months.

36. For the two courts, see SAHG, II, 309f., 317f.; SFC, VIII, 41f., 54f.; AZR, pp. 125–130; HE, IV, 230; CAS, pp. 128f., 142; CLA, II, 216f.

37. Serving on the court just under the *tlacateccatl* were the *quauhnochtli* and the *tlailotlac* (MON, II, 352f.). Note that Garibay translates *tlailotlacatl* as "one who returns" (GHL, I, 373) from the verb *iloa*. The *tlailotlac* was an official in charge of such immigrants.

38. For the thirteen members of the *tecxitlan*, see ANE, p. 59; SAHG, II, 318, 329; SFC, VIII, 55.

39. For the standardization of positions, procedures, and state practices, see DINE, I, 198, 214f., 242; CODRAM, pp. 78f., 83f.; CLA, I, 290; MON, I, 169.

40. On the great famine see, MON, I, 158; HMP, p. 230; CLA, I, 282f.; AOG, p. 61; DINE, I, 245–249; TMH, pp. 81, 120; SFC, VIII, 2; ATCT, pp. 16, 56f.; ROCA, pp. 99f., 156, 165, 200f., 204; AM, p. 63; AC, p. 52; CODRAM, pp. 183f.; CODAUB, p. 44; TEZ, pp. 164f. Two different designations are given of the famine, *necetochuiloc* (SAHG, II, 283) and *netotonac[a]-huilloc,* "when people went down among the Totonacs" (AM, p. 66). Because of the ruin associated with one-Rabbit, that year was felt by the Aztecs to be ill-starred (SFC, VII, 21f.). Thus the record of a famine fifty-two years later and also in the reign of a Moteuczoma gives the careful historian some pause. For the other natural disasters of Moteuczoma's reign, see AM, p. 63; IXCH, pp. 205ff.; AC, pp. 52f.; DINE, I, 165; CODRAM, p. 177; HMP, p. 230; CLA, I, 281f.; TCM, p. 132; MON, I, 157f.; OM, p. 273.

41. LS, p. 126; SAHG, I, 170; III, 351; TEZ, pp. 333, 384f., 425; DINE, II, 142f.

42. For the increase in flower wars as a result of the drought, see IXCH, pp. 206f.

43. Thirteen Aztec years formed a unit known as *tlalpilli*, "a bundle" (IXREL, p. 25); four of these comprised the sacred *xiuhtlalpilli*, "year bundle" (IXREL, p. 269), *toxiuhmolpia* (MOL, I, 23), or *toxiuhmolpilia* (SAHG, II, 269), "our years are bundled up." Two of these, or 104 years, formed "one entire old age," *ceueuetiliztli* (IXREL, p. 272; SFC, VII, 25).

44. Much has been written on the New Fire Ceremony. Here I will cite only C. A. Saenz, *El Fuego Nuevo* (Mexico: Instituto Nacional de Antropología e Historia, 1967) and the appropriate parts of A. Caso, *Los Calendarios prehispánicos* (Mexico: UNAM, 1967). For the sources, see DINE, I, 472; SAHG, II, 269–274; SFC, IV, 143f.; VII, 27ff.; MON, II, 293; CODHALL, pp. 5f.; TMH, p. 112; TMM, pp. 41f.; SER, p. 118; CLA, II, 161.

45. Today the Cerro de la Estrella.

46. MEN, I, 110; SAHG, II, 269.

7. THE WARS OF MOTEUCZOMA

1. Chalco probably means "on the edge of the Basin" (SS, p. 47; CODRAM, p. 18).

2. IXCH, p. 45; ROCA, p. 185.

3. ROCA, p. 57, 128f., 134ff.

4. ROCA, p. 155.

5. IXREL, p. 129.

6. For the supposed flower wars with Chalco in which Mexico was involved, see AC, p. 32; ROCA, pp. 82f., 89, 157, 182f.

7. For Mexican relations with Chalco under Huitzilihuitl, see ROCA, p. 184; AOG, p. 59; HMP, p. 229.

8. AC, p. 66; EST, VI, 223.

9. CLA, I, 276; DINE, I, 142; JAC, p. 347.

10. AM, pp. 65f.; DINE, I, 134f.; CODRAM, p. 174; TEZ, p. 81; ROCA, pp. 97f.

11. The year 1446 saw the Mexica demand aid from their neighbors and subjects in building their temple, and Chimalpahin says that Chalca refusal marks the beginning of the war (ROCA, pp. 97, 199; DINE, I, 134; AM, pp. 65.f.; CODRAM, p. 174. This appears to have been a preliminary sparring, and I have accepted the date 1452 (or 1453) as the true beginning of the Chalco war (AM, pp. 63, 66; ROCA, p. 99). For 1465 as the date of the termination of the war, see ROCA, pp. 102, 204; AC, p. 53; IXCH, p. 229; LPT, p. 228; AM, p. 66.

12. CLA, I, 277; IXCH, p. 223; MON, I, 151.

13. Accounts of the Chalco war are found in CODRAM, pp. 174ff.; DINE,

I, 134–152; CLA, I, 277–279, 289f.; MON, I, 151–154, 163f.; ROCA, pp. 99–102.

14. This brother or close cousin of Moteuczoma held the title of *ezuauacatl* (TEZ, pp. 89ff.; CODRAM, pp. 80, 175f.; CLA, I, 288f.; DINE, I, 146f.).

15. CODRAM, p. 80.

16. CLA, I, 289f.; ROCA, pp. 102, 110, 203f.

17. For the treatment of the conquered, see IXCH, pp. 229f.; ROCA, pp. 112, 205f., 218; AC, p. 53.

18. DINE, I, 152; CODRAM, p. 176.

19. GPN, II, 59. This poem has Chimalpopoca ruling in Tlacopan at the end of the Chalco war, which occurred in 1465. But almost certainly the ruler of that city then was Totoquihuatzin, whose date of death is usually given as 1469. For translation of an interesting poetic lament on the destruction of Chalco, see GHL, I, 219f.

20. SAHG, III, 214; SIM, p. 592; MOL, II, 136.

21. For Texcalla as the original name, see CAM, p. 55; ROCA, p. 75; GCNE, p. 118. It probably was an abbreviated form of Quauhtexcallan, "eagle crags" (SAHG, IV, 37).

22. On the Chichimec period of Tlascalan history, see MON, I, 198, 257ff., 265; VHA, I, 166; IXCH, p. 54; IXREL, p. 477; DINE, I, 14ff.; CAM, pp. 23, 27–56, 79, 89; CLA, I, 182ff.; II, 23. A great deal of pertinent material on Tlascala has been gathered together in C. Nigel Byam Davies, *Los Señoríos independientes del imperio Azteca* (Mexico: Instituto Nacional de Antropología e Historia, 1968), pp. 66–155.

23. MON, I, 199; CLA, II, 23f.

24. I have followed Barlow (TTT, X, 23) in his picture of the northern encirclement of Tlascala. Not much is known about this war (TEZ, pp. 105f.; CODRAM, pp. 177f.; DINE, I, 165–171).

25. DINE, I, 180.

26. On the Mixtecs, see Barbro Dahlgren de Jordan, *La Mixteca, su cultura e historia prehispánica* (Mexico: Imprenta Universitaria, 1954); also R. Spores, *The Mixtec Kings and Their People* (Norman: University of Oklahoma Press, 1967).

27. The Mixteca war was a notable event in Mexican history (AC, p. 52; AM, p. 66; CLA, I, 284ff.; ROCA, p. 100; AOG, p. 61; HMP, p. 231; DINE, I, 188–192; CODRAM, pp. 178f.; TEZ, pp. 132–137; MON, I, 159f.).

28. For the victory *temalacatl*, see ROCA, pp. 100, 201f.; HMP, p. 230; AOG, p. 61; DINE, I, 192ff. and atlas, chap. 23. Note that Duran calls it and depicts it as a *cuauhxicalli*, whereas he says that the *temalacatl* was dedicated after the Huaxtec victory (DINE, I, 174f.).

29. MON, I, 160f.; CLA, I, 285f.

30. ROCA, pp. 201, 206; AC, p. 66; MON, I, 164.

31. Poyauhtecatl is also found as Poyauhtlan (SAHG, I, 72, 140; MON, I, 262). Poyauhtecatl can apparently refer to any high cloud-capped mountain. Literally the word means "he of Poyauhtlan," where *poyauhtlan* means "colored land," i.e., a land painted with many colors. This designation is allied to the name of the mountain worshipped by the Tlascalans, Tlapaltecatl, "lord of many colors" (DINE, II, 205). Present-day Mount Tlaloc was called Poyauhtecatl (GHL, I, 489). Why this reference to coloration designates high mountains I do not know. Another name for the Pico de Orizaba was Citlalte-pec, "mountain of stars."

32. The name Ahuilizapan, "by the waters of delight," was corrupted by the Spaniards to Orizaba.

33. On the Cotastla campaign, see MON I, 161ff.; CLA, I, 286ff.; ATCT, pp. 57f.; TTT, X, 26, 28; TEZ, pp. 122–131; CODRAM, p. 178; DINE, I, 181–186.

34. ATCT, p. 59; TEZ, p. 197; TT, X, 26.

35. GHL, I, 226.

36. On the marriage and coronation of Moquiuix, see TEZ, p. 197; ROCA, pp. 203, 208; AOG, pp. 72f.; TCM, p. 111; MON, I, 162; DINE, I, 262.

37. ROCA, pp. 103, 206; DINE, I, 156, 164; CODRAM, pp. 176f.; TEZ, p. 100; MON, I, 164.

38. TCM, p. 113; TEZ, pp. 155f.; DINE, I, 230–237, 243f.; CODRAM, pp. 180ff.

39. For Moteuczoma's pious building, see ATCT, p. 59; MON, I, 161.

40. ATCT, p. 59.

41. DINE, I, 249, 251; TEZ, p. 170; JAC, p. 314; HE, III, 224.

42. AM, p. 64.

8. THE SACRED NATURE OF THE MEXICAN STATE

1. IXCH, p. 21.

2. Besides *iptla*, the Nahuatl-speaking peoples also used the stem *polo-*, "to erase, confuse," and therefore "to mask" (SS, p. 62). *Ixpoloa*, "to wear a mask," is literally "to confuse or make different the face."

3. For the office of *cihuacoatl* in Aztec cities other than Mexico, see EST, V, 103f.; GPN, II, 90, cxv; IXREL, p. 178.

4. On the duties of the cihuacoatl, TEZ, pp. 282, 435, 459; CLA II, 216; GCNE, p. 323. Note the monopoly of the office held by Tlacaelel and his descendency (TCM, pp. 123, 125).

5. On the *texiptla*, the person who wore the mask or face paint of the god, see DINE, I, 522; SAHG, I, 93.

6. For *Quetzalcoatl* as a term for high priest, see CLA, II, 157; MOL, I, 85; II, 89; POM, p. 17; SFC, 161; III, 67; SAHG, I, 307; II, 97, 212.

7. LPR, pp. 86–89; SAHG, I, 248.

8. On autosacrifice and its many forms, see POM, pp. 21f.; MEN, I, 108, 112–115; SAHG, I, 164f.; SFC, II, 202f.; CODRAM, p. 150; PRM, p. 25; CAM, p. 157; JAC, p. 245; DINE, II, 107f., 114, 209, 211; CLA, II, 124ff.; HE, III, 177.

9. MEN, I, 114f.; TMM, pp. 69ff.; MON, II, 182f.; TMH, p. 126; CAS, p. 69f.

10. There is a great deal of information on the *telpochcalli*, but often the Spaniards did not bother to distinguish it from the *calmecac*. For life in the *telpochcalli*, see CLA, II, 193f.; TMM, pp. 44, 255, 266; CAS, pp. 71f., 158f.; POM, pp. 26f., 29; SAHG, I, 150, 301; SFC, III, 53ff., 57; VIII, 43f.; HMP, p. 239; AOG, p. 75; DINE, II, 108, 229f.; MON, II, 187; EST, VIII, 34; MEN, I, 136f.; JAC, p. 315; CODRAM, p. 147; ANE, pp. 22ff.

11. SFC, VIII, 43.

12. For the *telpochtlato* or captain of the young, see MEN, I, 136; SFC, III, 57; SAHG, I, 137f.; II, 311; TMM, p. 254; CLA, II, 185; MON, II, 185; DINE, II, 113.

13. There were similar institutions in Tlascala, Tezcoco, and Huexotzinco (POM, p. 26; MEN, I, 136f.; AZR, pp. 138ff.; DINE, II, 132). In part, the *telpochcalli* functioned as a *cuartel*, one in each barrio (SFC, VIII, 58; SAHG, I, 301).

14. SAHG I, 299.

15. For life in the *calmecac*, see TMM, p. 248; COR, p. 52; CAS, pp. 70, 142; ANE, pp. 22, 24ff.; LPR, pp. 75–79, 88f.; ACN, p. 47; MON, II, 184f., 190; IXCH, p. 185; MEN, I, 132; OM, p. 285; POM, p. 28; DINE, I, 419; II, 104; SAHG, I, 234; II, 317, 327.

16. DINE, I, 328; SFC, VIII, 18f.; CLA, III, 89.

17. For a list of others *calmecacs*, see EST, VI, 178ff.

18. SAHG, I, 304; II, 213; SFC, II, 36f.; III, 59; ANE, pp. 22, 165.

19. The *mimixcoa* as a class were monsters who were also known as *tlacatetecolo* (sing. *tlacatecolotl*), literally "owl people," with the connotation of evil sorcerers. They lived in the north, which was an ominous direction (VET, pp. 49, 103; CODAUB, p. 22).

20. For the Mimixcoa in myth, see GPMX, pp. 29–32, 40, 131; CODAUB, p. 22; HMP, pp. 216f.; LS, pp. 122ff.

21. For Mixcoatl, see SAHG, II, 81; III, 207; RB, p. 310; LS, pp. 123ff.; DINE, II, 130f.; AC, pp. 5, 46; MON, II, 280. For his myths, see LS, p. 124; MEN, I, 159f.; SER, pp. 181, 189; SAHG, I, 204; GPMX, p. 35; TMM, pp. 9, 12; AC, p. 62.

22. TEZ, p. 6; AC, pp. 3, 51; LS, p. 124; GPMX, pp. 34, 133.

23. For Quetzalcoatl's lowland origin, see CAS, p. 55; MON, I, 255; SAHG, IV, 89.

24. Note another name for the whirlwind, *ecamalacatl*, "wind spindle."

25. The wind-jewel is the *ehecailacacozcatl*, "revolving-wind pendant."

26. Acallan, in southern Campeche, at least once substitutes for Tlapallan as Quetzalcoatl's objective (GPN, III, 1). This supports the historicity of the Quetzalcoatl migration eastward, for Acallan was a real Mayan community, heavily influenced by Nahuatl-speaking peoples, whereas Tlapallan, "red land" is a vague term meaning east in general.

27. For the form of the myth of Quetzalcoatl that Cortez heard directly from Moteuczoma, see ANE, p. 214; COR, pp. 42, 48; HE, III, 273; GCNE, p. 141; CDH, II, 580. This information was, however, already known to Cortez from the early days of his landing on the coast (CDH, II, 561).

9. THE REIGN OF AXAYACATL

1. I am assuming that the temple of Coaxolotl erected by Maquiuix was used as a prison for conquered gods; it appears to stand in apposition to Coatlan in Tenochtitlan (MON, I, 173; CLA, I, 292).

2. The temple of Huitzilopochtli in Tlatilulco was called Tlillan (MON, I, 178, 565; RCAA, p. 178; TTT, II, 36, 47, 53; CLA, I, 301; II, 96).

3. There are three acceptable dates for the death of Cuauhtlatoa and the installation of Moquiuix: 1460 (AM, p. 66; TCM, pp. 110f.; ROCA, p. 203), 1464 (SFC, VIII, 7; SAHG, II, 287), and 1467/1468 (LPT, p. 134; ROCA, p. 208; ATCT, p. 59). Along with Barlow (TTT, X, 26), I have preferred the latter, but 1464 may well represent some elevation of Moquiuix to high position beside Quauhtlatoa.

4. ROCA, pp. 103, 206; ATCT, p. 59.

5. On Axayacatl's parentage, see MON, I, 162, 172; ROCA, p. 197; RGL, p. 253; IXCH, p. 230; LPT, p. 133; TCM, pp. 114f., 135, 143.

6. SFC, VIII, 7; AOG, pp. 72f; MON, I, 162; TCM, p. 114; DINE, I, 262.

7. MON, I, 169; CLA, I, 291; LPT, p. 134; DINE, I, 254f.; TCM, p. 116; CODRAM, pp. 84ff.

8. HE, IV, 115; CLA, I, 291f.; JAC, p. 351; CODRAM, pp. 86, 89; MON, I, 172.

9. Axayacatl was a common Aztec personal name. For the full spelling of the insect's name as *axaxayacatl*, see SFC, XI, 64; MOL, II, 10. The *a-* in the word is generally, because of hieroglyphic writing, translated as "water," but it is more likely to refer to a class of small insects (SS, p. 41) in which case a better translation of the word would be "insect mask."

10. ROCA, p. 106; TCM, p. 135.

11. One source says definitely that Moquiuix was not a Tlatilulca (ROCA, p. 203).

12. ROCA, pp. 206f.

13. TEZ, pp. 143–146; CLA, I, 292; HMP, p. 231; AM, p. 67; DINE, I, 199ff.; AOG, p. 62; CODRAM, p. 180.

14. AM, p. 67; AC, 55; ROCA, pp. 104, 208; IXREL, p. 498.

15. For the completion of the temple of Coaxolotl, see MON, I, 173, 177f.; SAHG, I, 236; CLA, I, 292. Coaxolotl, "snake monster," is another name for the goddess Chantico.

16. For the part played by Teconal and Poyahuitl in bringing war, see DINE, I, 259, 263f.; TEZ, p. 179; MON, I, 177.

17. For Tlatilulco's search for allies, see AC, p. 55; AM, p. 67; DINE, I, 257f., 263; CLA, I, 299f.; MBG, pp. 50ff.; MON, I, 176f.; TEZ, p. 179; VHA, II, 233.

18. DINE, I, 256, 261f.; TEZ, pp. 178, 182; MON, I, 178.

19. Chalchiuhnenetl's name ("jade or precious vulva") no doubt gave rise to the startling prophecy of woe (DINE, I, 262). For her part in the approaching conflict, see MBG, p. 49; TCM, pp. 117, 119; RGL, p. 253; AOG, pp. 72f.

20. AM, p. 67.

21. For Tlatilulco's war preparations, see CLA, I, 300; DINE, I, 258ff.; MON, I, 177.

22. DINE, I, 265f.

23. DB, I, 70.

24. References to the actual fighting can be found in ACT, p. 37; IXCH, pp. 251f.; JAC, p. 352; ROCA, pp. 104f., 206–209; CODRAM, p. 90; ATCT, p. 5; CLA, I, 300–304; MBG, pp. 53f.; MON, I, 178ff.; DINE, I, 264–270.

25. For the treatment of the defeated Tlatilulca, see ROCA, p. 208; TCM, p. 120; TEZ, pp. 199f.; DINE, I, 270f., 437; TTT, IV, 23, 31; CLA, I, 304; MON, I, 180.

26. The subject of the style of military government imposed on Tlatilulco by Tenochtitlan is confusing. We know that Tlatilulco, until the rule of Cuauhtemoc, was never again to be sovereign (ANE, p. 123; SFC, VIII, 2); it was under a military governor appointed by Tenochtitlan but of Tlatilulca blood (MON, I, 180). We find interesting references to a group of four ruling Tlatilulca nobles (VET, p. 31; AOG, p. 73; SAHG, II, 340; III, 16; SFC, IX, 2 and ACT, p. 38, where eight are mentioned, two such groups). This may refer to a structure of rule in Tlatilulco in terms of the sacred number four, as was the case with Tenochtitlan, namely a council of four princes that included the military governor. At the same time we hear of a dual system in Tlatilulco at this time (ATCT, p. 61; AOG, p. 73; TTT, VIII, 23f.). I can make sense out of these two seeming conflicts only by assuming that, of a council of four, two were appointed by Tenochtitlan and responsible to it, whereas the other two were elected by the Tlatilulca or at least represented indigenous interests. The rule of two was ancient in the Aztec system, one ruler being a sovereign and the other a war leader (ROCA, p. 81; IXREL, pp. 255, 282; AOG, p. 53; HTC, p. 120; TEZ, pp. 413f.; MON, I, 78; PRM, p.

21. Itzcuauhtzin is said to have been the first military governor, installed in 1475, and to have held this post until murdered by the Spaniards (TCM, pp. 121, 148f.; ROCA, pp. 209, 236; SFC, XII, 43; RCAA, p. 170; AM, pp. 70f.).

27. For the punishment inflicted on Tlatilulco's allies, see MON, I, 180f.; CLA, I, 304f.; AC, p. 56; IXREL, p. 456.

28. Tolotzin is today the Nevado de Toluca.

29. The dates for the rulers of Tlacopan are not quite as confused as might at first appear. I have chosen to follow MON, I, 173, and CLA, I, 292, rather than to accept the date 1489 given in SAHG II, 291, where Sahagún is clearly confusing the date of the death of Chimalpopoca (IXCH, p. 89) with the date of his election.

30. For Mexico's attack on the Toluca basin and the settlement that followed, see ROCA, pp. 105, 209f.; DINE, I, 271–279; IXCH, pp. 256f.; LPT, pp. 165, 167; TEZ, pp. 202ff.; HE, IV, 238; AZR, pp. 263f., 266; AM, p. 67.

31. For the sacrificial stone and the sacrifice of the Matlatzinca, see TEZ, pp. 202, 216f., 222ff.; LPT, pp. 136f.; DINE, I, 272f., 281f., 285 (see also 298 and 300 for a possible confusion of Toluca victims with those from Tlateputzco).

32. JAC, p. 325f.

33. Tlaximaloyan, "the place of woodcarving," today Ciudad Hidalgo, was the great frontier fortress city of the Tarascans (CLA, I, 306); it was held by the Otomí (CM, p. 222).

34. For the battle and its aftermath, see DINE, I, 286–292; TEZ, pp. 224–231; CM, p. 232. For the date of the battle, see LPT, p. 138. A famous epic lament for this disaster is attributed to Axayacatl himself in LPT, pp. 149–153; GPN, III, 61–63; ROCA, p. 104.

35. Chichicha is the Nahuatl pronunciation of the Tarascan name Tzitzintza (GPN, III, xliv).

36. On the meaning of Zamacoyahuac, see MOL, II, 12.

37. DINE, I, 293.

38. ROCA, p. 210.

39. The wounding of Axayacatl at the city of Xiquipilco was a memorable event in Mexican annals. Tlilcuetzpalin, "black lizard," is also called Tlilatl, "black water," and identified as an Otomí (LPT, p. 167). For standard accounts of the attack on Xiquipilco and the wounding, see AC, p. 57; CODAUB, p. 47; MON, I, 181f.; DINE, I, 278f.; AOG, p. 62; HMP, p. 231; TEZ, p. 209; ROCA, pp. 104f., 208, 210, 215; CLA, I, 305; IXCH, p. 256.

40. DINE, I, 160ff.; TEZ, p. 368; see also TCM, p. 65.

41. For burial ceremonies for warriors who died in the field, see DINE, I, 154ff., 294, 453, 495; TEZ, pp. 232–235; TMM, p. 247; CAS, p. 185.

42. MON, I, 176, 181; CODAUB, pp. 46f.; ROCA, pp. 105, 211.

43. DINE, I, 302.

10. TWO KINGS OF THE MIDDLE PERIOD

1. The full form of the name Tizoc is usually written Tizocicatl. It appears therefore to be a gentilic formation, "he of Tizocitli*," though we know of no such compound. Arguing from the short form with its hard *c*, the gentilic would be "he of Tizoc," where Tizoc would be a place designation ending with the sign of the locative. This then would imply the existence of the word *tizotl** of which we do have knowledge (as in the word *tizocihuacoatl*) but no translation. The only translation given in our sources for the ruler's name is "pierced nose" or "the pierced one" (MON, I, 181), which is consonant with the hieroglyphic writing. He is also called either Tlalchitonatiuh (DINE, I, 318), "sun under the earth," or Chalchiuhtona (TEZ, pp. 245f., 252, 264), "shining jade."

2. CODRAM, p. 85; JAC, p. 350; TEZ, pp. 245f.

3. For the Metztitlan campaign, see TEZ, pp. 249–253; DINE, I, 312ff., 321.

4. TEZ, pp. 255f., 258–261.

5. On Tizoc's temple, see AOG, p. 62; ROCA, p. 106; CLA, I, 310; COD-AUB, p. 48; HMP, p. 231; AC, p. 57; ATCT, p. 59; AM, p. 68.

6. For the unrest in the Toluca Basin, see CLA, I, 306; MON, I, 182; ROCA, pp. 107, 109f., 217.

7. ROCA, pp. 107, 110f., 216, 219–222.

8. For the death of Tizoc, see MON, I, 184f.; HE, IV, 114; JAC, p. 312; DINE, I, 321f.; CLA, I, 309f.; II, 201; VHA, II, 236. In at least one source Tizoc's death is totally suppressed (CODAUB, p. 48).

9. For Ahuitzotl's election, see TEZ, pp. 266f., 272ff.; DINE, I, 323–327.

10. For Tlacaelel's demonic powers, see DINE, I, 174, 238ff., 281. For his ruling position, see DINE, I, 100; JAC, p. 350; TCM, pp. 97, 121; CODRAM, pp. 64, 85. He is once referred to as "world conqueror," *cemanahuac tepehuan[i]* (TCM, p. 121).

11. For the date of his birth, see ROCA, p. 188.

12. DB, II, 284.

13. For the title *atempanecatl*, see ROCA, pp. 91, 190; AM, p. 51. This title is found in Tlatilulco as well as Tenochtitlan (MBG, p. 50). In part it is a military title (TEZ, pp. 58, 60; SIM, p. 32), but more importantly it is a priestly title connected with Toci's shrine in Mexico called Atempan (SAHG, I, 194; IV, 322) where children were kept awaiting sacrifice, MON, II, 156. This is supported in AC, p. 29, where we find it used similarly in Culhuacan. In MON, II, 184, the high priest of Toci is called the *atempanteohuatzin*. Tlacaelel thus controlled the oracles of the two paramount goddesses, Cihuacoatl and Toci.

14. For the retention of Tlacaelel's privileges by his descendants, see DINE, I, 381; JAC, p. 351; TEZ, pp. 378f.

15. The word *ahuitzotl* is generally translated "otter" (SS, p. 73), but this is certainly incorrect. The word for otter is *aitzcuintli* (SFC, XI, 16, 67). The *ahuitzotl* is a water demon whose tail ends in a human hand and who makes a practice of drowning people; he has connections with Tlaloc (AA, pp. 106–111; SFC, XI, 68ff.; GLL, pp. 269ff., 334. Ahuitzotl as a man's name is distinctly unusual and in fact is found only here.

16. For indications of Ahuitzotl's character, see DINE, I, 404, 417; MEN, I, 166; CODRAM, pp. 91f.; JAC, p. 353; CLA, I, 317f.

17. TEZ, p. 289.

18. For the coronation of Ahuitzotl and his initial campaign, see TEZ, pp. 272ff., 286; DINE, I, 330, 335–339.

19. For the Teloloapan campaign and resettlement, see TEZ, pp. 338–354; DINE, I, 360–367.

20. For the Huaxtec campaign, see IXCH, p. 275; PRM, p. 91; MON, I, 187; ROCA, pp. 220f.; CLA, I, 312f.; AC, p. 58; TEZ, pp. 292–297; DINE, I, 339–343; AM, p. 68.

21. For the temple dedication, see DINE, I, 344–359; ROCA, pp. 111, 220f.; AC, p. 58; CLA, I, 311; ATCT, p. 60; HMP, p. 231; AOG, p. 62; MON, I, 186; ATH, p. 9; IXCH, p. 273; TEZ, pp. 313–338. Veytia has an excellent criticism of the numbers of victims reported as killed in the dedication (VHA, II, 243–246). The place where the file of victims on the southern causeway ended later became known as Malcuitlapilco, "place of the tail end [of the file] of prisoners" (VHA, II, 243). For a discussion of the date, see CP, p. 59.

22. ROCA, p. 113; CODAUB, p. 48; MON, I, 187; IXCH, p. 274; AC, p. 58; AM, pp. 68, 70.

23. AC, pp. 57f.; ROCA, pp. 112, 224ff.; LPT, p. 229; AM, pp. 68f.

24. A problem raised here is the great prominence allotted to the Pochteca by Sahagún, especially his emphasis on their Ayutlan venture, the four-year siege and the ensuing victory (SAHG, III, 16–21, 32, 63; SFC, IX, 3–25; VET, pp. 33–43). Almost all the other sources omit mention of this, only Duran touching it cursorily (DINE, I, 368f.). We should certainly expect to find reference to it in the *Anales de Tlatelolco* (ATCT, p. 60) but do not.

25. For references to trade with Anahuac in sources other than Sahagún, see GCNE, pp. 350–357; DINE, I, 164, 230, 368f.; MEN, I, 160.

26. It is evident that Tzinacantlan was of great importance to the commercial plans of Mexico (VET, p. 69; SFC, IX, 21; SAHG, III, 30f.). This was probably the period when the Mexica planted a garrison there (CLA, IV, 320; HE, VI, 123).

27. SFC, IV, 62f.; see also 65f.

28. For the Aztec armies in the Tehuantepec campaign, see DINE, I, 370–377, 395–399; ATCT, p. 60; CODAUB, p. 49; TEZ, pp. 355–376; ROCA, pp. 119, 157, 225; ATH, p. 10; IXCH, pp. 283, 289.

29. MEN, I, 144; DINE, I, 349, 426; CLA, II, 243; TMM, pp. 207, 296, 299; SAHG, II, 319; AC, pp. 24, 26.

30. For words for the various categories of spies, see MOL, I, 58, 60; II, 31. For the work of spies and their prevalence, see MEN, I, 142; SFC, II, 166; SAHG, I, 232f.; TMM, pp. 295f.

31. Heraldry was an important feature of Aztec life; the coat-of-arms or *tlahuiztli* of Mexico was called the *matlaxopilli* (IXCH, p. 401; CAM, p. 227; CLA, III, 177). For the Tlascalan arms, see HE, III, 181, 184; GCNE, p. 102; CLA, II, 237; CAM, p. 102.

32. DINE, I, 275; TEZ, p. 274; SAHG, IV, 41, 104; SFC, XII, 35.

33. For the numerous words for ambassador, see MOL, I, 50; II, 98, 141.

34. On the protocol and organization of embassies, see VHA, I, 347f.; DINE, I, 230, 364; AM, p. 52; HE, III, 138–142; TEZ, pp. 350, 364; CLA, II, 203f.; AC, p. 45.

35. CAM, p. 25.

36. For marriage politics in Mexico, see AZR, p. 90; EST, V, 107–114; CAM, p. 124; ANE, p. 33; DINE, I, 88. An interesting case of marriage politics can be seen in the case of the lords of Tochimilco who commonly married princesses from Petlauhcan (AOG, p. 77). For marriages with noble relatives, see RGL, p. 253; IXCH, p. 59; IXREL, p. 117; MON, I, 154.

37. For adultery involving a Mexican princess (married to a foreign ruler) as a *casus belli*, see HM, pp. 98f.

38. On the appearance of the phantom called *moyoallitoa*, "the night speaker," see ROCA, pp. 113, 223; MON, I, 186; CODAUB, p. 48.

39. ROCA, pp. 113f., 119, 224f.; CODAUB, p. 49; ATCT, p. 60; AM, 69; ANE, pp. 123f.

40. There was a persistent tradition that Tlacahuepantzin, the brother of Moteuczoma II, died in battle at Atlixco in 1494 or 1495 (DS, pp. 117, 125, 136f.; AC, p. 58; IXCH, p. 283; ROCA, pp. 106, 225). This is in contradiction to the tradition I have accepted that he died, along with another brother named Ixtlilcuechahuac, in a flower war early in Moteuczoma's reign (1507?); see ROCA, p. 228, IXCH, pp. 305, 309f. This tradition receives some support from allusions in poetry; see GPN, I, 80f. (and possibly GPN, II, 33); CAM, p. 115; GHL, I, 211. In any case this Tlacahuepantzin should not be confused with the famous warrior of the same name who died in the Chalca war.

41. The strike against Tlateputzco in 1498 is recounted in CLA, I, 313ff.; II, 11; AC, p. 58; MON, I, 187, 191.

42. For the flood of 1499, see DINE, I, 382–394; TEZ, pp. 379–388; CLA, I, 315f.; OM, p. 274; TMH, p. 263; MON, I, 192f., 292; AM, p. 69; IXCH, pp. 291f.; MEN, II, 16; HMP, p. 231; ATH, p. 10; SAHG, II, 284; SFC, VIII, 18; XII, 2; ROCA, pp. 119, 226f.; TMM, p. 141f.; AC, pp. 58f; CODRAM, pp. 92f.; ANE, p. 123; CODAUB, pp. 49f.

43. CLA, I, 316.

44. For the opening of the *tezontli* quarry and the rebuilding of Mexico, see CLA, I, 316f.; II, 306f.; MON, I, 193; DINE, I, 394f.

45. DINE, I, 404–409.

46. *Tonatiuhixco* is a word for the east, which was always considered to be the gathering place for dead warriors (CAS, p. 185; SAHG, II, 180f.; TMM, p. 246). For their lives as birds and butterflies, see SAHG, I, 298; ANE, pp. 48f.; CLA, II, 59.

47. For the ruler in Ximoayan, see TEZ, pp. 244, 264, 390, 392; SAHG, II, 69, 75; GPN, I, xxiv; II, xxi.

11. MOTEUCZOMA II AND THE PRESENCES

1. TEZ, p. 247.

2. MON, I, 194.

3. Note that Macuilmalinal, the *tlacateccatl* elected along with Moteuczoma, died almost immediately in the precoronation war with Atlixco (ROCA, p. 228).

4. DINE, I, 411; CLA, I, 8; JAC, p. 355.

5. CODRAM, pp. 97f.

6. MEN, I, 168; TEZ, p. 394. Veytia gives 1466 (VHA, II, 321).

7. SFC, IX, 23; TEZ, p. 502.

8. ROCA, p. 215.

9. GCNE, p. 214; DINE, I, 446f.; CLA, III, 166; MON, I, 187, 194; SAHG, III, 19.

10. CLA, II, 231.

11. TCM, pp. 125, 151f.; IXCH, p. 306; ROCA, p. 225; CLA, III, 167; VE, pp. 136f.

12. For his physical presence, see SFC, XII, 25; IXCH, p. 396; CLA, III, 166.

13. HE, IV, 132.

14. One of the best appreciations of Moteuczoma's character is in CLA, III, 165f. Otherwise I have utilized COR, p. 43; GPN, I, 14; TMH, p. 78; SAHG, II, 282; MON, I, 228; CODRAM, pp. 94–100; CLA, II, 8, 20; TEZ, p. 401; 508f.; IXREL, p. 337; IXCH, p. 396; DINE, I, 417, 419, 421f., 506f., 513f., 515; GCNE, p. 179, 182, 213f.; JAC, p. 355.

15. IXCH, p. 306.

16. RGL, p. 251.

17. CLA, II, 11f., 207; MON, I, 196; DINE, I, 417f., 421; JAC, p. 357; TEZ, pp. 399ff.; CODRAM, pp. 97f.

18. DINE, I, 418.

19. MON, I, 205f.; HE, III, 224; JAC, p. 358; CODRAM, p. 100.

20. IXCH, pp. 321–327.

21. MON, I, 212, 226; POM, p. 34; CLA, II, 55; IXCH, pp. 310f.

22. For the Atlixco flower war and Moteuczoma's subsequent punishment of the Tlatilulca knights, see TEZ, pp. 436–440, 452f., 462ff., 480f.; IXCH, pp. 309f.; DINE, I, 450–453, 462ff., 465–469, 479–483. The date given is either 1507 or 1508 (AC, p. 60; IXCH, p. 309; MON, I, 210).

23. For the Huexotzinca crushed by Tlascala and their residence in Mexico under terms of a treaty, see AC, p. 61; POM, p. 43; CODAUB, p. 52; MON, I, 227; TEZ, pp. 468ff.; ROCA, pp. 120, 232f.; DINE, I, 473f.; II, 127; ATCT, pp. 61f.; AOG, p. 63; HMP, p. 232.

24. For a poem composed on this Huexotzinca embassy, see GPN, III, 6f.

25. DINE, I, 475; TEZ, pp. 474–477; MON, I, 219f.; CLA, II, 28ff.; CAM, pp. 126f.

26. ROCA, p. 233; MON, I, 228; CAM, pp. 115ff.; TEZ, p. 478.

27. MON, I, 228; AC, p. 63; DINE, I, 476f.; ROCA, p. 121.

28. For the Nopallan campaign of 1503 and the affair of the tribute due from Tlatilulco, see DINE, I, 422f., 432, 435ff., 439; TEZ, pp. 403, 420–425.

29. For Moteuczoma's relations with the merchant class, see SFC, IX, 23f., 32; SAHG, III, 31f., 37; ROCA, p. 228.

30. DINE, I, 423, 439f.; TEZ, pp. 424f.

31. DINE, I, 438; CLA, II, 30; ANE, p. 200.

32. For the Mixtec rebellion, see IXCH, see, p. 309; MON, I, 207ff., 211, HMP, p. 231; ROCA, p. 120; TEZ, pp. 441–448; AOG, p. 63; DINE, I, 454ff.; CODAUB, p. 51; CLA, II, 31f., 34f.; VHA, II, 279.

33. TMM, p. 323; DB, p. 388; MON, I, 203, 235; II, 565; AM, pp. 69f.; ATH, p. 11; IXCH, p. 309; ATCT, p. 61; SAHG, II, 284, 309; SFC, VIII, 41; CLA, II, 30, 226; MEN, II, 16; AC, p. 59.

34. MON, I, 210; II, 542; CODAUB, p. 51; HMP, p. 232; CLA, IV, 65; DINE, I, 473; ATCT, p. 17; ROCA, pp. 120, 229; TMM, p. 42; SAHG, II, 273; SFC, VII, 31; AC, p. 59.

35. On Moteuczoma's religiosity, see ROCA, p. 62; MON, I, 197, 206; II, 164; SFC, I, 7; CLA, II, 19; HE, IV, 115; TMM, p. 71.

36. HMP, p. 231; AOG, p. 62; CLA, II, 30.

37. There is undoubted duplication in the omen stories referring to the inexplicable burning of temples. I have made little attempt to unscramble these. For the burning of the temple of Xiuhteuctli, see CLA, II, 44; MON, I, 234; MEN, II, 17f.; CAM, p. 170.

38. The great statue of Coatlicue in the Museo Nacional de Antropología in Mexico City (under the name of Ilamateuctli, CP, pp. 129–140) celebrated the closing of the fifty-two–year cycle as is suggested by the date, one-Rabbit, hidden under the base. Justino Fernández (EST, VI, 51) interprets the date as the year 1454, which occurred in the reign of Moteuczoma I. I am more inclined to attribute it to the succeeding *xiuhmolpilli* in 1506, in the reign of Moteuc-

zoma II. In fact, I believe that we have references to it in TEZ, pp. 454, 457, 459f.; DINE, I, 456f., 461f. Here we learn that Moteuczoma II built a temple called the Coateocalli for Coatlicue (Coatlan Tonan) just before the celebration of the New Fire Ceremony, and dedicated it with a large number of victims taken in the Teutepec campaign. The famous statue mentioned above is therefore quite likely to be the idol made for the occasion of the finale of this fifty-two–year period of time.

39. On the pillar of fire, see TMM, p. 154; DINE, I, 489; CLA, II, 35ff.; MON, I, 212f., 233f.; TEZ, pp. 485f.; GCNE, p. 294. For the part played by the *texiptla*, see DINE, I, 522ff. The confusion in our sources over dating this strange event is undoubtedly caused by the fact that the light was said to be visible for the sacred number of four years. Thus any date in this four-year spread would serve equally well. The year 1508 is given in AC, p. 60. The year 1509 is in SAHG, IV, 23; SFC, XII, 1; ROCA, pp. 231f.; CAM, p. 168. The year 1510 is in MEN, II, 16; ROCA, p. 120; IXCH, pp. 313f. The year 1511 is in MON, I, 211; AOG, p. 63; ANE, p. 117. The year 1512 is in HMP, p. 232. Sahagún well exemplifies the typical uncertainty in dating this event (SAHG, II, 285, 288f., 291; IV, 81). Moteuczoma's 1510 embassy to the Cakchiquel of Guatemala is surely connected with this event; see *The Annals of the Cakchiquels*, translated by Adrian Recinos and Delia Goetz (Norman: University of Oklahoma Press, 1953), pp. 112f.

40. DINE, I, 522ff.

41. DINE, I, 491.

42. DINE, I, 507f., 513f.; TEZ, pp. 494–498; MON, I, 214f.; CODRAM, p. 102; CLA, II, 44.

43. For 1515 as the date of Nezahualpilli's death, see AC, p. 61; ATH, p. 12; IXCH, p. 327. The year 1516 is given in CLA, IV, 70. Vaillant accepts the latter, following Clavijero, who is often off by a year in his calculations. Nezahualpilli appears not to have had a public funeral, which was very unusual. His fame as a sorcerer contributed to the popular understanding that he had not died but had returned to his ancestral homeland, Amaqueme (VHA, II, 292).

44. MON, I, 224–227; IXREL, p. 336; CLA, II, 52.

45. DINE, I, 518; IXREL, p. 130; BF, p. 153; AC, pp. 61f.; DB, p. 483; TEZ, pp. 46, 499. Note that the full name of the city of Cuitlahuac has the word *ticic* added, so that the whole means "Cuitlahuac, the place of the sorcerors" (AC, p. 17).

46. Inasmuch as Moteuczoma dedicated the new shrine of Coatlan in 1518 (MON, I, 228), I am assuming that he began it in the preceding year; see also TEZ, pp. 454, 457, 459f.

47. In our sources the arrival of Grijalva is occasionally confused with that of Cortez in the following year. The following relate the details of Grijalva's

arrival: CLA, III, 9f.; TEZ, p. 518; AOG, p. 63; ATCT, p. 62; HMP, p. 232; MON, I, 378ff.; DINE, II, 3–11; HE, III, 31, 103; ANE, pp. 196ff; COD-RAM, pp. 104f.; SAHG, IV, 25–29, 83–90, 110; SFC, XII, 5–9.

48. TEZ, p. 529; DINE, II, 13; SFC, XII, 9; JAC, p. 364.

49. Quoted from Burgoa, OB, II, 156.

50. DINE, II, 11–13, 78; TEZ, pp. 524–527.

51. DINE, II, 14; TEZ, p. 530.

52. San Juan de Ulua was on or near the site of Chalchiuhcueyecan (the full form of the more usual Chalchicuecan; DINE, II, 15), which is generally identified as the site of the landing of Cortez. The meaning of the name is "the place of the water goddess," which makes us think of the nearby Isla de los Sacrificios and which certainly marks the area as holy; quite possibly the name refers not to a specific location but to a whole stretch of coast. Near this landing site was the community and Aztec lookout station of Chianhuiztlan (HE, III, 119). Another Aztec name given to the site of San Juan de Ulua is Huitzilipan, "hummingbird waters," though our source translates it as "ultimate sea or littoral" (ANE, p. 195). The specific place of the Spanish landing is said to have been Tecapantlayacac (ATCT, p. 62; RCAA, p. 169), which was definitely on the shore (SAHG, IV, 31). The name means "the palace of the first-born."

12. THE FAILURE OF A MEXICAN *TLATOANI*

1. The Spaniards were called *teteo*, "gods" (SFC, XII, 21). One source gives *quiteteo* with the unaccountable translation of "many gods" (TMM, p. 84). A more specific identification of the Spaniards (conflicting with the picture of them as Quetzalcoatl's retinue) was as "sons of the sun god" (CDH, II, 13f.). The Negroes were referred to as *teocacatzactli* ("dirty gods" according to MON, I, 418), the word being referent no doubt to the word for crow, *cacalotl*. The Spanish horse was referred to as a *tlacaxolotl*, "servant-beast" (CAM, p. 174). *Tlacaxolotl* is the common Nahuatl word for "tapir" (SFC, XI, 3), but here the word may well be understood, as above, in terms of its separate components.

2. Tentlilli, the governor of Cuetlaxtlan, on his appearance before Cortez, was accompanied by a special envoy whom Moteuczoma had dispatched for the purpose from Mexico; his name is given as Cuitlalpitoc (HE, III, 100; CLA, III, 22; MON, I, 387f.; DINE, II, 3–9. The name Quintallan (CDH, 118f.; GCNE, p. 56) may be a garbled form of Cuitlalpitoc. He is almost certainly the *tlillancalqui* sent down by Moteuczoma and extravagantly rewarded later (TEZ, p. 524). The accounts of the first Mexican embassy to Cortez are legion. I offer the following citations upon which I have based my remarks: SFC, VIII, 21; XII, 9–20; COR, pp. 20–22; ATCT, p. 62; GCNE, pp. 56–59; MON, I, 381–403; CAM, pp. 174f.; AOG, p. 63; JAC, pp. 365f.;

CODRAM, pp. 106ff.; DINE, II, 8–17; IXCH, pp. 344–349; ANE, pp. 195f.; HE, III, 100–106; TEZ, pp. 518–534; CLA, III, 22–25.

3. For Moteuczoma's attitude toward the invaders, see ANE, p. 196; SFC, XII, 17; SAHG, IV, 36, 94; DINE, II, 17ff.; GCNE, p. 213; CLA, III, 90; TEZ, p. 534.

4. Twice Gómara mentions two nobles who were in close touch with Cortez on the coast before he left Cempoalla (GCNE, pp. 58, 61, 81f.). He does not mention their names, but in all negative respects they fit the persons of Atonal and Tlamapanatzin. The source from which the above account of the two named traitors is taken is the *Merced de Hernán Cortés a los caciques de Axapusco*, in CDH, II, 4–18 (the name Atonal is there spelled Atonaletzin). The garbled and mutilated condition of this important manuscript has in the past kept it from being properly credited. When it is taken under scrutiny, the astounding successes and certainties of Cortez, which make him out as a Machiavellian superman, must be considered as much the result of excellent intelligence as of native astuteness. Moteuczoma had no corresponding advantage on his side.

5. In his first remittance to Charles V of the royal share of the loot from the conquest, Cortez included some codices (GCNE, p. 86). It is most probable that these books were the ones referred to in the episode of Atonal and Tlamapanatzin.

6. DINE, I, 515–524; CODRAM, p. 108; SFC, XII, 26; SAHG, IV, 34f.; TEZ, pp. 503–507, 511–514.

7. HE, III, 115; MON, I, 403; COR, p. 43.

8. ANE, p. 205; GCNE, p. 82; Cortez may refer to it as Sienchimalem or Ceyxnacan (COR, p. 28).

9. DINE, II, 19f.; SAHG, IV, 34, 95; SFC, XII, 21f.; MON, I, 417ff.

10. GCNE, p. 94.

11. COR, p. 34; MON, I, 429ff.; IXCH, pp. 363–366; CLA, III, 63ff., 67; GCNE, p. 108.

12. CLA, III, 67; COR, p. 35; IXCH, p. 370.

13. CODRAM, pp. 192, 194; IXCH, p. 349; MON, I, 433; CLA, III, 63.

14. COR, pp. 37f.; SFC, XII, 30; MON, I, 441; CLA, III, 89; GCNE, p. 133.

15. For the exchange of embassies between Cortez and Moteuczoma after the massacre, see COR, pp. 37f.; GCNE, p. 132; HE, III, 195; CLA, III, 84; IXCH, p. 373.

16. CODRAM, p. 110; SFC, XII, 31–34; SAHG, II, 293f.; IV, 39–42, 103; ROCA, pp. 234f.; MON, I, 445; CLA, III, 89; GCNE, p. 135.

17. SFC, XII, 30 (I have changed the word "iron" used by the translators to "metal" as being less anachronistic).

18. CM, pp. 60–65; MEN, III, 24; MON, III, 332.

19. MON, I, 443; CODRAM, p. 185.

20. DINE, II, 31f.; SAHG, IV, 107.

21. SAHG, IV, 42.

22. The date traditionally accepted for the Spanish entry into Tenochtitlan has been November 8. In an as yet unpublished article on Christian/native synchronologies in the Codex Telleriano-Remensis, Cline comes to the conclusion that the native tradition of November 9 is correct. At least six thousand Indian allies entered Mexico City with Cortez (IXCH, p. 377; HE, III, 200).

23. SFC, XII, 37.

24. SFC, XII, 38.

25. Topantemoctzin is said to have been the *tlatlatlalicatl* in Tlatilulco. Dibble translates the word as "storekeeper" (SFC, XII, 43). I have not seen this word as a formal title anywhere else.

26. SFC, XII, 42.

27. There is overwhelming evidence that Cortez was greeted in Mexico as one sent by Quetzalcoatl (ANE, p. 214; HE, III, 273; MON, I, 452; DINE, II, 5, 7, 30f., 34; COR, pp. 42, 48; SAHG, IV, 43f., 108f.; SFC, XII, 42; GCNE, p. 141; CODRAM, p. 191).

28. SFC, XII, 42.

29. SFC, XII, 42.

30. JAC, p. 368.

31. SAHG, IV, 110f.

32. MON, I, 454.

33. For Spanish actions against the Mexican gods, see MON, I, 454f.; GCNE, p. 176; COR, p. 53; DINE, II, 173; HE, III, 242f.; ROCA, p. 121; CDH, II, 586.

34. SFC, XII, 43, 45; SAHG, IV, 44f.; ROCA, p. 235.

35. COR, p. 45; MON, I, 457, 467ff.; IXCH, p. 382; DINE, II, 23f.; CODRAM, pp. 194, 196; HE, III, 261ff.; GCNE, pp. 168–178; CLA, III, 85ff.

36. SFC, XII, 45.

37. MON, I, 468f.; HE, III, 262f.; GCNE, pp. 178f.; IXCH, p. 382.

38. CLA, III, 129–135; GCNE, pp. 182f.; CODRAM, pp. 194–197; COR, p. 48; HE, III, 268–271; IXREL, pp. 338, 438f.; IXCH, pp. 383ff., 396; ANE, p. 118; MON, I, 469ff., 476.

39. GCNE, pp. 184f.; COR, p. 49; HE, III, 272ff.; CLA, III, 137; IXCH, pp. 387f.

40. MON, I, 472f.; CLA, III, 140ff.; GCNE, pp. 188–191; HE, III, 278f.

41. For Alvarado's massacre, see CODAUB, pp. 56f.; RCAA, p. 171; MON, I, 489f.; IXREL, p. 340; GCNE, pp. 207f.; CLA, III, 148–151; CODRAM, pp. 114f.; ATCT, pp. 62f.; DINE, II, 41ff., 83f.; HE, III, 343f.; SFC,

XII, 54ff.; SAHG, IV, 116ff. Howard Cline has shown in the unpublished article mentioned above that the date of the massacre was May 21.

42. CODAUB, pp. 54f.

43. SFC, XII, 55f.; SAHG, IV, 47f., 118ff.; CODRAM, p. 198.

44. CLA, III, 153f., 163; HE, III, 344; MON, I, 494.

45. For Cuitlahuac's accession to power, see SAHG, II, 285; ROCA, p. 236; CODAUB, pp. 60f.; CLA, III, 163; IV, 69; GCNE, p. 238; COR, p. 78; TCM, p. 159; DINE, II, 52; IXREL, p. 341.

46. Statements concerning the death of Moteuczoma and the disposal of his body are numerous: OM, p. 276; RCAA, p. 171; CCH, p. 101; MON, I, 494–499, 511; JAC, pp. 369f.; ROCA, p. 236; CODRAM, pp. 115, 119, 200; GCNE, pp. 212f.; COR, p. 65; CLA, II, 202; III, 158f., 164f., 168ff.; IXREL, pp. 341, 441; SFC, XII, 63f.; SAHG, IV, 51, 123; ATCT p. 64; TTT, VIII, 25; DINE, II, 45–50; CODAUB, pp. 58f.; HMP, p. 233; AOG, p. 64; CAM, p. 217; IXREL, p. 441; IXCH, p. 395; HE, III, 348f.

47. For the burial of Moteuczoma's ashes in Copulco (VHA, II, 321).

48. DINE, II, 34.

49. On the events of the Noche Triste, see CAM, p. 219; CCH, pp. 96, 102; SFC, XII, 65, 69f.; SAHG, IV, 57, 125; HE, III, 354; CLA, III, 170; DINE, II, 186; ATCT, p. 64; EST I, 9.

50. For the battle of Otumpan, see SFC, XII, 75; SAHG, IV, 56; DINE, II, 50ff.; CLA, III, 176–180; IXCH, pp. 400ff.; CAM, pp. 225, 227; MON, I, 509.

51. For Cuitlahuac's activities as emperor, see HE, III, 375; SFC, XII, 76f.; SAHG, IV, 134f.; CLA, III, 183–187, 192; MON, I, 511, 513, 517, 519; CAM, pp. 85f.; CODRAM, p. 201; GCNE, pp. 238f.; COR, pp. 78f.; DINE, II, 53f. The Spaniards had a high opinion of Cuitlahuac's abilities (VHA, II, 325).

52. For the plague, see SFC, XII, 81; SAHG, II, 285; ROCA, p. 235; IXCH, p. 404; DINE, II, 255; TMM, p. 18; GCNE, pp. 204f.; ATCT, p. 64; CLA, III, 200. Note that the *huey zahuatl* spread instantly into Michoacan killing the *cazonci* there (CM, p. 67).

53. Cuitlahuac is said in most sources to have ruled eighty days, but this round number, being four Aztec months, is suspect. Some sources give as low as forty-seven days (IXCH, p. 404) or even twenty-four days (ROCA, p. 236). Clavijero insists that he ruled less than six months, probably referring to Aztec months (CLA, IV, 69).

13. OF WHAT ADVANTAGE PRIDE?

1. For Cuauhtemoc as a legitimate scion of the old royal house of Tlatilulco, see MON, I, 524; IXCH, p. 306; IXREL, pp. 342, 450. The statement in SFC, VIII, 2, that Tlatilulco legitimately elected a *tlatoani* in 1520, the first since Moquiuix, bears this out. His home was in Tlatilulco (MON, I, 524; GCNE, p. 287, does not necessarily deny this), and he is referred to as the

governor of that city before the advent of the Spaniards (ACT, p. 39; MON, I, 216; IXCH, p. 404; ATCT, p. 6; DINE, II, 43, 50; CODRAM, p. 202). There is no doubt of his close identification with that city, though he appears also to have been accepted as one of the Tenochca; he was the choice of both Mexican cities (DINE, II, 43).

2. RCAA, p. 172; VE, p. 136; CODAUB, pp. 59f.; TCM, pp. 163f.; ATCT, p. 65; VHA, II, 323.

3. As the siege began, Mexico's only allies were Cuauhtitlan with its dependencies. The Tlahuica cities, and the remnants of the old Tepaneca centers (DINE, II, 53; ROCA, p. 237; RCAA, p. 174; ATCT, p. 67; IXCH, p. 438). But in many of these instances the cities aided Mexico only in the persons of their rulers (those no doubt who claimed Mexican blood or Mexican appointment to office) and a few associated nobles; the bulk of the cities' population either were supine or fell into the camp of the Spaniards. The Chinampa cities at first were neutral (HE, IV, 58, 63; GCNE, pp. 270, 277), but as the siege progressed they moved over to the Spanish side; witness particularly the case of Xochimilco (SAHG, IV, 63f., 144ff.; SFC, XII, 91f., 100, 104; CLA, III, 258, 261).

4. For Chalco's part in the pre-siege events and Mexico's attacks upon her see IXREL, p. 348; HMP, p. 233; AOG, p. 65; MON, I, 537; DINE, II, 55; GCNE, pp. 136, 247, 255f., 259f.; COR, p. 102; HE, IV, 15, 27; CLA, III, 216–219, 227–229.

5. The estimate of the Mexican dead comes from a Spanish source and is no doubt exaggerated (GCNE, p. 293; VE, p. 136). More died of starvation and disease than in battle (DINE, II, 57; SAHG, IV, 149).

6. ATCT, p. 71.

7. The dates of the beginning of the siege and the surrender are certain (COR, p. 136).

8. DINE, II, 58.

9. For the initial Tenochca collapse and the murder of their leaders, see RCAA, p. 173. This initial break—after only three days of fighting—in Mexican morale (MON, I, 295) was noticed by the Spaniards (GCNE, p. 271; HE, IV, 63; RCAA, p. 173).

10. For the flight of the Tenochca to Tlatilulco, see ATCT, pp. 66f.; RCAA, pp. 173ff.; ACT, p. 42; SAHG, IV, 62; MON, I, 550. Some of the Tenochca appear to have been used later by the Spaniards in the siege against the Tlatilulca (ATCT, p. 7).

11. For the great lords who distinguished themselves during the siege, see SFC, XII, 87f., 92, 97, 106, 111f., 115f., 119; SAHG, IV, 62, 76, 152, 156, 158–163; ACT, p. 39; LPT, p. 171; MON, I, 565; RCAA, p. 175; CLA, III, 260; ATCT, p. 72.

12. GPN, III, 44. For other moving poetic elegies on the defeat, see GHL, II, 91, 93.

13. For the Spanish naval victories, see HE, IV, 56; IXREL, pp. 356f.; SFC, XII, 83f.; GCNE, pp. 266ff.; MON, I, 542.

14. HE, IV, 65–68; GCNE, pp. 281f.; CLA, III, 267; MON, I, 556; TTT, pp. 56–59; DINE, II, 58f.; COR, p. 125.

15. MON, I, 567; SAHG, IV, 72f., 158f.; SFC, XII, 113f.

16. RCAA, 180f; ATCT, p. 73.

17. GCNE, p. 291; SFC, XII, 118.

18. I have accepted Gómara's account of the capture of Cuauhtemoc as being essentially correct (GCNE, p. 292; HE, IV, 92f.). The other version has it that Cuauhtemoc voluntarily went to surrender himself (SAHG, IV, 74; RCAA, p. 181). This does not comport with his actions up to then.

19. I have used Cline's unpublished data that puts the Spanish victory on August 13 and the formal surrender by Cuauhtemoc on the following day.

20. Surviving Mexica were said to number thirty thousand (HE, IV, 93). Gómara's figure of seventy thousand seems inflated (GCNE, p. 292). Over forty thousand bodies were estimated as floating in the canals, a figure no doubt also exaggerated (DINE, II, 62).

21. SFC, I, 36.

CHRONOLOGICAL CHART

Until a lot more work has been done on the various pre-Columbian calendars in Mesoamerica, any chronology that gives exact dates must be considered tentative. This scheme is the one I have worked with in writing this book. Almost every date is, of course, subject to challenge, but the scheme is the result of care and much reflection and should therefore serve as a sufficiently reliable guide. Criticism of it, based on equal care and reflection, is welcome.

	200 B.C.–A.D. 650	Teotihuacan
	770–1168	Tula
	1168–1319	The Mexica wandering after leaving Aztlan.
	1319–1349	Mexica residence in Chapultepec. Tlotzin ruling in Tenayuca.
	1350–1352	Residence in Contitlan.
	1351	Some of Mexica go to Acocolco.
	1352–1366	Residence in Tizaapan.
	1366	Tezozomoc begins rule.
	1369	Tenochtitlan founded. Quinatzin ruling in Tezcoco.
	1375	Cuacuauhtzin begins rule in Tlatilulco. Acamapichtli brought to Tenochtitlan.
	1376	The Chichimecayaoyotl begins. Mexico begins series of flower wars with Chalco.
	1377	Culhuacan collapses. Mexico sends Nauhyotl as military governor there.
	1378	Tlatilulco temple inaugurated.
	1390	Huitzilihuitl elected. Tenochca cease paying tribute to Cuacuauhtzin. Mexico burns temple of Culhuacan.
Huitzilihuitl (1391–1414)	1391	Huitzilihuitl crowned. Mexican military rule in Culhuacan ends.
	1398	Mexico crushes Cuauhtinchan.

	1402	Mexico clashes with Chalco. Nezahualcoyotl born.
	1403	Fifth New Fire Ceremony
	1404	Acamapichtli dies. Huitzilihuitl marries daughter of Tezozomoc.
	1407	Commoners installed as *calpixque* in Amaquemecan.
	1411	Ixtlilxochitl begins rule in Tezcoco. Mexico backs down at threat of war from eastern league.
	1413	Mexico under Tezozomoc attacks Tezcoco.
	1414	Huitzilihuitl dies. Ixtlilxochitl crowned emperor in Huexotla.
Chimalpopoca (1415–1427)	1415	Chimalpopoca installed. Quarrel with Tepaneca over timber rights. Mexico again attacks Tezcoco.
	1416	Mexico burns temple of Tenayuca.
	1417	Ixtlilxochitl begins drive to crush Tepaneca.
	1418	Cuacuauhtzin dies. Tlacateotl takes his place. Ixtlilxochitl killed.
	1421	Tlatilulco brings the god Tlacahuepan from Tula.
	1422	Tulantzinco taken after year's effort.
	1425	Chimalpopoca dedicates a *techcatl* and a gladiatorial stone. Huitzilopochtli's temple under way. Mexico demands supplies from Tepaneca. Tepaneca boycott Mexico.
	1426	Tezozomoc dies. Maxtla siezes the rule.
Itzcoatl (1427–1440)	1427	Chimalpopoca and Tlacateotl killed. Itzcoatl elected to rule Tenochtitlan. Maxtla attacks Mexico.
	1428	Cuauhtlatoatzin elected to rule Tlatilulco. Mexico attacks and crushes Azcapotzalco.
	1430	Xochimilco conquered. Maxtla defeated in Ajusco and flees. Teotihuacan and Otumpan taken.
	1431	Tlatilulco breaks with Tenochtitlan. Coyoucan taken. Nezahualcoyotl crowned emperor in Mexico.
	1432	Conquest of Mizquic.
	1433	Nezahualcoyotl leaves Mexico for Tezcoco. Conquest of Cuitlahuac.

	1434	Tlatilulco submits to Tenochtitlan. Tenochca build temple to Cihuacoatl.
	1439	Cuauhnahuac taken.
Moteuczoma I	1440	Itzcoatl dies. Moteuczoma I ascends throne.
(1440–1468)	1441	Cuitlahuac rebels. Mexico takes its god captive.
	1442	Campaigns aimed at the Balsas country begin.
	1446	Mexico demands Chalco and other cities aid in building Huitzilopochtli's temple. Hostilities.
	1450	Tlatilulco conquers Cuauhtinchan. Beginning of natural calamities. Flood.
	1451	Snow and hail storms. Defeat of the Huaxteca.
	1452	First year of famine. War with Chalco begins.
	1453	Two Mexicos reunite. Huitzilopochtli's temple started.
	1454	Worst year of the famine.
	1455	Rains return. New Fire Ceremony. Dedication of temple. Moteuczoma and Tlacaelel have likenesses carved in rock of Chapultepec.
	1456	Mixtecs defy Mexico.
	1458	Coaixtlahuacan conquered. *Temalacatl* dedicated.
	1459	Cozamaloapan conquered.
	1460	Attack on Cuetlaxtlan. Quauhtochco taken. Yopitli temple dedicated.
	1461	Atezcahuacan conquered.
	1463	Cuetlaxtlan conquered after rebellion.
	1464	Great winds. Designation of Moquiuix to rule of Tlatilulco.
	1465	Chalco submits to Mexico. Oaxaca conquered.
	1466	Chapultepec aqueduct opened to Mexico. Tlatilulco builds new *tzompantli* and serpent house. Tepeyacac defeated.
	1467	Tezcoco completes temple. Moquiuix finally installed in Tlatilulco.
	1468	Tlatlauhquitepec attacked. Moteuczoma I dies.
Axayacatl	1469	Axayacatl installed. Temple of Coatlan built. Tlatilulco builds temple of Coaxolotl. Tlatlauhquitepec crushed.
(1469–1481)		
	1470	Inherited campaign against Cuetlaxtlan finished.
	1472	Nezahualcoyotl dies.
	1473	Civil war between Tlatilulco and Tenochtitlan.

	1474	Cuetlaxtlan rebels and is put down. Mexico opens attack on Matlatzinca. Itzcuauhtzin installed as military governor in Tlatilulco.
	1475	Great earthquake. Mexico takes Toluca.
	1476	Malinalco and Ocuillan conquered. Cuauhnahuac punished.
	1477	Icpatepec and Poctepec destroyed. Toluca revolts.
	1478	Tarascans defeat Mexico. Axayacatl wounded at Xiquipilco.
	1479	Xiquipilco surrenders.
Tizoc (1481–1486)	1481	Axayacatl dies. Tizoc installed. Unsuccessful attack on Metztitlan.
	1483	Huitzilopochtli temple begun.
	1484	Rebellion in Toluca basin put down.
	1485	Home rule for Chalco instituted.
Ahuitzotl (1486–1502)	1486	Tizoc dies. Ahuitzotl installed.
	1487	New governments set up in Tlahuica cities. Xiuhcoac subdued. Teloloapan revolts. Temple of Huitzilopochtli dedicated.
	1488	Teloloapan resettled. Home rule for Chalco confirmed. New governments in Tlacopan, Coyouacan, Xochimilco, and Culhuacan.
	1489	New governments for Azcapotzalco, Tula, and Iztapalapan. Phantoms seen.
	1490	Cuauhtla attacked. Temple of Tlacatecco completed.
	1492	Famine year. Acatlan crushed.
	1493	Xaltepec crushed.
	1495	Tlacahuepan the younger dies in flower war at Atlixco.
	1496	Pestilence, eclipse of sun, and earthquakes. Attack on Tehuantepec with losses.
	1497	Amatlan and Xochitlan subjected.
	1498	*Temalacatl* dedicated. Attacks on Tlateputzco repulsed. Ahuitzotl seizes waters belonging to Coyouacan.
	1499	Xoconochco surrenders. Mexico inundated.
	1500	Famine. Reconstruction of city begins. Xaltepec rebels.
	1501	Unsuccessful attack on Tlascala.

	1502	Ahuitzotl dies. Moteuczoma elected.
Moteuczoma II	1503	Xaltepec crushed. Moteuczoma II assumes
(1503–1520)		office.
	1504	Tlachquiauhco crushed. Temple of Quetzal-coatl erected. Heavy attack on Tlascala. First year of drought.
	1505	New Chapultepec aqueduct opened. Quetzal-coatl temple burned. War against Itzcuintepec. Temple of Cinteotl built. Year of great famine.
	1506	Famine continues. Yanhuitlan and Tzotzolan crushed. Teuctepec crushed. Coateocalli built.
	1507	Drought broken. New Fire Ceremony. Que-tzalcoatl temple rebuilt. New *tzompantli* dedi-cated. Quetzaltepec crushed.
	1508	Flower war against Cholula. Tlatilulca war-riors disgraced.
	1509	Light seen in the night sky. Omen lasts into following year.
	1510	Fruitless attack on Huexotzinco. Fire in the great temple. Failure of attack on Amatlan.
	1511	Rebellion of Icpatepec and Xochitepec crushed. Tlachquiauhco crushed. Temple of Tlama-tzinco built.
	1512	*Cuauhxicalli* dedicated.
	1513	Moteuczoma's effigy carved at Chapultepec.
	1514	Iztactlalocan conquered.
	1515	Nezahualpilli dies. Huexotzinca submit to Mexico and are settled there. War with Tlascala.
	1517	Death of *tzompanteuctli* of Cuitlahuac. News of Córdoba expedition in Yucatan.
	1518	Coming of Grijalva. Moteuczoma replaces many vassal rulers. Huexotzinca break away from Mexico. Tlascala again unsuccessfully attacked.
	1519	Cortez lands April 21. Cortez enters Tenoch-titlan November 9.
Cuitlahuac (1520)	1520	Alvarado's massacre, May 21. Death of Mo-teuczoma and Noche Triste, June 30. Cuitla-huac installed. Plague. Death of Cuitlahuac.

Cuauhtemoc   Cuauhtemoc installed.
(1520–1521)   1521   Siege of Mexico, May 31 through August 13.
                                  Cuauhtemoc surrenders August 14.

REFERENCES

(Abbreviations used in the notes follow each entry.)

Acosta, José de. *Historia natural y moral de las Indias*. Edited by Edmundo O'Gorman. 2nd ed., rev. Mexico City: Fondo de Cultura Económica, 1962. (JAC)

Alarcón, Hernando Ruiz de. *Tratado de las idolatrías, supersticiones, dioses, ritos, hechicerías y otras costumbres gentílicas de las razas aborígenes de México*. 2nd ed. 2 vols. Mexico City: Ediciones Fuente Cultural, 1953. (BRA)

Anales de la conquista de Tlatilulco en 1473 y en 1521. Translated by B. McAfee and R. H. Barlow. Vol. 5, *Tlatilulco a través de los tiempos*. Mexico City. (ACT)

Anonymous Conqueror, the. *Narrative of Some Things of New Spain and of the Great City of Temestitan, Mexico*. Translated by Marshall H. Saville. New York: The Cortes Society, 1917. (ACN)

Barlow, R. H., trans. "Anales de Tula, Hidalgo, 1361–1521." *Tlalocan* 3. Mexico City. (ATH)

Barlow, Robert H. *La Fundación de la Triple Alianza*. Anales del Instituto Nacional de Antropología e Historia, vol. 3. Mexico City: 1949, pp. 147–155. (BF)

Berlin, Heinrich, trans. *Anales de Tlatelolco y Códice de Tlatelolco*. Fuentes para la Historia de Mexico, vol. 2. Mexico City: Antigua Librería Robredo de José Porrúa e Hijos, 1948. (ATCT)

Bryan Davies, C. N. *Los Señoríos independientes del imperio Azteca*. Mexico City: Instituto Nacional de Antropología e Historia, 1968. (DS)

Burland, Cottie A. *The Selden Roll: An Ancient Mexican Picture Manuscript in the Bodleian Library at Oxford*. Berlin: Gebrüder Mann, 1955. (BSR)

Camargo, Diego Muñoz. *Historia de Tlascala*. Edited by Alfredo Chavero. Mexico City, 1892. Facs. ed., Guadalajara, 1966. (CAM)

Las Casas, Bartolomé de. *Los Indios de México y Nueva España. Una Antología*. Edited by Edmundo O'Gorman. Mexico City: Editorial Porrúa, 1966. (CAS)

Caso, Alfonso. *Los Calendarios prehispánicos*. Mexico City: Instituto de Investigaciones Históricos, UNAM, 1967. (CP)

Castillo, Cristóbal del. *Fragmentos de la Obra general sobre la Historia de los Mexicanos*. Translated by Francisco del Paso y Troncoso. Florence, Italy: n.d. Reprint, Ciudad Juárez: Editorial Erandi, 1966. (CCH)

Chimalpahin Cuauhtlehuanitzin, Francisco de San Antón Muñón. *Relaciones Originales de Chalco Amaquemecan*. Translated by Silvia Rendón. Mexico City: Fondo de Cultura Económica, 1965. (ROCA)

Chimalpopoca, trans. *Anales Mexicanos, México-Azcapotzalco, 1426–1589*. Anales del Museo Nacional, vol. 7. Mexico City. (AM)

The Chronicles of Michoacan. Translated by Eugene R. Craine and Reginald C. Reindorp. Norman: University of Oklahoma Press, 1970. (CM)

Clavigero, Francisco Javier. *Historia Antigua de México*. 4 vols. Mexico City: Editorial Porrúa, 1958. (CLA)

Códice Xolotl. Translated by Charles E. Dibble. Mexico: Publicaciones del Instituto de Historia, no. 22, 1951. (CODX)

Cortez, Hernando. *Cartas de Relación*. Mexico City: Editorial Porrúa, 1963. (COR)

Dibble, Charles E. *Codex Hall: An Ancient Mexican Hieroglyphic Picture Manuscript*. Monographs of the School of American Research, no. 11. Albuquerque: University of New Mexico Press, 1947. (CODHALL)

Durán, Diego. *Historia de las Indias de Nueva España e islas de la Tierra Firme*. 2 vols. and atlas. Mexico City: Editora Nacional, 1965. (DINE)

Estudios de Cultura Nahuatl. Vols. 1–8. Mexico City: Instituto de Historia, Seminario de Cultura Nahuatl, Universidad Nacional Autónoma de México, 1959–1969. (EST)

García Icazbalceta, Joaquin, ed. *Colección de documentos para la historia de México*. 2 vols. Mexico City: 1858, 1866. (Reprinted by Kraus Reprint Corp., 1971). (CDH)

Garibay, Angel María. *Historia de la literatura nahuatl*. 2 vols. Mexico City: Editorial Porrúa, 1953. (GHL)

———. *Llave del Nahuatl*. 2nd ed., rev. Mexico City: Editorial Porrúa, 1961. (GLL)

———. *Poema de Mixcoatl*. In *Epica Nahuatl*. Biblioteca del Estudiante

Universitario, no. 51. Mexico City: Ediciones de la Universidad Nacional Autónoma, 1945. (GPMX)

————. *Poesía Nahuatl*. 3 vols. Mexico: Universidad Nacional Autónoma de México, 1964–1968. (GPN)

Gómara, Francisco López. *Cortés: The Life of the Conqueror by his Secretary*. Translated by Lesley Byrd Simpson. Berkeley: University of California Press, 1964. (GCNE)

Granados, Rafael García. *Diccionario biográfico de historia antigua de México*. 3 vols. Mexico City: Instituto de Historia, 1952–1953. (DB)

Guzmán, Eulalia. "Un manuscrito de la colleción Boturini que trata de los antiguos señores de Teotihuacan." *Ethnos* 3: 89–103. (TPT)

Hernández, Francisco. *Antigüedades de la Nueva España*. Mexico City: Editorial Pedro Robredo, 1946. (ANE)

Herrera, Antonio de. *Historia general de los hechos de los castellanos en las islas y tierra firme de el Mar Océano*. 10 vols. Asunción, Paraguay: Editorial Guaranía, 1944–1947. (HE)

Historia de los Mexicanos por sus pintures. In *Relaciones de Texcoco y de la Nueva España*. Edited by Joaquín García Icazbalceta. Mexico City: Chavez Hayhoe, 1891. (HMP)

Historia de la Nación Mexicana: Reproducción a todo color del Códice de 1576 (Códice Aubin). Translated by Charles E. Dibble. Madrid: Ediciones José Porrúa Turanzas, 1963. (CODAUB)

Historia Tolteca-Chichimeca. Translated by H. Berlin and Silvia Rendón. Mexico City: Antigua Librería Robredo de Porrúa e Hijos, 1947. (HTC)

Ixtlilxochitl, Fernando de Alva. *Relaciones*. In *Obras históricas de Don Fernando de Alva Ixtlilxochitl*. 2 vols. Edited by Alfredo Chavero. Mexico City: Editora Nacional, 1965. (IXREL)

————. *Historia de la Nación Chichimeca*. In *Obras históricas de Don Fernando de Alva Ixtlilxochitl*. 2 vols. Edited by Alfredo Chavero. Mexico City: Editora Nacional, 1965. (IXCH)

Jonghe, M. Edouard de, ed. *Histoyre du Méchique*. Journal de la Société des Americainistes de Paris, nouvelle série, vol. 2. Paris, 1905. (JM)

León-Portilla, Miguel. *Trece poetas del mundo azteca*. Mexico City: Universidad Nacional Autónoma de México, 1967. (LPT)

Mappa Quinatzin. In *Recherches Historiques et Archéologiques, publiées sous la direction de M. E. T. Hamy*. Part one, *Histoire*. Paris: Imprimerie Nationale, 1885. (MQ)

Mappa Tlotzin. In *Recherches Historiques et Archéologiques, publiées sous la direction de M. E. T. Hamy.* Part one, *Histoire.* Paris: Imprimerie Nationale, 1885. (MTL)

McAffee, Byron, and Barlow, R. H. "La Guerra entre Tlatilulco y Tenochtitlan según el Códice Cozcatzin." In *Tlatilulco a Través de los Tiempos.* Memorias de la Academia Mexicana de la Historia, vol. 7. Mexico City, 1946. (MBG)

Mendieta, Fray Gerónimo de. *Historia ecclesiástica indiana.* 4 vols. Mexico City: Chavez Hayhoe, 1945. (MEN)

Die Mexikanische Bildeshandschrift Historia Tolteca-Chicimeca. Translated by Konrad T. Preuss and Ernst Mengin. Baessler-Archiv. Berlin: Dietrich Reimer, 1937. Reprinted by Johnson Reprint Corp., 1968. (PRM)

Molino, Alonso de. *Vocabulario en lengua castellana y mexicana.* Facs. ed. of edition of 1571. Madrid: Ediciones de Cultura Hispánica, 1944. (MOL)

Motolinía, Fray Toribio de. *History of the Indians of New Spain.* Translated by Francis Borgia Steck. Washington, D.C.: Publications of the Academy of American Franciscan History, 1951. (TMH)

———. *Memoriales.* Mexico: Luis García Pimentel, 1903. Facs. ed., Guadalajara: Edmundo Aviña Levy, 1967. (TMM)

Olmos, Fray Andrés de. *Fragmentos.* In *Teogonía e Historia de los Mexicanos: Tres opúsculos del siglo XVI.* Edited by Angel María Garibay. Mexico City: Editorial Porrúa, 1965. (AOG)

Origen de los Mexicanos. In *Relaciones de Tezcoco y de la Nueva España.* Edited by Joaquín García Icazbalceta. Mexico City: Chavez Hayhoe, 1891. (OM)

Orozco y Berra, Manuel. *Historia antigua y de la conquista de México.* 4 vols. Mexico City: Editorial Porrúa, 1960. (OB)

Pomar, Juan Bautista. *Relación de Tezcoco.* In *Relaciones de Tezcoco y de Nueva España.* Mexico City: Chavez Hayhoe, 1941. (POM)

Ponce de León, Pedro. *Breve Relación de los dioses y ritos.* In *Tratado de las idolatrías, supersticiones, dioses, ritos, hechicerías y otras costumbres gentílicas de las razas aborígenes de Mexico.* 2nd ed. Mexico City: Ediciones Fuente Cultural, Librería Navarro, 1953. (PP)

———. *Historia de México.* In *Teogonía e historia de los Mexicanos.* Mexico City: Editorial Porrúa, 1965. (HM)

———. *Tratado de los dioses y ritos de la gentilidad.* In *Teogonía e historia de los Mexicanos.* Mexico City: Editorial Porrúa, 1965. (PL)

Relación Anónima describiendo la división que tenían los Indios en tiempo de Moteczuma. Biblioteca de Historiadores Mexicanos. Mexico City: Ediciones Vargas Rea, 1953. (RELA)

Relación de la genealogía y linaje de los señores que han señoreado esta tierra de la Nueva España. In *Relaciones de Texcoco y de la Nueva España*. Edited by Joaquín García Icazbalceta. Mexico City: 1891. Facs. ed., Mexico City: Chavez Hayhoe, 1941. (RGL)

Relato de la conquista por autor anónimo de Tlatelolco, redactado en 1528. In Sahagún, *Historia general*. (RCAA).

Sahagún, Bernardino de. *Augurios y abusiones*. Translated by Alfredo López Austin. Fuentes indígenas de la cultura nahuatl; Textos de los informantes de Sahagún, vol. 4. Mexico City: Universidad Nacional Autónoma de México, 1969. (AA)

———. *Historia general de las cosas de Nueva España*. Edited by Angel María Garibay. 4 vols. Mexico City: Editorial Porrúa, 1956. (SAHG)

———. *General History of the Things of New Spain (Florentine Codex)*. Translated by A. J. O. Anderson and C. E. Dibble. 12 vols. Santa Fe, New Mexico: The School of American Research and the University of Utah, 1950–1963. (SFC)

———. *Relación breve de las fiestas de los dioses*. Translated from Nahuatl by Angel María Garibay. *Tlalocan*, vol. 2, no. 4, 1948. (RB)

———. *Ritos, sacerdotes y atavíos de los dioses: Textos de los informantes de Sahagún*, no. 1. Translated by Miguel León-Portilla. Mexico City: Universidad Nacional Autónoma de México, 1958. (LPR)

———. *Vida Económica de Tenochtitlan: Textos de los informantes de Sahagún*, no. 3. Translated from Nahuatl by Angel María Garibay. Mexico City: Universidad Nacional Autónoma de México, 1961. (VET)

Serna, Jacinto de la. *Manual de ministros de indios para al conocimiento de sus idolatrías y extirpación de ellas*. In *Tratado de las idolatrías, supersticiones, dioses, ritos, hechicerías y otras costumbres gentílicas de las razas aborígenes de Mexico*. 2nd ed. Mexico City: Ediciones Fuente Cultural, Librería Navarro, 1953. (SER)

Siméon, Rémi. *Dictionnaire de la Langue Nahuatl ou Mexicaine*. Reprint of 1885 Paris edition. Graz, Austria: Akademische Druk-U. Verlagsanstalt, 1965. (SIM)

Swadesh, Mauricio, and Sancho, Madalena. *Los Mil elementos del mexicano clásico*. Mexico City: Universidad Nacional Autónoma de México, 1966. (SS)

Tezozomoc, Hernando Alvarado. *Crónica Mexicana*. Mexico City: Editorial Leyenda, 1944. (TEZ)

————. *Crónica Mexicayotl*. Translated by Adrian León. Mexico City: Imprenta Universitaria, 1949. (TCM)

Tira de la peregrinación (Codex Boturini). Mexico City: Librería Anticuaria, G. M. Echaniz, 1944. (TP)

Tlatilulco a Través de los Tiempos. Memorias de la Academia Mexicana de la Historia. Mexico City. (TTT)

Torquemada, Fray Juan de. *Monarquía indiana*. 3 vols. Mexico City: Editorial Porrúa, 1969. (MON)

Tovar, Juan de. *Relación del origen de los indios que habitaban esta Nueva España según sus historias (Códice Ramírez)*. Mexico: Editorial Leyenda, 1944. (CODRAM)

Vázquez de Espinosa, Antonio. *Compendio y descripción de las Indias occidentales*. Washington, D.C.: Smithsonian Institution, 1948. (VE)

Velázquez, P. Feliciana, trans. *Anales de Cuauhtitlan*. In *Códice Chimalpopoca*. Mexico City: Imprenta Universitaria, 1945. (AC)

————. *La Leyenda de los Soles*. In *Códice Chimalpopoca*. Mexico City: Imprenta Universitaria, 1945. (LS)

Veytia, Mariano. *Historia Antigua de México*. 2 vols. Mexico City: Editorial Leyenda, 1944. (VHA)

Wauchope, Robert (general editor). *Handbook of Middle American Indians*. 11 vols. to date. Austin: University of Texas Press, 1964–. (HMAI)

Yáñez, Agustín. *Mitos indígenas*. Mexico City: Biblioteca del Estudiante Universitario 31, UNAM, 1956. (MI)

Zorita, Alonso de. *Life and Labor in Ancient Mexico (Brief and Summary Relation of the Lands of New Spain)*. Translated by Benjamin Keen. New Brunswick, N.J.: Rutgers University Press, 1963. (AZR)

INDEX

Tlateputzco: 3; cities of, 64, 66, 71, 73–74, 101, 129, 132–133, 147–148, 151, 154, 180–181, 218, 221, 235–239, 278, 283, 288
Tlatilulca: 28–29, 35, 44, 54, 72, 90, 111, 148, 155–156, 174, 180–181, 187–189, 236, 238–240, 280, 287
Tlatilulco: 28, 42, 45, 49, 51, 53–54, 66, 72–74, 83–84, 90, 122, 152, 156, 174, 178–183, 188–190, 211–212, 236, 239–240, 250, 265, 281–282, 285, 301, 319
tlatlatlalicatl: 329
tlatoani: 121, 128, 159–161, 190, 312. SEE ALSO ruler
tlatocapilli: 310
tlatocatlalli: 83
tlatocayotl: 121, 217
tlatolitqui: 219
tlatoqui: 205, 312
Tlaximaloyan: 196, 198
tlazolyaoyotl: 185
Tlilatl: 320
Tlilcuetzpalin: 320
Tliliuhquitepec: 133, 264
Tlillan: 95, 165–166, 238, 318
tlillan calmecac: 308
tlillancalqui: 115, 254–255, 311, 327
Tlilpotonqui: 184, 211, 230, 250
Tloque Nahuaque: 159
Tlotzin: 17, 26
Tochimilco: 323
Tochtepec: 151–152, 212
Toci: 161, 321
Tocual: 251–252
Tolotzin, Mount: 192. SEE ALSO Nevado de Toluca
Toltecatl: 221–222
toltecayotl: 20
Toltecs: 3, 5–11, 14, 23, 26, 49, 68, 101, 105, 115, 169–171, 192, 219, 225–226. SEE ALSO Tula
Toltitlan: 112, 150, 181
Toluca: 17, 19, 126, 185, 193–195, 202, 228, 300
Tonacateuctli: 232
Tonan (the goddess): 95, 161
Tonan (the mountain): 277
Tonatiuh: 93, 104–106
Tonatiuhixco: 226
Topantemoc: 265
Topiltzin: 6, 169–171, 254
Totec: 206
Toteotzin: 75, 138–140, 143–144
Totomatzin: 184
Totonacapan: 131, 152–153, 241, 257
Totonacs: 239, 260, 268
Totonac War: 142, 146, 152–156
Totoquihuaztli I: 89, 117–119, 192, 315

Totoquihuaztli II: 225, 230
Tototepec: 241
Totozacatzin: 239
Toxcatl: 273–274
toxiuhmolpia: 314
toxiuhmolpilia: 314
treason: 255–256
tribute: 84, 87–88, 92, 120–121, 124–127, 189, 193–194, 239
triumph: 199, 240
Tula: 4–6, 8, 10–12, 14, 20, 25, 97, 102, 170–171, 178, 210, 230, 235–236, 251; legitimacy of rule from, 10–12, 29–30, 39, 47, 68, 107, 122, 230, 296. SEE ALSO Toltecs
Tulantzinco: 125, 149, 169
Tuxpan: 251
Tuztlantli: 304
two-Reed: 134, 241
Tzihuacpopoca: 262, 281–282
tzihuactli: 8
Tzinacantlan: 212
Tzintzuntzan: 195, 320
Tzitzimicihuatl: 161
tzompanteuctli: 153, 248
tzompantli: 104, 155, 157, 174, 209
Tzonapan: 252
Tzonmulco: 50
Tzontemoc: 184
Tzotzolan: 241
Tzotzoma: 222

Uaxyacac. SEE Oaxaca
Ueuezacan: 108
uey zahuatl. SEE smallpox
urbanism: 217

Vera Cruz: 249

Wandering: 20–26, 33, 122, 150, 168, 302
warfare: 9–10, 13, 34, 61, 78–79, 96–102, 111, 121–122, 124–126, 133, 153, 158–159, 162–163, 165, 197–198, 207, 215, 218, 220–221, 238, 257, 308–309. SEE ALSO coronation war; flower war; warriors
War of Defilement: 182–188, 190–192
warriors: 10, 97–99, 133, 165, 183–184, 287, 310, 324; orders of, 105–106, 110–111, 162–163, 170, 230
water, potable: 34, 52, 82, 86, 92, 141, 152, 157, 182, 222–223, 286. SEE ALSO aqueducts; Chapultepec
waterspout: 169
whirlwind: 169
White Mixcoatl: 167
wind god: 168–169

wind jewel: 169, 266
Wolf Woman: 167

Xaltepec: 240
Xaltilulco: 299
Xaltocan: 16, 27, 29, 40, 44, 55–56, 71, 283, 299, 303
Xayacamachan: 237
Xictli, Mount: 95
Xihuiltemoc (ruler of Xochimilco): 191
Xihuiltemoc (son of Chimalpopoca): 305
Xiloman: 184, 191
Xilotepec: 123, 181
Ximohuayan: 226
Xipe: 106
Xippille: 184
Xiquipilco: 198
Xiuhcoac: 207
Xiuhtepec: 113
Xiuhteuctli: 50, 98, 242–243
xiuhtlalpilli: 134, 314
Xiuhtlamin: 242
xiuhtzitzquilo: 135
xochiatl: 308
Xochiatl River: 213
Xochicalco: 86
xochimicqui: 103
Xochimilco: 13, 17, 30, 44, 85, 87, 95, 181, 191, 210, 252, 284
Xochimilco, Lake: 32, 58, 85, 300

xochiyaoyotl: 99–101. SEE ALSO flower war
Xoconochco: 210, 213, 215
Xocotl, Mount: 297
Xocoyotzin: 203, 229
Xoloc: 15
Xoloco: 265, 286
Xolotl: 12–17, 25, 54, 82, 118–119, 136–137, 173, 219, 248, 296

Yacana: 216
Yacapixtlan: 284
Yacateuctli: 169, 212
Yanhuitlan: 241
Yaocihuatl: 102, 161
yaotl: 96, 165
yaotlalli: 306, 309
Yaoyotl: 97, 99
yaoyotl: 96
Yauhtepec: 284
yolatl: 196
Yopi: 123
Yopitzinco: 208
Youalli Ehecatl: 159–160
Yucatan: 171, 248

Zacateca. SEE Teochichimecs
Zacatepec, Mount: 81, 95
Zamacoyahuac: 196–197
Zapotecs: 151, 156, 214–215, 240–241
Zapotitlan: 299
zodiacal light: 244